# The FreeBSD Corporate Networker's Guide

D1610986

# The FreeBSD Corporate Networker's Guide

**Ted Mittelstaedt**

## Addison–Wesley

Boston • San Francisco • New York • Toronto • Montreal
London • Munich • Paris • Madrid
Capetown • Sydney • Tokyo • Singapore • Mexico City

The publisher offers discounts on this book when ordered in quantity for special sales. For more information, please contact:

Pearson Education Corporate Sales Division
One Lake Street
Upper Saddle River, NJ 07458
(800) 382-3419
*corpsales@pearsontechgroup.com*

Visit us on the Web at *www.awl.com/cseng/*

**Library of Congress Cataloging-in-Publication Data**
Mittelstaedt, Ted
   The FreeBSD corporate networker's guide / Ted Mittelstaedt.
      p.   cm.
   Includes index.
   ISBN 0-201-70481-1 (alk. paper)
   1. FreeBSD. 2. Free computer software. 3. Computer networks. I. Title.
   QA76.754.M58  2000
   005.4'4769—dc21

                                                    00-053577

Text printed on recycled paper

1 2 3 4 5 6 7 8 9 10 – CRS – 04  03  02  01  00
*First printing, December 2000*

# Contents

# List of Exhibits

# Preface

*The FreeBSD Corporate Networker's Guide* is written for beginning FreeBSD administrators who want to take advantage of the power and cost savings afforded by use of this operating system on their organizations' production network. FreeBSD takes its name from the Berkeley Software Distribution group, where the software originated. As with all network operating systems (NOSs), there is a "learning hump" that the administrator just beginning to work with the NOS must climb

In keeping with the spirit of freely available Open Source software, this book has operating with the Microsoft (MS) operating system and networking as a primary goal. FreeBSD and Windows can peaceably coexist on the same network without problems. As an administrator you can mix and match FreeBSD and Windows servers and clients as you see fit, as long as you follow good networking practices of using standards-based methods and protocols. It is important that a production network be based on standards as much as possible. Mixing FreeBSD and Windows on the same network is an excellent way to do this.

Newcomers to the UNIX computing paradigm will find it somewhat different than the Windows paradigm. Sometimes it is even more difficult for the administrator experienced in other operating systems (OSs) to pick up UNIX than it is for the raw newcomer. Preconceptions of how an OS works and how best to do things need to be shed. This mind expanding is a very good thing for the information system (IS) professional, even if he or she has no intention of using the material professionally. Some people are so bigoted that they carry on a crusade against the Macintosh and/or OS/2. This trap, more than anything else, blocks progress in the quickly shifting computer industry. Even Microsoft, once the standards' bearer of proprietary computing, has come to realize this. The Web front-end of MS's Hotmail service, for example, runs entirely on FreeBSD (look at the MS Help Wanted postings that require FreeBSD experience for Hotmail administrators).

## Organization of This Book

The first section of this book, Chapters 1 through 3, covers preinstallation and installation of FreeBSD. As with any other NOS, several questions must be answered before the installation CD even boots up in the server hardware. (This is one reason the DNS chapter is before the installation chapter.) I strongly recommend installing a FreeBSD system before tackling the rest of the book, even if all you do is install according to the directions without understanding them. In some ways, learning about FreeBSD is a catch-22 proposition. You need to know how FreeBSD works before you can install it properly, but you need an installed FreeBSD system before you can learn how it works! To solve this problem, just go ahead and install a system, even if it's the ugliest and worst option selection possible. All you need is something running on something, which will help you understand the rest of this book. You will want to go back later and reinstall FreeBSD anyway.

Chapters 4 through 9 are intended to be taken piecemeal. Do you need a FreeBSD router to connect to the Internet? If so, skip to Chapter 5. Do you need a FreeBSD mailserver? If so, skip to Chapter 9. Although there is some order, in that later topics do build on some material introduced in earlier chapters, the main idea is to concentrate first on the sections for which you have an immediate need.

In addition, the information in the chapters is not intended to be swallowed in one gulp but to be used more as a reference. Ignore the bits that are completely inapplicable to your situation. For example, most people will never need to connect a DOS-bootable disk to a FreeBSD network, but the information is there for the few who do need it.

Chapter 10, Advocacy, contains material that polarized the reviewers. Some loved it, some hated it; nobody lacked an opinion about it. This chapter presents all the reasons to use FreeBSD instead of Windows, and it includes some background information about FreeBSD. If you are an administrator who thinks that both Windows and FreeBSD have their strong points and you want to "marry" the two, you won't find agreement here. My goal is to see FreeBSD *replace* Windows, not to coexist with it forever. Although advocacy may seem out of place in a technically oriented publication, the truth is that this chapter is the real key to the essence of FreeBSD.

FreeBSD, and other Open Source software products, were not written by people who wanted to make a lot of money, or even any money at all. They are not in any way commercial products, yet they are being used as pillars for commercial enterprises! Without understanding Open Source software, why FreeBSD exists, or what drives it, any good administrator would be concerned about its longevity in the market; no administrator could persuade management to try FreeBSD or have any confidence in it. Thus, an understanding of advocacy is essential to the FreeBSD administrator.

## Open Source Software

Open Source software, like FreeBSD, generally follows this definition.

- The software is free when obtained electronically and has only a nominal cost if supplied on media (usually less than $30).
- No support, warranty, or suitability of fitness for use is implied. There is no guarantee that it will function at all.
- The entire source code needed to compile the software is freely available. In some cases binary versions of the software may not be available; the end user must compile it.
- There are no restrictions on the end user's personal use of the software. In a corporate or governmental organization, *personal use* is defined as entirely within that organization and benefiting members of that organization.
- The software is *not* intended to be available only for a limited time, at the end of which it converts to a commercial model (e.g., beta code, eval code).
- In general, no commercial support is available, other than targeted consulting. This is changing with the largest packages—FreeBSD, Linux, and Sendmail—which do have commercial support available.

Open Source software generally comes with a license applied by its copyright holder. The most important purpose of this license is to establish that the software is indeed Open Source and is not commercial, or pirated. Beyond this, Open Source licenses fall into one of two general categories.

**1.** *Limited or restricted license.* A good example is the GNU software license used on the GNU C Complier (GCC) in the FreeBSD operating system. This license permits GNU code to be included in commercial software, but any modifications to the GNU software must be placed under GNU also. Another example is the license used on the Sendmail version 8.9.X software package, which requires anyone using Sendmail in a commercial software project, such as a UNIX operating system, to obtain permission from Sendmail, with an exception for Open Source projects. These licenses also have language specifying source availability. There is *no* single standard for a limited or restricted Open Source license, despite what you may read about the GNU software license. Anybody can (and often does) sit down and write up a license document and apply it to his or her software; the existence of GNU does *not* prevent this.

**2.** *Unlimited or unrestricted license.* The classic example of this type of license is the Berkeley BSD license used on most of FreeBSD itself. It allows use of the source in other commercial projects without obtaining permission or opening the source of the commercial project. Another example of this kind of license is that of the Livingston Radius code; that license file can be found at `ftp://ftp.livingston.com/pub/le/radius/radius21.tar.Z`. Although the difference between limited or restricted and unlimited or unrestricted may seem trivial, in reality it is not. Unlimited licenses, such as that of BSD, exist because the developers *want* the code to be used commercially, even if the developer never sees a dime from revenue generated by sale of the software. The principal reason for this is the age-old human instinct for leaving a mark. If your goal is to write a piece of software that will become a standard for everyone, BSD is the best and quickest way to do it. In contrast, GNU and GNU public license (GPL) and those limited licenses force the software to stay alive and be improved or prevent people from profiting by reselling software under the limited license.

Software that is shipped with the source code and contains a software license that disallows mere use of the software in a commercial environment is *not* Open Source software. The FreeBSD Project does not use such software in FreeBSD because this practice would place most FreeBSD end users in legal trouble.

## PC Server and PC Local Area Network

In the old days of IBM XT-compatibles, building a fileserver on a PC was impractical as well as unbelievable. The 8088 hardware simply was not powerful enough, and the XT was extremely restricted in internal bandwidth and other resources. Back then, servers were big, powerful computers that sat in a glass house, if the organization had them at all.

As PCs became more powerful and Ethernet networks extended to all desktops, the Intel 80286 chip began to be used in the AT computer. Because these PCs were constructed with 8MB and 16MB of RAM and 300MB ESDI disks, their use as network servers became possible. These early machines were still very weak compared to a real UNIX server of the time, but because they were much cheaper, network operating systems began appearing—for example, NetWare and LanManager based on OS/2. Companies built large networks based entirely around these NOSs; these networks came to be known as PC-LANs since clients and servers were both PC-compatible computers. The primary difference between a PC used as a server and a PC used as a client was that the server was more powerful, with larger disks, more RAM, and a faster central processing unit (CPU). In addition to this, while PCs were becoming powerful enough to be used as servers, the original proprietary *server* computers also continued to become more powerful.

Today, vendors selling servers can be selling, in effect, souped-up PCs, or proprietary-hardware computers such as Sun Sparcs. In this book, the term *PC server* is used to designate a server built around a PC computer (e.g., Wintel) rather than a server computer built with proprietary hardware (e.g., Sparc).

The Token Ring, Latticenet, and Arcnet network media types originally had some marketshare, but Ethernet rapidly became the dominant network media. FreeBSD does support fiber distributed data interface (FDDI) network cards, but the Ethernet network standard is assumed in this book because it is what most 10BaseT and 100BaseT networks are made up of.

## Conventions Used

Over the years, the various Microsoft OSs have developed nicknames, although, according to Microsoft, the *proper* way to refer to them is to use their full names. This book is not an advertisement for MS products, therefore I do not use spelled-out product names for Windows, such as Windows NT Advanced Server, numerous times in a paragraph. Using full names would not only be very tiring for the reader, but it would also make the text read like Microsoft advertising copy. So, here are the shortened terms that are used:

- MS—Microsoft Corporation
- Win31—Microsoft Windows 3.0 and Microsoft Windows 3.1
- WfW—Windows for Workgroups 3.1 and Windows for Workgroups 3.11
- Win16—All Windows 3.0, 3.1, 3.11, Windows for Workgroups 3.1 and 3.11
- Win95, Win98, or Win95/98/ME—Windows 95, Windows 98, Windows Millennium
- NTWKS 3.51, NTWKS 4.0—Windows NT Workstation 3.51, 4.0
- NT Server 3.51, 4.0—Windows NT Server 3.51, 4.0 and Windows NT Advanced Server 3.51, 4.0 (This book doesn't differentiate Advanced from regular NT Server.)
- NT— used when there is no difference in the behavior of the NT Workstation and Server, as well as numeric versions
- Win2K—Windows 2000 Professional (successor to Windows NT Workstation)
- Win2K Server—Windows 2000 Server (successor to Windows NT 4.0 Server)

Normal text in this book is in Times New Roman. Text that is typed into the computer, such as commands, is represented in Courier. **Bold Courier** indicates computer output. You need to understand that space characters are just as important in command strings as they are in text characters; when typing commands, include the spaces. Special emphasis and keywords are represented in *italics*. In UNIX, the command interpreter assigns special meanings to double and single quotes. Text that is to be typed into the computer is always exactly what is to be typed, including all forward slashes, backslashes, and/or quote marks.

All URLs in this book are set using underlined Courier (e.g., http:// www.freebsd.org). URLs either follow the convention of linking to the root index or linking to the base of the item in question. For example, a Web site may have a separate area for a particular program that is substantively different from the rest of the site, in which case it's apparent that the Webmaster regards the separate area as being apart from the main Web site.

UNIX uses the forward slash (/) as the directory separator in the filesystem, not the backslash (\), as in DOS and Windows. In most cases, I use the fully qualified pathname so that "a file named /foobar is read as a file named "foobar" located in the root directory."

One other formatting convention I use is quad-X. In a command string where input must be substituted, the XXXX mark will appear, as in the following.

```
passwd root
Changing local password for root.
New password: XXXX
Retype new password: XXXX
passwd: rebuilding the database...
passwd: done
```

## Obtaining RFC Documents

TCP/IP is an open protocol originated by the Internet Engineering Task Force (IETF). This body creates standards through the Request for Comments (RFC) process. In addition to the TCP/IP protocol, RFCs exist for many programs found in UNIX, especially network programs. RFCs are identified by numbers, and this book contains references to specific RFCs.

A copy of any RFC can be downloaded from the Internet. Years ago, the master location was ftp://ds.internic.net/rfc. So many books and other publications linked to this machine name, however, that it was shut down. In any case, the InterNIC is not the network citizen it once was. Today, the master RFC site is http://www.rfc-editor.org/. The most popular primary repository is located at ftp://ftp.isi.edu/in-notes. There is a second repository at http://www.ietf.org/, but its RFC page lists the RFC editor's site as the primary one. It contains mainly text versions along with some PostScript versions. The PostScript versions of the RFCs are better than the text ones because some contain diagrams.

## Software and Hardware Mentioned in This Book

In keeping with the spirit of the FreeBSD operating system, practically all software discussed in this book is free, except for the Windows and DOS operating systems. Where specific needs exist on Windows OSs for which no free software package is available, I have used shareware alternatives, always attempting to use the least expensive shareware possible.

Many commercial software packages that manage UNIX-to-Windows interoperability would probably work *just as well or better* with FreeBSD and Windows desktops. For TCP/IP clients for Windows in particular, the market could use a $20-per-seat Network File System (NFS) client for Win95/98, although this is becoming a moot issue with the release of Win2K.

In some cases, buying hardware devices may be far cheaper and make more sense for many applications than would running software packages on a PC. You owe it to yourself to investigate these as well. Nothing in this book should be construed as a licensing statement for any specific software package. In the case of shareware and freeware, the licenses in the packages take precedence over any statements in this book. It is the end user's responsibility to make sure that all licensing requirements are properly met.

I mention various computer hardware devices that facilitate use of FreeBSD as a network server. Rest assured that I have not received any of these devices free as promotions from their manufacturers, which would influence my selection as to their suitability for use with the operating system. I have purchased all the hardware mentioned here, or used it at businesses that have employe me, where I used the FreeBSD operating system.

## Information Sources

An administrator can use a number of significant recognized sources of information about FreeBSD, including the following.

- *The manual.* All UNIX systems have a system manual, accessed by the man command.
- *Electronic documentation.* Many document directories can be found in /usr/share, such as the FreeBSD Handbook. If full sources are installed, detailed documentation is often available in source directories, along with the source code.

- *The FreeBSD Web site.* http://www.freebsd.org:
- *Mailing lists.* The FreeBSD group manages a number of mailing lists, subscription instructions, and a list of mailing lists on the FreeBSD Web site.
- *Usenet news.* Several Usenet news groups cover FreeBSD.

Usenet is an excellent source of quick information on FreeBSD, but new users should be aware of certain aspects of Usenet and its mailing lists. All users should read the "Netiquette" document in the newsgroup news.newusers before posting. In addition, please keep the following in mind.

- Usenet is not a manufacturer's technical support forum. If you post a question, nobody has any responsibility to respond, or to respond with correct information.
- Usenet is not very fast. In general it may take more than a week before your question is answered by those in the reading group who want to answer it.
- Before posting a question on Usenet, make sure that it is not answered in documentation or on the FreeBSD Web site in the documentation archives. In addition, check past postings at http://www.dejanews.com or some other major Usenet news archive.
- Most readers of the Usenet site visit it irregularly. The one person who can answer your question may not happen to be reading on the few days that you post. Post a question again after a suitable interval, such as a week, if no answer is posted.
- Don't say "send responses by e-mail" in your posting message. Most readers who answer questions on Usenet get annoyed at this because it indicates someone who is too lazy or too busy to bother to follow up on a query. An unreliable news server is not an excuse because DejaNews can be checked for possible missing postings.
- Don't post general questions asking for help. Make your posting as specific as possible. List all relevant details, such as machine, brand, disk size, disk model, amount of memory, exactly what you are trying to do, and so on.
- Always remember that people answering questions on Usenet are doing it for their own enjoyment and advancement of the FreeBSD Project. Your education is of secondary importance.

## Megabytes and Megabits

From almost the beginning of the computer industry, computer engineers have measured data by bits. A single bit in a computer can be either on or off, represented by decimal 0 or 1. Bits are grouped together into bytes, which are eight bits long. Bytes are grouped into words, then double words, and so on. All of these units are used with the octal (base 8) or the hexadecimal (base 16) numbering system.

People don't think in hexadecimal, however; they think in the decimal system (base 10). So do most engineers in other disciplines. Only software engineers can think in hexadecimal. So, bits and bytes are often converted from their hexadecimal and octal measurements into decimal by adding the powers of two: two to the zeroeth, plus two to the first, plus two to the second, and so on.

Two raised to the tenth is equal to 1,024. Very early on, software engineers decided to make things easier for themselves and began using the International System of Units (SI) designations—kilo, mega, giga, and so on. So, eight bits is a byte, 1,024 bytes is a kilobyte, $1,024 \times 1,024$ bits is a megabyte, and so on. Soon, the abbreviation KB came to be associated with kilobytes, MB with megabytes, GB with gigabytes, and so on.

When networking became important to the industry, confusion arose, so people began writing Kbt, Mbt, Gbt—kilobits, megabits, and gigabits—to satisfy the networking and telecommunications people. These people use the decimal measurement, generally, and to them 1Mbt means 1,000,000 bits, not 1,048,576 bits (a megabyte).

Everyone was pretty satisfied with the arrangement and things went along well enough until hard drive manufacturers came along. The problem was that generally the more bits a hard drive holds, the more expensive it is. So, to gain marketshare, hard drive manufacturers began to market their products based on the decimal measurement of bytes the drives could hold. Thus, instead of a 100MB hard drive holding $100 \times 1,024$ bytes, it actually held only $100 \times 1,000$ bytes. This allowed hard drive manufacturers to advertise a 10MB drive that didn't actually hold 10MB of data from the computer user's point of view.

As long as hard drives were fairly small, every computer user pretty much accepted the fact that a hard drive's usable capacity was somewhat smaller than its advertised capacity. In the 1990s, however, as hard drives became larger and larger, the advertised capacity began to diverge tremendously from the real capacity. The drive manufacturers, being hardware people, began complaining to the umbrella standards organization—the Institute of Electrical and Electronics Engineers (IEEE)—to do something about it.

Things came to a head, so in December of 1998, the IEEE (which the networking TCP/IP community had rejected in favor of IETF over the IP standards wars) decided to get involved. With a coalition of physicists and measurement purists, they persuaded the International Electrotechnical Commission (IEC) to issue a standard for data storage based on the decimal system. The new standard renamed all of the standard terminology used by the computer industry, with the exception of the hard drive manufacturers, into the base 10 terminology.

In this book, I do *not* use the Revised Data Processing measurements promoted by the IEC. Because this book is about a computer operating system, the classic measurement system used by software engineers is used *except* when referring to data transmission—the telecommunications people have never used the computer measurement system.

Sadly, the IEC justifies its standard by saying that more people don't know that 1K means 1,024 rather than 1,000. Therefore, the technical people should bow to the majority. An explanation of the IEC's views on this is located at http://physics.nist.gov/cuu/Units/binary.html.

## Reaching the Author and Errata

I am always interested in comments and questions from readers. I've set up an e-mail address for comments about the book, and I hope to incorporate readers' suggestions into a future edition. Please refrain from sending general FreeBSD questions until you have read the entire book, asked questions on one of the FreeBSD mailing lists, and searched the archives—http://www.freebsd.org. Unfortunately, I don't have the time (or money) to be a full-time, unpaid, technical support person for FreeBSD. Please send any book comments to *book@freebsd-corp-net-guide.com.*

Naturally, the publisher and I have tried to eliminate all typos and errors from the text. However, a book this size undoubtedly contains at least one mistake. I'll post any necessary corrections you send me on a Web site for this book. Check the Addison-Wesley site and see http://www.freebsd-corp-net-guide.com for postproduction information.

## Web Site URLs

No body of case law covers URL linking. I am aware that some people would like to make some sort of global, or at least federal, requirement that anyone linking to a URL first seeks permission from the Web site host. This idea may sound reasonable, but it is not. Because no right to control URL linking exists currently, seeking permission would merely confer a right that never existed to begin with.

In all URLs listed in this book, I have followed any instructions that are *posted* on the Web site by the Webmaster. However, a Web site that is intentionally made accessible to the public is fundamentally a public venue. If you as a Webmaster do not want others to link to a site that is plainly intended to be public, I respectfully suggest that you examine the definition of *public* and install IP number block filtering to prevent the general public from viewing the site. I believe that if you place a Web site on the publicly accessible Internet, then people should have the right to link to it, which is exactly the same as their right to visit it. If the Webmaster has placed a directive on the Web site requesting that links to it be made to a particular location, I follow these directives for the URLs in this book.

Because of the fluidity of the Internet, a book that names a significant number of URLs is likely to refer to some sites that have vanished or moved. I apologize for this and I'll try to keep a table of corrected URLs and links available at `http://www.freebsd-corp-net-guide.com`.

## ACKNOWLEDGMENTS

Portions of this book are based on material originally published in "The Network Community," a monthly column appearing in *Computer Bits*—a local computer periodical in Portland, Oregon. These can be viewed online at `http://www.computerbits.com`.

TCP/IP networking is based on many standards published by the IETF in RFC standards. These standards are copyrighted by IETF, if a copyright exists at all. It is not clear, however, whether the concept of copyright can be applied to a public standard. Standards can be considered specifications, for which copyrights cannot be obtained.

Some shell scripts and other data in this book are taken from Usenet online public postings and from mailing lists. It may be that some of these postings are themselves based on data published elsewhere. I have attempted to avoid using material that appears to have originated as copyrighted material, even if nothing obvious shows that it was copyrighted at one time.

It is not possible to list here the names of the enormous number of people who have contributed to the UNIX operating system. Special thanks are due to the many people who have contributed to the FreeBSD Project, including this book's reviewers: Sean Eric Fagan, a BSD developer; Rick Hamell, Portland FreeBSD User's Group; Bryan Helvey; Bill Swingle, *unfurl@dub.net*; and Bill Rabson, The Free BSD Project. Others who have contributed in one way or another are listed at `http://www.freebsd.org/handbook/staff.html`.

I also want to thank my wife Jean for her patience with a study stuffed full of computers, which I used to help write this book.

# FreeBSD Serving Windows Networks

Deciding to use FreeBSD as a production server on your corporate network is only the first step. Before the first installation floppy is inserted in the server's disk drive, a lot of planning and preparation work needs to be taken care of. Some of it is no different from the preparation needed for any other server. For example, you must decide where the new server will sit, how much money you want to spend on it, how you would prefer to have it backed up, and so forth. However, some preparatory work is unique to any UNIX server, and those issues are addressed in this chapter.

First, I'll describe the common tasks that a FreeBSD server can perform on the network to help you decide which of these to move from your Windows servers to FreeBSD and which to keep on Windows servers. Then I'll discuss the most noticeable differences between your interaction with a Windows server and with the FreeBSD server and operating system. The remainder of the chapter is an overview of server hardware selection, physical layout, and miscellaneous items.

In short, this chapter serves as a kind of executive briefing of what FreeBSD can do for your network and discusses figuring out how FreeBSD will fit into your existing network.

## TASKS OF A FREEBSD SERVER IN A WINDOWS NETWORK

FreeBSD is an extremely flexible and versatile network operating system (NOS), but like any operating system, there are some things that you cannot—and should not—do with it. For example, although you can run a large

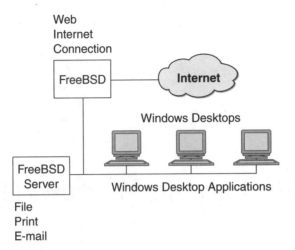

**Figure 1.1**  Typical use of FreeBSD servers on a Windows network

corporate mail system on FreeBSD, if you have already decided that Microsoft Exchange Server is going to be the central mailserver backbone on your net, then you can't use FreeBSD for it. Of course, this is also true of Windows NT. For example, if you have decided to use INN for your site's central Usenet news server, you can't use Windows NT for it. Indeed, it's almost impossible to use NT for any serious high-volume Usenet news serving.

One of the keys to using FreeBSD effectively in a corporate network is to view the tasks that you want to solve from a *forest* rather than a *tree* perspective. For example, a typical FreeBSD net is shown in Figure 1.1. FreeBSD and Windows are *not* the same thing and never will be. Each approaches problems differently. In many cases, perhaps most cases, the FreeBSD method is superior and results in a simpler and more effective solution. In other cases, such as end-user desktops, the Windows solution is called for. Unless you can look at each of these problem cases from a general perspective, you will have tunnel vision that will interfere with your ability to make a good decision.

The following sections describe the major server networking tasks done in most organizations, along with their FreeBSD implementation considerations.

## Domain Name System and the Dynamic Host Configuration Protocol

Since FreeBSD and other UNIX operating systems all use TCP/IP as their primary networking protocol, a network using FreeBSD must by default be a TCP/IP network. If your network has no TCP/IP running on it (e.g., a pure Novell NetWare IPX network or an NT network based on NetBEUI), there's not much point in running FreeBSD. The tremendous importance of the Internet makes this situation unlikely, however.

Any discussion of TCP/IP networks must start with IP numbering because the TCP/IP numbering scheme is such a fundamental part of the protocol. Don't make the mistake of starting your TCP/IP deployment with an ad hoc IP assignment scheme; you will create a mess and waste a lot of time later cleaning it up. If you currently administer a TCP/IP network that is disorganized, FreeBSD can help you to impose some order on it.

Today, all major TCP/IP client operating systems can automatically obtain their TCP/IP network assignments during bootup via the Dynamic Host Configuration Protocol (DHCP). This is superior to hard-coding the IP number manually in each client because it eliminates keying errors and inadvertent IP number clashes and allows the administrator to renumber the network easily if needed. Of course, it may be necessary to assign the system's IP number statically in the DHCP server for some client software, but the process is much easier to control when the static assignments for all systems are present in the central DHCP server.

Once the computer has its IP number, other systems may need to connect to the computer. If so, it is then *named*, and on TCP/IP networks the mechanism used to do this is the Domain Name System (DNS). DNS is the basic mechanism used to convert a hostname, such as a.root-servers.net, into an IP number, such as 198.41.0.4, which the computer uses to make a network connection.

DNS is not always required. If the corporate network is not directly connected to the Internet it is perfectly fine to use a *hosts file* on *every machine in the network*. The hosts file is specific to the operating system, and the TCP/IP stack on the client uses it to look up the IP number of a host if a DNS server isn't accessible on the network. In this case a central hosts file is usually edited on a convenient system and copied to each client periodically, perhaps with an rcp command executed out of cron under UNIX, or the at scheduler under Windows NT. Hosts files can be giant. Before the Great Renaming (when the entire Internet was shifted to DNS), the central hosts file at the InterNIC had many thousands of machines entered into it. In fact the principal reason that the Internet was shifted onto DNS was because it became too expensive to distribute hosts to every system in the network.

Putting the DNS and DHCP server on the same server also leads to another question: is it possible to somehow connect the two systems so that when the DHCP subsystem hands out an IP number, a DNS entry is created? Today, there is no standards-based way to do this. Several vendors are experimenting with solutions, such as Microsoft's Active Directory on Win2K. Another more serious obstacle is the concept of caching. With DNS, caching is a requirement:

when a DNS server obtains a name-to-IP number map, the server retains the map in its cache for a specified period. A DHCP/DNS server that is continually rotating IP numbers can create a lot of trouble with a remote DNS server's cache.

Until a standards-based mechanism is developed, for most client operating systems it is simple enough for the administrator to edit two files on the same server—the DHCP database file and the DNS zone file—when entering a host onto the network. Win2K does allow for dynamic DNS if an *allow-update* clause is placed in the DNS zone declaration and BIND version 8 is used. (BIND version 8 is the default in current versions of FreeBSD.) Dynamic DNS is detailed in RFC2136.

FreeBSD can provide excellent DNS and DHCP services. With it and other UNIXes, DNS is provided with the Berkeley Internet Naming Daemon (BIND) server program, and DHCP is provided with the Internet Software Consortium (ISC)–DHCP server program. BIND is part of the basic FreeBSD system, and ISC–DHCP is in the Ports directories. Chapter 2 discusses their deployment in more depth.

## Internet Connectivity, Wide Area Networks, and Dialup

Making a formal connection to the Internet can bring many benefits to the organization, and over time it can fundamentally change how the organization does its daily work. Setting up a usable connection is relatively inexpensive, even for an office of only a few people.

Internet connectivity can be roughly divided into two areas: the circuit hardware and the Internet software. The circuit hardware comprises the actual mechanisms used to pass packets between the internal corporate network and the Internet. The Internet software directs how those packets are manipulated once they're inside the internal network.

FreeBSD contains every piece of Internet software it needs, from Web servers to network address translation programs. In certain circumstances it can also serve as the connection hardware. For example, if the connection is Ethernet, as is delivered by many digital subscriber line (DSL) connections, inserting two Ethernet cards into the FreeBSD system provides most of what is needed to get it set up as a router between the outside Ethernet connection and the inside network. If the connection is a dialup V.90 modem, FreeBSD can handle that also.

Even though FreeBSD servers can have cards inserted that allow them to connect to very high-speed Internet circuits, most people use hardware routers, such as that made by Cisco, for the circuit hardware. FreeBSD can also be very useful to the hardware router from a support standpoint, for example, by providing a system log (syslog) drive for network syslog from the router.

Circuits connecting to the Internet can further be logically divided into two types: intermittent (dial-on-demand) or permanent (e.g., leased lines). Intermittent connections require special techniques to operate a mailserver successfully at the customer field office.

Because local Internet service offerings vary between Internet service providers (ISPs) and because circuit rates vary between areas, the best way to decide is to interview a number of local ISPs and get their opinions on the connectivity best suited to the organization.

FreeBSD can be of use in a wide area network (WAN) situation as a virtual private network (VPN) server. For example, an organization can set up two sites connected to the Internet via dedicated circuits. Each site can have a FreeBSD server as a network address translator, which allows them to use an RFC1918 Private network number range. The FreeBSD servers at both sites can then also be configured with point-to-point tunneling (ppp over TCP) to allow the two private networks to be tunneled over the Internet. The tunnel also can be encrypted by using the `ssh` program or IPSec and the gif driver in FreeBSD 4.X.

FreeBSD can also be configured as a dialup modem server, although unless the organization is bringing in its modem lines as ISDN Primary Rate Interface (PRI) circuits, it can only achieve 28.8K on analog Plain Old Telephone Service (POTS) phone lines. (PRIs are required for terminal servers to permit inbound V.90 dialup access.) The `pppd` program is used for this task. In this manner organization members can dial into the FreeBSD server and use it to access the Internet through the organization's Internet connection as well as the internal organizational network.

## Web Serving

Web serving today is nothing new; just about every network operating system in existence has had a Web server built for it. Vendors are even putting Web servers into embedded devices, such as routers and hardware print servers, to give configuration access to the administrator.

FreeBSD is a suitable Web server platform not because you can run a Web server on it but because of the kind of back-end Common Gateway Interface (CGI) programs and more advanced server-side programs, such as Perl Hypertext Preprocessor (PHP), that can be run on it. CGIs can certainly be compiled C programs, but they can also be flexible scripts written with the Perl scripting language.

Perl is probably the most powerful and useful scripting language in use today. Perl also has a giant library of contributed programs available in the comprehensive Perl archive CPAN. It can be used to put together just about any program rapidly. Some Web servers themselves are written in Perl, such as the `webmin` program.

Although Perl is available for other platforms, such as Windows NT, it does not have the vastness and flexibility on these other platforms that it has on UNIX. FreeBSD makes a fantastic platform to field Perl script applications on.

In addition to the versatility of the back-end CGI that can be run on FreeBSD, there are also secure socket layer (SSL) and FrontPage versions of the basic Apache Web Server available for FreeBSD. FreeBSD servers make an extremely powerful Web and FTP server. The Walnut Creek FTP server, `ftp.cdrom.com`, for example, can support 10,000 simultaneous users on a single Xeon 500Mhz-based PC!

## Fileserving

Fileserving is one of the core requirements of most corporate network servers. Historically, UNIX has always used Network File System (NFS) protocols for fileserving, and it is certainly possible to load NFS on a Windows client. However, adding NFS to each Windows client is costly, and presents another administrative burden on the client compared to a network of Windows clients and NT Servers. Rather than loading NFS on the Windows clients, Samba software can be installed and configured to load Windows networking on the FreeBSD server system. Since Samba uses the same networking protocols as Windows networking, the Windows clients can be set up out of the box with the default Microsoft Networking client.

Samba allows FreeBSD to serve file and printer resources to DOS, Win31, WfW, Win95/98, NT, and Win2K. (Samba version 2.0.7 or greater *must* be used for Win2K.) It can also serve file and printer resources to OS/2 Warp Connect and to later versions of OS/2 with networking support. Samba requires a TCP/IP stack loaded with appropriate network client software. WfW 3.11, Win95/98, NT, and Win2K all contain the client software; Windows 3.1 and DOS don't. Suitable clients for Win31 and DOS can be downloaded from Microsoft or obtained from the Windows NT Server CD-ROM. The WfW network client must use the TCP/IP protocol available from Microsoft.

In effect, Samba makes a UNIX system appear on the network looking like any other Windows NT Server running TCP/IP. Windows systems can browse and map drives on the FreeBSD server running Samba.

Samba does *not* participate fully in the Windows NT primary or backup domain controller system. A Samba system cannot currently be used as a Backup Domain Controller (BDC) to NT because the mechanism that Microsoft uses to replicate from a Primary Domain Controller (PDC) to a BDC is proprietary and undocumented. A Samba server *can*, however, be used as a PDC. An NT server cannot be used as a BDC to a Samba PDC for the same reasons listed previously.

An experimental version of Samba labeled Samba_TNG can be found at `http://www.kneschke.de/projekte/samba_tng/index.php3`. It *does* contain NT-to-UNIX/Samba replication. This work will be merged into the next major version of Samba.

For NT networks that are set up in the domain model, a FreeBSD system running Samba can be configured to use the NT PDC as the password server. This functionality is similar to that of a regular NT Server in a controlled domain when it is *joined* to the domain.

Kerberos security will be important to watch as Active Directory unfolds under Windows 2000. Currently, the Microsoft Kerberos is standard, but their Kerberos uses the *future extension* field to carry Windows-specific, proprietary information. As a result Windows cannot authenticate against a standard Kerberos Distribution Center, although this will probably change soon because Microsoft has finally released their documentation. FreeBSD *can* authenticate against a Win2K Kerberos KDC, however.

Although Microsoft has stated that the NT domain model will ultimately be replaced by Active Directory, Win2K servers built on Active Directory contain an interface that is used by all Windows clients that are not Win2K (e.g., NT4, NT3.5, Win98/95, WfW). This was designed to permit Win2K systems to use NT 4 servers; it also permits them to use Samba servers.

## Printserving

The topic of FreeBSD printserving in a Windows network generally involves two issues. The first is whether or not the FreeBSD system can accept print jobs from Windows clients and whether it can do this with either the Microsoft networking protocol (using Samba) or the Line Printer Remote (LPR) protocol. LPR is an optional networking component that comes with the operating system and can be installed and enabled on NT and Win2K systems. It can be added on to Win95/98 systems.

The second issue is whether or not the FreeBSD system can transmit print jobs to printers. FreeBSD can do this using the LPR protocol to remote printers, or via the LPT or COM port to directly connected ones. If the remote printer is plugged into an NT server, LPR must be turned on in the remote NT server. If the remote printer contains a hardware card, such as an HP JetDirect card, or is plugged into a remote hardware printserver box, such as a JetDirect EX external printserver, these printservers must have their line printer daemon

(LPD)/LPR turned on. Typically, directly connected printers use the LPT port because it is faster than a COM port.

Print jobs from the FreeBSD system are generally in one of two formats: plain American Standard Code for Information Interchange (ASCII) text and PostScript. While it is possible to convert PostScript to the more common HP-PCL format right on the FreeBSD system, using Ghostscript, which can also support some other printer formats, you will save yourself much time if you make sure that all printers you purchase for your organization have the Post-Script option turned on and installed. Also, the output of Ghostscript often varies greatly from the output of a PostScript printer, and usually not for the better.

## Electronic Mail

The FreeBSD system makes an excellent, stable, and fast e-mail server. A single FreeBSD server, on appropriate hardware, can serve up to 60,000 accounts using stock mail system utilities and the `Procmail` local delivery agent from the ports collection. BSD mailservers can be scaled to the millions of users by introducing Structured Query Language (SQL) into the mail system. For example, the Microsoft-owned Hotmail service uses FreeBSD for its Web serving.

The typical corporate FreeBSD mailserver contains four server programs that make up the core of the mail system. The first program is Sendmail, which acts as a railroad switchyard for e-mail. Next is the POP/IMAP program, which is used by users who run client e-mail programs, such as Microsoft Outlook, on their individual systems. The third program is the Lightweight Directory Access Protocol (LDAP) server, which allows remote client mail programs, such as Outlook, Netscape Communicator, and Eudora, to use the central corporate address book. Last is the Web-interface program which allows users to read their e-mail from the mailserver directly from a Web browser.

In addition to these server programs you may consider loading some subsidiary programs on the mailserver. There are client mail programs usable from a Telnet window, a password-changing server, a fax server, a content-filtering software program, and a listserver.

It is also possible to configure the mailserver to scan for virus or worm programs. Worm scanning has become particularly important after the ILOVEYOU and Melissa incidents. These worm programs are easily blocked with simple filters on the FreeBSD server; in fact, worm filters for these programs were released just hours after the worms themselves. It is a testimony to the flexibility of the UNIX mail system that even weeks after these worms were released, the commercial mailserver manufacturers, such as Microsoft, still did not have worm scanners available for their servers.

## Commercial Databases

SQL databases are one of the more important corporate server resources and are often used as back-ends for commercial software programs. FreeBSD also has a selection of Open Source databases, such as MySQL, which are frequently used to build active Web sites and commercial programs. Flat-file database tools, such as some Perl modules, use flat-file databases, such as GNU Database Manager (GDBM), Database Manager (DBM), and hashed files. Most Windows networks that have a commercial program, however, require a commercial database or one accessible over the network. One example is a server program using an Oracle database via Oracle's SQLnet. Another possibility is a script, such as a programmed Excel spreadsheet using ODBC, that accesses an Oracle database via SQLnet.

As of this writing Oracle is not available as a native program for FreeBSD. It *is* available for Linux, and it is possible to run Oracle on FreeBSD under FreeBSD's Linux emulation. BSDi is working with Oracle to release an Oracle for FreeBSD.

Another issue is connecting a FreeBSD server as a client to a commercial database server, so that an application running on FreeBSD can use the database. One possible method is to use freeTDS, which is a Transport Data Stream (TDS) protocol library used to connect to Microsoft and Sybase SQL Servers.

# FREEBSD USER INTERFACES VERSUS
# WINDOWS USER INTERFACES

There is no question that, if you have a pure Windows background, acquiring skill with the UNIX user interface (UI) will take some time. One central idea that will help you to gain proficiency fast is to understand that from a block-diagram point of view, Windows and Unix aren't much different. Windows is composed of a kernel that has a set of core function calls, a series of Dynamic Link Libraries (DLLs) that provide even more function calls, and two UIs. These are the graphical Windows UI and the character-mode DOS UI. Obviously, one UI is more capable than the other, but both can be used to do many of the same things.

UNIX also works pretty much like this. FreeBSD has a kernel that provides a set of core function calls and a series of shared and static libraries that provide even more function calls; these are all accessed by a UI. The only difference between UNIX and Windows in this respect is that Windows has only two UIs, but UNIX has a multitude. UNIX has many different character-mode UIs, called shells, and many graphical UIs, called X Window System Managers. Just as an administrator can get along in Windows without learning how to use the character-mode interface, neither does a UNIX administrator need to learn how all the UNIX UIs work. However, such an administrator won't have the same depth of knowledge and skill with FreeBSD as would a Windows administrator who understands the DOS command prompt.

## Character-Based Interfaces

Character-based interfaces are familiar enough to administrators used to dealing with DOS and Win31, somewhat difficult for NT and Win95 administrators, and shocking to Macintosh users. Although great strides in UNIX interfaces have been made with the graphical windows system called X, if the would-be UNIX administrator is unwilling to learn how to use the command line, he or she is forever condemned to pecking away at the fringes of the operating system.

This is true even for those who say X is the solution. For example, on a network I ran, there were several developers with Sun Sparc stations on their desks. One developer was particularly fussy about his X Window Manager. He used a Common Desktop Environment (CDE) and had all the icons for printers, e-mail, and such on his desktop, but every time I went into his office he was working in one of several command-line windows. I thought it was quite humorous that he insisted on turning on the graphical Sun login prompt (instead of just typing `openwin` after logging in to the character prompt, as I preferred to do) but once logged in, he spent the rest of his day in one of the command windows!

It is possible, by using the `webmin` program and other tools, to get just about all FreeBSD system administration into a graphical UI (GUI). However, if you never learn to do anything with the character-mode shell prompt other than fire up a GUI you will be cutting yourself out of a lot of FreeBSD's flexibility and power.

## Configuration Files

Practically all UNIX programs use configuration files that are ASCII text files. Although ASCII doesn't standardize layout of text on a page, in UNIX the convention is that an ASCII text file is standardized as a file containing lines of no more than 80 characters, with each line terminated by a newline character. The newline is the same character as the linefeed character usually referred to in Windows/DOS documentation, which is discussed in the ANSI X3.64-1963 standard. These lines are represented by a fixed-width font on a display screen. This is a historical convention, as early serial terminals used an $80 \times 24$ grid of fixed-width characters. These conventions make it easy to draw legible windows and other things in character mode, as long as the font remains at a fixed width. UNIX configuration files are hardly ever binary files, which are illegible to a text editor.

UNIX configuration files vary in readability. Sendmail, for example, uses a cryptic rules-based file, whereas Taylor UUCP has a configuration file so simple that the experienced UNIX administrator is left looking for the *real* configuration file!

Generally, UNIX configuration files use the hash character (#) for comments. It is placed at the start of a line, and most programs ignore text that follows a comment character in a configuration file. A few significant differences are DNS zone files, which use semicolons, and C code. Usually, tabs and spaces in configuration files are treated the same (i.e., ignored, other than as a separator character) and are referred to as white space.

## File Manipulation, Wildcards, and Special Characters

The experienced UNIX user gets in the habit of naming common files with matching characters to enable the use of wildcards. For example, the /etc directory contains a group of files starting with rc, such as rc.conf, rc.firewall, rc.i386, rc.local, and rc.network. This makes it easy to go to /etc and do a directory listing of only these files with the command ls -l rc*. The * character is a wildcard meaning *Pattern-match everything*. The line is interpreted to mean, "Match all files starting with rc and any characters after these two." This makes it easy to see that these files all have something to do with each other, which is true: all the files have to do with system startup.

Naming conventions become important when moving groups of files around. For example, the administrators may have used up all space on the disk drive on which /usr/local is located, and they attempt to correct the problem by adding a disk. However, they only want to put some of the directories in /usr/local on the new disk, specifically the bin, man, lib, and etc directories. To do so they might first go to /usr and create a new directory, local1. They then create a mountpoint for the new disk on /usr/local1. (With UNIX, unlike DOS/Windows, disks can be placed into any arbitrary point in the filesystem and are not restricted to a drive letter.) Then they move the directories from /usr/local to the new disk with the mv local/??? local1 command. The ??? means "Match a single character in that position." The result is that, since the directories they want moved are all three letters long, no more and no less, only those directories are moved.

UNIX users should not use certain special characters in filenames and directory names (i.e., characters that are reserved by the command processor, especially the forbidden "/"). Examples are <, >, &, and space characters. Some of these, such as the space character, may be allowed, but the file created with this character will be very difficult to manipulate. For example, UNIX generally allows a file to be created by a program with a space character, but it is annoying to have to enclose the filename in double quotes to manipulate it. These characters are listed in the man page for the command processor that the user decides to use; for example, at the prompt issuing the man sh command, will display information about the sh command processor and list characters reserved for use as control and redirection operators.

## Logging In

PCs historically have been used to run single-user operating systems. DOS and many Windows programs assume that they are the only things in control of the machine, writing directly to screen buffers and I/O ports and chewing up the CPU waiting for key input. From this perspective, many of the multiuser features in UNIX seem to be pointless overhead.

In a multiuser system, many assumptions about the program being able to *take over* the machine have to be cast aside. Significant differences exist between the computing experience on a single-user system and a multiuser one, the most important of which are separation of user and system files and separation of users from each other. Users tend to want to separate their work from other users' work. They may want to deny or give access to others. For the system to manage these preferences, it must be told who is doing what and where they are doing it. This is done by creating separate *login sessions* and assigning usernames and passwords to each user. Before users are allowed to manipulate data in the system, they must authenticate to the system. The UNIX system then keeps track of them all the while their login session is running until they log out.

The system keeps a list of allowed users in /etc/master.passwd. This file maintains some other personal information about each user, such as complete name, rather than login *handle*, and preferred shell program. It is generally manipulated by the vipw program. It should *not* be edited directly.

The password file also defines *home directories*. Since the system should not intermix its system files with the user's personal files, it establishes *file and directory permissions* to prevent users from manipulating files in inappropriate areas. Imagine the problems that would result if each user wanted to run a different version of the Telnet program and simply copied their versions over the system-supplied one. This is a big change from Windows operating systems, which allow user application install programs to copy executables and libraries wherever they please or overwrite library versions with their own. Under UNIX, there is no *right* directory to which user-supplied personal application programs can copy their files, except for the user home directories. Only the superuser is allowed to overwrite or change system binaries and files.

Because users do want to run their own programs and customize behavior of system programs, UNIX application software typically makes much more use of environment variables. Some of these, such as USER, HOME, and TERM, are set by the system when a user logs in. Others, such as EDITOR, are set by the user. The application software uses these variables to decide where to put personal configuration files. Therefore, one user running vi (vi is pronounced *vee-eye*, not *six*) can have a setting such as Visual Bell default to on, while another user simultaneously running the same program on the same system can have it default to off. A command in the personal login script places this setting in the environment for the user.

Logon variables are set in three major areas. The *user-selected shell program* and the system authentication programs (login) set some of these, the *system profile* file for the selected shell sets some, and the *user profile* file sets the rest. The following is a sample user login under FreeBSD and how it works.

**1.** The init program calls getty on an opened tty and invokes the login program to authenticate the user.

**2.** The login program discards any previous environment and then sets the HOME, SHELL, PATH, TERM, LOGNAME, and USER variables. It then executes the user-specified shell (/bin/sh).

**3.** The sh program runs and executes the system script /etc/profile, which sets additional variables. This is somewhat like the system AUTOEXEC.BAT under DOS. Common variables are PATH, MANPATH, or LD_LIBRARY_PATH, which the sysadmin may use to specify additional directories for software added to the system. LD_LIBRARY_PATH is sometimes used for test compiles of software. Usually, add-on software to UNIX systems, such as improved editors, network programs, and so on, are placed in a binary directory that is kept separate from the system-supplied binary programs. This practice facilitates easy system upgrading. A map of the FreeBSD filesystem is available from the system manuals with the command man hier.

**4.** The sh program then executes the .profile (*dot-profile*) file, which is located in the user's home directory specified in /etc/passwd. The home directory resembles a personal copy of an AUTOEXEC.BAT that the user can customize to his or her own environment. It sets user-specified environmental variables, such as EDITOR, and it can modify any system-defined variables, such as PATH, to allow for personal user programs.

The UNIX system doesn't count on anything as insecure as an environment variable to establish security, however. Security is controlled by the interaction of *permission bits* and /etc/group. The latter is changed by the system administrator, who uses a special user account known as the *root* account for administrative tasks. The root account is also known as the superuser account.

## The Root Account

A certain mystique has grown up around use of the root account. Newcomers hear that superusers have absolute control over the system and can do anything they want to any process, user, or file, and think that the root user account is supremely powerful. A user might think that the root account can somehow run programs better or make the system easily do a bunch of things that ordinary users strive to get the system to do. The root account may seem like the pinnacle of user accounts.

In reality, there is only one difference between the root user and ordinary users. The root user's security profile overrides all other system security. For example, ordinary users cannot manipulate files owned by other users that are not world-writable, but root can open any file regardless of who owns it.

Because many system-level commands deal with modification of the entire system, these commands are written and their permissions are set so that only the root user can execute them. This is a safety issue, not a rights issue. For example, what possible reason would an ordinary user have to run commands needed to add a hard drive to the system? Since this operation requires getting every user to log off, shutting the system down to maintenance mode, and in general creating a royal nuisance for all system users, such commands are restricted to the superuser. If they weren't, an ordinary user could accidentally wipe out every user's files as well as the UNIX system's directory structure.

As you can see, the root logon can be dangerous, even fatal to the system if the administrator makes an inadvertent mistake. So the individual designated as the superuser usually has an ordinary account for personal use, just like every other user. Superusers use the root account when it's necessary to do something special. To switch into superuser mode from a regular user session, use the su command. A user must be a member of the *wheel* group to be able to run su.

The Root account is analogous to the Administrator account under Windows NT or the Supervisor account under Novell NetWare. Unlike these NOSs, however, it is generally not possible to designate superuser abilities to arbitrary users. Under UNIX, only one Root account exists. "Assistant root users" either have the password to it or they don't. Unlike NetWare, it is also impossible to delete the Superuser account. Although the entry can be erased in /etc/passwd, if the system is rebooted at the console to single-user mode (in which case the system cannot be used from anywhere other than the console), the person logging in can simply stick the line right back in.

Microsoft Windows NT operating systems all use the username of Administrator for the privileged account that can override security. The Novell NetWare NOSs use the username of Supervisor for this account.

This book uses the term *Administrator* for the person who is charged with operating the Administrator, Supervisor, and Root accounts on their operating systems. *Superuser* refers to the appropriate privileged user account name used to log in to the operating systems.

## System Permissions and File Ownership

The UNIX system maintains a set of *permission bits* for every file in the filesystem. These are shown by use of the ls command with the -l option. For example:

```
$ ls -l
total 2
-rw-r—r—    1 tedm   staff     0 Nov 11 23:45 afile
-rwxr—r—    1 tedm   staff     8 Nov 11 23:45 asecondfile
drwxr-xr-x  2 tedm   staff   512 Nov 11 23:45 myfiles
$
```

The output of this command lists the permission bits on the left. The file named afile is an ordinary file, and the file named asecondfile is an executable, which is shown by the x in the fourth character position from the left. The file named myfiles is actually a directory.

The permission bits have three major fields, comprising positions 2 through 10 of the permission bits. Reading from left to right, the first three are *user* permissions, the next three are *group* permissions, and the last three are *other* permissions. *User* is the user logged in; *other* is basically a synonym for everyone. Group permissions allow the administrator to group like users together.

For example, Sally, Fred, and Mark are all employees of the marketing department who are responsible for putting periodic report files up for another employee, Sam, to collect. Since the first three employees collaborate on the reports and frequently modify each other's work, they have a separate directory, /home/reports, in which they are allowed to modify and delete files. Sam works for a different department and is always looking for the odd corner on the network servers to save extra files. (Sam is the bane of the network administrator.) The first three don't want Sam or any other employee from his group messing up their Reports directory with a bunch of stuff that doesn't concern them.

The administrator might set up a group called *market* and put the first three as members in it. The administrator would then set the Reports directory as writable by this group but only readable by others. Since Sam is not in the marketing group, he can only read the reports in the directory, not delete them.

Groups are defined in the file /etc/group. The line in this file that defines the marketing group listed here would look like this.

```
market:*:634:sally,fred,mark
```

A directory listing of the /home directory would show the permission bits set as follows. Note that not only do the group permissions need to be set writable, but also the Reports directory must be in the market group.

```
$ ls -l
total 2
-rw----      1 sally   users       0 Nov 11 23:45 sally
-rw----      1 fred    users       0 Nov 11 23:45 fred
-rw----      1 mark    users       0 Nov 11 23:45 mark
-rw----      1 sam     users       0 Nov 11 23:45 sam
drwxrwxr-x   2 sally   market    512 Nov 11 23:45 reports
$
```

The chmod command is used to manipulate file and directory permissions. The chown command changes file ownerships. The system manual page has a complete listing of the different permissions and what they do.

## Text File Differences

Almost all UNIX configuration can be done by editing text files. Even the graphical UNIX administration utilities are simply front-ends that modify the real text configuration files. Unfortunately, Microsoft operating systems, DOS, Windows, Windows NT, and so on, handle internal representations of text files differently than UNIX. UNIX text files terminate every line with a newline character, which is actually an ASCII linefeed character. Microsoft operating systems terminate lines in a text file with two characters: the carriage return character followed by the linefeed character. Apple Macintoshes use only the carriage return. Usually, text files created under MS operating systems are referred to as *DOS text files*.

This leads to a problem—creating and modifying a DOS text file on a Microsoft operating system and transferring it unmodified to UNIX results in a UNIX text file with an extraneous carriage return character at the end of every line. Sometimes this doesn't matter. For example, if a Hypertext Markup Language (HTML) text file is created under an MS system and dragged into a UNIX directory over the network, the Apache Web Server running under UNIX treats the file as if it were created under UNIX. Line printers, such as dot matrix printers, however, need the carriage return that UNIX text files lack.

There are many schemes to translate DOS text files to UNIX. The translation can be done before or after the file is transferred; it can be done by separate programs or by the application used to copy the file between operating systems. I'll cover some of these, but it is up to the administrator to decide what scheme to use. In all examples concerning text files, I assume that the file was created *on the UNIX system* and thus has no extraneous carriage return characters and follows UNIX text file conventions.

## Control Characters and Escape Sequences

When a PC is booted, the user sits down at a keyboard that is hardwired into the machine. When a key is pressed on the keyboard, the keyboard *scancode* is sent to the PC. Internally, the computer does a mapping between the scancode and a character representation. The PC operating system (actually the BIOS in DOS) must manage the keyboard input at a very low level, which is one reason it was so difficult to build multiuser versions of DOS. This hardware scheme is ideally suited for a single-user operating system, such as DOS, Windows, or Win95.

UNIX, by contrast, originated on time-shared systems where most users were connected at some distance from the CPU. In many cases the connection was several miles long, so modems were employed. In such a large system it is more efficient to distribute as much of the low-level computational load as possible. Thus, terminals that did the internal scancode-to-character mapping were used, with only the characters sent to the CPU. Originally these terminals lacked a screen and used printers for output. ASCII was developed for these printing terminals to use.

ASCII defines a number of additional characters, called *control codes*, to handle noncharacter keys and nonalphanumeric input. DOS also picked up this convention. The escape key (Esc), the carriage return key (Enter), backspace, and delete are control characters. In UNIX documentation, it is traditional to represent control characters with a prepended carat. For example, Ctrl-M is "^M," Ctrl-D is "^D," and so on. This book follows the UNIX convention.

In addition to the control keys, many terminals have function keys. There are vendor-standardized *escape codes* for these function keys. For example, the DEC VT100 terminal has F1 through F4 function keys and defines escape codes for them.

If the user running FreeBSD is typing at the PC keyboard, a kernel driver translates the scancodes to characters before passing them to the program. On the other hand, if the user is Telnetted in to the FreeBSD machine from a client machine such as a PC, the client Telnet program does the scancode conversion and sends the characters to the FreeBSD system. Thus, UNIX programs see identical character input whether they are run from the console or from a remote terminal.

Because of the reliance on a character stream, the operating system cannot assume that shortcuts such as Ctrl-Alt-Del on a PC, which brings up the task list under Win95 and NT, are available to the user. Therefore, the control characters are used to send special input directly to the operating system to override the currently running program, much as Alt-Tab is used to tell Windows to switch between Windows programs. Sometimes, these are referred to as *job-control* characters under UNIX.

Note that with FreeBSD, Ctrl-Alt-Del does reboot the machine—only on the system console, and only once the console driver has loaded. If you press the three-finger-salute while the system is booting, nothing happens because nothing is intercepting keyboard scancode output at that time.

## Shells

UNIX supports the concept of user-definable command processors, called *shells* (see Figure 1.2), much as the 4DOS command processor can be used to replace command.com under DOS. Shells are the character-mode interfaces with the UNIX system. The basic shell in practically all UNIX computers is

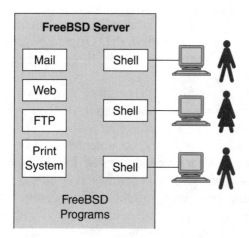

**Figure 1.2**  The shell program is the software interface to the system programs

known as the Bourne shell (named after S. R. Bourne, who wrote it), often seen as `/bin/sh`. Many introductory UNIX courses spend much time showing how to use various commands of this shell and constructing complex scripts with it. The truth is that the vast majority of administrators, let alone users, have no need to learn these commands. Today, most modern scripting on UNIX is done using the Perl utility; many people even use Perl as their shell.

The Bourne shell presents the dollar sign ($) as the prompt when the user logs in; when the user switches to the root user, the prompt is changed to the hash mark (#). Most other shells follow the Bourne convention and use $. The prompt character is also user-configurable, so don't assume that if $ is the prompt, the Bourne is the shell in use. The $ is a carryover from the Digital Equipment Corporation TOPS-20 operating system that ran on the PDP-10. This operating system used @ as the regular user prompt, and $ as the superuser prompt. The Bourne shell designers considered `/bin/sh` superior to TOPS-20, and so the $ sign stuck.

The Korn shell that later written to supersede the Bourne shell also uses $. Another shell older than `/bin/ksh` was `/bin/csh`, the "C" shell (pun intended). The "C" shell has also been superseded by a newer variant, `/bin/tcsh`. These shells use % as the prompt, which is a carryover from the original V6 UNIX for the PDP-11 before either Bourne or C shells were written.

The Bourne shell is not a very user-friendly shell and is not popular as a daily-work shell with most UNIX users, except, perhaps, system administrators. UNIX users usually change their shell to a preferred shell. For example, `chpass -s /usr/bin/ksh` changes the user's shell to the Korn shell (assuming that the Korn shell is installed). However, `/bin/sh` is the most popular shell for use with scripts because it is standardized; generally small, with lower resource requirements; and guaranteed to exist on all UNIX systems. Another advantage is that it does not require shared libraries. If the system's hard drives crash, in some cases `/bin/sh` is the only shell available to repair the damage. Because it is so important to administrators, it is the shell used for all examples in this book. Users with DOS backgrounds who like the DOSKEY command history may want to use the Bash shell, which is installable from Ports.

## SELECTING FREEBSD HARDWARE

At least an entire chapter could be written on the topic of FreeBSD hardware selection, but the computer hardware market changes too fast to make such a thing practical. Today, a mere $500 buys a clone system built from modern parts that are generally compatible with FreeBSD, and it is 100 times more powerful than new systems available only three years ago. It is simply not cost effective to bother with the older hardware anymore in a commercial organization, at least not for FreeBSD.

My rule of thumb, drawn from experience, is that FreeBSD boots and runs flawlessly on 95 percent of all new hardware and 80 percent of all hardware that is older than three years. So, if you have an older machine in the closet that you want to try running FreeBSD on, go ahead and try it. However, if it doesn't work, then don't waste your time trying to get it to work.

At any rate, most commercial organizations want hardware that is supported under FreeBSD by the manufacturer, and this is now a reality. For clone hardware, the page at `http://www.freebsd.org/commercial/harware.html` gives a list of vendors that custom-build FreeBSD hardware. For name-brand hardware, the page at `http://testdrive.compaq.com/` has a FreeBSD link that shows FreeBSD running on a Proliant 550 and an XP1000a EV6.7 Alpha-architectured system.

For administrators who would like to get a commercial name-brand desktop computer and run FreeBSD on it, some sample configurations follow. Since these are desktop systems, using them as a server is not optimal, but they would probably perform satisfactorily anyway. All have been operational at one time.

## Compaq Deskpro EN

Compaq makes a wide variety of Deskpro EN computers. They are all built around the same general low-profile chassis, but models vary depending on the amount of RAM, size of hard drive, speed of CPU, and so on.

Compaq Deskpro EN came with 64MB of RAM on a single DIMM, a 6.4MB hard drive, and a 400Mhz Celeron processor. The system has two PCI slots and an onboard Intel Pro 100 network adapter and sound card. It was targeted for a dual-use Ethernet router and Web server. In the first PCI slot was an Intel Pro/100+ Dual Port Server adapter card. The second slot held an Adaptec 2940UW. An external rack-mounted hard drive bay was connected to the external SCSI adapter port. FreeBSD 4.0 was then installed on the internal 6.4GB IDE hard drive.

FreeBSD recognized all devices out of the box except for the sound card and USB port. A subsequent kernel recompile added the drivers for these devices. The three network adapters (the one on the motherboard and the two on the dual-port card) were recognized by the fxp0 device as full-duplex 100BaseT. The IDE controller on the motherboard was recognized as a bus-mastering Intel PIIX4 ATA33 controller, and the IDE disk was recognized as an Ultra DMA device. The CD-ROM was recognized as a PIOmode4 device. The SCSI adapter was recognized by the ahc0 driver, and during the kernel reconfiguration, the AHC_ALLOW_MEMIO option was selected to turn on memory-mapped mode to the SCSI card. The sound card was recognized as an ESS card by the sbc0 and pcm0 drivers after kernel recompilation. The USB port was recognized as an Intel 82371AB/EB port by the usb0 and uhub0 drivers.

## Older Deskpro

The older Deskpro system, a 386/33DX EISA-bussed Compaq Deskpro model 386/33L with 12MB of RAM, was also set up as a router. The system originally shipped with 12MB of RAM in a weird memory card configuration, and it was judged not worth the money to attempt upgrading. The system shipped with a 300MB ESDI disk plugged into a Compaq-modified ESDI controller.

FreeBSD version 2.1.6 would load but couldn't boot off the ESDI controller, which was removed and replaced with a standard Western Digital WD1007 ESDI controller. The system was reloaded and then booted fine. It had two internal COM ports on the motherboard, both nonbuffered. One was disabled, and a serial port card with a 16550AFN chip was added. An external Supra 2400bps modem was attached for remote access. Three SMC8013 Ethernet cards were added and recognized by the ed0 driver. The system saw a total of three years of continuous duty; during its life, it was upgraded all the way to FreeBSD version 3.2.

## CompuAdd

The CompuAdd 486/33 EISA system running NetWare 3.11 on two 500MB IDE disk drives and four 4MB SIMMS was retired from NetWare and set up for FreeBSD. Disks were removed and replaced with a BusLogic 742A EISA controller and a 2GB DEC 5.25 refurbished SCSI disk. A Wangtek 5525ES QIC drive was added for backups, and a Sanyo double-speed CD-ROM was added for loading software.

A load attempt on FreeBSD revealed problems with the SCSI controller, which were solved by an upgraded ROM chip and a firmware chip for the controller. This also revealed EISA probe problems with this controller. A problem report (PR) was filed with the FreeBSD Project. Several years later, during the CAM cleanup for version 3, one of the core developers became interested in the problem. I mailed him the EISA card and several other BusLogic cards, and about three months later, the BusLogic driver was completely overhauled. The completed code appeared in version 3.2 of FreeBSD; I tested it and the PR was closed.

## Micron P90

The Micron P90 desktop with Neptune chipset and motherboard was limited to a top CPU speed of 100Mhz, which was judged too slow for an end-user system; the motherboard contained five ISA slots and four PCI slots. It was upgraded to 32MB of RAM and a 3.2GB IDE disk drive. An Adaptec 1520 SCSI card was added, with two internal modems, an ISA video card, and an ISA NE2000 clone card. A 2GB Wangdat tape drive and SCSI CD-ROM were added. FreeBSD 2.2.6 was loaded, and the system was set up with two external modems, for a total of four modems. The Apache Web Server and PPP were both loaded, and the system was turned into a dialup remote access server and internal Web server for a 50-person office. It saw two years of continuous duty before retirement.

## PHYSICAL LAYOUT SECURITY

Since a central company fileserver by definition should contain all the organization's valuable data, the integrity of the server is of paramount importance. Unlike a desktop, a server's accessibility is not as important as its security. For example, if the administrator has only two locations to place a server, the first an open, easy-to-work-on location, the second a narrow, enclosed closet, the closet is the better choice if it can be fitted with a lock.

A PC is inherently physically insecure. Typical cases are small enough to lift, which means an intruder breaking in over the weekend can make off with the hardware. Some PC cases have fancy locks that can easily be drilled out. At any rate, PC cases are cheap enough that the thief can destroy the existing case and still make money selling the parts. Other cases have holes to pass a chain or cable through. This deters a *smash and grab* but not a determined attacker because the cases are all made of soft steel. Power tools can cut this steel in a matter of minutes, or bolt cutters can be used on the chain or cable. Even worse are the all-plastic cases made by some major manufacturers, such as Dell. The only sure way to keep a system from being stolen is to place it in a locked room with an alarm on its door.

Keeping the server in a locked room does have one drawback: connecting printers directly to parallel ports on the server is difficult. Many smaller organizations like to hang parallel printers off their servers, and a parallel cable is limited in how long it can be run. Generally, locking the server doesn't allow enough proximity for a printer.

It is also very common to keep spare hard drives for a production server on the shelf so that they can be rapidly substituted in case of a hard drive crash.

Many sites also keep spare motherboards and other critical server components. These parts must also be protected against theft or damage. A good way to handle this is to place all server accessories, such as spare parts, manuals, and software installation sets, in a locking metal cabinet next to the server.

## FREEBSD INSTALLATION MEDIA

Historically, UNIX installations were usually done from nine-track open-reel tape and from DEC TK50 cartridge tape. Later, quarter-inch cartridge (QIC) tapes came along. Tape is rarely seen now that CD-ROM drives are available. Unlike PCs, most UNIX workstations had ROMs that allowed them to boot from the QIC tape drive for this reason. FreeBSD carries on this tradition by permitting tape or QIC installation, as well as the other more popular installation mechanisms. Since the PC can't boot from the tape drive, however, to do a tape installation, the PC must have an equivalent amount of free space on the hard drive to extract the entire distribution. One other note about a tape installation: if you wish to *create* a tape installation with `tar` you must set the `tar` blocksize to 10.

Although tape installation may be useful, most people install their FreeBSD server by simply booting from a FreeBSD CD-ROM in the server's CD-ROM drive. Typically, in a corporate network environment the administrator obtains a CD of FreeBSD and installs it first on a main server. Additional installations of FreeBSD on computers acting as lesser servers can be done by mounting the CD in the first server and using the FTP method of installation. These are the quickest and most trouble-free methods of installation.

## DUAL-BOOTING WINDOWS NT AND FREEBSD

Although the thrust of this book is to set up FreeBSD as the only operating system on a server, someone might want to create a test system to dual-boot both operating systems. One approach is detailed at `http://www.devious.com/freebsd`. It discusses how to modify the NT boot loader menu to load FreeBSD from a second hard drive in the system. Another approach is to install NT and its boot selector, followed by FreeBSD, and then to install the FreeBSD boot manager. When the system boots, it first runs the FreeBSD boot manager, which allows a choice of FreeBSD or DOS. If DOS is selected, the NT boot manager runs, allowing the choice of NT (or NT and Windows). It's a bit cumbersome, but it works.

# DHCP, DNS, and TCP/IP
# on the Corporate LAN

Because FreeBSD uses the TCP/IP protocol as its primary network protocol, there is little point in running BSD unless you are committed to running TCP/IP on your organization's network. TCP/IP can be run as the primary network protocol or in conjunction with another protocol. Common protocols are NetBEUI, which is often used in peer-to-peer Microsoft Networking, and IPX, which is often used with Novell NetWare networks. However, it will save a lot of trouble later on if you can switch your organization's network completely over to TCP/IP, and indeed both Microsoft and Novell now recommend doing this.

Switching over to TCP/IP is far easier said than done, however, and it is also easy to make uninformed decisions during its initial deployment that cause problems later. Also, TCP/IP is much more than a simple network access protocol, such as NetBEUI. A whole suite of programs are part of the TCP/IP protocol suite and are unique to the protocol. Deploying the protocol and these application programs on the organizational network is the focus of this chapter.

I begin with a discussion of basic IP numbering and numbering schemes. Also covered are DNS, its relationship to the network, and basic IP services from a protocol standpoint. The chapter concludes with a discussion of all major TCP/IP application programs and instructions for loading the TCP/IP stack on several client systems.

## INTERNET PROTOCOL DESIGN VIEWPOINT

TCP/IP and the Internet grew in response to the networking needs of research, military, and governmental organizations. It was originally designed to network

UNIX and other mainframe systems together over very wide areas, up to world-wide, and to be redundant so as to withstand a nuclear attack that would destroy some nodes and links. Initially, few corporations used it as their primary network protocol because most early corporate networks were *dumb* terminal-based networks connected to mainframes with serial cables (Figure 2.1) or running Novell-based or IBM-based WANs. TCP/IP wasn't commonly used until the mid-1990s after the importance of the Internet became clear. After IP's initial development, the protocol became standardized with the Request for

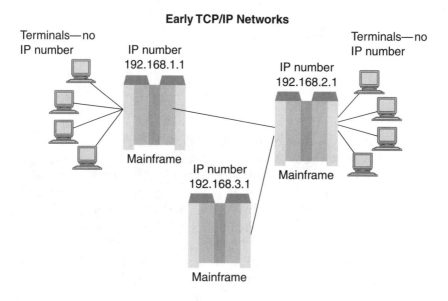

**Early TCP/IP Networks**

Terminals—no
IP number

IP number
192.168.1.1

IP number
192.168.2.1

Terminals—no
IP number

Mainframe

IP number
192.168.3.1

Mainframe

Mainframe

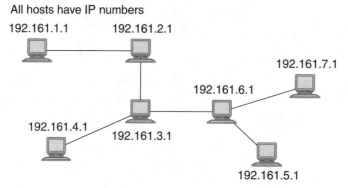

**Modern TCP/IP Networks**

All hosts have IP numbers

192.161.1.1          192.161.2.1

192.161.7.1

192.161.6.1

192.161.4.1          192.161.3.1

192.161.5.1

**Figure 2.1**  TCP/IP networks

Comments (RFC) process of the IETF (see Obtaining RFC Documents in this book's Preface). Although IP was still extensible, additions could be made only within its general framework.

Since most early timeshare systems were built out of a network of dumb terminals, such as VT100 terminals, these terminals weren't assigned IP numbers. The original designers of the IP protocol did not expect every user's access to the network to require a separate IP number; it was thought that only the hosts serving the terminals would need to be numbered. As a result of this, TCP/IP was not built from the ground up around a dynamically assigned network numbering scheme, such as that employed by Novell's IPX, AppleTalk, or NetBEUI.

In the original TCP/IP, all devices on the network were assigned a fixed IP number. Devices knew where to find each other by using DNS, which depends on a fixed IP number assigned to the device.

## Initial Networking Considerations

The first issue for many sites is knowing whether multiple networking protocols will run on the same network. Will TCP/IP will be the only protocol, the primary, or the secondary? If the site is converting to UNIX from an existing NetWare, Windows NT-over-IPX, or LanManager/LanServer NetBEUI-based network and plans to maintain overlapping file access to both server platforms, there isn't much choice. Clients will have to run both protocols and both types of networking clients for the duration of the conversion. User confusion may result over the locations and names of server resources. Almost certainly, two protocols and networking clients will generate much more work for the administrators. Larger sites planning a transition may be better off simply combining as much of the existing server resources on as few master servers as possible and doing a mass conversion over a major holiday.

Application compatibility with TCP/IP is another starting issue. If any current network applications are IP applications, or strict file and print applications, there should be no problem. Unfortunately, some earlier network programs that originated on NetWare networks used the additional function calls that Novell provides in its client. Novell is such a strong proponent of NetWare Directory Service (NDS) because software programs built requiring NDS cannot be run on any other kind of network. Theoretically, as long as the organization uses these applications, they won't switch away from Novell. For example, many accounting packages originating on NetWare used the Btrieve function calls. These applications *cannot* be reloaded on UNIX without purchasing an entirely new version from the manufacturer, assuming a UNIX version exists. Application compatibility with TCP/IP must be tested in advance of any conversion.

Microsoft has gotten the Novell "religion" on directory access and is promoting its own, competing, incompatible directory standard, Active Directory (AD). AD is a better replacement for the Microsoft Networking NT Domain Model, but any application programs that are specifically written to require AD cannot run on any other type of networking. When selecting applications, do not choose ones that require either NDS or AD, or your network will be forever locked in to a specific manufacturer's proprietary network implementation.

If you don't know right off what network-aware applications are running on client computers in your network, you may need to do a site software inventory of all computers before starting anything else. If you do have applications tied to a specific NOS, you will need to take them into account when planning what applications will be fielded on FreeBSD and what will be fielded on the proprietary NOS.

## Internet Protocol Number Range

Sites that implement TCP/IP must first decide how IP numbering is to be handled and choose an address range to use.

Historically, an organization that was going to use TCP/IP for their internal network numbering was advised to request a set of *legal IP numbers*. These were first assigned from the Network Information Center at SRI's numbering registry and then from the InterNIC's IP numbering registry. (The InterNIC controlled all IP numbering on the global Internet.) The numbering registry allocated IP numbers so that no organizations would use the same set of IP numbers on their internal networks. This way, in the event that the organizations were connected, through the Internet or directly, their internal numbering schemes would not overlap.

The Internet Assigned Numbers Authority (IANA) has sole authority for all IP number assignment. IANA has a contract with ARIN, `http://www.arin.net/`, a nonprofit corporation whose sole purpose is to manage IP number allocations among ISPs. The U.S. government funds IANA but is attempting to get rid of it. Besides ARIN, two other IP registries have been created: Réseaux IP Européens (RIPE) and Asia Pacific Network Internet Center (APNIC). All registration authority for IP numbering has been transferred from IANA to ARIN, RIPE, and APNIC. All three registries are funded by yearly fees for IP number blocks.

Due to the enormous popularity of the Internet and the way TCP/IP routing is structured on it, it is impossible to assign enough IP numbers to allow every organization to have a large set of unique numbers. Compounding the problem is the fact that years ago organizations requesting IP numbers would often request tremendous allocations of IP numbers, so that as they expanded their internal networks, they would have plenty of spares. For example, according to the whois[1] records, Microsoft has an entire class A IP number assigned to themselves, which totals approximately 16 million separate addresses. However, the entire company and its affiliates have only 22,000 people according to the corporate backgrounder on its Web site. Even assuming that everyone in the company has eight computers, Microsoft is still using less than 2 percent of its entire assigned address range. In reality, though, since most of the corporate Microsoft network is behind a firewall, only a small part of the company network must use legal numbers, perhaps a few hundred machines. Many other companies did the same thing. In addition, many more class B addresses were assigned.

Several technical solutions to this problem have been proposed, the principal one being IP-version-6 (IPv6). Unfortunately, this solution is completely incompatible with practically all TCP/IP implementations today, although implementation is proceeding slowly in the core Internet. FreeBSD 4.X now has IPv6 support, imported from the KArigoME[2] (KAME) project, as does Win2K. No one knows when Ipv6 will be required on the Internet, but most people hope that it won't be soon.

For these reasons, an organization switching over to IP today really has only one option: it must implement some kind of proxy between its internal network and the external Internet. It is then able to use what are known as RFC-Unassigned IP numbers (RFC1918) on their internal network. These are number blocks set aside specifically for use on inside networks and not allowed to be routed on the Internet. Most large ISP routers block them to *convince* organizations to abide by this. The ranges are 10.0.0.0 to 10.255.255.255, 172.16.0.0 to 172.31.255.255, and 192.168.0.0 to 192.168.255.255.

The proxy server can be implemented as an older-style *services proxy*, such as the Microsoft Proxy Server, or a newer-style *transparent proxy*, such as a Network Address Translation (NAT) program on FreeBSD, or a NAT running on version 11.2 or later Internetwork Operating System (IOS) on a Cisco router. Proxy servers have a side benefit to conserving IP numbering address space: they also serve as good firewalls.

Using RFC1918 addresses does have one drawback, however: if the organization connects its internal network to another organization by a direct connection (i.e., not through the Internet), and if both organizations are running

---

[1]*Whois* is a network TCP/IP program that is used to see what IP ranges are used by who, and what domain names are owned by who.

[2]Karigome is the city in Japan where the IPv6 KAME project is located.

RFC1918 addresses, they may have duplicate networks. For example, suppose a drug manufacturing company decides to use RFC1918 addresses 10.0.1.0 through 10.0.100.0 for its internal network. It connects to the Internet through a NAT. A year after its network is set up, its largest customer decides to connect to it directly for an order entry system. The customer is also connected to the Internet through a NAT and is also using RFC1918 addresses 10.0.1.0 on its internal network. Unaided, the connection won't work because hosts on the drug company will think that hosts on the customer are actually within the drug company network.

There are five ways to resolve such a connection clash.

1. One organization can obtain a set of legal numbers from its ISP, renumber its network, and use a NAT in between the two companies. The disadvantage here is that a few TCP/IP protocols, such as Microsoft NetBIOS Networking used for filesharing and browsing, cannot pass through a translator. If the application is something like SQLnet, it will have no problems passing through a translator.
2. One organization, usually the smaller one, can have the administrator of the bigger company make an assignment from the big company's RFC1918 range, and the smaller organization can renumber into this range. The smaller organization can generally do this once; for the next directly connected company they won't be able to renumber again without breaking the connection to the first company.
3. One organization can renumber into a different subnet of RFC1918. For example, if the big company is numbered from 10.0.0.0, the smaller company can renumber from 192.168.0.0. The drug company is unlikely to use this subnet because it is discontiguous from its existing numbering plan.
4. One company can renumber into a subnet on the Internet that is extremely unlikely to be used but is not set aside for RFC1918. For example, a number of legal subnets are tied up in military networks that will *never* be connected. This is risky, of course, because there is no guarantee that this net will stay unconnected.
5. The company-to-company connection can use proxying, but this is limited to Web/HTTP. Also, since fake IP numbers would need to be used on the *client* side, the proxy configuration would be horrendously complicated. Certainly, filesharing is also greatly complicated through a proxy, and some HTTP-based applications don't work properly through a proxy.

All these issues of corporate-to-corporate connectivity deal only with IP numbering and routing; DNS lookups present an additional set of problems.

# AUTOMATIC NUMBERING—DHCP

Once the IP number range is set, the next decision is how to assign it to the hosts in the network. TCP/IP originally assumed that hosts would be assigned a static IP number and would be locatable via DNS. At first, this worked out fine, but later on the deficiencies of static numbering became apparent. With static numbering, the administrator maintains a list by hand or on a spreadsheet that contains the names of every machine in the network and the TCP/IP network number assigned to each one. Whenever a machine is set up, the IP number must be entered into it. This can be very tiresome for the administrator, and typos can result in duplicate IP numbers being applied to multiple hosts on the network. Finding duplicates can be a very frustrating exercise.

To solve this problem, the Dynamic Host Configuration Protocol (DHCP) was codified in RFC1533 and RFC1534, with additional suggestions in RFC2132. DHCP was based on work done with the earlier auto-assignment protocols RARP and BOOTP and is used to assign an IP number to a workstation automatically. The main benefit of DHCP is that it greatly simplifies administration of the IP by not requiring each workstation to be specifically configured. I can state from experience that, especially in a mobile computing or development environment, where users are constantly trashing their machines' configurations, the headaches of static IP assignments make DHCP a requirement.

A DHCP network can be automatically assigned or statically assigned. With automatic assignment (i.e., floating IP numbering), a pool of IP numbers is defined by the administrator in the DHCP server. The DHCP server is configured to allocate IP numbers out of this pool to any client's Medium Access Control (MAC) address that happens to request one. The numbers are leased for a reasonable period, such as 24 hours. The client is required by the standard to request permission from the DHCP server to continue using the IP numbering when the lease expires. If the lease expires without a re-lease request, the server waits a bit for a re-lease request from the client. If none is forthcoming, the server then assumes that the client has been shut down and marks the IP number as available to other lessors. In this way IP numbers can transfer between clients over time.

While at first glance it may seem advantageous to number every host automatically, this is not a good idea in a production network. Devices such as printers, routers, servers, network switches, SNMP agents on hubs, and other network devices must continue to retain the same IP number, even if they are shut down for long periods. In addition, hosts often require fixed IP numbers, too. Many legacy IP applications depend on a fixed IP number assigned to the server that they are communicating to, like NFS and `rcp`, or because their security is based on a fixed IP number. Also, fixing IP numbers to a host greatly helps in tracking network problems (or illegal employee cracking) in logs. Very few sites need to allow IP numbers to float between hosts, and most prefer the opposite. In fact, in most cases on most production networks, the only hosts that clearly require floating IP numbers are portable hosts, such as laptops.

This is where static DHCP numbering comes into play. The DHCP server is configured with a table of MAC addresses and IP numbers. (The MAC addresses can be determined by setting up the DHCP server initially as an automatic server and then reviewing `/var/db/dhcpd.leases`.) When a client boots up on the network, it sends out a broadcast packet that contains its MAC address and a request for an IP number. The DHCP server matches the MAC address and assigns the IP number allocated to that client. When the lease has expired, the client requests the IP numbering again. The numbering handed back out is always the same for that client.

Unfortunately, there is a lot of misinformation about DHCP. Partly because of ignorant marketing by DHCP server vendors, but mostly because of horrible management of static assignments of addresses by network administrators, many inexperienced networking people have the impression that DHCP somehow conserves IP numbers. This is simply not true *if* the administrator is managing static assignments correctly. The only thing a DHCP server does is ease administration. If an organization has 100 nodes on the network, no amount of DHCP configuration is going to change the fact that the organization needs at least 100 IP numbers when all those hosts are switched on at 10:00 AM. It's like a game of musical chairs: just because everyone is dancing around doesn't change the fact that an extra chair is needed. When the music stops, someone is missing a chair.

If the network administrator is running a sloppy network, with numerous IP numbers statically assigned to hosts that no longer exist, DHCP works very well in reclaiming IP numbers! Of course this works only one time; once the pool of checked-out IP numbers shrinks to the actual number of hosts, no further gains are possible. Thus, the DHCP network is the same as a well-managed static network, with one IP number for each host.

In any case, the idea that IP numbers must be *conserved* in the internal network is foolish. In just about all modern corporate networks today, RFC-Unassigned TCP/IP numbers are used on the *inside* network, behind either a proxy or an address translator. For example, the Class A Unassigned range 10.0.0.0 gives 16 million addresses to use. Thus, there is no need to "conserve" IP numbers or artificially restrict their use. DHCP can be relied on to reduce administration, which it does very well, but it does not make additional IP numbers appear out of thin air.

Following are several other issues to be aware of with DHCP servers.

- A DHCP server assigns addresses only in its *broadcast realm*. If a large, multisubnetted network is to be switched over to DHCP, it requires either *DHCP helpers* on each router or separate DHCP servers on each subnet. By default, TCP/IP broadcasts are *not forwarded between routers*.
- Only one DHCP server per subnet can be active at a time; multiple servers can clash with each other. This restriction may reduce network reliability: if the DHCP server goes down for an extended period, the entire network can be taken offline. To fix this problem, a DHCP Server Failover protocol is being written that will appear in a future version of FreeBSD in the Internet Software Consortium (ISC) DHCP server.
- DHCP cannot restrict an assignment to a host, unless the server assigns addresses only to already entered MAC addresses. Otherwise, if the DHCP server can hand out addresses automatically, it hands them out to any client that asks. Thus, the DHCP server cannot exercise any security control.
- A DHCP server should be run on a lightly loaded, powerful machine with great network connectivity that's not going to be affected by a power glitch or some user tripping over a dangling cable. Otherwise, clients can fail to obtain an IP number in time during the boot process.

Several popular DHCP servers are available in the FreeBSD distribution. The two major ones are the Widely Integrated Distributed Environment (WIDE) DHCP server (wide-dhcp-1.3b) and the ISC DHCP server (isc-dhcp2.b1.0) Both of these are available as precompiled packages and in the Ports directory. The official home of the current ISC DHCP server is at <ftp://ftp.isc.org/isc/dhcp/>.

## Installing the ISC DHCP Server

At this point, if you are reading the book sequentially, you may not have an operating FreeBSD server. If so, you can skip this part and come back to it once your server is operating. I include these instructions here because they are relevant only to this chapter.

The precompiled ISC DHCP server can be installed on FreeBSD by selecting it from the packages listed in /stand/sysinstall, but for production use the current server code should be obtained from ISC and built in the Ports directories. Use the instructions shown in Exhibit 2.1.

### Exhibit 2.1  Installing the precompiled ISC DHCP server

1. Change directory into `/usr/ports/net/isc-dhcp2`.

2. Run `make`, followed by `make install`. The DHCP server is installed in `/usr/local/sbin` as the `dhcpd`, `dhcrelay`, and `dhclient` programs.

3. Now, build a dhcpd.conf configuration file in `/usr/local/etc`. A sample one that can be copied and then modified will end up in the `/usr/ports/net/isc-dhcp2/work/dhcp-2.0/server/dhcpd.conf`. The manual page on the `dhcp.conf` file is also very useful. Note that some builds of this server look for the file in `/etc`, not `/usr/local/etc`.

   An example of a `dhcpd.conf` file* for Windows hosts is as follows:

```
option domain-name-servers 192.168.1.1 , 192.168.1.2;
subnet 192.168.2.0 netmask 255.255.255.0 {
        range 192.168.2.10 192.168.2.254;
        max-lease-time 172800;
        default-lease-time 86400;
        option routers 192.168.2.1;
        }
host ahost {
        option netbios-node-type 2;
        option netbios-name-servers 192.168.3.2;
        hardware ethernet 00:a0:ca:58:da:41;
        fixed-address 192.168.2.8;
        }
```

4. If the FreeBSD kernel doesn't have support for the Berkeley Packet Filter, rebuild it and add BPF support.

5. In the `/usr/local/etc/rc.d` directory, create the `dhcp.sh` file with the following lines.

```
#!/bin/sh
[ -x /usr/local/sbin/dhcpd ] && /usr/local/sbin/dhcpd -q && echo -n
    'dhcpd'
```

   After a reboot, the server is activated. Note that with some versions of this DHCP server, Windows clients do not like the option `server-name` passed to them, so this option should not be in the `dhcpd.conf` file.

   Note that if you have a WINS server on the network, then, option `netbios-node-type` and option `netbios-name-server` *must* be present in the configuration file!

   This DHCP server stores DHCP dynamic leases in `/var/db/dhcpd.leases`. It does *not* store static DHCP assignments in this file. To track activity of static DHCP leases, syslogging must be turned on in `/etc/syslog.conf` with the line
   `daemon.info      /var/log/daemon`

---

*Note:* In this file the `domain-name-servers` option is the only global option, and the subnet declaration is for most of the subnet. The few IP numbers that it doesn't cover are either statically assigned on the host or assigned to specific hosts in the DHCP server. Be sure that a subnet declaration exists for every interface on the FreeBSD system; it must be present even if no range is defined because the administrator doesn't want the DHCP server handing out IP numbers on the network on that interface.

## DOMAIN NAME SYSTEM

Once a method of assigning IP numbers to all computers in the network has been determined, the next consideration is how—or if—you will use DNS on your network. DNS is the protocol used to convert a human-readable name, such as `ftp.uu.net`, into a TCP/IP network number, such as 192.48.96.9, which the computer requires to make an IP connection. It is something like a telephone directory: a person needs a telephone number to phone another person, and a computer needs a TCP/IP network number to reach another computer using the Internet. On the Internet, DNS is used to locate any host offering services. For example, typing in `http://www.freebsd.org` to a Web browser generates a DNS query from the browser that goes to a DNS server.

Today, millions of machines on the Internet provide publicly reachable services such as the Web and FTP. All these machines must be entered into a DNS server. Countless additional hosts are not providing services but are named in DNS to facilitate their management on organizational networks. Also, with most domains and networks, hosts are constantly being reassigned to different IP numbers and renamed.

It is practically impossible to build a single DNS server with a database large enough and powerful enough to act as a central directory repository with a record for every host on the Internet. Even if it could be done, the network traffic alone needed to reach the server would be much larger than the largest long-haul network connections in existence. Thus, the DNS is actually implemented as a database distributed across many hundreds of thousands of DNS servers, called *nameservers*, on the Internet (see Figure 2.2). Each nameserver has a small part of the total database, and each knows how to find some other nameservers on the Internet that know some more bits of the database.

Most DNS servers are run by ISPs. If your network is small (i.e., less than 50 hosts), access to the ISP's DNS server may be all you need. Furthermore, if you're running a proxy server, none of the inside computers need access to a DNS server at all; only the proxy would need access to a DNS server.

If you don't plan on using DNS at all, not even an ISP's DNS server, it is perfectly fine to use a `hosts` file on every machine in the network. This file is referred to by the TCP/IP stack on the client to look up the IP number of a host if a DNS server isn't accessible on the network. Typically a central `hosts` file is edited on a convenient system and copied to each client periodically, perhaps with an `rcp` command executed out of `cron` under UNIX or the `at` scheduler under Windows NT.

If your network is larger than 50 hosts, however, or you wish to control your own namespace, or your network is not directly connected to the Internet,

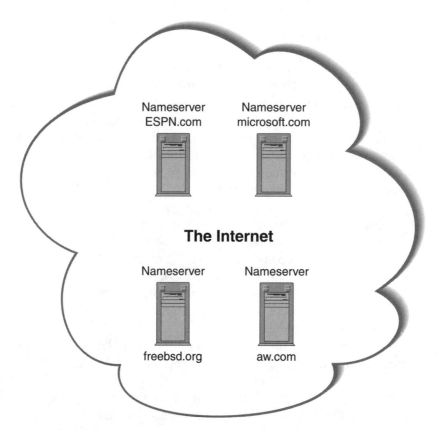

**Figure 2.2**  DNS on the Internet

you may want to run your own nameserver. If you plan on doing this, purchase the name services "Bible."[3] It explains in depth how to configure Berkeley Internet Nameserver Daemon (BIND) on a UNIX system. BIND is a free UNIX utility originally written by Kevin Dunlap working under a Department of Defense contract at the University of California at Berkeley. FreeBSD through version 2.2.8 ships with BIND version 4. FreeBSD version 3.X and later uses BIND version 8. The current version of BIND is 8.2.2 and is located at `ftp://ftp.isc.org/isc/bind/src/`.

With some operating systems, such as Windows 95/98, the client checks the `hosts` file for a lookup first; if it's not found there, the client attempts a

---

[3]Paul Albitz and Cricket Liu, *DNS & BIND, Third Edition*. O'Reilly, September 1998 (ISBN 1565925122).

DNS query. This is an extremely useful hack for one or two machines but an administrative nightmare with many machines. FreeBSD has a configuration file, `/etc/host.conf`, that controls this behavior, but this configuration file generally won't need to be modified except under unusual circumstances. In most cases, however, it's better to set up a DNS entry instead of hacking things in this file.

You can run a DNS server as a public or a private server. A public DNS server is a DNS server that is accessible to hosts on the Internet and is registered in the root nameserver. It is used if you wish to offer names of your externally accessible hosts to the Internet at large. A private nameserver is used for your own use only, such as local name caching or local name resolution. If you're serving RFC1918 numbers with a private nameserver, it will not be reachable from hosts on the Internet.

If you run a public nameserver, don't use any version of BIND older than version 8. Older versions of BIND contain security holes, which are addressed in Computer Emergency Response Team (CERT) advisory CA-96.02 (available online at `http://www.cert.org`).

## The DNS's Relation to DHCP

Naming all your internal TCP/IP devices in a local DNS server is a very useful way of keeping track of systems. If you use DHCP to assign IP numbers on your local network, however, and you want to use DNS, special care is required. If you want the same name to refer to the same host all the time, any host that is defined in the DNS server *must* be defined with a static IP number in the DHCP server by hard-coding it in its configuration file with a fixed IP number. Otherwise, you can simply name all the IP numbers and use DHCP or other random assignment, but then the hosts will not have the same name all the time.

Some people, however, cannot accept the use of fixed IP numbers in a DHCP server. As a result, there are a number of proposals that modify the DHCP server or DNS server, or the clients, to send various messages between the DHCP server and the client. RFC2136 and RFC2137 describe a way to create DNS entries dynamically. Additionally, the latest version of the DNS server, BIND version 8, which is supplied with the current version of FreeBSD, allows for dynamic updating from Win2K and BSD DHCP clients. Version 3 of the ISC DHCP client must be used for FreeBSD dynamic updating.

One major problem with these schemes is how other DNS servers on the Internet handle them. Unlike changing a Web page, a change made in a DNS server does not immediately take effect across the Internet. A tremendous amount of caching is deliberately designed into the DNS server network. It may take up to a full day before changes to a host's IP number are propagated across the Internet.

With all the propagation problems on dynamic DNS, it's amazing that there's still widespread interest in it. The only reason that it even works at all is because DHCP servers usually continue to hand out the same IP number to a client. Dynamic DNS is useful in large networks of laptops or other mobiles, but for most fixed IP networks, controlling your IP numbering from the beginning and tracking MAC addresses is still the best way of handling DHCP and DNS on your network. In particular, tracking the MAC address pays dividends later when you need to troubleshoot your network.

## Client DNS Queries

When a computer in the network makes a DNS query (Figure 2.3), it's not just a simple name-IP number pairing. Many kinds of DNS queries are possible, but the primary ones are Address and Mail Exchanger queries (see Exhibits 2.2 and 2.3).

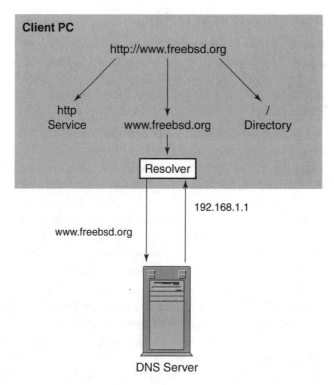

**Figure 2.3** Client DNS querying

This is an example of how a Web browser running under an operating system uses the DNS system (*not* hosts or other resolution protocol) to make an address query.

1. The user types in a URL, such as `http://www.freebsd.org/`.

2. The Web browser breaks the URL into three parts: `http`; the hostname, `www.freebsd.org`; and the directory requested, "/".

3. The browser passes the hostname to a function call in the operating system that returns with an IP number. This function is part of the local resolver.

4. The local resolver checks the operating system settings looking for the IP number of a DNS server. It then opens a connection to the DNS server on UDP port 53 and passes the server the hostname.

5. The DNS server returns the IP number of the hostname to the local resolver.

6. The local resolver returns to the Web browser application with the IP number.

The procedure in Exhibit 2.3 on the next page shows that e-mail is actually routed based on the entry in a host's MX record, *not* on its address record. Much e-mail is addressed to domains instead of hosts. With that kind of mail, the process is exactly the same, except that the destination domain name is passed to the nameserver in the MX query instead of the destination hostname. The MX record for the domain returns a hostname or list of hostnames.

## Server DNS Queries

How does the nameserver find out IP numbers? It sends DNS queries to other nameservers (see Figure 2.4). These nameservers make queries to even more nameservers. Consider for a moment all the domains currently on the Internet. Each one of those is served by a minimum of two nameservers, a *primary* and a *secondary* nameserver. Each of these nameservers exchange information with each other, creating a gigantic nameserver network referred to as the *Internet namespace*.

The Internet namespace is organized like a pyramid. At the top of the pyramid are the root nameservers. Currently, there are 13 root nameservers, and they are the single most important servers on the entire Internet. If some catastrophe were to occur and all these servers were to crash simultaneously, from the point of view of most users, within 6 hours the entire Internet would be so much useless wire. The catastrophe would have to be global in nature because the servers are spread over the entire world. The list of root nameservers is maintained on `ftp://ftp.internic.net/domain/named.root`.

**Exhibit 2.3  Mail Exchanger queries**

TCP/IP applications that transfer e-mail make a DNS query that returns a special kind of
address known as an *MX record*. Here is an example of how these work with a POP mail
client sending mail to `user@domain.domain.com`.

1. The user on the computer running the e-mail program composes an e-mail message and
   clicks Send.

2. The e-mail program looks for the name of the *smart* mailer (the SMTP server), and goes
   through the regular lookup process to gain its IP address.

3. The e-mail program then passes the mail to the smart mailer.

4. The smart mailer receives the e-mail address and reads the receipt address, `user@`
   `domain.domain.com`.

5. The smart mailer strips off the username part of the mail address and sends the hostname
   to the local resolver, asking for an MX query instead of an address query. If no MX
   record exists for the host, a last-ditch attempt at delivery is made to the number listed in
   the A record.

6. The local resolver contacts the DNS server and sends the query to it on port 53.

7. The DNS server returns the MX record to the local resolver, which returns it to the smart
   mailer.

8. The smart mailer checks the MX record looking for the name of the highest-priority mail
   relay.

9. The smart mailer passes the name of the mail relay to the local resolver, asking for an
   address query.

10. The local resolver queries the DNS server and returns to the smart mailer with the IP
    number of the mail relay.

11. The smart mailer attempts to establish a connection to the IP number of the mail relay
    and passes the e-mail.

12. If the mailer cannot establish a connection to the mailserver, it goes back to the MX record
    returned to it in step 7 and checks for the *next-highest-priority* mail relay for that domain.

13. The mailer then gets an IP number for this server and attempts to contact it.

14. If the mailer fails to contact this server, it repeats steps 12 to 13 until there are no more
    next-highest-priority mailservers left on the MX record. If no MX records are referred
    back, an error is generated.

---

Within the group of root servers is a single master root server—the "A"
server. All other root servers replicate the database on the A server. The A
server is operated by Network Solutions Inc. (NSI) and is funded by domain
registration fees and the U.S. government. Some of the other root nameservers
are owned and operated by other governments. NSI controls all root nameservers through the A server replication, regardless of ownership.

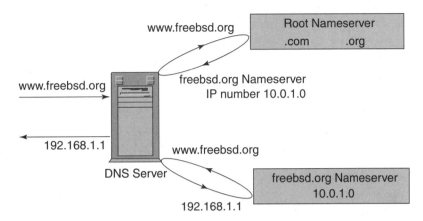

**Figure 2.4** Server DNS querying

Every nameserver in the world has a copy of `named.root`, and name service queries begin at those servers if they are not answered from the name cache of the originating server. In 1991, those servers handled six queries per second; today there can be hundreds of queries per second. These servers are basically servers of nameservers. In other words, a root nameserver doesn't know what the IP number of `ftp.uu.net` is, but it does know the IP number of the second-level nameserver for `uu.net`. That second-level nameserver knows the IP number of `ftp.uu.net`.

When a nameserver queries a root nameserver, all it gets back is a pointer to a nameserver that is authoritative for the domain it is querying on. It does not get back the IP number for the query; the root nameservers do not have a copy of every IP number assigned to every host!

Completely unconnected networks use a special DNS configuration on their server to make it a *fake root* nameserver, if they use nameservers at all, that is. These nameservers are not able to resolve domain names on the Internet; they are used to supply names for internal servers, such as Web, mail, FTP, and news. They can also be used to name any and all clients within that domain. Fake root servers are not used much anymore because most TCP/IP networks large enough to require a nameserver are now connected to the Internet.

## Differences Between WINS and DNS

It is very common for people who work with the Microsoft OSs, particularly with Windows NT, to become confused the first time they start working with DNS. Before 1995, Microsoft's literature seemed to regard DNS as a kind of competitive name service. Microsoft didn't really understand the Internet yet, and they weren't the only ones. This is no longer true, but the legacy of damage remains. For example, Microsoft refers to groups of Windows systems organized into a lookup group as belonging to members of a *domain*. The domain referred to in the MS technical literature has absolutely nothing to do with the domain in DNS.

The Internet in the Windows Internet Naming Service (WINS) also has nothing whatsoever to do with the actual Internet. What this Internet is referring to is an internet of networks. Before the Internet became so popular, the networking term *Internet* was used in this manner by Network Basis Input/Output System (NetBIOS) proponents. WINS is actually a marketing label applied to the NetBIOS Name Service (NBNS), which was standardized in RFC1001. This RFC also standardizes NetBIOS Datagram Distribution (NBDD) servers, which is referred to as *Master Browsing* in the Microsoft literature.

A WINS server is *needed only* in Microsoft Networking NT-style domains that span TCP/IP routers. It is *useless* to look up hosts on the Internet; DNS services are needed for that.

A summary of the differences between NBNS (WINS) and DNS follows.

**1.** NBNS is not guaranteed across the Internet; there is no master root server listing; and no mechanism exists for resolving hosts via NBNS that aren't entered into the organization's NBNS server (WINS server).

Because of this, organizations are often surprised to find that their NT Web server is resolvable inside the network, unresolvable outside of it. Entering an NT server into a WINS server *does nothing* to make it resolvable to hosts on the Internet.

**2.** DNS has a hierarchical structure: the root domain " . ", the top-level domains (e.g., `.com`, `.edu`), the second-level domain name (`freebsd.org`, `xfree86.org`, `cdrom.com`, etc.), and any third-, fourth-, or higher-level domains that the organization wants to set up.

NBNS has a flat structure. All hosts have a single name. Even if hosts are set up in different *NT domains*, if they are in the same broadcast region, they must have unique NetBIOS names.

**3.** NBNS servers *cannot* resolve DNS names, unless specially modified. The IP number of a normal Windows NT Server with WINS loaded on it *cannot* be used as the DNS server IP number in a Windows client. Of course, if a DNS server is also loaded on the same NT server, this is possible.

**4.** WINS servers automatically acquire names to add to their databases, which can be a huge security problem if someone on a network deliberately tries polluting the WINS server with bogus data. DNS servers have names statically assigned unless the site has implemented Dynamic DNS, in which case they can also be dynamically assigned, with the same security implications.

**5.** NBNS/WINS resolver queries return things other than an IP number. Do *not* try using a DNS server to resolve NetBIOS queries; it will work for crude lookups, but many Windows services depend on the additional data typing returned by a WINS server. Unfortunately, Microsoft NT has a button labeled "Use DNS for NetBIOS lookups" that can be turned on, but *do not do this*. If you need a WINS server on your network, then run one; don't substitute a DNS server for it.

In summary, if an organization has connected their internal network to the Internet, DNS is a requirement, regardless of whether the DNS server is operated by the organization or by the ISP.

An organization with a wholly unconnected internal network (not even a proxy connection)—and that describes virtually all Windows hosts—may elect to make a static entry for the few FreeBSD servers they run in their WINS server. This may be an easy way to avoid putting host files in each Windows client.

DNS–WINS interoperation is discussed more thoroughly in Chapter 7. Win2K replaces WINS with Active Directory, which is based on LDAP and other protocols, but a Win2K server still installs a WINS server for backward compatability. Indeed, Active Directory is useless unless every Windows system in the enterprise is changed to a Win2K system of some kind.

### Installing the BIND DNS Server

FreeBSD comes with BIND prebuilt and a skeleton set of BIND files in `/etc/namedb`, but its database must be created before the DNS server can run. The instructions in Exhibit 2.4 show how to build a quick and dirty primary nameserver using the h2n utility. These instructions use the following names as examples.

Machine name: `ns.testdomain.com`
Random host in domain: `www.testdomain.com`
Machine IP number: 192.168.1.45

In addition, an `/etc/hosts` file should be filled in with IP numbers of hosts in the network. See the example entries in the `hosts` file itself. The h2n utility was written by the authors of *DNS & BIND*, which should be purchased by anyone planning on setting up a production nameserver on the Internet. In particular, those who have *broken* Class C addresses (i.e., a subnet assigned by their ISP that is less than a full C) should *also* read RFC2317 *before* attempting to run a production primary nameserver.

## Exhibit 2.4  Building a primary nameserver using the h2n utility

1. Start by obtaining the h2n Perl script from `ftp://ftp.uu.net/published/oreilly/nutshell/dnsbind/dns.tar.Z` and put it into `/etc/namedb`. Make absolutely sure to back up the existing example files in this directory.

2. Make a directory called `tools` in `/etc/namedb` and change the current directory to it.

3. Extract the tools with the `tar xfz ../dns.tar.Z` command.

4. Some of the scripts may be UNIX-goofy, with DOS CR/LF text files. These can be fixed with the `cat foo | tr -d '\015' > foo2` command, where `foo` is the source file and `foo2` is the destination file. This may need to be done with the `h2n.man` manual page.

5. Change the h2n script to be executable with the `chmod u+x h2n` command.

6. h2n works by building the database files from the system `hosts` file in `/etc/hosts`. Start the initial test run with the `./h2n -d testdomain.com -n 192.168.1` command, substituting your domain name and network numbers, of course. The network number is the first three octets.

7. If that works, change one directory back into `/etc/namedb` and run h2n again. Use the `-v 8` flag if you are running under FreeBSD 3.4 or later because it uses BIND version 8. For example, `./h2n -d placo.com -n 192.168.1` builds some BIND files for my test network.

8. If running BIND 4, modify the `named.boot` file, comment out the `primary` line under the `cache` line, and then substitute these lines:
   ```
   primary 0.0.127.IN-ADDR.ARPA    db.127.0.0
   primary 1.168.192.IN-ADDR.ARPA  db.192.168.1
   primary testdomain.com          db.testdomain
   ```
   Otherwise, if running BIND 8, rename `named.boot` to `named.conf`, find the line `zone "." in {`, and under this, where it says `file db.cache` substitute
   ```
   zone "." in {
           type hint;
           file "named.root";
   };
   ```

9. Test the nameserver with the `/usr/sbin/named -b /etc/namedb/named.boot` command for a BIND 4 nameserver or just `/usr/sbin/named` for a BIND 8 server. If everything is OK, the console shows the message **named[some number] Ready to answer queries.** If the console is not active, this message can be seen with the `tail /var/log/messages` command.

10. Make a further test by running the `nslookup www.testdomain.com 127.0.0.1` command.

11. To permanently turn on the nameserver, modify the `/etc/rc.conf` file lines as follows
    ```
    named_enable="YES"
    ```
    and reboot the server to make sure it comes back up. When everything is working, modify the `/etc/resolv.conf` file and put the IP address of the system in it for the nameserver.

> **NOTE**   Do *not* set up this test nameserver as your primary nameserver on the Internet until you are familiar with how DNS database files should look. Read the *DNS & BIND* book before setting up a production nameserver! Also, read the example files in `/etc/namedb`.

### Note on BIND

The following error message has been noted on particularly heavily loaded nameservers under FreeBSD 2.X:

```
Too many open files
```

This is followed by bouncing mail and other bad behavior. It is probably caused by the `named` program reading the per-process limit on the number of open file descriptors.

The default limit of 64 descriptors can be lifted by running `limit descriptors 256` or `ulimit -n 256` before starting `named`, or by running `sysctl -w kern.maxfiles=256`. A better solution, however, is to build a new kernel with a higher default, using

```
options      "OPEN_MAX=256"
```

Note that this should not happen on current FreeBSD versions. Don't run `sysctl` on them.

## Your DNS Name

A domain name is an organizational asset, just like a published 800 number or a successful advertising campaign. Because the Internet has no single central directory, as the telephone system does, potential customers who may be surfing the Web usually collect lists of interesting URLs or e-mail addresses containing a domain name. A business that wants its Web site or e-mail address to be noticed and saved by online users must advertise its domain name. Advertising requires a large commitment of time and people, and, as with anything valuable, the organization must continue to invest in the domain name.

## Registries

A registry is an organization that assigns domain names. Ever since the Internet started, and through September 1999, there was only one authorized registry, the InterNIC, owned by Network Solutions Inc. Many organizations wanted to be registries and proposed alternative DNS naming schemes, but unless the organization registered the domain through NSI, it was not official. This means that there was no guarantee across the Internet that the organization's domain name was resolvable because just about everyone on the Internet used the InterNIC's root nameservers. Only NSI-approved domain names were guaranteed to be resolvable across the Internet.

Needless to say, the monopoly enjoyed by NSI caused a tremendous amount of controversy, especially among organizations that looked with greed at the guaranteed revenue stream currently going into NSI. Because the root nameservers must be maintained, it was very unlikely that a domain name registered in the commercial part of the DNS namespace would be registered for free, forever. InterNIC currently charges a fee of $70 for two years' registration in the `.com` domain.

In an attempt to get around NSI, some of the alternative registries did set up registration and solicited domain name registrations from organizations, but their system worked only with the very few organizations that modified their `named.root` files. It soon became clear that propagandizing organizations to modify their `named.root` files wasn't going to work, and that only control of the root nameservers, specifically the A root nameserver, would allow participation of alternative registries. Most DNS administrators were not interested in complicating their troubleshooting by introducing additional root registries. As a result of all this and the death of Jon Postel, the father of the DNS system, the alternative registries finally got their wish: in January 2000, a new scheme came into existence.

The first thing that happened is that operation of the A root nameserver was taken over by the Internet Corporation for Assigned Names and Numbers (ICANN). ICANN's charter prevents it from profiting from domain name registrations. Therefore, all other registries must submit their lists of domain name updates to ICANN for inclusion into the roots.

The second thing that happened is that InterNIC/NSI effectively split into two companies (NSI is transitioning away from using the InterNIC name), NSI/Business and NSI/WorldNIC. NSI/Business handles domain name submissions from bulk users (e.g., ISPs, corporations with many vanity domains). NSI/WorldNIC handles *retail* domain name submissions from end users via the Network Solutions Web page.

Note that registration in the `.gov` domain as well as the `.us` domain and other ISO country-code domains is currently *not* handled by commercial registries. In some areas of the world, such as Taiwan, most commercial organizations register in the ISO country-code domains. The country-code domains do not enter into the monopoly controversy because the way registration occurs in these domains is up to the government of that country. However, the root servers controlled by the InterNIC do serve for these domains as well. The

.com domain is the one in dispute because registrations in .com are open to anyone and far exceed registrations in all other domains combined. Many foreign companies, in fact, maintain dual registrations: one in the ISO-country code domain for their geographic location and one in the .com domain.

A fairly complete list of ISO country codes is available at <u>ftp://ftp.</u> <u>ripe.net/iso3166-countrycodes</u>. There is also one in /usr/share/ misc/iso3166 on FreeBSD if the misc documentation is installed. The Inter-NIC, at <u>http://www.internic.net/</u> contains the current list of official registrars and should be the first stop for any organization planning to register a domain name.

> **NOTE**    *All two-letter domain endings are country codes* and are thus specific to the country. In some cases the country has entered into a contract with an outside registry to manage their top-level domain (TLD), and in those cases the registry currently has a *monopoly* on registrations in that country. For example, the .cc domain is served only by a single, monopoly registry.

*Do not* attempt to pull a fast one and register a trademark that you do not own under an alternative country code! For example, if you think you can register cocacola.cc as a domain name, you may find yourself the subject of civil action by Coca-Cola to recover lawyer's fees and damages. Recent court rulings are showing that the courts are getting tired of this and are starting to slap more serious civil penalties on would-be squatters.

## THE MICROSOFT NETWORKING CLIENT AND SMB

After determining an IP assignment and DNS plan, the next consideration to make on the TCP/IP network is what TCP/IP applications will be fielded. Since filesharing is almost always central to an organizational network, on a Windows network it's important to be aware of the issues between FreeBSD and Microsoft Networking. Microsoft Networking is based on Server Messaging Blocks (SMB), which are based on NetBIOS, which can be run over TCP/IP. Support on FreeBSD for this is provided by the Samba suite of programs.

### NetBIOS over TCP/IP

IBM developed NetBIOS as a software layer that isolated the lower-level networking driver software and hardware from the higher-level software network client. Originally it was implemented with proprietary protocols, such as the LLC2-based NetBEUI. NetBIOS found its way into the MS LanManager product, which was later sold to IBM and renamed LanServer. Microsoft continued to use NetBIOS in its NT Server product.

In 1987, the Air Force wanted to use NetBIOS but didn't want to be tied to a proprietary network protocol. As a result, RFC1001 and RFC1002 were written to standardize a means of implementing NetBIOS with the TCP/IP protocol. This became known as NetBIOS-over-TCP/IP (NBT) and was incorporated into the LanManager and LanServer products and their DOS, OS/2, and Windows clients. Besides proprietary protocols, such as NetBEUI, and open ones, such as NBT, both Microsoft and Novell have also implemented NetBIOS with IPX.

## Server Messaging Blocks

The IBM and Microsoft LanManager, LanServer, and Windows NT Server products all implement file and print sharing using the SMB protocol. This protocol requires a NetBIOS layer and therefore runs on top of NBT. SMB is partially documented by Microsoft at the following Web sites.

```
ftp://ftp.microsoft.com/developr/drg/CIFS/
http://msdn.microsoft.com/workshop/networking/cifs/default.asp
http://www.cifs.com/
```

SMB is proprietary to both IBM and Microsoft, and in general both of them use identical implementations, with the exception of domain and some browsing differences. For example, NT networking and Win95 file- and print-sharing both have settings to enable LanManager 2.2-style network broadcasting.

In 1998, Microsoft made an effort to promote SMB as an open standard under the banner Common Internet File System (CIFS). Since then they have quietly allowed the effort to drop, many links to CIFS on their Web pages are broken, and information there is old. It's possible that the company intends to make the protocol proprietary once again, especially since SMB servers have been built using Samba-on-UNIX that have been benchmarked faster than the fastest Windows NT Servers in existence. Of course, doing this would break all existing Windows NT Servers, so it's unlikely to happen.

In the absence of a concerted effort from Microsoft to open CIFS or to adhere to an open standard in this area, the Usenet news group `comp.os.ms-windows.networking.tcp-ip` and the Samba home page are likely to stay the most current areas for information on this protocol.

## TCP/IP SERVICES

In addition to basic file and print services, an organization running TCP/IP should consider offering other services, such as FTP, the Web, mail, directory, time, dialup, news, and list services. *Icing-on-the-cake* services are mail-to-fax, mail-to-news, and Web gateways. All these services have been implemented for years under UNIX and FreeBSD. Overviews of some of them follow.

### E-Mail

Electronic mail, including both internal and external organizational mail, is perhaps the most important network service after basic fileserving and printserving. The speed at which companies have connected to the Internet has made Internet mail protocols the single most important part of the electronic messaging infrastructure in the world today. Increasingly, business deals between organizations and individuals are moving into e-mail.

E-mail can be offered with a number of value-added services. Chief among these are automated mailing list services that are almost completely managed by software. Companies can sponsor mailing lists for their internal users and their external customers. Subscription to the mailing lists can be either user or administrator-controlled. Control and access to mailing list archives can also be done via a Web interface.

Other kinds of e-mail gateways can also be set up, such as mail-to-fax. In this kind of gateway, a user might send e-mail to an address of `5551212@`
`companydomain.fax`. The mailserver then takes the mail message and faxes it to the phone number 555-1212. In a mail-to-pager gateway, e-mail that goes to `username@companydomain.com` sends a page to a beeper the user is wearing, as well as forwarding the mail message to the user's inbox.

### Directory Services

In large organizations, it is becoming increasingly important to find e-mail addresses and locations of individuals. Toward this end, years ago a unified directory standard called X.500 was created as the OSI directory service. This standard was not widely adopted because it required an OSI protocol stack, but it did form the basis of the Lightweight Directory Access Protocol (LDAP) standard, documented in RFC1777. LDAP has found greater acceptance over the past few years. Version 4 of Eudora and Netscape Communicator both support LDAP directories, as does Microsoft's Outlook mail clients, both Express and regular, Microsoft Active Directory, and Novell's directory service.

## World Wide Web

A Web server is a very versatile network server. It can serve up informational pages, but this is only a small part of its capability. Web servers can field pages that allow users to control such things as print spools; perform searches, such as a Web-to-LDAP or Web-to-Finger gateway; allow mail and discussion group access; and perform group calendaring and numerous other functions. A Web server is usually the nucleus of a company's *Intranet* effort, which allows a company to categorize corporate documents on the Web server for easy access. A Web server also serves as the focal point of external customer access to information on the organization and its products. More complex Web servers can extract credit card information from customers and, with the addition of credit card verification software, such as Cybercash, can complete an entire purchase transaction for the customer without employee intervention.

## FTP

FTP is a client-server protocol used to copy files over TCP/IP networks. Unlike internal fileserving protocols, such as NetBIOS-over-TCP/IP, the FTP protocol is session-based. Clients connect, validate, transact, and disconnect. It also crosses platforms, in that practically every known operating system that has implemented the TCP/IP protocol has an FTP program. So, FTP is typically used to offer external TCP/IP users, such as company customers, a way of obtaining files that the company makes available. These files can be anything from company marketing presentations and other information files to software programs.

Due to the recent activity of worm programs that propagate through Internet e-mail, many network administrators are discouraging users from sharing files through e-mail. As a result, FTP is becoming even more important than ever as a file transmission program. FTP also works through proxies and network address translators, unlike CIFS and NetBIOS.

FTP has two modes of operation: active and passive. Since passive FTP generally runs better through a firewall, more browsers and FTP clients are using it as the default.

## Dialup

Remote access to the company network by organization members is also a very important part of building an internal company net. Modem pools connected to the internal network can allow e-mail access for traveling executives; working at home for telecommuting employees; access to specialized servers, such as

SQL servers for client-server packages; and remote network access for off-hours administration. Modem pools also allow the administrator to close off many services from access through the company's Internet connection, its electronic front door. For example, a company without a modem pool might have to allow incoming FTP from the Internet to internal hosts to allow a remote employee to transfer files to the host.

## INTERNAL ORGANIZATION SUBNETTING

When a TCP/IP network becomes too large, it begins to have the same kind of traffic problems common to other network protocols and networks. Thus, TCP/IP networks are often broken into subnets that are connected with a router or routers. Many administrators use switched hubs to help alleviate traffic, but ultimately the IP subnet will limit itself anyway. For example, all members of the accounting group may be placed on a separate subnet, a practice which improves security as well.

In a large internal network of many subnets, there may be multiple redundant connections between subnets, separated by gateways. To avoid sending traffic intended for a network behind one of the gateways to the wrong gateway, the Routing Information Protocol (RIP) was developed to allow gateways to *advertise* TCP/IP routes to each other.

Unfortunately, the vast majority of Windows clients up to and including NTWKS cannot listen to RIP advertisements and select the appropriate gateway for forwarding out-of-network traffic. As a result, the gateway IP number is a fixed number supplied by DHCP or by physically setting it up in the control panel. Typically, the client setup in such a network is given the gateway IP number that is closest to the outside gateway network. If other internal gateways exist, the client learns about them through ICMP redirect packets from the router. The gateway routers can use RIP to communicate routes to each other. In this way, if a redundant link dies, the other routers learn about it and change their route tables accordingly. Once the network gets to be more than a few subnets in size, the organization must run a routing protocol.

DHCP, being broadcast-driven, is also affected by introducing routed subnets. Hosts attempting to configure via DHCP send out broadcast packets. If the DHCP server is on a different subnet, it doesn't see these packets and thus does not issue an IP number response. It is possible to install a `bootp/dhcp` *helper* application under FreeBSD (if a FreeBSD system is the router) or use a `helper` command under IOS if a Cisco router is used. The DHCP server must recognize multiple subnets. Version 2 of the ISC DHCP server under FreeBSD, covered earlier in this chapter, does so, as do the DHCP server in Win2K and the post-SP4 Windows NT 4.0.

## BASIC SETUP OF IP CLIENTS

Here is an overview of TCP/IP setup on all potential clients in the corporate network. The setup presented here is only an example; refer to your vendor's documentation for an authoritative guide to setting up TCP/IP. Coverage of IP setup here is more thorough for IP clients with less readily available setup documentation.

### TCP/IP on DOS

DOS is rarely used today for general-purpose computing in corporate settings, but DOS-only workstations may still be applicable in special-purpose machines, such as gateways, and as a platform for running diagnostic utilities. One of the great benefits of DOS is that the OS and all networking utilities needed to gain access to the network can be fit onto a single, bootable 1.4MB disk. With such a boot disk, a service technician in an organization can bring up a workstation that has a problem and run a host of diagnostic utilities on it, including utilities to reformat the disk and reinstall higher-level operating systems. This is a great aid in laboratory or classroom environments.

The DOS operating system contains several drawbacks to TCP/IP implementation. First, processing of code must be done in the first 1MB of RAM by the CPU in real mode. Since DOS software programs consume most of this memory, little memory is left for network drivers. Because TCP/IP is much more complex than a simpler protocol, such as IPX, and so requires a lot more software overhead, it is very difficult to fit a good TCP/IP stack into DOS. Second, DOS is not multithreaded. With most IP implementations, a number of network services must listen continuously. These other services cannot respond if the TCP/IP stack is in the middle of servicing a request under DOS.

Because DOS shipped with no networking of any kind, over the years four ways were developed to implement TCP/IP on DOS.

**1.** The Microsoft NDIS stack started out as the LanManager for DOS clients and is now the current Microsoft Networking client for DOS. A few Microsoft-supplied programs have used this stack directly, such as utilities and a few other programs. The most important use of this stack, however, has been to provide an interface for the DOS client, which allows file and print access to SMB servers, such as LanManager, Windows NT, and Samba-on-UNIX.

**2.** The Novell ODI and TCP/IP stack contained in the Novell Lan-Workplace for DOS software, later available directly from the Novell FTP site. This was the original way to access mainframes and larger hosts concurrently on a Novell network because it provided full implementations of Telnet, FTP, and numerous other TCP/IP networking programs. For a short time this suite included an NFS client.

**3.** The packet driver stack for which TCP/IP programs were written, such as the NCSA Telnet and its suite of TCP/IP programs. The set was very popular in the educational community because it allowed virtually useless XT computers to be used as dumb terminals to access UNIX hosts.

**4.** The FTP software's PC/TCP interface and its suite of TCP/IP software for DOS. Unlike the previous three, this implementation was not free. Most of the TCP/IP-aware commercial DOS software required the presence of FTP software TCP/IP interface. Originally the software was built on top of the packet driver specification; later FTP made NDIS an option. The FTP PC/TCP Onnet software also includes an NFS client that runs under DOS.

To install any of these clients, refer to the detailed instructions for preparation and setup in the clients. General instructions for the client written by the National Center for Supercomputing Applications (NCSA) are listed in Exhibit 2.5. The Microsoft DOS client setup is covered in Chapter 7, and the Novell TCP/IP client setup is covered in Chapter 8. The FTP software TCP/IP client setup is covered in its manual. I have not included it here because its functionality is duplicated by the other three free clients and it is unlikely that anyone would pay for a DOS TCP/IP implementation today.

### Exhibit 2.5  NCSA Telnet for DOS and DOS TCP/IP setup instructions

Here are the setup instructions for NCSA Telnet for the DOS and DOS TCP/IP suite of programs using a Compaq 386 Deskpro, with a 3Com 3C579 EISA network adapter card.

1. Obtain a packet driver for the network adapter card used in the machine. The network card adapter driver disk file often has a packet driver. For example, the 3Com 3C579 adapter card disk has a directory PKTDVR with a packet driver named 3C5X9PD. COM. A collection of packet drivers are also available from ftp://ftp.cdrom.com/pub/simtelnet/msdos/pktdrvr/pktd11.zip or ftp://ftp.crynwr.com/drivers/pktd11.zip. If a packet driver is not available for the network card and a Novell ODI driver is, a program called odipkt can be used to place a packet driver interface on top of a DOS ODI stack. Currently, this program, as well as many other useful networking programs, can be obtained from http://www.danlan.com/.*

2. Load the packet driver with the appropriate command-line options. Packet drivers often require the network card hardware port and hardware interrupt, sometimes the memory

**Exhibit 2.5** (*continued*)

region (if the card uses shared memory), and always the software interrupt numbers on the command line. For example, the 3Com card packet driver loads on the 3C579 as follows.

```
C:\3C5X9PD 0x60

3com Etherlink III Packet Driver v1.1
(C) Copyright 1993 3Com Corp. All rights reserved
Slot:                     6 (0x6)
I/O base:                 24576 (0x6000)
Interrupt:                10 (0xA)
Transceiver:              External (AUI)
Ethernet Address:         00:20:AF:74:E0:38
Packet Driver Interrupt: 96 (0x60)

C:\
```

3. Obtain the NCSA Telnet program from <u>ftp://ftp.ncsa.uiuc.edu/Telnet/DOS/</u> <u>tel2308b.zip</u>, along with an unzip utility. Alternatively, an older version of NCSA Telnet with a 3270-type terminal is available as the cutcp package, from <u>ftp://</u> <u>ftp.amu.edu.pl/pub/msdos/network/cutcp/cutcp-s.zip</u>. Binaries only can also be found somewhere on ftp.nstn.ns.ca as the cutcp-b.zip file. Unfortunately, the full source and binary of cutcp is becoming hard to find. Rutgers University was supposed to be maintaining it, but they seem to have lost it from their server. The cutcp package is particularly useful since it has a Ping program, as well as the full documentation for DOS LPR programs, both of which are missing from the NCSA distribution. The 3270 terminal emulation in cutcp was written to support IBM mainframes.

4. Create the C:\NCSA or C:\cutcp directory and expand either or both packages into the appropriate directories with pkunzip. Use the -d option to expand the directories as well.

5. Edit the config.tel files and install the IP number. Make any other changes that need to be made. The files are fairly self-explanatory. With the preceding packet driver example, the following parameters would be set in config.tel.

```
hardware=packet
interrupt=A
ioaddr=60
```

6. Test by running the Telnet program or another program, and attempt to log in to a FreeBSD host.

---

*\*Note:* It may be possible to run NCSA Telnet under Win95 using the NDIS-to-packet driver on this URL. Proceed with caution.

## TCP/IP on OS/2

There have been four major TCP/IP implementations on OS/2.

**1.** The FTP software TCP/IP for OS/2. Several other TCP/IP software vendors, such as Ipswitch, also produced OS/2 TCP/IP stacks that provided software interfaces intended to comply with the FTP software OS/2 interface.

One major TCP/IP program that required the FTP software interface under OS/2 was the Lotus cc:Mail multiprocessing mail router, which allowed a single OS/2 machine to serve a number of remote mail modems, as well as a post office to post office mail router. FTP OS/2 software is completely incompatible with the IBM TCP/IP software included with OS/2 3.0 Warp Connect and later versions of OS/2.

**2.** The IBM TCP/IP software for OS/2. This was available in 16-bit implementations for OS/2 versions up to 1.3 and in a 32-bit TCP/IP 2.0 implementation for OS/2 versions 2.0 and 2.1. With OS/2 3.0 Warp Connect, most of this client was moved into OS/2, with the exception of NFS and DNS, which are still compatible with the 32-bit IBM TCP/IP software in the OS. OS/2 3.0 Warp nonConnect included the network layer of this stack, with only the serial SLIP and PPP drivers. Later, instructions were posted to the Internet that explained how to load parts of the Microsoft OS/2 client and this stack to duplicate the network card driver interface of Warp Connect.

**3.** The Microsoft LanManager TCP/IP client. This client was originally written for OS/2 versions up to 1.3 and contained both network drivers and the networking client. The client part of this software was later patched to run under OS/2 versions 2.0 through 3.0 and to run on top of the IBM TCP/IP NetBIOS kit. With OS/2 3.0 Warp Connect and later versions, the functionality of this client is duplicated by the TCP/IP software that ships with OS/2.

**4.** The Novell LanWorkplace for OS/2. This client never achieved the popularity of LanWorkplace for DOS, however, and little OS/2 network software required it.

## TCP/IP on Windows 3.1

Win31 contained little networking besides the Windows DLL section of the Novell NetWare client that worked in conjunction with the Novell NETX.EXE NetWare DOS client program. TCP/IP implementations under Windows revolve around the use of the Winsock TCP/IP sockets interface specification, which was created by Microsoft and others to promote TCP/IP under Win31. Some of the major Win31 Winsock implementations are listed here.

1. FTP software PC/TCP for Windows, which used part of FTP software's DOS client and a number of Windows .DLL files.
2. NetManage Chameleon TCP/IP for Windows, which was entirely implemented in .DLL files.
3. Novell TCP/IP for DOS and its Winsock addition.
4. Microsoft's DOS client and its Winsock.dll addition.

5. Trumpet Winsock DLL, which was the first shareware Winsock implementation, used a packet driver interface.

In addition to the network card Winsock interfaces, there have been several
major dialup PPP-only Winsock implementations.

1. The Microsoft dialer that comes as part of the Microsoft Internet Explorer
   Web browser freely downloadable from Microsoft.
2. The Netscape dialer that is downloadable on a trial basis from Netscape.
3. The shareware Trumpet Winsock dialer.
4. The Shiva LanRover dialup client that is used with WfW and Microsoft
   TCP/IP to allow a remote WfW client to establish SMB networking connections.

## TCP/IP on Windows for Workgroups 3.11

WfW was developed to meet the needs of companies that wished to internetwork NOSs other than NetWare under Win31. In the released version of WfW
3.11, Microsoft didn't include TCP/IP, but a full 32-bit NDIS and Winsock
TCP/IP implementation was released later. This included rudimentary Telnet
and FTP clients as well as the file and printsharing of SMB networking protocols. Additional TCP/IP networking tools included are Ping, netstat, nbtstat,
route, and traceroute.

WfW is very configurable, and virtually all DOS and Win31 TCP/IP client
programs previously mentioned can be run under it. However, because WfW
adds nothing other than networking to Win31, it is assumed that anyone
spending the extra money on WfW 3.11 is using the Microsoft-supplied
TCP/IP client. Installation of Microsoft TCP/IP for WfW 3.11 is discussed in
Chapter 7.

## Windows 95/98

The Win95 OS is an outgrowth of WfW. Microsoft greatly expanded networking support in Win95, and one of the most notable additions was the dialup networking PPP client. It has greatly helped increase the ability of organizations to
support remote-node dialup networking clients. Win98 is virtually identical to
Win95 in the networking areas covered in this book.

Because the TCP/IP networking support is so good in Win95/98, the
TCP/IP stack vendors, such as FTP software (which doesn't exist anymore),
have pretty much gotten out of the TCP/IP stack business and are mainly concentrating on TCP/IP applications. The exception to this is in NFS implemen-

tations: since Microsoft didn't include NFS in Win95, several stack vendors still replace parts of the Win95 TCP/IP stack with components that are optimized for use with NFS.

If a network adapter card is inserted in a PC and the Win95 system is installed on a fresh disk, the PC automatically detects the network card and sets up networking. To add TCP/IP to Win95, merely select Protocol→Microsoft→TCP/IP during the installation. If a network adapter is installed in a running Win95 system, it is often autodetected. Otherwise, "Add New Hardware" can be selected to add support for the card. TCP/IP can be added as a protocol from the Networking icon in the control panel.

## Windows NT

Since Windows NT version 3.1, Microsoft has supplied some TCP/IP networking in Windows NT. This is similar to the 32-bit TCP/IP networking in WfW. Additional items include FTP server and LPR client and server support, RCP/RSH programs, and, in version 3.51 and later versions, HTTP (Web) and Gopher server support. NT has also included client remote access support (RAS) since version 3.51. RAS is a Microsoft acronym for dialup PPP.

With the release of Win2K, Microsoft has greatly added to the core TCP/IP support. Access filtering, routing protocol, and address translation are now available.

## Macintosh Operating System

TCP/IP on the older Macintosh systems is provided by one of two programs. The first is MacPPP, which is intended for use with a modem connection to provide TCP/IP support. The second is MacTCP, which is used to provide TCP/IP support in conjunction with an Ethernet card in the Macintosh. Under the newer Mac OS, TCP/IP is included as part of Open Transport. A rich set of TCP/IP utility programs is available over the Internet for the Macintosh, including Fetch, the Mac FTP client.

## TCP/IP WINDOWS NETWORK AND APPLICATION PROGRAMS

TCP/IP includes a number of networking programs that are directly tied to protocols within the TCP/IP suite. These are almost a required part of any complete IP diagnostics toolkit. Unfortunately, unlike UNIX systems, Microsoft didn't include many of these TCP/IP networking programs. Although this omission has spurred the development of third-party Winsock TCP/IP applications, it has also retarded development past a certain level. This is because most new TCP/IP users get their first taste of TCP/IP on a Windows platform and so only learn about the few applications available in a stock installation. It also makes it difficult to maintain consistency in look and feel across an organization. Following are the most-missed TCP/IP utility programs for Windows, their uses, and where they can be obtained, with an emphasis on free programs.

## Archie

Archie is an early program that is used to search for other programs located on public FTP sites. The user needs to have a good guess of the filename to use it. Archie servers are located across the Internet, such as `archie.rutgers.edu`. Archie can be gotten from `ftp://ftp.cdrom.com/pub/simtelnet/win95/inet/wsarch32.zip`, which also has a 16-bit version for Win31. Archie has been largely replaced by Web-based search engines, but a few Archie servers still exist.

## FTP

A browser can do anonymous FTP, but it is difficult to perform many FTP operations with a browser. A dedicated FTP program can be used to select multiple files to transfer at once, log in with a username and password other than anonymous, and put files onto an FTP site. An FTP client is included with Win95, WinNT, and WfW 3.11, but people who use the dialer stack in the Win31 version of the Microsoft Web browser may appreciate the unrestricted WinFTP program available from `ftp://ftp.uni-mannheim.de/systems/windows/winsock/winftp.zip`.

## Trivial FTP

Trivial FTP (TFTP) is generally used to copy ROM images and other such code to network devices; it is not generally used for obtaining files on the Internet. It is particularly important for backup of network device configurations. An excellent TFTP server is included with FreeBSD, and in conjunction with Simple Network Management Protocol (SNMP) commands, it can be used to set up a nightly job on the FreeBSD server to copy a router configuration. For Windows, a shareware TFTP server is available from Walusoft at `http://www.walusoft.co.uk/`. Also, no-cost TFTP servers that require Win95 or NT are available from Cisco, located at `ftp://ftp.cisco.com/pub/netmgmt/utilities/tftp-dll.zip`, and from 3Com, located at `ftp://ftp.3com.com/pub/utilbin/win32/3cs117.zip`. There is also a TFTP server there that runs as a service under WinNT.

## Telnet

A Telnet client is included with Win95 and WfW 3.11. For those using a stack such as the Microsoft dialer stack in the Win31 version of the Microsoft Web browser, a popular Telnet client is the EWAN Telnet client, available from `ftp://ftp.cdrom.com/pub/garbo/garbo_win/winsock/ewan1052.zip`. A nicer Telnet program for Win95, Win31, and Win32 is also available at `http://www.vandyke.com`.

## Secure Shell

Secure Shell (SSH) is rapidly becoming the preferred connection program or protocol for access to UNIX systems, replacing both Remote Shell (RSH) and Telnet. SSH encrypts the datastream and thus is particularly important on academic networks, where many people run sniffers and little switching takes place in the network (switches block promiscuous packet sniffers). SSH uses the patented RSA encryption algorithm

SSH is included with current versions of FreeBSD; for Win95/98/ME, Van Dyke Technologies sells SecureCRT. Another SSH Telnet client called PuTTY, it is located at `http://www.chiark.greenend.org.uk/~sgtatham/putty/`.

## Usenet News

News readers are available from many locations. Microsoft includes one with Internet Explorer 3.0x. In later versions of the Web browser, the news capability is folded into Outlook Express. A popular news reader for Win31 is WinVN, located at `http://www.winsite.com/info/pc/win3/winsock/winvn926.zip/`. Unfortunately, this news reader is unable to execute LIST commands on the news server if the number of news groups exceeds approximately 27,000, so the NEWSRC file must be obtained from a Unix system running RN. A more modern news reader that is able to manage current news group sizes is Free Agent, located at `http://www.forteinc.com/getfa/download.htm`. Also, Microsoft now includes Outlook Express with the current version of the Internet Explorer Web browser, which contains a news reader.

## Ping

Ping is a network testing program used to test reachability and latency between two hosts. It is included in WfW 3.11 Microsoft TCP/IP, Win95, and Windows NT. Users running the TCP/IP dialer under Win31 may want to use a ping program located at `ftp://ftp.cdrom.com/pub/simtelnet/win3/inet/ws_ping.zip`. This `ping` program only works with Win31 plus the Microsoft dialer.

## Finger

Finger is a program used to find information about individuals who have accounts on machines on the Internet. It returns the full name of a person when given his or her login name, or the login name and e-mail address when given the full name. A version of Finger that runs under Win31 and Win95/98 is located at `http://www.winsite.com/info/pc/win3/winsock/wfingr10.zip/`.

## Nslookup

Nslookup is used to test domain nameservers to see if they are returning correct address records, or to convert between a hostname and an IP number. A version of Nslookup that runs under Win31 and Win95/98 is located at `ftp://ftp.demon.co.uk/pub/trumphurst/nslookup/nslookup.zip`. Nslookup is included with Windows NT/2K.

## Whois

Whois is somewhat like Nslookup, except that it is a more generalized lookup. Usually, it is used to check the correctness of a site's DNS records in the root DNS servers. Whois is part of the Finger package. Whois programs usually default to using the server `whois.internic.net`, but other servers of importance are `whois.arin.net` and `whois.networksolutions.com`.

## Tar

TapeARchiver (tar for short) is used to back up hard disks to tape drives and to create archive files. An *archive* is a file with many other files inside it, much like a `zip` archive. UNIX `tar` programs can be piped in conjunction with RSH to other UNIX machines, which allows a number of UNIX systems to back up to a single machine with a tape drive on it. Unfortunately, Windows machines don't support piping, but a version of `tar` for Windows that will do this is located at `ftp://ftp.cdrom.com/pub/garbo/garbo_win/winsock/wtar15u.zip`. This version runs under Win31 and Win95/98.

## RSH/RCP

The R-utilities are used on UNIX for quick network and file copy commands. They do not use username and password validation but instead depend on validation by IP number, which helps to keep cleartext passwords off the network. Unfortunately, IP spoofing makes the security implications of using these commands on public machines even worse. They are useful on internal networks, however. A version of RSH for Win31 is located at `ftp://ftp.cdrom.com/pub/garbo/garbo_win/winsock/wrsh16.zip`.

A version of RCP used to be located on `ftp.cdrom.com` with the filename of `wrcprs16.zip`. It has disappeared but may still be available on older CD-ROMs of the Simtel collection. A shareware RSH/RCP client available for both Win31 and Win95/98 is located at `http://www.denicomp.com/`. Windows NT has command-line `rcp` and `rsh` commands that are part of the distribution.

## The X Window System Software

The X Window System from Massachusetts Institute of Technology (`http://www.x.org`) is the software used to run graphical programs under UNIX, such as Web browsers. X also allows programs, called clients, to run in such a manner that their graphical output is displayed on a different machine on the network, called an X Server. There used to be a freeware X Server for Win95/98 located at `http://www.microimages.com/freestuff/mix/` that allows X programs to run on FreeBSD servers and their output to display on Windows workstations. It's now a try-before-you-buy commercial product costing $25 per server. It's reputed to work well, although some users have had problems opening Xterms with scrollbars.

Users who are looking into running X on their Windows workstations to connect to FreeBSD servers should also consider using VNC Viewer. Details are located at `http://www.uk.research.att.com/vnc/`.

There are many commercial X Servers for Windows and other PC OSs. Often they ship with a suite of tools. If you need a good X Server for Windows, you may want to buy one first and look through its tools before getting any of the tools listed here.

## Other TCP/IP Utilities

Other TCP/IP utilities exist, such as mail clients, LDAP directory lookup clients, LPR clients, and many others not listed here. Mail and LDAP clients are covered in Chapter 9, and LPR is covered in Chapter 8. Some tools, such as traceroute, exist in Win95 under slightly different names. Traceroute under Windows is `tracert`, `ifconfig` is `winipcfg`, and so forth. Looking through the major FTP archive servers on the Internet should allow the user to gather everything under Windows necessary for basic TCP/IP networking.

## Other References

Unfortunately, few cross-platform references are available on the topic of running TCP/IP on an internal corporate network. Practically everything is written from the viewpoint of a single operating system on the organizational network. Although these references, such as the Microsoft Windows NT Resource Kit and the various guides from Sun, are good sources of information on TCP/IP, they are obviously slanted toward their vendors' products. Following instructions in these kinds of materials will produce a TCP/IP network that lacks integrated support for other vendors' OSs.

It is possible to take a general text on TCP/IP and, with experience, apply it to your organizational network. Probably the best general-purpose guide to TCP/IP that I've come across is the *Internetworking with TCP/IP* series of books (Comer, 2000).[4]

---

[4]Douglas Comer, *Internetworking with TCP/IP, Fourth Edition*. Upper Saddle River, NJ: Prentice-Hall, 2000.

# FreeBSD Installation

I wrote this chapter assuming readers would have an operating TCP/IP network and a small understanding of UNIX, and thus be ready to start construction of their FreeBSD server. For many readers this is the real first chapter of this book. If you don't have an IP network and are just installing FreeBSD as a non-networked standalone server, that's OK, but you might consider placing a network card in your FreeBSD system and plugging it into a separate Windows system. Although most die-hard UNIX proponents would disagree, I feel that UNIX is best experienced as a network server; this is its strongest point. If you don't agree with me after reading this book, it's unlikely you would agree that FreeBSD would make a better desktop system. So, let's get started and set up our FreeBSD server.

## OBTAINING INSTALLATION CDS

FreeBSD is truly a free operating system. If desired, the administrator can FTP the FreeBSD files and install the system without spending a dime on distribution media. However, it does cost money and time to maintain the servers on the Internet that host the FreeBSD Project, not to mention the time of helpful people on the various mailing lists and news groups who will assist in installation problems. The project itself receives monetary sponsorship from Walnut Creek CD-ROM, which makes money from selling installation CDs. The Walnut Creek CDs are very reasonably priced (approximately $29.95 for a subscription) and are available in many large electronics stores, such as

CompUSA, as well as many bookstores. If your favorite local software store doesn't carry the CDs, encourage it to stock them.

FreeBSD also receives sponsorship from several other CD-ROM vendors (see the sponsorship list on `http://www.freebsd.org`). Purchasing the installation CDs from one of these vendors helps to ensure their continued sponsorship of the project.

Even though Walnut Creek is now merged with BSDi, CD sales of FreeBSD continue to be one of the most effective and easily measured indicators of market penetration of the software. When the computing trade press compares FreeBSD and Linux installations, they aren't talking about numbers of copies downloaded for free from some server. In fact, it can be argued that the superiority and reliability of the FreeBSD-based fileserver that offers FreeBSD for download is in no small way responsible for significant underreporting of FreeBSD installations.

The production versions of FreeBSD used to write this chapter are versions 2.2.8, 3.4, and 4.0. By the time this book is in print, version 4.2 will have been released, and version 2.2.8 will no longer be directly available from Walnut Creek or the FTP sites. The general installation procedures between versions haven't changed much. I've attempted to make the instructions applicable to as many versions of FreeBSD as possible, but they are focused on version 4.X.

The most recent 4.X version of FreeBSD should always be used; *however*, the FreeBSD committers have *not* continued to bring forward *all* hardware device drivers from the older kernels to the newer kernels. In addition, some device drivers for older hardware, such as the Intel EtherExpress 16, have been brought forward but are now broken. It is unfortunate that this has occurred, but FreeBSD is not limited to this behavior; the current version of Solaris 8 removed EISA support, which is about as fundamentally destructive to backward compatibility as you can get. So, if you have older hardware and you want to run FreeBSD on it, you may need to boot up an older copy to get support for your devices.

## INSTALLING NONPRODUCTION VERSIONS OF FREEBSD

As of this writing, there are several nonproduction versions of FreeBSD that the administrator may consider installing. The oldest, 1.1.5.1, contains the infamous "Copyright AT&T" kernel code. On the right hardware, 1.1.5.1 is wonderfully stable. Although it lacks the features of current versions, history buffs, students, or those involved in porting projects of ancient UNIX code to FreeBSD may be interested in running it. The kernel is also slightly smaller than current versions, making a production 4MB 386SX a reality. However, 1.1.5.1 is hard to find, so don't try obtaining or installing it unless you have a real need. If you don't know whether or not you need it, you don't. It's also full of enough security holes to excite even the novice *script kiddie*. A *script kiddie* is a cracker who is such a loser that he or she can't develop his or her own system cracks and therefore relies on crack scripts written by other losers.

The other major nonproduction versions of FreeBSD to consider installing are the SNAP releases of FreeBSD. SNAPs are snapshot releases of code that is currently in development; in effect, the SNAP releases are continuously rolling beta code. SNAPs are *not* recommended for production work and should be avoided unless your intent is to participate in FreeBSD development. SNAPs are located at `ftp://current.freebsd.org/pub/FreeBSD/snapshots/`.

In the history of FreeBSD, there have been only three times that SNAPs have really been needed for production usage.

1. During the transition from 1.1.5.1 to 2.0, and thence to 2.0.5. The transition away from the AT&T code was difficult, and it wasn't until the 2.1 versions came out that FreeBSD regained the stability of 1.1.5.1. A number of sites committed to FreeBSD were forced to run SNAP releases to get stable 2.0 code.
2. The insertion of *divert sockets* into the FreeBSD kernel, which occurred during the transition from 2.1 to 2.2. Divert sockets are what make NAT possible on FreeBSD. Many sites ran early SNAPs of 2.2 to field NAT, although there was a long, convoluted patch file that could be applied to 2.1.X.
3. The entrance of symmetric multiprocessing (SMP) into FreeBSD with the 3.0 release. SMP support was added months before the version 3.0 release, so the only way to get SMP was by running the SNAPs.

Anyone running SNAPs should be doing it for testing and development. Use the currently shipping release version for production use.

## Dual-Booting Windows NT and FreeBSD

Although the thrust of this book is to set up FreeBSD as the only OS on a server, someone might want to create a test system that could dual-boot both OSs. One approach, detailed at `http://www.devious.com/freebsd`, discusses how to modify the NT Boot Loader menu to load FreeBSD from a second hard drive in the system. Another approach is to install NT and its boot selector, followed by FreeBSD, and then install the FreeBSD boot manager.

When the system boots, it runs the FreeBSD boot manager first, which allows a choice between FreeBSD and DOS. If DOS is selected, the NT boot manager allows a selection of NT (or NT and Windows). It's a bit cumbersome, but it works.

## PREINSTALLATION

With name-brand computer hardware not optimized for FreeBSD, the first thing the installer should do is search the FreeBSD Web site, `http://www.freebsd.org/`, for any references to his or her computer. Ideally you would find a recent post on the mailing list from an individual with the identical make, model, and configuration of computer and who is running the version that you have. If a match is found, send an e-mail to that person asking about any abnormal installation experiences.

The next step is to open up the system and carefully note all peripheral cards, their manufacturers, and their model numbers. In particular, if X is to be installed later, check the XFree86 Web site—`http://www.xfree86.org/`—to be sure the video card is supported. If the system has an existing Win95/98 installation, it may be helpful to get some of this information from Control Panel → System → Device manager.

After this, access any online Web sites or computerized bulletin board systems of the hardware components and obtain all utility diskettes, configuration programs, or EISA-configuration files used to set up cards. For non-plug-and-play (PnP) jumpered cards, such as ISA and EISA cards, obtain any jumper diagrams available. It is also useful to obtain any installation guides or manuals for cards and the motherboard used in the system. At this time, do any necessary card swapping with other systems and remove all cards that won't be used in the server.

Make sure that the system has no difficulty recognizing its disk drive on boot. Many older systems, especially ISA-bussed 486s, have BIOS code that does not allow them to access all the space on an IDE disk drive that has more than 1,024 cylinders (i.e., 500MB). Programs, such as DiskManager (often supplied on a floppy disk with boxed hard drives, or downloadable from the drive maker's Web site) or EZ-Disk, are used to get around these limitations with Win95 and DOS. Although FreeBSD usually still recognizes the entire amount of drive space on a computer with this kind of limitation, it increases the chance that the installation will fail. FreeBSD does know about DiskManager and will make allowances for it, but that is the only disk manager it does know about. In any case, it's preferable to attempt installation without using DiskManager. If such an ISA system must be used, it would be better to replace the IDE disk with a SCSI device, using a good SCSI controller such as the Adaptec 1540. Many of the cheaper ISA SCSI controllers, such as the Adaptec 1520, still have the same BIOS limitations on the controller card's BIOS. Alternatively, two IDE disks could be used in such a system, the primary IDE disk being small (less than the 1,024 limitation) and the secondary disk being any size. With this setup, the UNIX driver directly addresses the second disk, and thus the BIOS limitation on the second disk is not active.

Upgrade any flashable firmware in the computer to the latest version. It is common for motherboards today to have flash BIOS code available. However, be *extremely* careful before flashing a motherboard; if in doubt, don't do it. A bad motherboard flash can ruin it.

As a last task, if it's possible and reasonable (i.e., you have a fast machine), attempt a scratch Windows 95/98 install on the computer. If the system cannot run Win95/98, it most likely cannot run FreeBSD. It is very rare that an Intel computer that cannot run Win95/98 can run FreeBSD.

## STEP-BY-STEP INSTALLATION

The sections that follow describe the steps to use for a FreeBSD installation. They are intended to produce a running system with basic options for use as a server. The process was done from a CD of version 3.3 mounted in a second computer accessible via FTP. Notes are also made for a target computer with a CD-ROM drive.

### Installation Phase 1

Keep in mind that these directions are written for the worst-case scenario in that they assume the hardware cannot simply boot from the FreeBSD CD-ROM. By all means attempt to do this *before* reading these directions, and if the system can boot from the CD, ignore all the instructions about making disks.

> **NOTE**   A production server should probably be placed in "quarantine" right after installation and watched for a week before placing it into production.

### *Step 1*

Start by mounting the first FreeBSD CD into a convenient computer (not the target installation computer) and reading the `*.TXT` files in the root of the CD. On the 3.3 CD, there are 12 such files. In particular, read through the

INSTALL.TXT, HARDWARE.TXT, and ERRATA.TXT files. Get the newest ERRATA.TXT file from the FTP site location specified in ERRATA.TXT, and read it also. Among other things, INSTALL.TXT contains instructions explaining how to set up a FreeBSD CD-ROM in another FreeBSD system to allow FTP installations to be made from it. Read the paper booklet in the CD case.

### *Step 2*

Make a list of all resources used by the peripherals in the computer, and if possible, change any of the settings on the cards programs to match those in HARDWARE.TXT. It may be necessary to boot the computer into DOS and run configuration utilities or to unplug cards and change jumper settings. It may be helpful to write out each card model number and setting on a piece of scratch paper. It may also be helpful to place all configuration utilities on bootable DOS diskettes and leave the diskettes inside the case of the computer. This was a common trick with EISA systems, which all required an EISA-configuration diskette. It is important to understand that the port, memory, and interrupt settings listed in HARDWARE.TXT are defaults; if a better arrangement of settings should be used in your hardware, the installation sequence allows the defaults to be overridden.

If X will be installed on the FreeBSD system, make note of the video card model, chipset, ramdac, and clock chip. Properly configuring X with all color modes and resolutions is complex, especially with older cards, and may require some trial and error. However, adequate configuration for use with the most commonly used modes is usually possible with just the video card model.

It is critical that the hard disk, CD-ROM, and network adapter are properly set up and detected by the installation kernel. For example, if the computer has a PnP sound card with a PnP IDE controller on it and a CD-ROM drive plugged into that, the CD won't be accessible for installation. In that case, the CD-ROM should be moved to an IDE controller that is active when the system is booted, such as a secondary on the motherboard.

**NOTE**    If you're installing on a system that has a CMD640 IDE controller, the CD-ROM should probably be the secondary device on the primary IDE controller. This controller is an early attempt at an enhanced IDE controller, and the chipset is buggy; even with the workaround in the device driver, the installation often crashes anyway. (This problem also occurs when installing Windows NT on such a controller; it is not a FreeBSD-specific problem.) Fortunately, these controllers were used on early Pentiums and aren't used on modern hardware. If possible, *don't* install on a system with a CMD640; if you must, use it for a test server.

Avoid the use of PnP ISA network adapters in a FreeBSD version 3.4 or earlier system; versions 4.0 and later don't have this problem. Many ISA NE2000 network card clones have a configuration utility that sets them into either PnP mode or standard configurations. Some go into manual configuration mode only if the system they are plugged into is *not* a PnP system! A FreeBSD system built with a PCI bus will have superior network performance if a supported PCI network card, such as an Intel EtherExpress Pro 100b, is used in place of an ISA network card. Most PCI cards are PnP cards, and supported PCI cards are OK for use under FreeBSD. If a PnP ISA network card is used, the computer's BIOS will program it with port and interrupt settings after boot, and the cards' utility program should be run to determine what these are before installation.

Avoid IDE drives. Although the cost per megabyte of IDE is about half that of SCSI, there is a reason for that: IDE drives are slapped together fast on the assembly line. Hard drive manufacturers make IDE disks for use in end-user workstations. Their quality is abysmal compared to SCSI, their failure rate is far higher, and they don't belong in a server. In addition, most early IDE controllers were programmed input/output (PIO) mode, and many ugly parts of this standard still survive even in the present-day Ultra Direct Memory Access (UDMA)/Busmastering drives and controllers. If you must use IDE, stick to one disk per IDE port; otherwise, you will greatly reduce your data transfer rate.

Unlike DOS, FreeBSD does not tolerate misconfigured system resources. There should be no memory, port, or interrupt clashes. For most ISA cards, with the exception of PnP sound cards, FreeBSD cannot autodetect their settings, which must be entered manually. PCI cards are generally autodetected. Make sure to set the PnP OS in the motherboard to *OFF* (or UNIX). Take care not to allow PCI cards and jumpered ISA cards to assume the same interrupt. Many motherboards have BIOS settings that can be used to reserve interrupts for ISA cards that will prevent PCI cards from grabbing them. In the event of a BIOS that doesn't allow this, such as the Original Equipment Manufacturer (OEM) Phoenix BIOS used in Dell computers, it is necessary to remove all ISA cards, boot the installation diskette, and note the interrupts detected by the kernel that the PCI cards have seized. Then, the ISA cards must be rejumpered to avoid conflicts.

As a final measure, turn off Advanced Power Management (APM) in the BIOS; it frequently interferes with servers built on desktop hardware.

### *Step 3*
Low-level format the hard drive. If the drive is a SCSI drive and is plugged into a PCI SCSI controller, such as BusLogic or Adaptec, pressing a control sequence (such as Ctrl-B for BusLogic or Ctrl-A for Adaptec) during boot

usually calls up a menu that can be used to format the drive. For ISA SCSI controllers, there is often a formatting program to be downloaded from the SCSI card manufacturer's Web site. For example, with Adaptec 1540 ISA SCSI cards, a bootable DOS hard drive can be made up with the DOS ASPI drivers, and the Adaptec SCSIFMT.EXE program can be used. For IDE drives, download the appropriate formatting program from the drive manufacturer.

At this stage of installation, the primary purpose of the low-level formatting program is to try to make the drive fail by stressing it. On a server, a weak disk should be out of production before any time is wasted attempting to install it. Also, although all defects are supposed to be locked out at the factory, why trust them? Generally, low-level formatting isn't necessary on on-off test or client installations.

> **NOTE** Modern SCSI and IDE disks, low-level formatting from the appropriate program or menu does not actually rewrite the surface of the drive with new tracks and sectors. Instead, it makes the controller do a single-pass reverification of the surface of the drive and in most cases locks out any bad sectors. UNIX in general assumes perfect drive media. The intelligent electronics in an IDE or SCSI drive maintains a defect map that maps out damaged drive sectors and, if formatted, reprograms the drive to appear as though no damaged sectors are present.

When low-level formatting a drive, for truly optimum stability, perform the format with the drive in the orientation that it will be in during production, and do so only after the system has been sitting turned on all night. This allows the drive temperature and expansion to stabilize.

FreeBSD versions 3.4 and earlier contain a program, bad144, that can be used to remap bad sectors on hard drives that cannot map out broken sectors transparently. Bad144 was removed from version 4.0. This program was originally written for use on large ESDI drives, which routinely had several bad sectors and contained no remapping software that would work on UNIX. Unfortunately, bad144 only works if the drive has 1,024 cylinders or fewer, which is a problem since most large ESDI drives run to high cylinder counts. Setting up large ESDI drives is a somewhat arcane art because ESDI controllers are very particular. ESDI controllers with the same chipset often use different BIOS code, and one BIOS may allow a successful ESDI setup while another doesn't. I have set up ESDI controllers successfully with 600MB and larger drives under current versions of FreeBSD using bad144, but I do not recommend it for the uninitiated.

Bad144 is sometimes recommended for IDE drives with bad sectors, but do not use it for this. Although it works, in general an IDE drive that still shows bad sectors after a defect remap (done by low-level formatting with the appropriate manufacturer-supplied program) is getting close to crashing. Such drives should be either thrown away or returned for warranty service to the manufacturer. SCSI drives should be treated the same way: if bad sectors are still present after a low-level format done by the SCSI controller, do not use the drive.

FreeBSD 4.X has no support for bad144. Thus, the last version of FreeBSD that can be used with drives that require defect remapping (e.g., RLL, MFM, ESDI) is the last version in the 3.X series.

It has been observed that some SCSI drives have shipped from the factory with automatic remapping switched off. According to FreeBSD FAQ, to enable this, you must edit the first device page mode, which can be done on FreeBSD 2.X and earlier by giving the command (as root)

```
scsi -f /dev/rsd0c -m 1 -e -P 3
```

or, on FreeBSD 3.X or later, by giving the command (as root)

```
camcontrol modepage da0 -m 1 -e -P 3
```

and changing the values of AWRE and ARRE from 0 to 1

```
AWRE (Auto Write Reallocation Enbld): 1
ARRE (Auto Read Reallocation Enbld): 1
```

## *Step 4*

After low-level formatting, if the system will be used as a production server, it is strongly recommended that a testing application be run on the drive. Usually, this means the disk must be partitioned and formatted with DOS and a utilities program and then run to test the drive. Novell used to supply a utility, EISADISK.EXE (filename ESDIDR.EXE on the Novell FTP site), that was used for ESDI drives. Central Point Software also had Diskfix, which could perform repetitive pattern testing on a hard drive. The aim here is to run a utility that repeatedly writes and rewrites all surfaces of the hard drive. Programs such as SCANDISK, which is included in DOS, are not suitable for this because they perform only single-pass read/write testing. Some server manufacturers, such as Compaq, contain a drive-testing diagnostic utility that can be run from the diagnostics diskette.

With a brand new disk, it is unlikely that a drive-testing utility will uncover any bad blocks. The important function of a good drive-testing utility is to stress the disk for many hours. If the disk has a hardware assembly flaw, this process should flush it out.

Most repetitive drive-testing utilities are real-mode DOS programs and, as such, do not access the hard drive in 32-bit protected mode, as UNIX does. Although modern PCI SCSI controllers and drives have no difficulty in 32-bit mode, older controller cards may work fine in real mode and fail in protected mode. I have observed this with a number of protected-mode operating systems, such as OS/2 and Windows NT on the same hardware; the problem is not limited to FreeBSD. There are some *very* cheap SCSI adapters on the market.

### *Step 5*

After the drive subsystem is thoroughly tested, if the system is to be used as a production server, the memory and processor should be evaluated. Before commencing this evaluation, the system *must* be vacuumed to get rid of all dust. It also must be checked for proper cooling; many cheap cases have inadequate cooling or not enough fans, or cheap plastic fans with sleeve bearings, not ball-bearings, and faults. Improper cooling can result in errors developing in the silicone chips in the computer. Mounting three fans in a server is not too much—one in the power supply and two in the case—and keep a few spares on the shelf as well.

In addition, consider using ECC memory: it's not much more expensive, and the newer motherboards and processors (Pentium 2 and later) generally support it. Unfortunately, few Pentium-series chipsets support ECC.

Memory testing presents a problem. The UNIX community generally agrees that all commercial memory and processor testing programs are useless. To test memory and processor, load an OS on a computer, stress the OS, and see if the system crashes. There are several good commercial operating systems that can be helpful in this regard. One of the best that I have found is OS/2. Second to this is the Microsoft Windows NT/2000 OS. OS/2 in particular is very sensitive to weak hardware; it has been known to trap bad RAM that was not detected with any other testing program. OS/2 also has the benefit that the kernel can be loaded off a boot floppy, whereas NT requires a full installation.

Windows NT also can be helpful in this regard. It traps and blue-screens on bad hardware, often during installation. In fact, many of the same garbage-grade hardware that FreeBSD has problems with, such as floppy-controller tape drives, NT also has problems with.

A practical benefit of using a commercial OS to stress-test the hardware is that if it crashes, it is still easier to get leverage against the hardware vendor to fix the hardware.

It is surprising how many people complain about hardware problems loading FreeBSD on hardware that cannot load Windows NT or OS/2 without crashing. UNIX is the highest-performing OS that can be loaded on a computer, and it is just as intolerant of weak computer hardware as any high-performance commercial OS. If the computer is unable to boot a high-performance commercial operating system, such as OS/2, without crashing, it probably will not be able to boot FreeBSD.

If the hardware passes the commercial test, another stress test is to load a scratch installation of FreeBSD onto it, with full sources, and do a *make* world. If the compiler crashes even once, often with a Signal 11, you have a problem. An excellent resource at http://www.bitwizard.nl/sig11/ contains many suggested solutions, but I would recommend replacing the hardware since you'll never be sure if you have corrected the problem or merely decreased its frequency.

### *Step 6*

The FreeBSD boot floppy must be prepared if the system cannot boot from the FreeBSD CD. In the root of CD 1 is a ../tools directory, which contains two programs that can be used to create the boot floppy, rawrite.exe and fdimage.exe. The boot floppy is created from an "image" file, which is an exact sector-by-sector copy of the diskette. These programs read this file and use BIOS function calls under DOS to write it out to a new diskette.

In use, one of these utilities and the image file or files (depending on the FreeBSD version) located in the ../floppies directory on the CD are copied to a DOS hard drive. It is best to boot the computer into pure DOS or Win95/98 DOS (accessed by pressing Ctrl-F8 during the Starting Windows 95 message on a Win95 boot) with nothing else loaded, and run the utility with a blank, formatted diskette. The diskette must not have any bad sectors.

There is also a method to create the boot floppy on an existing UNIX system with the dd program, which you can use once your FreeBSD system is operating, for the next time you wish to install FreeBSD.

Sometimes floppy disk drives are slightly out of alignment between computers. If problems with the boot floppy occur, try creating it in the floppy disk drive of the target computer. If this doesn't work, try a different floppy disk, and if that fails, replace the floppy drive.

If your CD of FreeBSD is missing ../tools, you can FTP the programs from ftp.freesoftware.com.

### *Step 7*

If the system is a Compaq or HP system with a *diagnostics* partition, set up the diagnostics partition with the appropriate Compaq or HP utilities. Leave the rest of the drive as a DOS partition; it will be deleted later. If the system is an EISA system, you may want to install a 10MB bootable DOS partition containing EISA-configuration utilities. If the system uses RAID or has much complex hardware in it, you may also want to install a small DOS partition with the various utilities on it. For example, DOS network card-testing and configuration programs, video adapter programs, or other utility programs can easily be stored on a small bootable DOS partition; these may greatly aid the administrator if the server should develop a hardware fault. Keep the diskettes in case the hard drive crashes.

### *Step 8*

If the system will be installed from a CD in a CD-ROM drive, insert the CD before power up. If the system is relatively modern, it should boot from the CD. If it does not, then boot the system with the created boot floppy. For FreeBSD 2.2.8, after a few messages, the Kernel Configuration menu displays. If it is 3.x or later, the second MFSROOT disk is required; after booting from that, the Kernel Configuration menu displays. If the system has any ISA cards that are not PnP, including network cards, CD-ROM controller cards, SCSI cards, or multiport serial cards, or if it has APM enabled (generally APM is disabled on servers) the "Start kernel configuration in full-screen visual mode" entry *must* be selected. It is also a good idea to select this item, even if all cards are PCI, and disable all ISA card entries.

In this menu go through the Storage and Network entries and delete all specifications for cards that are *not* present in the system. Also, for cards that are present, such as network ones, make sure that the port, memory region, and interrupt number displayed agrees with how the card is set up. If it doesn't, change it.

> **NOTE**   If the SCSI card is a Buslogic, the bt0 driver is a dual-use driver, which works on the ISA, EISA, and PCI versions of these cards. If the card is not an ISA card, delete the bt0 driver from the storage area, which disables the ISA probing. The driver will automatically load on the EISA or PCI probes.

Deleting the ISA probe should also be done if the network card is a 3Com 3C579 EISA card. These cards should have the "ep0" probe disabled in this menu because the EISA-probe routine automatically attaches these cards, and the ISA probe is redundant. This may also be the case with other dual-use device drivers (i.e., a single driver that works for ISA, EISA, or PCI card versions). Save and quit the menu to allow the kernel to complete booting.

If the system doesn't boot at all from the boot floppy (e.g., the screen goes blank), most likely a problem occurred when creating the boot floppy. Try creating the boot floppy under DOS with *no* drivers loaded, not even `himem.sys`.

Many FreeBSD CDs are also bootable: if the CD-ROM drive is an IDE drive and the motherboard supports it, or if the SCSI adapter supports booting from the CD, then FreeBSD versions after 2.2.6 should boot from the CD.

### Step 9

When the kernel finishes loading, the /stand/sysinstall program is run. This is a character-based installation program and, unlike many UNIX installation programs, it is extremely useful. The program opens at the Welcome to FreeBSD! [2.2.8-RELEASE] or Main Menu screen with 12 menu options. Take some time to become familiar with them and read the Usage and Doc menu selections and documents. Then go back to the Main menu.

### Step 10

For installers in the United States, at the Main menu, just skip the Keymap menu item. Foreign users who have keyboards with non-U.S. character layouts should select an appropriate entry here.

### Step 11

Select the Installation Options: item 4 (on v2.2.8) item O on 3.3. If the installation is done directly from a CD drive mounted locally or via PPP from a designated FreeBSD FTP server on the Internet, this item can be skipped. If the installation is done from a local FTP server, such as a system with a CD-ROM set up per the instructions in INSTALL.TXT, go into this item and change the FTP username entry to the username and password, and the Release Name entry to None.

### Step 12

Select Enter at the Novice installation, and follow the menus to the FDISK Partition Editor screen. Review the entries in the DISK Geometry: line at the top. In some cases, if the drive is going to be dual-booted with multiple partitions on it, such as a DOS partition, this geometry must agree with the geometry used by the other partitions. The detected geometry can be changed with the G command. For example, if the disk will be split between FreeBSD and DOS, install DOS first, run the MSD program installed in the c:\DOS directory, and note the geometry figures. If FDISK detects a different geometry, it can be changed to match the reported geometry to DOS.

Another method of verifying geometry figures is to use the ide_conf.exe program in the /tools directory on the FreeBSD installation CD-ROM. It must be run under DOS before the next installation attempt. If the system has a very large IDE disk and the BIOS is set to LBA mode, these geometry figures can most likely be ignored.

Under FreeBSD 2.X and earlier, it is not unusual for SCSI disks, especially those freshly low-level formatted, to have unusual or differing geometries. This is true because the FreeBSD device driver queries the SCSI drive hardware directly during the boot process and is given the number of total blocks, not the disk geometry. Geometry is later calculated. Often, the SCSI BIOS computes a geometry that results in a total number of tracks under the 1,024-cylinder boundary. For SCSI drives, the FDISK program mainly guesses what a reasonable approximation would be.

In FreeBSD 3.X and later, the adapter device driver can designate the correct geometry to use for the drive, and so this problem should be greatly reduced. As long as the first bit of the SCSI drive has been zeroed out through a low-level format, the adapter can supply a correct default geometry. If the wrong geometry is used for the installation, the disk does not boot.

If it is critical to have the FreeBSD installation use correct hard drive geometries because the FreeBSD FDISK program makes a wrong guess on your hardware, boot the server with a DOS bootable floppy, create a small primary DOS partition, and format it with DOS. Now, when the FreeBSD installer loads its FDISK, it reads the geometry of the disk from the DOS partition. In the FreeBSD FDISK screen, create a FreeBSD partition with the remaining space.

For server applications, the safest method is to select A for "Use entire disk" and use a true partition (cooperative partition) entry. This is done because some BIOSs have problems if they don't see an IBM-FDISK-style partition table on the drive. If this fails, however, on a second attempt go ahead and use the *dangerously dedicated* method *without* using a true partition entry. Since a server is supposed to be up all the time, it won't need to be able to dual-boot. After the partition is created, select the "Set Bootable" entry and quit the menu.

If a 10MB DOS utility or diagnostics partition was created (e.g., Compaq hardware) and the rest of the disk was set to a DOS/95/98 partition, delete the other larger DOS partitions, recreate a partition for FreeBSD, and leave the diagnostics partition alone.

If the cooperative partition is selected, after quitting the partition manager, the Install Boot Manager screen displays. Select "BootMgr," the FreeBSD boot manager, for dual-booting (i.e., a system split between FreeBSD and Windows NT). Otherwise, select the Standard MBR or, on FreeBSD 4.0 and later, select "None."

The later sysinstalls automatically select booteasy if they detect a DOS partition on the hard drive that is kept with the FreeBSD partition. Just accept the default and continue.

On older EISA-based hardware it was not uncommon for the system administrator to create a 10MB DOS partition on the server drive and place all EISA-configuration utilities in it. Even with modern hardware, many devices, such as motherboards, network cards, hard drives, and so on, have DOS firmware flashing programs for upgrades.

### *Step 13*

The next task is to determine the BSD partition layout. BSD "partitions" are different from DOS/Windows partitions in that they exist within a single DOS-style partition on the drive that is allocated to FreeBSD.

Historically, partitions under UNIX were used to speed up file access. Early UNIX versions ran faster if the drive was split up into multiple partitions instead of one large one. It was also safer because less of the drive would get corrupted as a result of a crash. Modern UNIX operating systems don't have the same constraints, but multiple partitions are still a good idea. Some of the reasons to use them are these.

- Partitions are sometimes created with different block sizes for specific applications (e.g., a news server spool directory disk could be built with a smaller block size to avoid running out of inodes).
- Backups with the dump program are facilitated if the backup tape used in the system is smaller than total hard drive storage. For example, a server might have a 4GB tape drive and a 9GB SCSI drive. If one BSD partition was around 4GB, it could fit on a single tape using dump. Otherwise, the dump would have to span tapes.
- If the UNIX system runs out of space in its temporary directories, some unattended programs can crash.
- Some partitions can be mounted asynchronously, others synchronously.

If there will be users on the FreeBSD system, it is also wise to place the home directories on a separate partition; that way if the users fill up the home partition with data, it won't affect the system partitions.

For a new installation, the "Auto Defaults for All" option is useful for a scratch testing installation. It may be useful for people new to FreeBSD to install the entire UNIX system, install all the user applications, and then check to see if any changes need to be made in the filesystem. If some partitions have too little free space, just scratch the FreeBSD installation and reinstall, repartitioning with the desired space in each partition, before extensive customization on the system has been done.

For production work, the current recommendations for partitioning the drive are shown in Table 3.1. If X will be installed, my rule of thumb is for swap space under 200MB to increase the amount of space autoallocated to the swap partition by about 20 percent or 25MB, whichever is larger.

**Table 3.1**  Drive-Partitioning Recommendations

| a | / | 128MB |
|---|---|-------|
| b | swap | 2 * memory |
| d | /var | 128MB, or more if extensive logs will be kept |
| e | /usr | 1,000MB |
| f | /usr/local | 1,000MB |
| g | /usr/src | 500MB |
| h | /home | Rest of disk |

**Table 3.2**  Determining Optimal Swap Space

| System RAM MB | Swap Space |
|---------------|------------|
| 4 to 32 | 2 × total system RAM |
| 32 to 64 | 1.5 × total system RAM |
| 64 to 256 | Equal to total system RAM |
| 256 to 512 | 0.75 × total system RAM |
| More than 512 | 0.5 × total system RAM |

Determining an optimal amount of swap space is kind of a black art on hard drives with limited space, but for a typical system (i.e., one not running many processes or programs that consume an exceptional amount of RAM), you can use the *guesstimate* chart shown in Table 3.2.

Keep in mind that it's a lot easier for swap space to be taken away by the system during operation than for it to be added on the fly. Only use the chart if you are running short on drive space; if you have the space, set swap to 2 × the system RAM. Being generous with swap will never hurt you, but being stingy with it can.

With the partitioning determined, quit the Disk Label Editor, which brings up the Choose Distributions menu.

### Step 14

At the Choose Distributions menu, a number of options are possible. If this is a first-time installation on the target hardware, selecting the "Full binaries and doc, kernel sources only" option is better than attempting to specify a custom distribution. That way if something goes wrong with the installation and it needs to be restarted, there won't be much time invested in distribution selection.

The DES Cryptographic Software Installation screen displays. Unless there is some compelling reason, select the Basic DES installation. Many pieces of software require it, and in addition this makes the password file compatible with other UNIX-based computers. For example, if a group of users went to FreeBSD from Sun's Solaris, the `password` file could simply be copied over, if DES is used.

Kerberos 4 is also shown here, and this can be installed if desired. Kerberos is not discussed further in this book; I do *not* recommend that new FreeBSD users load it. In my opinion, Kerberos is most applicable in environments where many hostile people have direct access to the physical network and routinely run password sniffers looking for passwords. This fits academic environments to a T, and it's no surprise that Kerberos originated there. However, most smaller corporate networks don't need this level of additional complexity, and in my experience, well-run, larger corporate networks have significant switching in their network fabric. In many cases every port may be switched, and in this environment a sniffer is useless. For unswitched flat networks, SSH can provide good wire password security.

### Step 15

The next screen asks for the FreeBSD Ports collection. This installation is strongly recommended, and Yes should be selected unless you are installing an extremely minimal system, such as one for use on a remote printserver. Even if only prepackaged software will be installed on the FreeBSD system, the Ports system may be required. Sometimes prepackaged binaries are not built with the desired options selected and must be compiled in the Ports directories. Exit the Choose Distributions menu.

### Step 16

The Choose Installation Media screen displays. Select option 1 if the FreeBSD CD-ROM is in a CD-ROM drive in the target system. If FTP is selected for local installation from another machine with an FTP server and a FreeBSD CD-ROM loaded in it, the "Specify some other FTP site by URL" option should be selected. For the URL, use the IP number of the FTP server, along with any subdirectory specification needed to reach the root of the installation CD.

### Step 17

The Networking Interface screen asks for the name and IP number of the system. Fill this out with the numbering selected for the system. Make sure to put in all numbering, including DNS numbering. If the system is on a local network that is unconnected to the Internet and has no DNS server, use 192.168.1.1 as a *fake* DNS server IP number, and use the IP number of the FTP server in the "Specify some other FTP site by URL." This is necessary because some versions of sysinstall hang if no DNS IP number is supplied. If there is truly no DNS server on the network, once the system is installed, remove the `/etc/resolv.conf` file.

**NOTE**   FreeBSD 3.X and later can obtain IP addressing via DHCP if a DHCP server is on the network.

### Step 18
Now the installation starts. The drive is formatted, and the installation sets are copied from the CD or FTP server and decompressed onto the hard drive. When the installation is complete, if an FTP installation was done, the system asks to go back and configure any last options. Answer No. If a CD-ROM installation was done, the system asks to configure Ethernet or PPP interfaces; answer Yes. Select the Ethernet card and enter the IP numbering and system name. The system then asks another set of questions that represent additional options. Don't set any of these at this time. The system then reboots.

### Step 19
If the system reboots and properly loads, it displays a Login prompt. The system is now ready for the next phase of installation.

## Troubleshooting

Many things can go wrong with a first-time FreeBSD installation. Some common problems are listed here.

### Boot Problems
The system hangs on the Install Floppy boot. If the system hangs with a blank screen and is unable to boot the installation floppy at all (no twirlie symbol), this usually points to a problem in how the installation floppy diskette was created. Make sure to run RAWRITE under a system booted with DOS, with no other drivers loaded. The problem can sometimes be traced to floppy drives that are badly out of alignment. Also, the disk used to create the boot floppy cannot contain any bad blocks. Run SCANDISK on the floppy before using it with RAWRITE.

If the system boots the installation floppy but hangs while the kernel is loading, it may be that an IDE controller was left enabled on a system with no IDE disk drive, such as a SCSI-only system. Sometimes the switchover may take a while in these situations; give it about five minutes. This symptom can also point to IRQ assignment problems on ISA cards. If the kernel load completes but doesn't switch to the Main Installation Menu screen, usually a hard drive wasn't found. If the hard drive is SCSI, there may be a mismatch between the kernel and the SCSI card port and interrupt setup.

Drive controller problems can also be the result of incorrect probes of controller hardware. For example, some hardware cannot be properly probed: the probe always assumes the same port and interrupt values no matter how the hardware is configured. In that case check the kernel messages during boot—the values it probes are listed—and make sure these agree with the hardware setup.

If the system properly boots the installation floppy, loads the OS, and then cannot reboot from the hard drive into FreeBSD, improper disk geometry may have been chosen in the FDISK screen. In rare instances, the problem can be due to bad firmware on the drive controller card. For example, the BusLogic 742A EISA card must have G or later firmware on it; it does not boot with early firmware chips on the controller. I once had a Compaq Deskpro with a Compaq-supplied ESDI controller that would go through a FreeBSD load completely but then refuse to boot the OS from the drive once it had been installed. The problem here was a Compaq-modified ESDI controller BIOS that required Compaq utilities to format the disk and always formatted the drive with sector sparing turned on.

### Write Errors

These are system errors during attempts to write to the hard drive. This problem is most commonly caused in IDE drives as a result of geometry mismatches. In SCSI (and some ESDI) drives, it can be caused by device driver problems within FreeBSD. In SCSI, it can also be caused by not formatting the hard drive with the SCSI utilities. It also can be caused by port and interrupt mismatches between the SCSI controller and the driver in FreeBSD. Some SCSI device drivers are not as good as others, particularly ISA SCSI card drivers, such as the Adaptec 1520 card driver. Typically, PCI SCSI drivers, such as the NCR/Symbosis, Adaptec 2940, and Mylex/BusLogic, don't exhibit these kinds of problems.

### FTP Problems

FTP install hangs on login. If the installation gets to the point where it attempts to log in to the FTP server and simply hangs, the problem is usually caused by an incorrect interrupt setting for the network adapter. Generally, modern PCI 100BaseT network cards are autoprobing and do not have this problem. Older ISA network cards may have jumpers that need to be set to the same interrupt that the Visual Configuration is set to.

### Read Problems

The system cannot read the installation media. If the CD-ROM is local, make sure that the drive is detected. Typically, SCSI CDs give the least trouble, followed by

ATAPI CDs. Proprietary CDs, such as ancient single- and double-speed Mitsumi, Sony, or Panasonic drives, give the most trouble.

If installing via FTP, the problem is often caused by network card problems, PPP-level problems, or incorrect subdirectory specifications. If installing by local FTP, make sure the installation options use the keyword *None* for Release Name and the proper subdirectory as part of the local FTP server URL.

### Startup Problems

The system installs fine, boots, and then hangs during startup. If the system boots, loads the kernel, and then stops partway through executing the initial boot script, there is often a network problem. If this happens, let the system sit for at least five minutes. If it eventually continues with the startup script, it ends up at a login prompt that can be used to log in and correct the problem. A common problem is that the ISA card interrupts were set to the same interrupt number as a PCI card. Run the dmsg command and check to see what interrupts that the video cards and other cards in the system seize; make sure they don't conflict. Also, check the DNS IP number in /etc/resolv.conf to be sure it's correct. If no DNS is present, remove the resolv.conf file.

### Geometry Problems

The system installs fine, then issues an error message such as "Cannot find system." If this happens, the BIOS of the PC cannot load the FreeBSD bootstrap. This is a disk geometry problem, and the suggestions to correct this in the Boot Problems section should be followed.

## Installation Phase 2

With the basic installation completed, it is the time to set up the miscellaneous options in preparation for the third phase of installation. Many of these are optional.

### Step 1

Start by logging in to the system as root and setting the root password. Then run /stand/sysinstall. From the Main menu select "Do post-install configuration of FreeBSD."

### Step 2

Start with User Management and add a user name for yourself.

## *Step 3*

Go to Customize system console and select a screensaver *only if* you're running a workstation. If the system is to be used as a server, don't select a screensaver unless you select the "Green" saver; otherwise the screensaver chews up CPU cycles that should be used for serving files. In fact, on some hardware the screensaver can seriously affect performance. Keeping the monitor off on a server or on a switchbox is a lot better than a screensaver.

## *Step 4*

Select "Option 3" and set the time zone. Some administrators like to set the BIOS clock to Universal Time (UTC, formerly Greenwich Mean Time), and others, especially those on dual-boot systems, like to set it to local time (referred to as wall-clock time). The UNIX kernel always keeps time in UTC. This is extremely important on a large network such as the Internet, where all hosts should agree on a single time at any instant.

The rule of thumb here is that if there is a DOS partition on the system, such as a diagnostics partition, use wall-clock time because when the diagnostic utilities are running this is the time they use. Running with UTC is not out of the question on a dual-boot Windows system, however; just set the Windows side to UTC, and uncheck the "Adjust for Daylight Savings Time" box.

Because it is well known that PCs have inaccurate clocks, FreeBSD assumes that any system running on a network will have access to an accurate Network Time Protocol (NTP) source and periodically readjust the running kernel time with a program like `ntpdate`. If the organization is connected to the Internet, the FreeBSD system has access to NTP. FreeBSD runs the adjkerntz program, which keeps the PC's BIOS clock synchronized with the kernel clock, which should be getting it's time via NTP (*not* by querying the inaccurate PC BIOS clock). Both `ntpdate` and `adjkerntz` use the `timezone` file, as do any UNIX utilities (like Mail) that must calculate wall-clock time.

Note that some people have reported that enabling APM in their systems' BIOS can make the PC clock drift. Others have reported that enabling APM can make their system lock up!

## *Step 5*

If desired, configure any mouse device that is connected to the system. This mouse configuration is for the `moused` daemon program, which handles mouse activity in any console-based, character-mode FreeBSD programs that support a mouse, as well as the command prompt. This daemon also acts as a pass-through for the mouse used in the X Window System.

### Step 6

If the system will be routing or providing NFS services, select the "Configure additional network services" option, and select any desired options, such as `-n` for nonroot mounts.

### Step 7

If the system has a printer attached or will run a nameserver or run any Linux binaries, select "Configure system startup" options. In particular, select the "Linux" entry if the X Window System will be loaded because many programs, such as the Adobe Acrobat reader, require Linux emulation. For example, the free CuSeeMe reflector at `http://www.dimensional.com/~bgodette/` requires Linux emulation. Note that the Linux compatibility libraries *must* be installed to activate Linux emulation.

### Step 8

If the installation was done from an FTP server, go into "View/Set various installation options" and change the release name or username and password if needed, then quit back to the Configuration menu. Go into "Change the installation media type," and reset it.

### Step 9

For version 2.2.8, go into "Install additional distribution sets" and select `doc` and then `man` to install the online documentation. Version 3.X and later installs these as part of the earlier selection. When you exit this menu and return to the Main Configuration menu, the options are automatically installed. If online documents are installed on a system without the X Window System, Lynx can be used to view them.

> **NOTE**   Lynx should *always* be installed unless the system is going to be completely brain-dead (e.g., it is used as a remote printserver) or will permit inbound user Telnet (because Lynx has a number of security holes). Install Lynx by selecting it from the additional software sets in the following step or building it in the Ports directory. Besides its use as a browser, Lynx is also used by the CPAN module in Perl.

### Step 10

Select "Install prepackaged software for FreeBSD." The system loads the index file listing all prepackaged software. Load any software that looks interesting, and in addition consider loading some or all of those shown in Table 3.3. (The

**Table 3.3** Available Software

| Software | Description |
| --- | --- |
| Xaw3d-1.5 | Makes X programs look like they are using Motif |
| apache-1.3.9 | To set up the system with a Web server |
| bash-2.03 | Popular shell with users; it has a DOSKEY-like scrollback buffer |
| bing-1.0.4 | Measures bandwidth of point-to-point links |
| cdplay-0.92 | Plays music CDs in CD-ROM drive |
| dnswalk-2.0.2 | DNS debugger; useful for a nameserver administrator |
| doom-1.8 | The infamous game; may be useful to prove to naysayers that FreeBSD works; not available in prepackaged software in version 3.X |
| emacs-20.4 | The ultimate programmer's editor, at least according to its proponents, who are almost as fanatical as Macintosh users |
| fetchmail-5.0.5 | Useful for organizations attempting to run a site behind a single dialup IP number |
| gated-3.5.11 | Powerful routing program used if the FreeBSD server is going to be routing in an enterprise network |
| gmake-3.77 | GNU make; used by a number of other programs as part of their `install` process |
| hylafax-4.0.2 | Fax software; requires Ghostscript—see Installation Phase 3 |
| hypermail-20b3 | Web front-end for mailing listservers |
| jpeg-6b | JPEG library; required for Hylafax and many other programs |
| linux_lib-2.4 | Linux compatibility libraries for programs such as `acroread`; this is for version 2.2.8 |
| mgetty-1.1.21 | Allows both dialup shell and PPP accounts to use the same indial modem; see the PPP manual page for setup information |
| mhonarc-2.3.3 | Web front-end for mailing list listservers |
| mpack-1.5 | Used to create and decode MIME mail messages for scripts |
| mpd-2.0b2 | Multilink PPP daemon used instead of built in MP in PPP |
| netscape-3.04 | Netscape Web browser; requires X Window; choose the preferred version |
| netscape-communicator-4.61 | Netscape browser; choose the preferred version |
| netscape-navigator-4.08 | Netscape browser; choose the preferred version |
| perl-5.00404 | Perl5; the Perl version included by default is version 4, this is for 2.2.8 only; version 3.X of FreeBSD includes Perl5 already |
| pidentd-2.8.5 | RFC1413 identification server; some mailservers like to make `ident` calls; the new Sendmail version has hooks for this program |
| pine-4.10 | One of the most full-featured UNIX character-mode mail clients; many claim it's better than Elm |
| poppassd-4.0 | Allows remote mail clients, like Eudora, to change their passwords |

**Table 3.3** (*continued*)

| Software | Description |
| --- | --- |
| procmail-3.13.1 | Used by many people to filter their mail automatically |
| qpage-3.2 | Sends pages to digital or alphanumeric pagers |
| qpopper-2.53 | POP3 mailserver for POP3 mail clients; very stable |
| samba-2.0.5 | Allows WfW, Win95, and WinNT systems to access files on the server |
| squid-2.2 | Caching HTTP proxy server, used on firewalls |
| tiff-3.5.1 | TIFF library; required for HylaFax faxing software |
| trafshow-2.0 | Popular network traffic monitor; requires BPF configured in kernel |
| upsd-2.0 | Monitoring software for the APC SmartUPS UPS |
| wu-ftpd-2.6.1 | High-security FTP server used for public FTP servers |

list is from 2.2.6 CD; later CDs may not have all of these prepackaged, but they are in the Ports section.)

In some cases, precompiled software packages require other packages, known as *dependencies*, installed. `Ghostview`, for example, requires `Ghost-script` to run. If the dependency package is available as a precompiled package, it is automatically installed. Due to licensing issues, however, some packages may not be precompiled. In these cases, the administrator must note the dependency packages that the precompiled binary calls for, and then build and install them from the Ports collection.

## Installation Phase 3

Unfortunately, due to licensing restrictions or other issues, not all useful software that is often needed for the FreeBSD server is available as precompiled binaries that can be installed from the menu in `sysinstall`. This is where the Ports directories come into play, and this is why it is so important to install them.

Also, many precompiled binaries supplied on the FreeBSD CDs may not be right for your server. For example, the precompiled versions of `popper` and `poppasswd` both may abort with the following error messages.

```
ld.so failed: Can't find shared library "libkrb.so.3.0"
```

This error occurs because these packages were linked with the Kerberos libraries, and if your FreeBSD system was installed without Kerberos, these libraries won't be on the system. In this case, the precompiled binary is useless; to use the program, the administrator must recompile it in the Ports directories.

**Table 3.4** Ports Programs

| Software | Description |
| --- | --- |
| elm-2.4ME+38 | The Elm mail program; the most popular character-based UNIX mail program |
| ldap-3.3 | Lightweight Directory Access Protocol server; many mail clients now support LDAP |
| lynx-2.7.2 | Character-mode Web browser; extremely useful to read info documents in a pinch, such as while Telnetted into the system |
| pgp-5.0i | Pretty Good Privacy; this is mainly useful for command-line mail clients |
| pilot-link-0.8.13 | Communications utilities for use with the 3Com PalmPilot |
| ucd-snmp-3.2 | SNMP daemon software to allow the FreeBSD system to be monitored by a network management console |

The following sections describe useful programs that are built in Ports (see also Table 3.4). Ports is designed to be used on a machine directly connected to the Internet since the builder automatically FTPs the software packages needed. However, if the package is obtained and placed in `/usr/ports/distfiles`, the builder checks for it there and won't need to FTP it. Note that all dependent packages should be installed or placed in `/usr/ports/distfiles` along with the target package.

### Acroread-3.01
The Adobe Acrobat Reader, this program requires the X Window System to be installed. It also requires Linux emulation to be loaded and activated by `/stand/sysinstall`.

### ApacheSSL-1.2.5
A secure socket layer (SSL) implementation of Apache.

### Ghostscript
Several `Ghostscript` versions are available in the Ports directory. `Ghostscript` is used by many programs; simply put, it is a PostScript interpreter. Faxing with Hylafax and PostScript-to-HP-LaserJet conversions are two areas that require `Ghostscript`. `Ghostview` (the PostScript previewer) is another program that requires it.

A number of versions of `Ghostview` are supplied because some programs have dependencies on specific versions. Unless you are installing (manually building, usually) one of these programs, select the most current `Ghostscript` version, and install it before installing other programs, such as Hylafax, that depend on it.

### Inn-1.7.2

The InterNetwork News (INN) program is the principal Usenet news server program used to handle the vast majority of Usenet news serving on the Internet today. At one time Cnews was the reference Usenet implementation, but INN surpassed Cnews several years ago. INN requires more core memory than Cnews, but it doesn't use as much disk channel I/O and can handle a greater volume of articles on the powerful UNIX hardware used today.

### Kermit-6.0.192

Kermit is one of the oldest mainframe serial communications programs and is very useful for connecting with elderly mainframes. Kermit is both a program name and a File Transfer Protocol implemented in this program. Kermit can also be useful for remote shell access over very poor or slow phone lines.

### Majordomo-1.94

Among the most popular mailing list managers available for FreeBSD, majordomo is unrestricted and can be used in a commercial environment. The other major UNIX listserver, ListProc, has some restrictions for commercial use.

Note that ListServ is the name often given to mailing list managers, but ListServ is actually the name of a mailing list program from DEC/VMS, Digital Equipment's OS originating on the VAX. Majordomo requires Perl to be installed. It works with Perl4, the default Perl installed with FreeBSD, but Perl5 is recommended. (Perl5 is the system Perl in FreeBSD 4.X.) Future versions of majordomo don't guarantee compatibility with Perl4.

### Patch-2.5

The current version of the Patch program is 2.5. Patch version 2.1 is already included in FreeBSD, and for practically any source patching that the average administrator will need to do, it is sufficient. However, developers may want specific features in this later version.

### Rzsz-3.48 or lrzsz-0.12.20

Rzsz is the original implementation of Zmodem; there are some license restrictions on its use. Lrzsz is a GNU version built on the older, public-domain Zmodem code. Like Kermit, this program is a good reference implementation to have around, but you will have to find rzsz on an older archive site or CD. The current version is unworkable and isn't supplied anymore; use lrzsz instead.

### Skip-1.0
This program was designed by Sun as a competitor to IP-Secure, the IETF's secure TCP/IP standard used to build Virtual Private Networks (VPNs). Skip came out several years before IETF finally standardized, but now that standardization has occurred on IP-Secure, it is on the decline. However, it is still very useful for building VPNs.

### Ssh-1.2.27
The Secure Shell is used to obtain secure login in insecure environments, such as college networks, where students often run sniffers and other password grabbers. It can also be used to build VPNs, encrypt over-the-wire backups, and secure unattended automated network data transfers.

> **NOTE** This is SSH1. A later version, SSH2, is available, but it cannot be used in commercial enterprises without paying a license fee. Be cautious with SSH-1.2.27; it makes an unprotected library call into the RSAref libraries, which themselves don't do bounds checking, thereby creating a security hole. It is possible to patch the RSAref libraries to close this hole (see the CERT advisory and accompanying patch if working with FreeBSD 3.4 or earlier).

A Windows Telnet client named SecureCRT has support for `ssh` built right into it. It's located at `http://www.vandyke.co`, and it has an excellent vt220 emulation.

FreeBSD 4.X and later should use OpenSSH instead of this one, which is included preinstalled in the system.

### StarOffice-5.1a
This commercial office suite (it requires X Window) originated in Europe and is popular on many other operating system platforms. This is the lightweight version. StarOffice is now owned by Sun, which distributes it on CD. The current version is 5.2. StarOffice uses file formats compatible with Microsoft products.

### Tripwire-1.2
This is a network monitoring program that is used to detect crack attempts.

## Installation Phase 4

With package fetching and installation complete, the next step is recompiling the kernel. Start by reading the handbook section on kernel configuration to get the basics. At this point, if X Window isn't installed, Lynx can be used to read the handbook.

> **NOTE**   If Lynx starts with an error message, edit the `/usr/local/etc/lynx.cfg` file and change `STARTFILE` to `STARTFILE:file://localhost/usr/share/doc/handbook/handbook.html`. This allows access to the online FAQs and the handbook.

Despite the sound of it, recompiling the UNIX kernel is a very simple process as long as you read the GENERIC and LINT kernels and their documentation. It is a good idea to recompile as soon as the server is up and running because recompilation is one of the more electrically stressful things that can be done on the system. If the FreeBSD system is able to recompile the system, it is likely to be stable enough to use as a production system.

There is nothing about recompiling the kernel that a slower or older machine cannot do. I have recompiled flawless FreeBSD kernels on an 80386/25Mhz system with 8MB of RAM, but this extremely restricted system took hours to recompile.

Be wary of any compilation error messages claiming that errors exist in the kernel source code. The production FreeBSD kernel is recompiled thousands of times before it is committed to the CD-ROM and simply does not contain syntax errors or other gross problems that would cause the system compiler to abort a compilation job. Spurious kernel compilation errors, such as claims of missing parentheses, are a red flag marking bad hardware or possible configuration errors. If problems like this develop, attempt to recompile the generic kernel to be sure that the system itself is not at the root of the problem. If the generic kernel causes the compiler to emit errors, reboot the system with the internal and external cache RAM switched off. If that doesn't help, check the system bus speed, and run an exhaustive memory checker on the system. If the FreeBSD server is unable to recompile the generic kernel, do *not* use it as a production server!

If the system can recompile the generic kernel without a problem but is unable to compile the kernel configuration file that the administrator is attempting to use, recheck it for syntax errors. Exhibit 3.1 shows a rough guide to a kernel recompilation.

Once a good kernel is done, the server is on line, and configuration is complete, run the `dmesg` program when Telnetted into the server (or print out `/var/run/dmesg.boot`) and send its output to a printer. Tape the printout to the back of the server case.

### Exhibit 3.1  Kernel recompilation guidelines

1. Log in, su to root, then change directory to /sys and list the directory. If /sys doesn't exist or the directory is empty, kernel sources haven't been installed. These can be installed by running /stand/sysinstall, and then selecting Do post-install configuration. Select "Install additional distribution sets" and then "Sources for everything but DES." From the Sources option, select the "/usr/src/sys" subgroup.

2. Change the directory to i386 and then to conf. This is the Configure directory, where the initial configuration file will be created.

3. Copy the generic file to a name of a new kernel configuration file, such as SMOKED, or use the host name of the system. It can be almost any name, but don't use numbers as part of the name (e.g., KERNEL1, or KERNEL2 because the configurator won't like it.

4. Read the LINT file, which lists all the device drivers that are available for inclusion into the kernel and the syntax used in the regular configuration file to enable them.

5. Delete all unnecessary device drivers in the new kernel file (the SMOKED file) and add in any device drivers needed for hardware that is not supported in the GENERIC kernel. Set the port and I/O addresses of any drivers.

6. Run the config command with the new file as an option (e.g., config SMOKED). If this runs properly, the output of the command will be
   `kernel build directory is ../../compile/SMOKED`.

7. Change directory to /sys/compile. Change the directory into the Kernel Configuration filename subdirectory.

8. Run make depend, make, and make install, in that order. This copies the new kernel to the root directory. Do *not* do this if you have deleted /kernel.GENERIC.

9. Reboot to test the new kernel. If the kernel fails, reboot. At the boot prompt, quickly type in /kernel.old to boot off the previously working kernel.

## THE X WINDOW SYSTEM

The X Window System is the graphical front-end that is used as the basis of all graphical interfaces on all UNIX OSs. Its use is not required for anything that is covered in this book, so skip this section if you want. However, even if your primary method of access to the FreeBSD machine is a command-line window, you may want to install X anyway.

The X System was originally developed at MIT and eventually turned over to the X Consortium. The Consortium managed a number of versions, ending with X11R6.3 in 1997. At that time the X code was turned over to a new organization, The Open Group (TOG). Currently, X implemented under FreeBSD (and Linux) is built on XFree86, which is built on the X11R6.3 *sample* implementation. The XFree86 group, at `http://www.xfree86.org/`, concentrates on a free version of X originally implemented on the Intel 'x86 series of processors.

Because the X Window System is the only way at this time to put a graphical front-end on UNIX, possession of X on a UNIX has always been kind of a political football. This is probably due to the commercial OS vendors making a basic assumption that a graphical front-end is a requirement to sell UNIX to the average system administrator. It is also due to several UNIX vendors, such as Silicon Graphics, being dependent on X for many years to produce intensely powerful modeling software that is difficult or impossible to create under Windows.

When MIT turned over the X Window System to the X Consortium, the Consortium funded itself by charging a membership fee. A group of UNIX industry leaders came forward and donated Consortium membership fees to XFree86 so they could join. Consortium membership allowed a say in future development on X. When TOG took over, the licensing was set up so that the *sample implementation* was open and freely available. X funding was built on charges applied to the Motif libraries, which were not free. Motif is much desired for X installations because the Motif libraries provide a rich toolkit of objects that make X programs compiled with Motif look much more visually appealing. TOG was happy to allow XFree86 to use new releases of the sample implementation as their code base. XFree86 didn't concern itself with Motif distribution, leaving that to the end user to purchase from some vendor.

Unfortunately, however, with TOG's release of X11R6.4 a change was made in the licensing. This required anyone distributing a UNIX containing X11R6.4 versions for profit to pay TOG a royalty fee. If XFree86 were to use TOG's X11R6.4 code, XFree86 wouldn't be required to pay a fee because they don't distribute XFree86 for a profit. However, any commercial UNIX vendor that uses XFree86 would have to pay. FreeBSD doesn't fall into this category, but Caldera's Open Linux (which sells at $100 a copy) almost certainly does, and the group is the bestselling implementation of Linux today. This put XFree86 in a hard place: if it used the 6.4 code, Caldera would cut itself off if they didn't then restrict other innocent groups, such as FreeBSD, to the older code.

Needless to say, this licensing change created intense controversy in the industry. XFree86 solicited input from all of the Open Source users and as a result formally announced they would not develop on 6.4 code. TOG began vacillating between threatening and pleading to get XFree86 back into the fold. To add salt to the wound, TOG documentation described XFree86 users as "hobbyists and students," pretending a UNIX world where no commercial users of systems like FreeBSD and Linux exist. This is insulting at best, completely misguided at worst. In the past, most of the good improvements and advances in the X Window System originated from the noncommercial UNIX world, and TOG knew this and wanted it to continue. On the other hand, TOG is mainly funded by commercial UNIX vendors and has felt threatened by the increasing use of XFree86 in commercial installations such as Linux.

The issue was finally resolved when TOG again revised their licensing fees. Although all parties have been publicly silent as to why TOG backed down, it is very likely that they did so because of a combination of pressure applied by commercial UNIX vendors, bad press, and the fact that XFree86 has the biggest market share for X. There's no question that the commercial UNIX vendors benefit from work done by the Open Source community, and they would see little benefit in a code split with XFree86 going one way and TOG going another.

## X Advantages

It is strongly recommended that the X Window System not be left running all the time on any FreeBSD machine that is used as a server, because X consumes a lot of core memory and resources. However, X is handy to have configured on the FreeBSD server for four reasons.

1. It allows a graphical Web browser to operate. Note that the FreeBSD handbook and FAQ documents are both in HTML.
2. It allows for multiple windows to be open at once on the console monitor. If you're running FreeBSD at home just to play with it, this can be very useful.
3. It allows for viewing of documentation that is not in ASCII format, such as PDF, PostScript, and other graphical formats.
4. Unlike cheap Telnet clients, Xterms can be dynamically resized and will notify programs running in the window of this capability. Some of the better Windows Telnet clients can resize Xterms.

For many people, X has a number of other advantages. To start with, many people are more comfortable using a text editor that has more of a WYSIWYG than a *character-based* feel to it. Also, a good X Window manager can be set up to allow commands to be listed in a menu, or on icons, to keep from having to remember their names. Some people are more comfortable with file manipulation using a graphical file manager rather than a command line with wildcards.

Whatever the preference is, if X is going to be run regularly, the following items will make the experience much more pleasant.

1. A large monitor—the larger the better. Unlike Windows, X programs are generally written using very small fonts, icons, and so forth, because the program author generally assumes that the user is going to be at a full-blown UNIX workstation plugged into a 21-inch monitor. These workstations often have resolutions of up to $1,600 \times 1,200$ dpi, which allows many windows to be open on the screen. Thus, it is very hard to use most X programs with resolution under $1,024 \times 768$ dpi on a 14-inch monitor. A *virtual desktop* capability can be used in a pinch to improve this, but don't rely on it.

2. The version of X supplied with FreeBSD is very, very fast, but, as with any graphical system, the more hardware acceleration available in the video card, the better. X runs acceptably on an SVGA card, such as a Western Digital WD90C30 chipset-based card (Paradise VGA), but these lower-end chipsets often have 256-color mode only. Screen acceleration like that provided by an S3-based card, such as a Diamond Speedstar, greatly speeds operations such as scrolling through HTML or PostScript files and allows for higher color modes.

3. Many X programs run better when more colors are available. The standard resolution for X is 8 bits per pixel (bpp) (8-bit color), otherwise known as 256 colors, and it is most compatible with many programs. However, 16- and 24-bpp TrueColor modes are available. The video card must have enough video memory in it to support millions of colors at a high resolution, preferably 4MB.

4. The part of the X Window System that actually manipulates the video card hardware is the X Server. FreeBSD comes with a basic X Server named XF86_SVGA, which supports most kinds of video card chipsets. Other X Servers take advantage of special hardware in certain cards, such as programmable dot clock chips, and have more colors available.

Because all the servers are written by different people, some are buggier than others, even SVGA. For example, under the S3 server, my ISA Orchid Fahrenheit VA card runs fine, but under SVGA, its pointer is messed up. Before buying an expensive video card for FreeBSD, carefully read the documentation on the appropriate servers. Depending on the application, it may be preferable to purchase a commercial X Server from Xi Graphics (http://www.xig.com/) that supports additional features and resolution of the video card in use. Xi Graphics also sells Motif v2.0 for FreeBSD for about $150. The Xi Graphics X Servers may be a requirement for a laptop. A list of supported laptop video chips is on the Xi Web site.

5. Finally, like everything, the faster the CPU and the more system RAM, the better X runs.

The X Window System is divided into two main parts, which perform different tasks and need separate configuration. The first part is the X Server, which is controlled by the `/etc/XF86Config` file. It can be generated easily or in a very complicated way, depending on how well the hardware is supported. In general, newer and more expensive monitors and video cards are easier to configure.

The second part is the X Window System's manager. This is largely a matter of personal preference. The X Window manager is a bit like the choice of Active Desktop, Classic Desktop, and Win31 Desktop available under Win95. (Win31 desktop is indeed available for Win95, but it is an option buried in the initial installation.) However, unlike those managers, the X Window manager doesn't interfere with a program's look and feel in the same way. A particular window manager is not a requirement for virtually all of the X Window System's programs.

For example, Sun used to offer the OpenLook window manager for its older Solaris products under its X derivative, OpenWindows. Later, Sun offered the Common Desktop Environment (CDE) window manager, and it is now standard on Solaris 2.6. CDE was developed by a collection of commercial UNIX software vendors and is not freely available. UNIX users who started with the earlier window manager under Solaris may prefer the `olvwm` window manager under FreeBSD, which is included in the prepackaged software list. Users who like CDE may prefer to use the `fvwm` window manager in conjunction with the `xfce` program, also in prepackaged software. Users with a Windows background may prefer the `fvwm95` or `qvwm` manager.

A collection of screen shots of most X Window managers is available at `http://www.plig.org/xwinman/index.html`.

Note that the X Server *doesn't need to be run* on the same machine on which X programs (called X clients) are run. X contains a protocol that allows remote machines to display the output of X applications that are running on the server. For example, users may run Netscape on the FreeBSD system with the output displaying on their workstations. This is very useful if custom applications are running on the UNIX server. One caveat is that the X protocol is "noisy" and very sluggish over a dialup serial line.

Originally, when UNIX workstation prices were high, many organizations purchased X terminals that used a single server on which to run X client programs. The X Servers that displayed the output would run on the cheaper X terminals.

A free X Server that can be run under Win95 used to be available at `http://tnt.microimages.com/www/html/freestuf/mix.htm`. I have successfully used this as well as the IBM-supplied X Server for OS/2 to run X programs on FreeBSD. Unfortunately, this server became so popular that the manufacturer incremented the version number and added a 15-day cutoff.

It now costs $25 to register, and the new location for it is <u>http://www.</u>
<u>microimages.com/mix/</u>.

## Installing X on the FreeBSD Machine

The following instructions show how to place on a FreeBSD machine a desktop as close to Win95 or Windows NT 4.0 as possible. It can contain a Start
menu with the Netscape browser (for HTML), Adobe Acrobat Reader (for PDF
files), Nedit (for text editing), Ghostview (for viewing PostScript files), and
Explorer (a Win95-like file manager). This setup can then be used as the front
end to the FreeBSD machine, if the administrator prefers a Win95- or
Windows NT-like interface.

The first step is to install the X Window System distribution. Keep one
thing in mind with getting X up and running: the higher the monitor resolution
and the better quality monitor you have, the easier it is to get X operating. Most
configuration problems I have run into with X occur because most video cards
can easily put out very high refresh rates that a cheap monitor cannot handle.
The remaining problems are usually due to various adapter card issues.

Just like installing kernel sources, the X Window System can be installed
by running /stand/sysinstall and then selecting "Do post-install configuration." Select "Install additional distribution sets" and then The "XFree86
3.3.5 distribution." Next, select the following for an X installation.

- Everything in the Basic Component menu except for the PC98 entries and
  the standard and contrib sources, unless you want to recompile X completely, which may be required to install patches at a later time.
- The SVGA, VGA16, and any other specific X Servers desired, such as the
  S3 and S3V servers. The VGA16 server is required for the graphical X
  setup program, the SVGA server is the suggested default server for most
  cards, and the other individual servers are useful for specific instances. A
  specific instance would be that SVGA doesn't run for your video adapter
  card or the individual server has more colors for your card than SVGA. If
  you don't know what other servers are desired, just select SVGA and
  VGA16.
- Standard, 100dpi, and Speedo fonts will extract the X distribution and
  install it into /usr/X11R6. As a last item, edit all system login script profiles for the various shells to place /usr/X11R6/bin into the PATH
  variables. For example, the system profile for the /bin/sh shell is
  /etc/profile.

After the X Window System is installed, generate the /etc/XF86Config
file. There are two ways to do this: run the graphical /usr/X11R6/bin/

XF86Setup program or run the command-line /usr/X11R6/bin/xf86config
program. The original configuration program was the command-line one; the
graphical program was added later. They take different approaches to the problem, and neither works in all circumstances.

My rule of thumb is that the more modern video cards and monitors work
better with the graphical program, and the older or more esoteric video cards
and monitors work better with the command-line configurator.

Start by running the graphical program and following the steps. If this fails,
run the command-line version. One of these will be sufficient to generate a
usable /etc/XF86Config file. After this is done, test the server by running
startx to start it.

To tune the file, read the manual pages for XF86Config with samples of
output runs from both programs. For older cards, one of the trickiest things is
generating proper Modeline entries. Sometimes, working Modelines from the
output of the graphical configurator can be used in a configuration file generated by the command-line configurator, or vice-versa.

After tuning, it's time to install the default window manager, unless you are
planning on continuing to use tvm, which is installed by default. It can
be installed from sysinstall in the prepackaged software. For a Win95-like
screen, select fvwm95-2.0.43a. This places the window manager binary as
/usr/X11R6/bin/fvwm95. To make this the default window manager used by
the startx  program, edit the /usr/X11R6/lib/X11/xinit/xinitrc file
and replace tvm with fvwm95. Or, edit the .xinitrc file in a user's home
directory to change it for that user.

This window manager places an init file that lists a number of X programs
under the start menu. If these programs aren't installed, clicking on them does
not produce a result. Run sysinstall and install any that you wish.

A running X Window on the FreeBSD console can be cycled through its
various resolutions with the Ctrl-Alt+ and Ctrl-Alt-key sequences. It can be
started with a different number of colors, with the color specification following
the startx command. For example, startx − -bpp 16 starts X with 16-bit
(HiColor) color.

## Graphical Login

FreeBSD can also be set up to present a graphical Login screen on boot instead
of the character-mode login prompt. This is *not* recommended if the FreeBSD
system is being used as a server because running X to present the Login screen
consumes server resources that would otherwise be devoted to the job
the server is supposed to be doing. If the administrator prefers using X for maintenance tasks (perhaps to allow cut and paste between Xterms on the desktop),

the recommended method is to log in to the character-mode prompt, run `startx`, and, when exiting, simply log out of the login window to close X down.

However, if the administrator wants to present the graphical Login screen, X can also be run by adding the following into the `/usr/X11R6/lib/X11/xdm/Xservers` file:

```
:0 local /usr/X11R6/bin/X :0 vt04 -bpp 16
```

This forces the X Server to start up on VT4, as opposed to the first free one it can find, so it won't interfere with the `init`-spawned `gettys`. This example shows the Login screen started with HiColor mode; if the display can only do 256-color mode, the last part of the line will be `-bpp 8`. With this example, the script `xdm.sh` placed in `/usr/X11R6/etc/rc.d` and containing

```
#!/bin/sh
[ -x /usr/X11R6/bin/xdm ] && ( /usr/X11R6/bin/xdm ) && echo -n ' xdm'
```

will be used to start the graphical Login screen on boot. Set the script as `executable`.

The `xdm` program is what presents the graphical login screen; `xdm` uses `xsm` as its session manager. When using the graphical login screen, the administrator may also want to modify the file `/usr/X11R6/lib/X11/xsm/system.xsm` and replace `tvm` with their preferred window manager, such as `fvwm95`. Users can, of course, override this with their own `.xsmstartup` files in their home directories, and they may want to do it if their home directories are NFS mounted on multiple systems. On standalone systems, the `.xsmstartup` file makes little sense unless several people will be logging in at different times at the same system console.

Note that setting up the system in this manner does not preserve the user's environment for the session manager, as `startx` does. Xterms and such started by the startup script won't contain the right environment for the user. Users can start their own Xterms after login with the correct environment.

## The Issue of the Netscape Browser Java Applet under X

When installing the Netscape Web browser under the X Window System of FreeBSD, the user may experience problems attempting to display Java applets. If this happens, run the following commands as the root user.

```
cd /usr/X11R6/lib/X11/fonts/misc
/usr/X11R6/bin/mkfontdir
chmod 444 fonts.dir
```

Then exit and restart X. These commands rebuild the `fonts.dir`, which must be correct for any X Window System version to display applets. This is also detailed in the Netscape Ports section under FreeBSD.

## PPP Installation

PPP is used for virtually all dialup ISP accounts these days; for example, an AT&T Worldnet Internet account uses PPP. If the installer can run a Win95 Dialup Networking connection to the ISP, it has access to a PPP account. FreeBSD can be installed using this kind of account only, without an Ethernet connection through a router to the Internet. However, the sheer quantity of data means that this is a project that the administrator initiates in the late afternoon and then lets run all night long.

If this kind of installation will be done, a modem must be installed on a serial port, either external or internal. External modems are generally preferred on UNIX systems because useful diagnostic information can be gotten from their front panel lights. The installer should also know the following IP numbering information: IP number, netmask, gateway number, and DNS server IP number. A properly configured PPP server should supply all these items, but plan for problems. These numbers can often be determined by using Win95 Dialup Networking to dial into the ISP and, when the connection is established, running the Windows program `winipcfg`. At the top is a box with the Ethernet Adapter listed. If PPP Adapter is not showing here, click the down arrow to the right and select it. The IP numbering will be listed in a box underneath. The DNS number is not listed in this screen. Click the More Info >> button and it will be displayed. Usually, on most ISPs supporting PPP dialup, the IP number that the dialup server hands out changes from call to call; however, the gateway, DNS, and subnet mask numbers usually stay the same.

In addition to numbering, the method used to log in should be known. Most ISPs authenticate dialup users using the PAP or CHAP protocols. When the user dials in with software, such as Dialup Networking, the server they connect to answers. When it detects a PPP initialization sequence from the user's system it launches PPP. The username and password is authenticated within the PPP stream. Some ISPs, however, run UNIX systems and require the user to "log in" at a regular Login prompt and then run the PPP program. Under Win95 Dialup Networking, this is done in a little terminal window that pops up.

For the FreeBSD installer the `/stand/sysinstall` program has a PPP compiled into it, as well as a simple, terminal interface used to create the PPP connection. The instructions in Exhibit 3.2 are for a sample PPP installation that uses an ISP account requiring PAP authentication; it does not use a login

**Exhibit 3.2  A sample PPP installation**

1. Start with steps 1 to 10 in the Installation Phase 1 section, except that, since the FreeBSD CD won't be present, log onto `ftp.freebsd.org/pub/FreeBSD` and select the desired version directory. Download the `boot.flp` file and diskette creation programs and build the boot floppy, then boot the system with it. Since this is an FTP installation over PPP, leave the installation options under item 4 of `sysinstall` alone.

2. Continue with steps 11 to 14, and at step 15 select FTP installation and a convenient FTP server.

3. The next screen is Network interface information requested screen. Select the ppp0 device, depending on which COM port the modem is on.

4. At the next screen, fill in as much as you can about the network information.

5. The next screen asks for the maximum baud rate of the modem, which is actually the modem-to-computer speed. A 28.8K modem normally uses the default of 115,200bps.

6. The next screen takes the IP address you entered earlier and asks if you want to use it. Set this to zero unless the PPP server you're dialing in to cannot negotiate this.

7. The terminal emulator is started on an alternate terminal; press Alt-F3 to switch to it.

8. At the > prompt, enter `set Authname fred` and `set AuthKey barney`. You can enter the `show auth` command to make sure these have been entered properly.

9. Enter the `term` command, which switches to the terminal mode. Type the modem dial command string, in this case `ATDT1234567`. When the modems link up and the **Connected** response is shown, enter ~. to switch back to the PPP > prompt.

10. If the PPP link hasn't come up, enter the `dial` command, which should kick it into operation.

11. Switch back to the Install screen with Alt-F1 and press Enter. Continue with the rest of the Phase 1 installation instructions.

12. The remaining installation phases can be done by running the PPP program, establishing the connection to the ISP, and then switching to a different console screen and running `/stand/sysinstall`.

---

prompt. The username is `fred`, the password is `barney`, and the phone number is 123-4567.

## Manual PPPD Connection

Depending on the ISP, some users may have difficulty establishing a PPP link with the user-mode PPP program used by `/stand/sysinstall`. In this case it is possible to use the kernel-mode PPP program, `/sbin/pppd`, to establish the connection. Unfortunately, it can't be used to do a PPP installation over the

## Exhibit 3.3  PPPD manual connection instructions

1. Log in to one of the console logins as root, making sure that at least three virtual consoles are available. Alternatively, run X and open multiple Xterms.

2. Copy `/etc/uucp/port.sample` to `/etc/uucp/port` and change its ownership to `uucp`.

3. Modify `/etc/uucp/port` and change the `port1` entries in it as follows.
   ```
   device /dev/cuaa1
   speed 115200
   ```
   Note that `cuaa0` is connected to COM1, `cuaa1` is connected to COM2, and so on. Exit the editor and save changes.

4. Go to the `/etc/ppp` directory and create the file `pap-secrets` with the following line in it:
   ```
   fred   *  barney
   ```

5. At the command line, type `cu -p port1`. The `cu` program should connect to the modem.

6. Type in the following to the modem:
   ```
   atz
   at&c1 (type any other command codes here to set the modem into high-speed mode)
   atdt1234567
   ```

7. When connected, press Alt-F2 to the next virtual console and log in as root.

8. In this virtual console type in
   ```
   pppd /dev/cuaa1 115200 crtscts defaultroute user fred
   ```
   The PPP daemon program should respond with a printout of the local IP address and the remote IP address.

9. Modify the `/etc/resolv.conf` file and enter the IP number of the DNS server of the ISP. At this point, the administrator can log in to an alternative console window and should have Internet connectivity (i.e., should be able to ping hosts on the Internet).

Internet; installation must take place with a CD-ROM first. Use the quick setup instructions in Exhibit 3.3 to verify if user-mode PPP is broken with your ISP. If it is, and `pppd` works, you might want to look at using a different ISP. User-mode PPP is much better suited for dial-on-demand uses than is `pppd`.

Although PPPD has scripting that can be enabled, as well as many options and automatic dialing, the instructions in Exhibit 3.3 can be used as a quick way to establish a manual connection using `pppd`. The example assumes an Internet account with a login of `fred`, a password of `barney`, a telephone number of `1234567`, and a 28.8K modem on COM2.

## DISKLESS BOOT

Occasionally, administrators who manage large installations may use diskless boot. Diskless boot was much more popular when hard drives were expensive, but it still has some utility today. To start with, all client configuration is stored on the server, so when the diskless workstation is booted every morning, its configuration is always exactly the same. Diskless boot is also popular in laboratories, to allow administrators to reconfigure large numbers of test machines rapidly. Instructions for setting up FreeBSD systems for diskless boot are available at <u>http://apollo.backplane.com/FreeBSD/diskless-1.00.tgz</u>.

## FREEBSD SUPPORT FOR THE UPS

Many UNIX versions contain monitoring support for UPSs, and FreeBSD is no exception. This support allows the FreeBSD system to shut itself down automatically in the event of a power failure. The FreeBSD UPS support is implemented in a daemon program that periodically (e.g., once a minute) checks the status of the UPS. When a blackout or power failure occurs, the UPS tells the polling program that the main power has failed. Typically, the UPS daemon program then waits a reasonable amount of time and checks the UPS again. If power has still not returned, the daemon program calls the /sbin/halt program. The daemon can also send a command back to the UPS to shut it off too, which is important because even though the OS is shut down, the PC may still be running. The /sbin/halt program closes all open files and stops all processes. The system must then be restarted by the administrator pressing the Reset button. This prevents file corruption as a result of a sudden loss of power.

Two UPS daemon programs are full-featured and can query the UPS for statistics and so on. The first is a third-party daemon written for the APC SmartUPS series; the second is written by Best Power Technologies for their line of UPSs.

A third, stripped-down UPS daemon program will work with any UPS that uses a simple interface. It was developed for the APC BackUPS. If an APC Smart Switch with UPS splitting is used to carry a signal to an entire rack of UNIX servers, it is required even if an APC SmartUPS is in use.

The APC UPS daemon program for FreeBSD 2.2.5 is located on FreeBSD installation CD-ROM 3, in the /cdrom/experiment/upsd directory. Later versions of FreeBSD, including version 4.0, have this program in the /usr/ports/sysutils/upsd Ports directory. It works only with the APC SmartUPS series of UPSs. The less expensive APC BackUPS or a simple-signaling UPS requires the /usr/ports/sysutils/bkpupsd program.

When using an APC UPS, make sure to get the correct cable for smart or dumb signaling, whichever you are using. APC UPS ships with the smart signaling cable that will work *only* with the special APC-only UPS program in the Ports directories. If the generic UPS program for BackUPS is used, the dumb signaling cable must be purchased for APC UPS.

The APC program in the Ports directories for SmartUPS is optimized for APC UPSs of European design (i.e., running 220 volts). A few years back Doug White at Oregon State University modified it for 120-volt UPSs. The patched daemon program is located at `http://resnet.uoregon.edu/dwhite/upsd-2.0.1.6.1.tgz`.

There is also a UPS daemon program that is written for BSDi UNIX at `http://www.bestpower.com/software/`. There are two different programs in the UNIX distribution of this software. The first is a bidirectional program, which works with Best Power Technologies UPSs, just like the program written for the APC. The second is a basic program that works with a UPS that has a single contact indication. The BSDi versions of these software packages, both supplied in the archive on the Best Web site, compile under FreeBSD without a problem.

Other UPSs may not have a serial port. They may have only one line with an on-off signal: on for power available from the wall and off for a loss of wall power. Or they may have a contact open-close indication of power. The System V UNIX program that monitored these kinds of UPSs was `powerd`. Unfortunately, this program used kernel structures not available in FreeBSD. For those interested in the code, it is located in the Obsolete directory of the SysVinit package, available from `ftp://sunsite.unc.edu/pub/Linux/system/daemons/init/sysvinit-2.74.tar.gz`.

Besides monitoring with a `powerd` port, or the basic program in the Best distribution, or the APC BackUPS program, these kinds of UPSs could also be monitored by a Perl script that is called once a minute out of `/etc/crontab`, which checked the joystick port on button 1. Part of a sample Perl script is in the manual page for the joystick device driver. The Joystick button would need to be wired to a relay that was wired to UPS indication power. When power is present, the button is connected, and the Perl script exits. When power is off, the button is unconnected, and the Perl script calls `/sbin/halt`.

It is also possible to monitor a UPS by *blocking* on the Carrier Detect (CD) port of one of the serial ports. This can be done in two ways: with a script or with a daemon program. Basically, all the script needs to do is attempt to open a serial port that has modem control applied to it; the script or program will hang while waiting for the Carrier Detect line to go high. If the power is on, this line is low; if it goes off, the line is raised high. If a UPS goes to battery voltage and raises the CD line, the script that was hung waiting for the CD line to come up then continues to run. The next statement in the script is the `halt` statement that shuts down the computer.

Construction of a cable is fairly simple. To trigger it, pin 7 (Ground) and 8 (Carrier Detect) of the DB25 COM port or pin 5 (Ground) and pin 1 (Carrier Detect) of the DB9 COM port on the PC must be connected to the UPS signal wire. Typically, PC computers use DB9 for COM1 and DB25 for COM2. The signal should be limited to 12 volts and go positive when the UPS is supplying power; it should go zero when the AC power is present. If the UPS has only a set of relay contacts available, the Data Terminal Ready line from the PC COM port can supply the positive voltage to one relay contact, and the other contact can be wired to Carrier Detect. Pin 20 is Data Terminal Ready on a DB25, and pin 4 is Data Terminal Ready on a DB9.

If the UPS doesn't have a set of relay contacts or a serial port for UPS indication, it is possible to plug a single-pole double-throw 120-volt relay into the AC power that the UPS is plugged into. When the AC power is energized, the relay is closed, and the Normally Closed (NC) contacts are open. These are wired to pins 8 and 20 of a DB25, or pins 1 and 4 of DB9. When the AC power fails, the relay opens, and the NC contacts connect the pins of the serial port and turn on Carrier Detect, signaling the computer that the power has failed.

A Shell script that does essentially the same thing as `pf.c` follows (originally posted by Joe Moss).

```
#! /bin/sh
#
# Shut down system in case of extended power failure
#
# This should be used with the serial port to which the UPS
# is connected.
#
# This port must be set to block on open until the CD line
# is asserted - many UNIX systems have this determined by
# the minor device number, if not, see if there is some way
# to enable this behavior on your system
#
# Note: FreeBSD /dev/ttyd? serial ports block on open as
# the default behavior
#
# Note: The serial port must be shut off in /etc/ttys
#
# FreeBSD serial ports are:
# COM1 = /dev/ttyd0
# COM2 = /dev/ttyd1
# COM3 = /dev/ttyd2
# COM4 = /dev/ttyd3
#
PORT=/dev/ttyd0
```

```
#
# Ok, this should block until there is a power failure
#
: > $PORT
#
# If we reach this point, we've lost power
wall << EOF
Loss of AC Power - initiating controlled system shutdown
EOF
#
# call shutdown (or init or whatever)
/sbin/shutdown -h +10 Emergency shutdown, AC power loss!
#
```

These methods of UPS monitoring handle a power drop with a software shutdown, usually by calling /sbin/halt. There is one problem with this method. Although /sbin/halt has a -p option, which turns off power on the system if possible, only hardware that uses a *soft* power switch, such as ATX-style motherboards, will support this. As a result, on standard or older hardware, although the UNIX OS is not active, the FreeBSD server computer is still running and drawing power from the UPS. If the blackout is extended, eventually the UPS batteries run low and the UPS shuts itself off. If the UPS isn't shut off, once power comes back on, the UPS batteries need some time to recharge. If a second blackout occurs during this time, the UNIX system may be vulnerable to an uncontrolled shutdown that could corrupt files.

## KERNEL RECOMPILATION

If you are setting up FreeBSD as a general-purpose server, you most likely do not need to concern yourself with recompiling the kernel. Most of the time, the generic FreeBSD kernel that is supplied on the boot diskettes will give satisfactory performance. The performance cost of the generic compared to an optimized kernel is not tremendous, and by using the generic kernel you don't have to use up a lot of disk space loading the FreeBSD kernel sources. An advantage is that if hardware changes in the future, the kernel can still be used because the generic kernel is configured to support as many hardware devices as possible.

For specialty servers or servers that are intended to have their bandwidth and resources optimized, you may want to recompile the kernel. Tradeoffs have been made in the generic kernel that are there because this kernel is intended to be used to install FreeBSD and so kernel optimization is traded off for flexibility.

If you *do* wish to recompile the kernel, the process is fairly simple. The following instructions make use of the generic kernel; if you have never compiled one before, it may be useful to leave this kernel configuration file alone and test to see if you can get a running kernel from it.

1. Make sure that kernel sources are installed on the FreeBSD system.
2. Log in to the console as root, and issue the `cd /sys/i386/conf` command.
3. In this directory, issue the `config GENERIC` command.
4. Change the directory again with the `cd ../../compile/GENERIC` command.
5. Issue the `make depend` command, followed by `make`, and then `make install`.
6. Reboot the server and see if it comes up on the new kernel.

If you want to build a custom kernel, you need to modify either the generic file or a backup of it and delete all statements that aren't needed. See the system manual pages on the various device drivers listed in the kernel.

## SPECIAL HARD DRIVE CONFIGURATION

Some FreeBSD servers have special applications that call for hard drive configuration that deviates from the default out-of-box setup. These applications may make use of soft updates, large inode counts, or asynchronous mounts. The configurations are primarily performance enhancements and should be treated with caution.

### Asynchronous Mounting

By default, FreeBSD drives are synchronously mounted. Basically what this means is that when a program modifies data on the disk, the data is flushed immediately from the disk cache (which the program writes to) to the disk drive. The advantage of doing it this way is that if the server should suddenly crash, very few files are going to be in an inconsistent state (changed in the cache without the changes being committed to the disk), and thus the filesystem most likely won't be damaged. The problem with it is that for most operations it is a tremendous performance drain. Writing to an open file that has just been created is done asynchronously, which is somewhat faster. The disk driver has little choice in how to group writes onto the disk, although the filesystem guards against fragmentation. Worse, if a file is changed in a sequence (i.e., written, changed, rewritten, changed), it really should remain in the cache and be written to the disk during an idle period.

Sync mounts can be switched off by making the disk mount asynchronous. To do this add the *async* keyword to the Options column in /etc/fstab for the disk partition that should be asynchronously mounted and reboot the server. (See the manual page for fstab for warnings and instructions on adding the keyword.) The asynchronous disk mount is frequently done on Usenet news servers and can result in cutting disk-bound process execution time in half, or even more. A news server that might have taken 22 hours to run the expire program might end up taking only six hours with the right hardware and asynchronous mounts on the spools. However, if the server crashes or is powered down unexpectedly, files *will* be damaged. In fact, if the filesystem is in a write state, the system itself can easily be damaged.

Asynchronous mounts are most useful on partitions such as Usenet news spools or proxy server caches, which contain a lot of transient data that is moved in and out because these partitions can be quickly and easily destroyed and recreated by the administrator if they are trashed. For example, when I ran a 50GB news spool on FreeBSD 2.2.8, I had to reformat the news spool about once every six months due to crashes.

## Soft Updates

Soft updates are a new development in the standard UNIX File System (UFS) filesystem. The idea is to speed hard drive access, as asynchronous mounts do, while retaining the crash protection of synchronous mounts. Soft updates should be enabled only on servers with several months of stable service to use as a baseline. A pointer to instructions to enable them are in the LINT file used when recompiling the kernel. The kernel must be recompiled to enable soft updates.

## Large Inode Counts

Servers such as Usenet news servers write many hundreds of thousands of itty-bitty (1K) files into their spools. Because each file requires an inode entry, it's possible to fill the inode table up long before the disk has actually run out of space. To prevent this, the disk or disk pack must have a filesystem created on it that uses a higher inode-per-sector count.

The newfs -f 512 /dev/rccd0c command creates a filesystem with a fragment size of 512 bytes and 2,048 bytes per inode on a disk stripe set that has already been labeled. The default without this option is a 1,024-byte fragment size and 4,096 bytes per inode. The newfs command automatically calculates the number of inodes based on the fragment size.

## GENERAL TROUBLESHOOTING

Despite the best attempts to select optimum server hardware for UNIX, a small percentage of installations inevitably fail or have some problem. If your installation is one of these, you must troubleshoot it. Following is a general FreeBSD troubleshooting installation guide.

### Step 1

The first step is to determine if the observed behavior is indeed a problem. For example, if FreeBSD crashes when a particular device driver is activated in the kernel, but the device isn't present, this is not a product defect. This step is often referred to as separating user error from machine error. Of course, it can take some experience with FreeBSD, or at least reading documentation or manual pages, to recognize appropriate behavior.

### Step 2

Next, outline the problem clearly. Did the installation complete? Did it fail part way through? Is the system running but having problems? An excellent way of doing this is to get a copy of the bug report form used by the `/usr/bin/send-pr` utility. In general, this involves writing up a report, in a text editor, word processor, or on paper, that details all the hardware items in the PC on the top part and exactly the steps that were taken to arrive at the problem. Note any error messages that may appear.

### Step 3

The next step is to determine how to duplicate the problem. Computers are machines, and no matter how unpredictably they may appear to be behaving, they all follow patterns. Of course, in some instances it may be that a random problem may be following a pattern that is impossible to discern externally. For example, a failed memory chip with a missing bit may be failing repeatedly, but the computer it is in has so many variables that the failures appear random. You must start by assuming that the failure has a pattern that is not immediately obvious; If all other explanations don't pan out, assume the hardware is flaky.

Often, problems that appear to be random are not. I once had an HP Netserver that would reboot for what seemed to be no reason. After several days of observation, we noticed that the rebooting happened when the room the computer was in got warm. After the machine was moved to a cooler room, the rebooting stopped. Obviously, some part in the Netserver began to function improperly after reaching a specific temperature. If I had six months and a battery of thermocouples, I could say precisely which chip on the motherboard was heat-sensitive and the exact temperature that would cause the fault to appear. However, since internal computer warming depends on many variables (e.g., fan speed, ambient room temperature), the system appeared to reboot randomly.

Most of the simpler computer problems have obvious repeatability components; it is generally the more complex problems, which arise from a combination of faults, that require effort to be isolated.

### *Step 4*

Determine if the same problem, or a manifestation of it, exists with other OSs or programs loaded on the computer. For example, if the problem is that FreeBSD cannot see a CD-ROM drive, then try loading Win95 on the machine. If Win95, OS/2, NetWare, or some other OS cannot see the drive as well, it is more likely that the CD-ROM drive itself or the cabling to it is at fault. If possible, obtain an OS/2 boot disk and attempt to boot the computer with it; OS/2 is well known to trap on hardware that is weak.

### *Step 5*

The next step is to attempt to determine if the same problem exists on completely different computers. For example, if FreeBSD is loaded on three computers built with different hardware, and all three display the identical problem, the problem is likely to be in FreeBSD. If it exists on only one of the three computers, the problem is more likely hardware. There should be enough information to attempt to determine in what general subsystem the trouble is located. For example, if the system crashes with a kernel panic when access is gained to a tape drive connected via a SCSI adapter, the problem is more likely to be in the SCSI or tape subsystem than in the keyboard or video card.

### *Step 6*

Thoroughly read all the documentation for the subsystem in question, looking for a mention of the particular problem. This includes all hardware documentation for the computer itself, especially hardware documentation on the suspected subsystem. To effectively troubleshoot, it is vital to understand every part of the subsystem under suspicion. Start with the FreeBSD Handbook, located in `/usr/share/doc/handbook`, or the FAQ, installed in `/usr/share/doc/FAQ`. Search the mailing lists for mention of the problem. Search the gnats database on `http://www.freebsd.org/`. It is important to be familiar with basic PC functioning. For example, if the administrator doesn't know what a PCI bus does and looks like inside a computer, it's going to be difficult to troubleshoot any problems originating in the PCI bus.

Up to this point, the troubleshooting steps have been designed to narrow down the possibilities and zero in on the faulty software or hardware. The simple act of going through this process usually leads the administrator to stumble across the answer. If this doesn't work, follow these steps.

**1.** Make sure you're not making completely obvious mistakes. For example, is the correct CD in the CD-ROM drive? Did you skip an installation step? Are all cables and peripherals plugged in and turned on? Did you check that the FTP password is correct? Are the correct IP numbers being used? Are you trying to compile the kernel, or run X, without these software options installed? It's easy to make these kinds of mistakes under pressure when rushing and not thoroughly reading the documentation.

**2.** Run a diagnostic on the computer. MSD run under a DOS boot floppy is a good beginning, and many other *check-it* type of system utilities exist. If the problem is a grossly obvious one, sometimes these utilities can catch it.

**3.** Upgrade all firmware to the most current levels. Many computer subsystems have firmware, including modems, motherboards, and disk drives. This goes for BIOS code as well. Although BIOS code is not usually executed while FreeBSD is running, it is executed when the machine first boots up, for PCI devices and APM, and is responsible for *setting up* many internal registers and things on the motherboard and peripherals.

**4.** Check the CMOS on the motherboard and make sure to turn off any *go-fast* or specialty settings. Examples of these are setting the bus clock speed faster than normal or setting the memory wait states lower than normal. Such speedups generally make little observable difference and often cause trouble. These settings may work under a real-mode PC OS, such as DOS, but fail under protected-mode operating systems, such as UNIX.

Poorly documented CMOS options are one of the worst problems in computer hardware, even for an experienced builder. As an example of how bad it can be, I recently filed a bug report on FreeBSD 3.0 SMP failing to boot on a Tyan Tomcat 3 motherboard. After no one on the development team could figure it out, I stumbled across the solution—changing a BIOS setting on the Tomcat to *enabled* fixed the problem. This option is completely undocumented in the Tyan documentation, apparently does not exist on previous versions of the motherboard, has nothing to indicate that it has anything to do with SMP, and, last but not least, makes no difference in how it is set under other SMP OSs, such as Windows NT. The name of the option? Enhanced Features!

**NOTE** It cannot be overemphasized how important it is to use very conservative BIOS settings. Many motherboards give the user lots of opportunities to modify parameters such as bus speed, memory wait states, bus cycle wait states, and other settings that are best left alone. When a motherboard is run too far out of spec as a result of these settings, behavior of the system becomes unpredictable under any protected-mode OS, such as UNIX, WinNT, or OS/2. Most of these settings (particularly in AMI-BIOS derivatives) can be properly changed only by using information from design chipbook settings. Reducing things such as the number of memory wait states or the RAS/CAS speeds can make good memory act like bad, intermittent memory. One of the most common markers of incorrectly adjusted CMOS settings is a nonsensical failure under heavy load. For example, the C compiler may complain about code syntax or `dump` core with a `sigsegv` (Signal 11) on code that has been verified as correct on other machines during one pass, and then compile it properly in a second pass. Signal 11 almost always indicates bad hardware, usually RAM but sometimes failing cache memory. A backup or heavy FTP might cause the system to panic with a memory allocation error when there is plenty of swap and RAM.

**5.** Change hardware settings on subsystems under suspicion. For example, I had a machine with an EISA BusLogic SCSI card in it. The card worked only when set to a Port setting of 330 and an Interrupt setting of 9; no other setting would work. Since I could change settings on other peripheral items in the computer to avoid a conflict, I could work around the problem. (It was eventually fixed in later FreeBSD versions.) As another example, many SCSI devices only work properly when set to asynchronous mode. Here is a situation in which it is particularly important to be familiar with the documentation on the computer hardware itself. Don't discount the possibility, especially if the system is older, that it wasn't properly built to start with. For example, I managed a Micron that was built around the 430NX chipset; it ran DOS just fine but crashed under FreeBSD. It turned out that someone had inserted EDO simms into the motherboard; the 430NX chipset doesn't support EDO, and in fact this particular motherboard could only take parity memory to begin with!

**NOTE** One of the first indicators of a SCSI problem is that the installation hangs while reading from the SCSI installation CD or while writing to the SCSI disk.

**6.** Try running the system with all internal caching turned off (i.e., in BIOS settings). Bad cache RAM or poor cache designs are a very big problem with non-DOS operating systems. If this works, try turning caching back on gradually: first turn on internal cache, then both internal and external, and then try changing from write-through to write-back.

**7.** Remove all boards that aren't absolutely necessary for the functioning of the computer. For example, if the main disk is IDE, remove any SCSI cards. If the serial or parallel port cards aren't required, remove them. If an add-in video card is used with a motherboard that has a disabled on-board video card, remove it and re-enable the onboard video.

**8.** Attempt a hardware swap. These days, with motherboards increasingly placing systems—such as IDE, floppy, serial, or parallel—on the motherboard, this is becoming less effective because there are fewer cards to swap.

If you have followed all these steps and the problem still exists, you should know exactly which subsystem is at fault. The problem should then be isolated either as a hardware-caused problem (bad hardware or a hardware bug) or a software-caused problem (a software bug). The question now is what can be done about it. Traditionally, the responsibility for repair of a hardware defect rests with the computer manufacturer. This repair *should* be made by a hardware repair such as a board or chip revision or replacement. With a software bug, the usual response is to apply a patch.

A software patch presents several problems. First, unlike commercial software, FreeBSD software bugs are repaired by anybody—a user, a core member, or a company. All bugs are repaired on a *whenever we get to it* basis, which is generally the way that freely available software works. To the FreeBSD core team's credit, major showstopper software bugs have been repaired immediately in the past. Minor ones, however, may still exist. Here's an example: in some FreeBSD versions, the vi editor core dumps when the LINES environmental variable is set to null. Since LINES should never be set to null, this is arguably not a bug, but it still shouldn't happen.

Organizations that plan on using the OS as a commercial platform and find a software bug that they must fix immediately generally have only two options: (1) they repair it themselves or (2) pay someone else to do it. (Option 3: They could also *hope* that a committer will fix the bug.) Fortunately, software bugs that are large enough to derail projects are rare in FreeBSD; it's more common to have problems with device drivers. If a software bug is determined, a bug report should be filed. Do *not* limit bug reports to observations of the immediate subsystem that you feel has failed—just because you don't think it's related to your problem doesn't mean that it isn't.

> **NOTE**   The fact that the end user even has the option of repairing soft-
> ware defects in the OS is a major advantage of FreeBSD. With commercial
> OSs, such as Windows NT, software defect repair is entirely at the discre-
> tion of the vendor and usually doesn't happen unless the defect is highly
> visible, such as a security hole.

Hardware bugs are a different matter. With computer hardware, it is sometimes possible to work around the problem with a software patch. For example,
software patches exist for the famous Pentium floating-point processor bug.
Obviously, a software patch is a quick-and-dirty way of fixing a problem, and it
is cheap. Consequently, hardware vendors often prefer this to replacement, if it is
possible. Unfortunately, although they may release a patch for a Windows OS,
they are unlikely to write one for FreeBSD. They should, however, supply source
code for their Windows patch to allow someone else to write a FreeBSD patch.

For hardware defects that cannot be patched, replacement or substitution is
the only option. The problem then becomes one of convincing the hardware
vendor to do this. For name-brand, expensive computer equipment from a
major manufacturer that is a new purchase, the 30-day guarantee that most of
these products carry is usually enough leverage to make a change or replacement. For older or *house-brand* clone hardware, this may be a problem.

When you determine that the problem is hardware, if possible you should
immediately return the hardware to the retailer and get it replaced with hardware from a different manufacturer that does the same thing. If the system is too
old for this and you can't use it for some other OS, start by calling the technical support department of the company that sold you the PC you're using.
Don't be put off by blanket statements such as "We only support Windows,
etc., on that PC." Explain to the support person that your decision to run an
alternative OS doesn't relieve them from the responsibility of providing a piece
of hardware that is compatible with the industry-standard PC. (This is why it is
important during the troubleshooting process to determine if the problem
appears under other OSs.) This falls under the category of basic warranty support. Explain also that the claim that "most people don't use the OS" isn't a
valid reason for withholding support. After all, no computer hardware vendor
is a majority market holder; why alienate any customers?

If this gets you nowhere on the phone, as is likely, write a letter to the manufacturer and send it by U.S. mail, *not* e-mail. Explain all the steps you have
taken to solve the problem and list all contacts that you have had with them.
Politely explain that you don't have a problem with their providing a computer
that contains some specialty components that may not be compatible with

FreeBSD (e.g., software modems such as Winmodems aren't compatible with any UNIX versions and probably never will be until someone writes a driver). The problem is that they refuse to support the OS on major subsystems, such as the motherboard. Make sure to list other manufacturers that do currently provide support for hardware for FreeBSD, and ask them to reconsider their position. This is the same tactic that the OS/2 community used several years ago when OS/2 2.0 and 2.1 were first released, and although it took persistence, it did eventually pay off because OS/2 drivers are now available for all major new hardware items today. The Linux community has also taken this tack with much success.

Of course, whenever new equipment fails to work, it should be returned immediately after any contact with the vendor technical support fails to result in a repair of the problem. Do not fall for the trick of having you send in the equipment to be repaired—by the time it is sent back to you, the retailer's 30-day warranty will have expired. If the computer works under Windows but not FreeBSD, having a factory *repair* is a waste of time.

There is one other area to go for support: attempt a posting on the FreeBSD mailing lists or the Usenet news groups. The more difficult the problem, the fewer responses you will receive. Don't hesitate to ask for pointers to further information sources. If you get no responses after two weeks, repost.

If none of the preceding suggestions fixes the problem, keep the following in mind.

**1.** A clone PC that runs FreeBSD satisfactorily is very inexpensive these days. Although it may be a great disappointment that that elderly NetWare Server that someone paid thousands of dollars for back in 1992 won't run the OS, a brand new motherboard and chassis that runs five times faster is available for pocket change.

**2.** Hundreds of thousands of people run FreeBSD in production environments and don't experience the problem you are having. Resist the urge to condemn the entire OS just because it fails to run on one computer that you own. It may be annoying to be stuck with the only model of the FuzzBar Gronkulating PeeCee that doesn't run FreeBSD, but it happens.

**3.** If defect correction requires the replacement of only one component in the PC, count yourself lucky. The money you spend purchasing a new video card, or sound board, is a fraction of what a commercial multiuser UNIX OS would cost.

**4.** FreeBSD, by and large, was developed by committed volunteers. Generally, people who are willing to spend that much time on something they don't get paid for are dedicated enough to buy fairly-high-quality computer equipment for themselves. Unfortunately, the majority of PC equipment on the market today is of poor quality. People buy IDE/ATAPI drives and CD-ROM drives instead of SCSI. They buy no-name clone Trident-chipset-based video cards instead of high-quality ones, such as Matrox Millennium. They buy NE2000-compatible clone network adapters instead of name-brand SMC or Intel ones. They buy no-name clone motherboards instead of high-quality Intel or ASUS boards. They buy inexpensive Gateway or Dell or Compaq systems made with these components. Problems can show up on low-end hardware that don't appear on good-quality hardware. Buy high-quality computer hardware from the start and you will be better off no matter what OS you run.

> **NOTE**   Many name-brand computer hardware box makers actually have two separate product lines, business and retail. For example, Compaq's business servers are Proliant, but their retail servers are Prosignia. The Prosignia systems are less expensive than Proliants simply because their components are of lower quality. Don't make the mistake of buying a computer intended for home word processing and games for use as a business server.

**5.** As a famous detective said, "Whenever all impossibilities have been eliminated, what remains, no matter how improbable, is the truth." In other words, sometimes logical problem solving simply doesn't provide an answer that is believable or reasonable. For example, if the server runs flawlessly with three SCSI drives but crashes when a fourth is added, even though everything *should* work, just accept that it doesn't. You probably will never know the reason.

**6.** Computers are incredibly complex and sophisticated machines, and it is quite possible to have a problem in one subsystem that shows up in another. For example, it is quite possible for a badly designed video card that is plugged into the same bus as a good network card to cause problems that look exactly like network failures. It is also quite possible for this particular video card to run flawlessly under FreeBSD in one computer and not work properly in another.

**7.** Particularly in a commercial setting, you can always play musical chairs and find some other use for the incompatible machine.

## Tape Installation and Some References

Historically, UNIX installations were usually done from QIC tapes, which are rarely seen now that CD-ROM drives are available. Unlike PCs, most UNIX workstations had ROMs that allowed them to boot from the QIC tape drive because most UNIX distributions were only available on tape. Since the PC can't boot this way, the target hard drive must have an equivalent amount of free disk space to extract the entire distribution. One other note about a tape installation: if you want to *create* a tape install with `tar`, you must set the `tar` blocksize to 10.

The FreeBSD Handbook is the most authoritative guide to installing the software. It is available from the FreeBSD Web site at `http://www.freebsd.org`. The installation documentation on the FreeBSD CD that is included in this book should also be reviewed. There is no substitute, however, for diving in and following the directions in the `sysinstall` program.

# FreeBSD System Administration

Basic FreeBSD system administration comprises maintenance of your FreeBSD server, including keeping it running and making your interface environment more pleasant. All UNIX systems require basic administration. Even if you have an infrequently used test server, you still must do administrative tasks from time to time.

Basic administrative tasks are things such as setting up your environment, adding and removing users (including yourself), and interfacing terminals with the system to allow others access to the server. I cover hardwire terminals here because, although users can access the FreeBSD system via Telnet over the network, having a hardwire terminal is smart. If the FreeBSD console driver crashes while networking isn't enabled (perhaps you're testing a console program or script), a hardwire terminal provides a point of access to the system that allows you to reboot gracefully. The same procedure is used to set up a modem on a serial port for dialin access with a terminal program, and having such a setup can be a lifesaver for the administrator trying to access a remote FreeBSD server. Besides, it's a nod to history, and going through the motions of setting up an inexpensive terminal can help you gain insight into why things are the way they are on the UNIX system.

# QUICK ENVIRONMENT SETUP

New users of FreeBSD often want to set up a system rapidly and learn about the nitty-gritty later. It is understandable, after the effort involved in setup and installation, to want to see the system actually *do* something useful. However, before you embark on a complex server configuration, such as installing Samba or a Web server, you can remove many small annoyances by properly setting up the *computing environment.*

UNIX at heart is a multiuser, multiprocessing OS. To support multiple users effectively, it allows a user to custom-configure the environment. This is in stark contrast to OSs such as DOS, Windows 95, or even Windows NT. When a user sits down at a computer running Win95, for example, he or she sees the same desktop that any other user sees and has access to the same programs as any other user. Even WinNT, which maintains separate profiles for each user, presents the same basic desktop to the user logging in to it.

When a fresh FreeBSD system is installed, it has a default environment. One of the first tasks of the administrator is to configure his or her own environment. Later, the administrator will configure the environment of any users having shell access to the FreeBSD system. UNIX users can have environments as different from each other as can be imagined.

Most UNIX configuration is done by running programs or editing text configuration files with a system editor. Many system editors exist (see Chapter 6 for more detail); but for most DOS/Windows users migrating to UNIX, the ee editor will probably be their first choice. ee was written by Hugh Mahon as a simple, easy-to-use editor for all normal UNIX system-editing tasks. It is much like the DOS EDIT editor supplied with DOS 5 and later.

## Shells

When FreeBSD is first installed, the sysinstall program asks if the installer wants to set up any new users. These users are set up with a default of the Bourne shell. By contrast, when the system sets up the root user, it uses the C-shell. Neither the Bourne nor the C-shell is optimal for new users—tcsh is actually more popular among C-shell users and bash is more popular among Bourne shell users. Many other additional shells are available for installation under FreeBSD; they can be selected with the chsh (Change Shell) command.

The shell is equivalent to the DOS command processor (command.com). It is what the user or administrator interacts with immediately after logging in to the system.

To be considered a valid shell, any program that is used as a shell program must be listed in the /etc/shells file. The precompiled binary installation programs do this automatically. Programs such as the FTP server don't allow access if the shell program isn't listed in this file.

Following are some popular shells and some of their features. It is by *no means* a complete list of shell programs.

### Sh

The shell /bin/sh is the Bourne shell and is among the oldest UNIX shells still in current use. The real Bourne shell is copyrighted by AT&T; FreeBSD's Bourne shell is actually the ash shell, a clone. The Bourne shell is preferred for scripting because it is very standardized across UNIX vendors and is available on practically every UNIX ever sold.

The Bourne shell supplied with FreeBSD has been enhanced to add job control and command history, neither of which is in most implementations.

### Csh

The C-shell—csh—is also very old. Many C programmers prefer it because of its C-like scripting syntax. csh was the first shell to introduce command history and user job control to UNIX, which made it popular rather quickly. It does have a few bugs and has largely been superseded by tcsh.

### Ksh

The Korn shell—ksh—is the "new and improved" Bourne shell, written by AT&T for inclusion in System V. As such, the code is copyrighted by AT&T, which has never made its source available. It is popular as a Bourne shell replacement among System V users. Two versions of ksh are frequently used under FreeBSD: ksh and pdksh.

- Ksh93 is a binary-only version of ksh that is currently available at http://www.research.att.com/sw/tools/reuse/. This is the real ksh code. A BSD/386 version of this ksh, found in the ast-base-97-99 distribution listed on the Web site, runs fine under FreeBSD.
- pdksh is a public domain implementation of ksh98 that is available both as a prepackaged binary and source code on the FreeBSD CD-ROM.

Some users like to set their prompt to the current directory. Do this in ksh with the .profile statement

```
PS1='$PWD  \$'
export PS1
```

Some users like to add a carriage return and linefeed character to the PROMPT variable with an editor to make the cursor come to rest on a new line. To insert raw control characters into text files with the vi editor, press Ctrl-V, then the control code.

### Tcsh

The extended C-shell—tcsh—is an enhanced version of csh that has become popular among the same people who liked the C-shell to start with. It features an improved command-line editor and history and is also available as a prepackaged binary on the CD. This shell's command-line history is much like the DOSKEY program, in that it uses the arrow keys to recall previously typed commands. Like csh, it also contains job control. FreeBSD 4.1 ships with tcsh replacing the original Berkeley csh.

### Bash

The GNU Bourne Again shell, bash, is a different view of the implementation of the Bourne shell. It contains job control and a tcsh-like, DOSKEY-like command history editor accessible with the arrow keys. Bash is also very popular.

### /sbin/nologin

The nologin shell is a special restricted shell that allows the user limited network access to the FreeBSD system but not to log in to a command prompt. An example is a mailserver which users can have POP3 access to in order to retrieve their e-mail but cannot Telnet into it. Another example might be a PPP access server. Nologin is not normally listed in /etc/shells, so users with this shell cannot FTP into the system. The administrator can choose to list it, but this may open up other security holes.

## Initial Environment Variables

When the user logs in, the login program checks the password file to see what shell the user account is set to use. If the shell is Korn, Bash, or Bourne, the login shell program first runs /etc/profile, then looks in the user's home directory for a file named .profile (dot-profile) and runs that. If it is the C-shell, it runs /etc/csh.cshrc, /etc/csh.login and then the .csh and .login files in the user's home directory. These initialization files are used to define environment variables that will be present in the user's login session. DOS and Win95 command processors also operate this way, except that the initialization file used to set the environment variables is the AUTOEXEC.BAT.

When the FreeBSD system is installed, sample .profile and .cshrc files (as well other samples) are installed in /usr/share/skel as an aid to administrators setting up new user profiles. These can be copied to the home directory and modified the adduser command can do this automatically. Table 4.1 contains a list and description of some of the more important variables a user can set.

**Table 4.1** User Profile Variables

| *Variable* | *Description* |
| --- | --- |
| TERM | Sets the terminal emulation type used when logging into the FreeBSD system. Network logins such as Telnet determine this automatically, typically with a dialup and hard-coded connection the user sets in a login prompt script. |
| LINES | Used in conjunction with TERM as an aid in setting the number of screen lines. Typically, it is used to extend terminal capabilities easily for terminal emulations, such as VT100, that would normally support only 24 screen lines of text. Some Windows Telnet programs have automatic line-renegotiating abilities. |
| EDITOR | Used by programs such as `mail` and `vipw` that call editors to determine which editor the user prefers to use. |
| MANPATH | Used to add additional manual page directories for the `man` command to search. It is typically used for programs that a user has built for personal use that contain manual pages. Under FreeBSD, MANPATH is not as important as it is under earlier UNIX because the `man` command gets its global path from the file /etc/manpath.config. |
| PS1 | A customized prompt. Some users set this to the name of the FreeBSD system, which can be useful in an environment with multiple FreeBSD systems. A common example is to set `PS1 = !$`, which under the `ksh` shell puts the current command number on the screen, where it is used for command history editing. PS1 doesn't apply to the `csh` or `tcsh` shell. |
| PATH | The same as it is in DOS, namely, a list of directories in which to search for programs. |
| DISPLAY | This is set to the system and screen on which the X Window System output will display should the user run an X program. It is often used when the user is located on a remote system with an X Server running on it. |

Besides variables, several other important settings are made in a file called /etc/login.conf. Some of these are the default UMASK, the default PATH (before modification by /etc/profile), the maximum number of open files the user can have, the maximum amount of system resources that programs run by the user can have, and the default character set. These settings exist as a safety measure to prevent runaway processes, such as forkbombs, from greatly slowing the system.

If a user complains that an exceptionally system-consumptive program of theirs is crashing or printing error messages about not enough resources, check the settings in /etc/login.conf and raise the limits for the group he or she is in.

## Job Control

UNIX is both a multiuser and multitasking operating system. Users can make many processes run at the same time or have multiple programs running and displaying output in different Xterms on an X Window System desktop. Under earlier, simpler shells, such as Bourne, to run multiple programs, a user would run the program followed by the & sign, as in `getreport &`. This runs the shell script named `getreport` in the background.

Under the more advanced shells available under FreeBSD (including `ash`, the Bourne shell clone), the user can also implement *interactive* job control. This mechanism lets the user press Ctrl-Z to push the current program the user is running into the background. If the program is an interactive program waiting for input, such as an editor, it remains inactive in the background. If, however, the program is batch-oriented, such as `getreport`, it continues processing.

When the user logs out, if any of these background jobs are still running, the message **You have stopped jobs** displays. In that case, issuing the `jobs` command displays a list of currently running jobs and their processor numbers. These can be brought to the foreground by running the `fg` command and then terminated.

## TERMINAL ACCESS

UNIX was developed before the advent of the PC. At the time the only way to support multiple users on a single computer was to connect *terminals* to serial ports on the computer. These terminals could be scattered throughout the building, with the UNIX host in a single location. Today, UNIX systems like FreeBSD are typically accessed over a network using the X Window System or the Telnet protocol. Whether Xterms or Telnet session, however, command-line sessions under UNIX still carry the characteristics of the original ASCII terminals.

The most important characteristic of terminals is that their screens are directly addressable through *cursor control codes*. These sequences of special characters can make the terminal do various things, such as position the cursor immediately anywhere on the 80 × 24 character screen. Cursor control codes can switch the screen into 132-column mode or double-wide characters, draw separate character windows, or, with advanced terminals such as the Tektronix 4010, draw colors and graphics. Each terminal uses a different set of control codes, which are documented in the manual for the particular terminal of interest. To see some examples of what cursor addressing can do, if you're running a VT100 emulation, run the `vttest` program.

Most Telnet programs today have a number of *terminal emulations* built into them. The most popular emulation is the VT series of terminals manufactured by Digital Equipment Corporation (DEC). The most common of these are the VT100, VT102, VT220, VT320, and VT330. Among dialup terminal programs, the ANSI terminal emulation is the most popular due to its use by all major bulletin board services (BBSs). The VT series is popular because DEC PDP systems were once very common (the PDP was the original DEC minicomputer on which UNIX was built) and, unlike ANSI, the VT emulation has remained fairly constant.

When a Telnet or, better yet, `ssh` program is used to access FreeBSD, the following are automatically set up during the initial negotiation.

- Terminal type is set in TERM environment variable.
- X-display (for the network of the X Window System) is set in the DISPLAY variable.
- Other environment variables specified in RFC1408 and RFC1572 are set up.

Additional information items can be exchanged as well.

Often, users who access the FreeBSD system like to do so with Xterms. This requires an X Server running on the remote computer, which can be a PC running Windows or another FreeBSD system running the X Window System on the console. An Xterm allows dynamic resizing and mouse support for character-mode programs that support it, such as `Emacs` and `vi`.

To use Xterms under the Microsoft Windows OSs as a substitute for Telnet windows, perform the steps in Exhibit 4.1.

Advanced Telnet programs, such as CRT, available from `http://www.vandyke.com/` also support dynamic resizing of the display without having to run Xterms.

Poorer-quality Telnet programs, such as the Telnet applet included in WfW TCP/IP and Win95 and NT, often set only the TERM environment variable. The Terminal applet in Windows NT is a particular nuisance because it frequently reports itself as an ANSI terminal instead of a VT100, and only the VT100 TERM environment variable setting really works properly with it.

FreeBSD installs the `vttest` program, which can be used to see how compatible a terminal emulation really is with the original VT100 terminal. Run this at a command line in a Telnet window while connected to FreeBSD and follow the instructions.

Character mode games, such as Rogue, can also be used to test a new terminal emulation, especially one that is not of the VT serics. They are also fun to play.

**Exhibit 4.1  Instructions for using Xterms with an MS Windows OS**

1. Load X on the FreeBSD server.

2. Load X on the Windows system. The Microimages X Server mentioned in Chapter 2 is an example.

3. Telnet into the FreeBSD system from the Windows system.

4. At the command prompt, run the w command and look in the From column to determine the hostname or IP number of the system from which you're telnetting.

5. Set the DISPLAY variable to `hostname:0` or `hostIP:0`. For example, the w command reveals that you are Telnetted in from IP number 192.168.4.5. The DISPLAY variable is then set to 192.168.4.5:0. If the w command reveals that you are Telnetted in from hostname `ppp45.domain.com`, the DISPLAY variable is set to `ppp45.domain.com:0`.

6. Make sure that the `/usr/X11R6/bin` directory is in your PATH variable.

7. Run the `ifconfig -a` command to get the IP number of the FreeBSD server.

8. Make sure that the X Server running under the Windows system allows X access from the FreeBSD IP number (or hostname). If you're running the Xterm from another FreeBSD system, you may want to issue `xhost +` to turn off X security. Keep in mind that if you are using X more than just casually, you should set up X security properly in the network.

9. Give the `xterm &` command.

## Hardware Terminal Access

Most people accessing the FreeBSD system are doing it at a console, via Telnet, via X, or dialing in via modem and terminal emulation software. The last-named access method is more like access via hardware terminal than access via network. However, it is still possible to connect an original ASCII terminal to a FreeBSD system and log in this way. It is particularly wise to do this if the FreeBSD system is a standalone non-networked system such as a single system running in someone's home. On such a system, if the console driver ever crashes or is disabled by an X Window misconfiguration, a terminal provides a back door to allow the user to log in and restart the system gracefully. Terminals can also find much utility in a UNIX classroom setting.

A number of computer surplus dealers sell used terminals. A recent check of pricing showed Wyse 60s selling for approximately $45, DEC VT330s for about $30, and Wyse 30s for $15. I have seen terminals selling for less than that at garage sales, thrift stores, and other odd places. This makes them quite viable options for user groups and others wanting to have a group training session.

It is also possible to make terminals out of old, worthless XT computers running old DOS terminal emulation programs. (Of course, it is also possible to run NCSA Telnet on these systems in conjunction with eight-bit network cards, which are available at computer scrap dealers for a few dollars, and Telnet directly in to the FreeBSD system.) Terminal emulation programs exist for the even older hobby computers, such as the Radio Shack TRS-80 (affectionately referred to as the Trash 80), the Apple II, and even the original Mac Classic (sometimes called the Toaster). These hoary, archaic systems can be rescued from the backs of closets, attics, basements, and garages and given a second lease on life as a terminal.

When a terminal is used on a serial port of a FreeBSD system, the TERM variable and all other variables are *not* set up. Variables must be defined in the `.profile` or another user startup profile file. Users can write a script that asks for the terminal type to be input and then export this into the environment.

Hardware terminals should be initialized with the `tset` command. This command is run in the login script after the terminal type is defined in the environment startup script. `tset` also initializes terminal emulation software, but this is not usually recommended because Telnet terminal emulation software initializes itself when it is started. Hardware terminals do this also, but since their initialization settings depend on stored `nvram` settings, they are more prone to coming up with odd settings. Sometimes poor terminal emulation programs crash when sent an initialization string, even the correct one for the emulation.

The `/etc/ttys` file is modified to install a terminal (or dialup modem) on the system. Change the entry in the Status column to on and the entry in the Getty column to `local.9600`, instead of `std.9600`, to turn on terminal login at 9600bps on the COM port desired. The `std.9600` type turns on carrier sensing, which is used for modem dialins. The `local.9600` disables carrier detection, so when the terminal is turned on and raises the Data Terminal Ready line, the system prints a login prompt.

Hardware terminals also depend heavily on *flow control*. With modern modem-based terminal emulation programs, flow control is not a problem. The `terminal` program is typically run on such a fast computer that even at the modem's highest speeds it won't be overrun. With hardware terminals, their internal buffers are often small enough to overflow.

There are two major flow control methods used with hardware terminals: DC3/DC1 (software flow control) and hardware flow control. However, flow control settings are pointless on Telnet and other network connections.

### DC3/DC1

DC3/DC1 is often referred to as XON/XOFF or *software flow control*. With this method, flow control is embedded in the datastream by sending a start control code and a stop control code. The terminal sends a stop code when its buffer is full, and when its buffer is empty it sends a start code.

Software flow control is useful *only* for ASCII text data, which is what most terminals display. Some modems, especially older ones, support software flow control, but this should never be enabled unless the modem is connected to a hardware terminal that displays text only.

The DEC VT100 series of hardware terminals supports *only* software flow control. (Later VT models support hardware flow control.) Many hardware terminals have VT100 or VT220 emulation selectable in their setups; these should usually have XON/XOFF enabled if VT100 emulation is selected. The exception is a terminal that supports hardware flow control, even when VT emulation is selected. A true VT100 emulation would disable hardware flow control because the real VT100 terminals didn't have it.

The user can disrupt software flow control by typing a control start or stop code. For example, many Emacs users got used to mapping Ctrl-S to Search. This control code is the DC3 control code. (DC1 and DC3 are defined in the ASCII standard.) Use a mapping like Ctrl-/ instead.

A hardware terminal user using software flow control should make sure it is turned on in the FreeBSD system with the `stty` command. For example, the command `stty ixon ixoff -ixany` in the `.profile` file takes care of this, as does the `local.9600` entry.

Software flow control on terminals was popular because the serial connection to the terminal could be *three-wired*. Thus, old four-wire telephone cables in buildings could be used with terminals, using only the send, receive, and ground wires. Most of the time the DTR wire was also brought back to the UNIX server so that the server would know if a terminal had been turned on or off at a remote location.

Typically, a terminal that uses software flow control, such as a VT100, can't run much above 19.2Kbps. In fact, on most routers and hub equipment, 9600bps is the de facto standard.

### Hardware Flow Control
Hardware flow control is handled by the CTS and RTS wires in the RS232 serial cable used to connect to the terminal. RS232 cables on a hardware flow control setup typically require a minimum of eight wires: TX, RX, DSR, DTR, CTS, RTS, GND, and CD. Hardware flow control is superior because it does not interfere with whatever control code the user might type. However, both the host and the terminal must support it, and the serial cable must be properly wired, for it to work. Most older hardware terminals don't support it, so check the terminal manual or, better yet, test the terminal with an RS232 *mini-breakout box* on the serial cable.

All modern high-speed modems require hardware flow control. On the FreeBSD host, hardware flow control can be turned on with the `stty crtscts` command in the `/etc/rc.serial` startup file.

## User Accounts

The FreeBSD administrator should always set up a user account for himself or herself and use the account to access the FreeBSD server. This user account should be listed in the *wheel* group to allow the administrator to `su` to the root user ID.

User accounts under most UNIX computers have a practical restriction of eight characters. FreeBSD through 2.2.8 set this limit to eight, but later versions have a maximum of 16 characters. Although it is possible to change UT_NAMESIZE in `/usr/include/utmp.h`, it requires recompiling the world. The `make world` command recompiles the kernel and every single system utility in the UNIX system. However, it can also break things in binary programs with hard limits and when managing a group of UNIX systems with the Network Information Service (NIS). NIS is restricted to eight-character usernames and passwords. So, even though under FreeBSD it's possible for a username to exceed eight characters, that would make the FreeBSD system incompatible with most other UNIXs. Another practical restriction in a mixed UNIX and WinNT system is that even though Windows NT allows longer usernames, setting them breaks NT and UNIX interoperability. Longer usernames can easily be accommodated as e-mail aliases if the only reason for having them is to have a long e-mail name.

The system user password file, `/etc/master.password`, can use one of two encryption methods, DES or MD5. If the system is a standalone server, the default MD5 hashing may be fine. However, if the system participates in an NIS group with other vendors' UNIX systems, it *must* use DES encryption. This is also the case if UNIX binaries requiring DES are run on the system. Other UNIXs, such as Sun's Solaris, use DES in their password files. Encrypted passwords can be copied wholesale from Solaris systems to FreeBSD systems if DES is selected, which may be useful if the organization is migrating to FreeBSD from Solaris.

The `adduser` program run by the root user easily and rapidly creates large numbers of user accounts, such as a new server setup. `Adduser` uses a configuration file, `/etc/adduser.conf`, which is generated on its first invocation. The defaults for `adduser` assign user ID numbers sequentially, starting with user ID number 1001. `Adduser` gets its list of valid shells from `/etc/shells`. It also creates a unique group in which the user can start out. UNIX permissions and groups are discussed in Chapter 1.

**Exhibit 4.2  Manually adding a user account**

1. Log in as root.

2. Change the directory to `/etc`.

3. Run the `vipw` command.

4. Scroll through the `password` file, find a free user ID, and make the entry there. Leave the Password field blank (two colons next to each other).

5. Write and quit the `password` file, and make sure the message says that the file rebuild was successful.

6. Edit the `/etc/group` file and add the user to any groups.

7. Change to the parent directory that the user's home directory will be located in and `mkdir` the home directory.

8. Copy the skeleton profile files from `/usr/share/skel` to the new home directory and rename them appropriately

9. `chown -R` and `chgrp -R` the home directory with the appropriate username and group IDs.

10. Run the `passwd username` command and set the user's password.

Another way of adding lots of users under script control is to use the `pw` command. To add a user account manually, follow the steps in Exhibit 4.2.

Deleting users is done by reversing the steps in the exhibit, but there is a problem area. When a user ID is created on a UNIX system, the user can create files in various locations in the system that he or she will own. When the user is deleted, the files owned by the user still exist and still contain the ownership of the ID that created them. A long listing, created with `ls -l`, shows the ownership as the user ID number on these files, rather than the name, if the user is deleted. The group can also be shown by a number if the group is deleted. This may block others from accessing the file until the root user can change ownership with the `chown` command.

Users can change their shells and other information about their account with the `chpass, chfn`, and `chsh` commands.

## Breaking Root

One of the more embarrassing questions asked by new FreeBSD administrators goes something like this: "I accidentally changed the root password to something, I don't know what, and now I cannot log in as root. How do I break the root password?"

Most of the time the questioner is honestly in a bind, although no doubt a few are probes for attempts to break into systems. The first thing to determine is whether the administrator is logging into an unsecure terminal. Under FreeBSD, direct root logins are allowed only at secure terminals, and the only secure terminal under the default installation is the physical console. With all other terminals, including Telnet prompts, root login is not allowed. Instead, the administrator should log in under his or her own account and run the `su` command to change to the root user. Terminals can be defined as secure in the same configuration file—`/etc/ttys`—for defining terminals, but if you modify secure and insecure, *never* set the console to insecure. If you do and you lose the root password, you will have to reinstall FreeBSD.

If the problem is genuine, and the administrator really cannot log in to the console as root, there is a procedure to regain the root user. This *must* be performed at the physical console of the FreeBSD system, which is one reason the physical FreeBSD server should always be in a locked room. In addition, the original password *cannot* be regained but must be replaced. In this case, any other administrators on the system will know immediately if an unauthorized root password change has occurred. This also requires rebooting the system, so don't do it during the middle of the day on a production server. It is a very good idea to *practice* this on a new system *before* ever having to do it. Of course, it is even better to be careful with the root password!

Regaining root is also part of the catastrophic repair process. Exhibit 4.3 lists the steps to regain root. UNIX gurus can undoubtedly find a simpler way to do this, but this is intended to teach, too.

## Migrating Password Files

Some administrators install FreeBSD to replace an existing UNIX system, such as a Sun system. Although migrating from a UNIX such as Solaris can be fairly simple, one problem that anyone doing this encounters is how to move the user passwords from the old UNIX system password file.

Most UNIX-type computers use the same general password system: a user password entered at login is run through the DES crypt program, and the output is compared to the crypted password stored in the password file. Since the crypting process is one-way only, just knowing the crypted password does not help anyone to obtain the real password. However, it is possible to move the account with the crypted passwords between UNIX systems by simply copying the password file between machines. The administrator does not have to know the actual decrypted password.

The problem with migration is that no UNIX stores the password file in quite the same way on the hard drive. The following is a comparison of how Sun's Solaris 2.5.1 stores the raw crypted passwords and how FreeBSD 3.4 stores them.

**Exhibit 4.3  Instructions for regaining root**

1. Reboot the system using Ctrl-Alt-Delete. Pressing these at the console makes the system display the message `syncing disks... done`, shut down, and then warm-boot.

2. For FreeBSD 2.X or earlier, after the BIOS POST messages and at the `boot:` prompt, quickly type in `-s` and press Enter. For FreeBSD 3.X and later, press the spacebar during the initial countdown boot message, and at the `ok` prompt type `boot -s`. This boots single-user mode.

3. The system comes up single user without a login prompt and asking for the full pathname of the shell. Make sure it shows `/bin/sh` and press Enter. The Hash Mark prompt displays, indicating maintenance mode.

4. Run the `fsck -p` command as a safety measure to make sure that any light filesystem corruption is corrected.

5. Run the `mount -vat -ufs` command. This changes the root directory to mount read-write from read-only.

6. If the system is a good system, the administrator can simply run the `vipw` command to modify the password file to remove the password. Alternatively, run the `passwd root` command to change the password. If `vipw` cannot run as a result of a file corruption, continue.

7. Change to the `/etc` directory and run the `cp master.passwd backup.passwd` command and then `cp master.passwd worktemp` command.

8. Run the `ed worktmp` command. The ed editor prints out the number of characters in the password file, and the cursor sets at the left side of the screen with no prompt.

9. Type in `/root/` and press Enter. This changes the current line to the line with the root entry in the password file and displays it, as in
`root:sfhjhj^fdsGds:0:0::0:0:Charlie &:/root:/bin/sh`

10. Type the `d` command and press Enter. This deletes the line.

11. Type the `i` command and press Enter. This inserts a line and places the editor into insert mode.

12. Type in the root line without a password and press Enter, as in `root::0:0::0:0:Charlie &:/root:/bin/sh`.

13. Type in a single period and press Enter.

14. Type the `w` command and press Enter. The number of characters displays.

15. Type the `q` command; this quits the editor.

16. Rebuild the password file with the `/usr/sbin/pwd_mkdb worktmp` command.

17. Reboot with the `reboot` command. When the system comes up, the root user's password will be reset to no password. Log in as root and enter a new password with the `passwd` command.

- *Sun* Solaris has two password files that are significant: `/etc/passwd` and `/etc/shadow`. The password file contains complete user account descriptions but not the crypted password. The shadow account holds only the crypted password.
- *FreeBSD* FreeBSD uses an `/etc/passwd` file, but this is just for show. The real passwords and usernames are kept in `/etc/master.passwd`.

To migrate the Solaris password file to the FreeBSD system, the first step is to recombine the `passwd` and `shadow` files. One of the simplest ways to do this is to FTP these files to a PC in ASCII mode and import both files into a spreadsheet such as MS Excel. Before doing this, go through the `passwd` file on the FreeBSD system and remove any commas in the username description area. In the "File Open and Import wizard," select the colon (:) as the delimiter. Once both spreadsheet files are open, copy and paste Column B of the `shadow` file into Column B of the `passwd` file. Make absolutely sure that the length of the column is the same and that each username corresponds with its password. Then save the file as a `comma-delimited` file, and FTP in ASCII mode back to the UNIX system.

Next, replace all commas with colons, and add the additional colon fields that are present in FreeBSD. This can be done with the `awk -F, '{print $1":"$2":"$3":"$4"::0:0:"$5":"$6":"$7}' <passwd.csv>master` command. When this is complete, open up the master file and verify that its lines look like the following:

```
.
.
hmfolk:PcjTEFdWeAxr6:513:60001::0:0:The Realtor:/home/hmfolk:/bin/sh
sjccstw:MCJBR96eZWsHM:519:60001::0:0:SJCC:/home/sjccstw:/bin/sh
.
.
```

Make sure to go through the entire `passwd` file to correct any syntax errors.

When the `passwd` file has been verified as correct in the editor, run the `vipw` command and read in the new `passwd` file (with `vi`, do an `:r filename`). Delete any redundant usernames, and do an `iw` and exit `vipw`. The FreeBSD hashmarked `password` files will be properly rebuilt.

## Redirection and Piping

Redirection and piping are two of the fundamental ideas employed in the UNIX OS. In UNIX a group of smaller programs are tied to each other in a pipe, often with a script, which is used to create a larger system.

DOS users are familiar with the `more` program. In a DOS window the `dir | more` command produces a screen-by-screen directory listing, which is similar to the UNIX pipe created by `ls -l |more`. Although on the surface these look the same, there is a big difference between the DOS method and the UNIX method. With DOS, the `dir` command is run first, and the output is then saved in a temporary file. Then, the `more` program is run against the temporary file. Under a UNIX system like FreeBSD, both programs actually run *at the same time*. In fact, in multiprocessing systems they might even be running at the same *instant*, as one CPU works on one program and another CPU works on the other. The UNIX kernel opens a pipe that allows the output of the first program to be sent to the input of the second program without needing any kind of access to the hard drive for temporary files. Later Microsoft operating systems, because of their graphical orientation, have abandoned the piping concept because it is extremely difficult to take graphical output and feed it into another program.

Redirection is another idea that DOS borrowed from UNIX. Under UNIX, programs output their data to *standard out* or *standard error*. This can be redirected to a file with the > character. Programs also take their input from *standard in*, such as the keyboard. This input also can be fed to the programs from a file with the < character. For example, the `man ls |col -b > ls.txt` command pipes the output of `man` into `col` and then redirects `col`'s output into the `ls.txt` file.

## UNIX EQUIVALENTS OF DOS COMMANDS

Table 4.2 shows some UNIX versions of common DOS/Windows command-line commands. Note that the options to the commands may not be the same (see the FreeBSD system manual for proper use guidelines).

### Common User Commands

When Microsoft wrote DOS, it took many ideas from UNIX, and even many of the DOS commands (e.g., `mkdir`) are the same as the equivalent UNIX commands. If the user knows DOS commands (or Win95 DOS-in-a-window DOS commands), he or she already knows a number of UNIX commands. Some of these work slightly differently; in addition, UNIX is case sensitive where DOS isn't. For example, under DOS the `mkdir` command, `MYfiLEs` is the same as `MKDIR myfiles`. Under FreeBSD, `MYfiLEs` and `myfiles` are two different directories.

**Table 4.2** Comparison of Equivalent DOS and UNIX Commands

| DOS | UNIX | Description |
| --- | --- | --- |
| attrib | chown, chmod | Sets ownership and attributes on files and directories |
| chkdsk | fsck | Repairs filesystem corruption on hard drive |
| cd | cd | Changes directory |
| pwd | pwd | Prints working directory |
| dir | ls -l | Shows directory listing |
| deltree | rm -r | Recursively deletes entire directory tree (be careful!) |
| Erase | rm | Removes or deletes a file (UNIX has *no* undelete; be careful!) |
| Diskcopy | dd | Block-copies media |
| edit | ee, vi | Runs system text editor |
| format | newfs | Creates new filesystem on media |
| help | man | Shows system manual pages |
| mem | top | Shows system status |
| mkdir | mkdir | Creates subdirectories |
| move | mv | Moves files from one place to another |
| rename | mv | Renames files |
| sort | sort | Sorts things |
| type | cat | Dumps file to screen |
| xcopy | cp -R | Recursively copies a directory tree |

Following are a few common commands and what they can do.

- cd is the Change Directory command. Under DOS, it prints out the current directory; under UNIX, it changes back to the home directory. If cd is issued, followed by a directory location, the user moves there.
- ls, the List command, does the same thing as the dir /w command does under DOS, namely, listing the files in the current or specified directory. ls -l is equivalent to dir; ls -lR is similar but not exactly equivalent to dir /s. ls -la and shows hidden files and directories similar to the DOS attrib *.* command.
- cat is the Concatenate command. Run with no options, it displays the file contents on the screen, like the DOS type command. With options, it smashes the files together, which is similar to the DOS copy file1+file2+file3 endfile command.

- rm is similar to the DOS command del; it deletes files. rm -r is equivalent to the DOS deltree command, which deletes a subdirectory full of files and other subdirectories. rm -i removes the file but prompts for delete confirmation. The only major difference is that there is absolutely, positively *no* undelete under UNIX; once it's deleted, it is completely gone, and even if the system is immediately turned off, the file clusters on the disk (called inodes under UNIX) are mostly overwritten. If you are used to using the undelete crutch under DOS, get in the habit of using the UNIX mv command and put the file into a *garbage pail* directory.
- mv is similar to the DOS move command; it moves files from one place to another.
- find is similar to the graphical Find under Win95. find locates files, and it is typed in with the parameters "starting directory", "filespec", and "action". Wildcards *must* be enclosed in double quotes. For example, the find . -name "*.tar" -print command lists all files with the extension .tar in the current directory and below.
- ps is the Process Status command and has no DOS equivalent. ps -ax lists all the running processes on the system. ps has a number of options; test some that are listed in the system manual pages.
- man is the command for running the system manual pages, somewhat like the DOS command help. The command man -k keyword lists all commands that have something to do with the keyword. Run man command to see the manual page for the command. See Chapter 8 for information on how to print system manual pages.
- top shows a list of running processes, similar to the task list under Windows.
- systat shows system status, similar to some of the third-party utilities for Windows. The options -vmstat and -iostat are useful in conjunction with this command.

## Common Superuser Commands

The root user can run commands that regular users cannot. Most of these are located in the /sbin and /usr/sbin directories and must be in the root user's path to be found. Some of them are listed here.

- shutdown has no equivalent in DOS. shutdown now shuts down the system immediately. shutdown -r now reboots the system, as does the Reboot command or Ctrl-Alt-Delete. *Never* simply press the Reset button.

- `mount` is used mainly to access CD-ROM disks and NFS directories. The superuser must run this because removing media, such as a floppy, that is mounted without running the `umount` command can crash the system. For example, to mount a CD-ROM the `mount -r -t cd9660 /dev/cd0a/cdrom` command might be executed.
- `dump` and `restore` are the UNIX backup commands.
- `pkg_add` is the FreeBSD command for adding prepackaged binaries without using the `/stand/sysinstall` menu-driven installer.

## MISCELLANEOUS ADMINISTRATION INFORMATION

### Manually Compiling Software

Eventually, the FreeBSD administrator is bound to run across a utility on the Internet that has not yet been ported to FreeBSD and is not available in the Ports collection. New ports are being added to the FreeBSD collection all the time, but some packages still aren't available for FreeBSD. The following guidelines can help the administrator who is thinking of compiling software on the FreeBSD server.

- Consider how dependent your installation will be on this package. If 300 users depend on this package and as far as you know you are the first site to try to compile this package on FreeBSD, you are in a fairly high-risk situation. It might be advisable to have a supported installation available as a backup.
- Software originating from System V may be slightly more difficult to compile than that originating on Berkeley UNIX.
- If the software is encumbered by a legal license, support will be much harder to get from the free community, no matter how useful it is. The entire point of projects like FreeBSD is sharing—volunteers working on it aren't interested in donating their precious time to a purely commercial venture. Many of them would be happy to work on your code for a fee, however, and some make their livelihood doing these kinds of projects.
- Many X software packages require Motif, which is available, but because they require it, there may not be much interest in the package. A package called lesstif is a Motif clone, and many people have good results building their Motif-requiring package with lesstif substituted.
- FreeBSD is an excellent development environment, but an experienced C programmer is not made in a day. Know your limitations.

- Simpler packages are easier to port.
- Packages that already have definitions for different UNIX versions, especially Linux, are much easier to port since the developer of the package has already had to deal with cross-platform portability.

Always try compiling a new package under FreeBSD before making any planning decisions. Despite the cautions, many packages compile under FreeBSD without modification and work wonderfully.

The FreeBSD Handbook, located in `/usr/share/doc` if the additional documentation is installed, contains a section on how to create an official *Port* of the package for inclusion in the Ports directories. If your package compiles and installs easily, the process of creating it as a port is simple. Consider fame and fortune by building it as a port and submitting it for inclusion!

## Backups

Making system backups is a critical part of any production server, and FreeBSD is no exception. Backup frequency can range from once every two months for a home system to once a day for a commercial fileserver. Backup storage can range from offsite to under the desk.

Two programs are used to back up most UNIX systems: `tar` and `dump`. Tar is very useful when the backup media may not necessarily be reread on the same machine it originated on, or may be restored onto a system with a much different layout than the one on which the backup was made. It also can compress data before writing it out to the tape drive. `Dump` is useful because it can copy the entire filesystem, including special files. It allows a server to be brought back completely from a hard drive crash without having to rebuild the FreeBSD system on it. `Dump` also works if part of the filesystem is corrupted as a result of hard drive corruption and is thus somewhat safer on an unattended backup.

Both programs can be set to back up over the network to a remote FreeBSD server with a tape drive in it. Tape drives with automatic changers require use of the `Amanda` program (from Ports).

Use the following examples with `tar` (weekly backup script with local tape drive).

```
#!/bin/sh
TAPE=/dev/nrst0
export TAPE
rm /backupfull.log
mt status
mt rewind
```

```
mt weof 1
mt rewind
tar cX /tarexclude /
mt rewind
tar t
tar -dv /*
mt rewind
tar -tv > /backupfull.log
```

Here are the contents of /tarexclude file:

```
proc
dev
cdrom
```

> **NOTE** The tape is then positioned at the end of the backup. This is intentional because once the primary system's backup is completed, additional FreeBSD systems in the enterprise can add their own backups to the tape in the primary system's tape drive.

Here is a weekly backup script for a tape drive that is located on system tapemaster.mydomain.com:

```
#!/bin/sh
rm /backupweekly.log
rsh tapemaster.mydomain.com mt -f /dev/nrst0 status
TAPE=tapemaster.mydomain.com:/dev/nrst0
export TAPE
tar cvX /tarexclude / > /backupweekly.log
```

Contrast that script with how the same thing would need to be done on a Sun Sparc workstation, running Solaris, to another Sparc workstation.

```
#!/bin/sh
rsh tapemaster.mydomain.com /usr/bin/mt -f /dev/rmt/0n status
cd /
/usr/bin/tar cbfX 20 - /tarexclude . | rsh tapemaster.mydomain.com dd
of=/dev/rmt/0n obs=20b
```

Here are the contents of Solaris the /tarexclude file:

```
./cdrom
./lost+found
./dev
./proc
./devices
```

## Reviewing Daily Logs

If the FreeBSD system is placed on the Internet and made accessible, ultimately there will be crack attacks made against the server. To stave off any cracker activity, it is vital that the administrator review the server logs on a daily basis.

Most FreeBSD logs are located in `/var/log` and are generated by programs or by the syslogger, `syslogd`. It is common for the system administrator to set other network devices, such as routers, to send syslogging data to the FreeBSD server. The two most important logs to review daily are `/var/messages` and `/var/maillog`.

The FreeBSD system *also* e-mails the results of its daily housekeeping scripts to the root user. It is a good idea to review the results of these scripts. Many administrators with multiple FreeBSD systems set up aliases that mail the script output to a single e-mail account, which they review at their convenience.

It is easy to insert your own daily scripts, such as system backup, into the system daily maintenance scripts. Run the `man periodic` command to learn more about how these are handled. To insert a script is simple; for example, a daily backup script can be copied to `/etc/periodic/daily`.

## UNIX System Administration Books

There are a number of good books that contain a wealth of non-FreeBSD-specific UNIX system administration information. They include O'Reilly's *Essential System Administration*, *Learning Perl*, and *Learning the vi Editor*; and Prentice-Hall's *UNIX System Administration Handbook*, *The UNIX Shells by Example*, *A Guide to vi—Visual Editing on the UNIX System*, and *The KornShell—Command and Programming Language*. This is not a complete list, but it's a place to start.

# Chapter 5

# Internet Connectivity and Corporate WANs

Making a formal connection to the Internet can bring many benefits to an organization and in time can fundamentally change how the organization does its daily work. FreeBSD contains all the software needed to connect to the Internet, and if you have read the previous four chapters, you have the information to use FreeBSD to make the connection. Connecting to the Internet, like anything else, goes much more smoothly if it is carefully planned. This chapter presents a framework to use when planning the connection and the technical details of making the connection.

## WILL YOU CONNECT?

Most people in business today have been bombarded by advertising and trade articles promoting Internet connectivity as the latest *must have* for a business. However, few people who have not gotten online on the Internet can appreciate its benefits, let alone begin to understand how Internet connectivity can be used to help an organization. Even those *power surfers* who have been on the Internet for years may not be aware of all the functionality available. There is as much misinformation about Internet connectivity as there is information.

As a result, it is often assumed that permanent Internet connectivity is an absolute necessity for an organization. It is worthwhile, however, to ask whether to connect at all. The administrator can start to answer this question with a dedicated dialup account to an ISP.

One of the first things an administrator should do in the planning process of connecting the organization is to obtain at least one dialup Internet account.

This dialup account should be a permanent account the organization owns, but the ISP should not be considered permanent. Even after the organization builds its own Internet connection, the account should be maintained separately because it will be needed for testing the dedicated connection from time to time. With this dialup account, the administrator should try out the services listed in Chapter 2 to get a feel for what services the organization might want.

In addition, the person in charge of researching the Internet connectivity decision might interview people from other companies in a similar industry who have set up their own connections to the Internet. This may help in deciding what services to use and what benefits can be realized from them.

It is important that the company have the required infrastructure; otherwise, the benefits of connectivity won't be realized. For example, e-mail is the *killer app* that most businesses cite as their reason to connect. Unless all users in the organization have access to e-mail, however, e-mail service will not be used fully. Even more important, what if the business has no internal network or if not all employees of the business have a computer? Don't put the cart before the horse and hook up to the Internet before you establish an internal network.

An Internet connection adds a permanent monthly cost to the organization. Often contracts must be signed that commit the organization to one or more years with a phone carrier or ISP. A direct connection also adds permanent technical administrative duties. An organization that is not prepared to commit additional personnel resources and time to an Internet connection should not bother with a direct Internet connection. Organizations should not use grants or other one-shot funding vehicles to *get* online unless they have mechanisms to continue a certain funding level after the grant money is gone. A dedicated Internet connection is not a panacea: it will not pull a sliding business out of bankruptcy or bring in a flood of new customers overnight. For most businesses it becomes just another service, at best like a fax line or phone system, that is just an additional required cost of doing business. It is a service that can add to the business if used well, but there is no free lunch: an Internet connection will provide benefits in proportion to the effort expended on it. Expend lots of time and money and it will reward you tenfold; expend nothing and it will return nothing.

## HOW TO CHOOSE AN INTERNET SERVICE PROVIDER

Once the organization understands what Internet services they need, they will be in a much better position to select an ISP. This section presents the information needed to decide who will provide your Internet connection.

## What Are We Plugging in To?

People often speak of "connecting to the Internet" as though the Internet was a unified entity that someone could point a finger at. The truth is that there is no single backbone to the Internet (Figure 5.1). The Internet Mapping project at `http://cm.bell-labs.com/cm/cs/who/ches/map/index.html` tries to make some sense of the network. The Internet is actually a web of high-speed TCP/IP circuits owned by the world's major telephone carriers. In the United States, AT&T, Worldcom/MCI, and Sprint own practically all these circuits. These circuits run over a giant network of high-speed fiberoptic data lines, some owned by the carriers and others leased from other providers, such as Global Crossing. Many millions of miles of fiberoptic cable are also owned by oil and gas pipeline companies, electric utilities, railroads, and other non-telecommunications-oriented enterprises.

This *backbone network* is referred to as the Internet core, on which transmission speeds are 155Mbps to 622Mbps and possibly even higher. The core connections are made in giant routers, mostly manufactured by Cisco, that are scattered around the world and administered by a loose confederation of administrators. Occasionally, squabbles break out. One nasty problem was precipitated by Sprint deciding to drop high-order Class C IP address routes from its

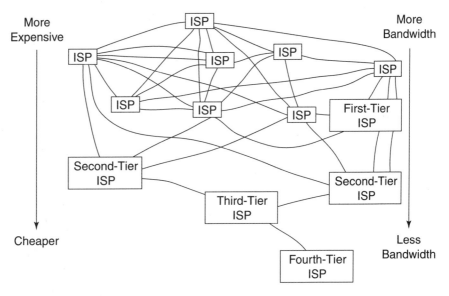

**Figure 5.1** A simplified version of the Internet

router's tables. Another was caused by UUNET canceling its peering agreements with smaller ISPs.

Surrounding the core is a larger network of fiberoptic lines owned by so-called second-tier ISPs. These lines are connected at multiple access points to the core net, usually through fiberoptic cable.

Third-tier providers are typically smaller, locally owned ISPs that can be connected just to their own ISP, or to each other, with a single line or multiple lines. The speed of T1 lines—high-speed leased circuits—typically is 1.54Mbps. Fourth-tier providers operate on the fringes. Often, such an ISP is a storefront with a modem bank connected via a single frame line to a third-tier provider. These businesses are generally concerned only with end-user modem connections or sometimes with dedicated 28.8K modem lines. A provider can straddle the fence between two classes. For example, a large ISP may have a single 45Mbit line, multiple T1s, and perhaps even a modem bank. In addition, merger mania thrives among ISPs, so the lines between tiers are getting even more blurred.

## Peering Agreements

Internet traffic is based on a large network of peering and transit agreements set up between ISPs. Peering works pretty simply: ISP A signs an agreement with ISP B, with each ISP allowing its network to be used by the other ISP's traffic. This helps to strengthen Internet redundancy, moving the network closer to the Web model used by the U.S. power grid, and away from the trunk-and-branches model of former times. Peering is done when both ISPs have roughly similar coverage area and a given point in the coverage area is accessible to both ISPs' networks. Transit is a little more complex: an ISP may set itself up with multiple connections to points on the Internet and permit traffic between these connection points to cross over its network. For example, an ISP may connect to both Sprint and AT&T and allow traffic from Sprint to cross its network to go to AT&T's network; the ISP then receives payment for access from Sprint.

Here's a simplified peering example: UUNET might have a DS3 connection between San Francisco and New York. UUNET signs an agreement with Sprint, which also has a line from San Francisco to New York. Normally, if a peering agreement didn't exist and a UUNET customer in San Francisco wanted to send traffic to a customer in New York, it would pass over UUNET's line. If that line got congested, the additional traffic would be dropped. With a peering agreement, traffic could go over either Sprint's or UUNET's lines. This example is so simplistic that it is almost meaningless. Real peering agreements and the networks they cover are far more complex. It does illustrate an important point, however: the larger the ISP, the more valuable the peering access to its network. In addition, more ISPs have peering agreements with it, and thus, the better integrated the ISP is with the Internet core.

## Multihoming

ISPs can be connected to the Internet core in two basic configurations: multihomed or single-homed (Figure 5.2). A single-homed ISP is connected to a single, larger ISP. The connectivity may operate at a high bandwidth, such as a DS3, but the ISP effectively has all its eggs in one basket. If the larger ISP should develop a fault and go offline, even for a short period, the ISP that is single-homed to it also goes offline. A multihomed ISP has connections to several larger ISPs, and it participates in Border Gateway Protocol (BGP). BGP routes the TCP/IP traffic flows between ISPs. To direct traffic effectively from its customers to anything more than a single upstream Internet feed, an ISP must have registered as a BGP provider and must exchange routing information with the larger ISPs via BGP. Multihoming allows the ISP to continue to provide service to its customers even if one of its feeds to the Internet core goes offline.

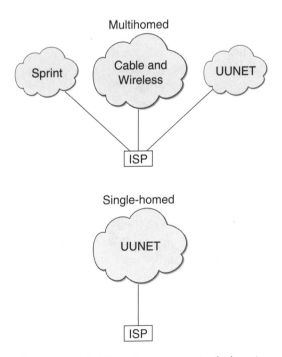

**Figure 5.2** Multihoming versus single homing

## Portable Internet Protocol Addressing

ISPs obtain the TCP/IP numbers they hand out to their customers via one of two mechanisms. They can go to their parent ISP and request blocks of IP numbers referred to as nonportable numbers. They can also go to the Internet Assigned Numbers Authority (IANA) registry that is authoritative for their geographic region and request a block of portable numbers. Currently, the three IANA-authorized registries are ARIN, RIPE, and APNIC.

If a customer of an ISP is assigned TCP/IP numbering from nonportable numbers and the ISP is ever forced to renumber by its feed, the customer is forced to renumber as well. If the assignment is made from portable numbers, the customer doesn't need to renumber unless the ISP goes out of business. Even then the ISP will probably include the portable block in its sale of assets, and if a different ISP buys it, which is likely, the customer can continue to use the numbers if it reconnects to the new ISP. Of course, renumbering is not a problem if the customer uses private numbers internally, which is recommended.

## Where Is the Bandwidth That Is Needed?

New administrators who purchase leased line connections to ISPs often wrongly assume that their access speed to servers on the Internet is determined by the speed of their connection to the ISP. Users within the organization are often far worse about this. They tend to say, "If I get a frame connection at 512K CIR, I'll be able to connect to my sites at that speed; if I get a T1, I'll be able to connect at 1.5Mbps."

In reality, the circuit speed from the end user to the ISP is just the first piece of the entire connection bandwidth equation. For example, most users at Company A want regular access to a server owned by Company B, which is connected to a small, regional ISP with a dial-on-demand ISDN line running at 128K. If Company A purchases a T1 connection to its ISP, even though its end of the connection path is running at 1.54Mbps, it doesn't get any more than 128K worth of bandwidth through Company B's Internet connection. Thus, it is very important to define the uses of an Internet connection *before* purchasing the connection. If most of the servers that the organization's users need are behind slow connections, such as some foreign servers, a high-speed Internet connection won't speed up anything.

This problem also arises if the remote servers that the organizations' users want to reach are extremely busy. Suppose in the previous example that Company B's server has a limit of ten simultaneous user connections. Because this server gets so many hits, Company B decides to upgrade its Internet connection to a full-blown T1 and raise the connection limit to 100 simultaneous users. Company A *still* cannot obtain any faster bandwidth to the server than it did before if the server is continuously running close to its connection limit.

## Hop Counts

Even if the servers that an organization's users want to reach are sitting behind large high-capacity circuits that run at very low capacity, it is also important that the network distance to these connections is short. Consider what happens if Company A is plugged into a third-tier ISP and sends traffic to Company B, which is also connected to a third-tier ISP. The data passes through two ISPs on its way to the core, then through two more ISPs on its way from the core to Company B. The return traffic also passes through these links. If Company A and Company B are both connected to first-tier providers, traffic passing between them goes through two hops, not four. Thus, the traffic passes between sites on much higher-capacity pipes. Of course, because these circuits have higher bandwidth, they cost more and therefore carry much larger amounts of traffic. However, consider the difference between a smaller ISP's T1 running at 95 percent capacity and a larger ISP's DS3 running at 95 percent capacity. Five percent of a T1 is a lot less spare bandwidth than 5 percent of a DS3!

Besides the circuit traffic, routers also introduce a delay in packet transfer. Although the delay doesn't affect the base throughput, it can affect applications such as Telnet, which send small amounts of data but need a quick response. For example, satellite links introduce a tremendous amount of latency because of the great distance from the Earth's surface to the satellite. If a megabit of data is transferred through such a link in one direction only, the user doesn't notice that transmission is not instantaneous. However, a user of an interactive program, such as a Telnet or an SQL-based program, definitely notices the two-second turnaround time! Multiple routers between the source and destination can also have the same effect. Using the traceroute tool can help provide a map of these routers.

## Where Does the ISP Connect To?

Connection points exist at every nodal location in the core and at the endpoints owned by the ISP to which your organization connects. Obviously, connection points closer to and inside the core receive greater bandwidth to the core, along with a higher probability of higher-speed connections to larger numbers of nodes. Naturally, connection to the points located closer to the core cost more. For example, Netcom, a second-tier provider, charges $1,000 per month for a T1 port. In contrast, AT&T charges more than $2,000 per month for a T1 connection, but this connection is with the core itself. The important thing to understand is that although both connections can carry the same amount of bandwidth because they run at the same speed, the practical bandwidth is determined by the relationship to the core. As a rule, the first-tier core connection can deliver faster, longer-sustained speeds to a greater number of points on the Internet.

A mistake that people frequently make when selecting an ISP is to compare price alone, without considering where the ISP is located in the bandwidth hierarchy. This is reinforced by the ISPs, who generally do not divulge the details of their connections to the Internet. Even if you can get that data out of them, it may be impossible to obtain a list of their subscriber's bandwidth, and if you can get this, it will be out of date within a few months. For example, a local ISP that advertises a total of four T1s to the "Internet core" is actually serving 30 separate T1s to different businesses from the four T1s! On average, these businesses will never be able to realize the full capacity of the connection to the local ISP all at the same time.

On the other hand, large ISPs sometimes aggregate many customers onto smaller amounts of bandwidth, so there is a lot to be said for connecting to a well-run smaller ISP rather than a badly run larger ISP. The most important single aspect of bandwidth allocation is reasonable utilization of the network circuits that connect the ISP with the upstream provider. The ISP must make a regular policy of measurement and monitoring to avoid circuit overload; ask to see these reports when shopping for ISPs.

## ISPs: Bigger Is Sometimes Better

Managing a well-run ISP requires lots of detailed advance planning; adequate funding; knowledgeable, highly paid staff; and a talent for juggling. ISPs spend enormous amounts of cash under contracts to the telephone companies (Telcos) and higher-tier ISPs and must take in enormous amounts to maintain a cash balance. An ISP that makes a mistake, such as spending lots of money on expensive servers for value-added service offerings that are never used, may be forced into spreading bandwidth too thin in order to pay for it. The result is a cascade into a vicious circle: customers get disgusted and leave, the incoming cash flow drops, but the outgoing cash flow is locked up in contracts and stays the same, thereby forcing bandwidth to be spread even thinner, angering more customers, who then leave, and so on. Eventually, the struggling ISP cannot afford to pay good networking staff, who leave, and the ISP collapses. Such mistakes have put many small ISPs out of business or forced them into a merger, and most larger ISPs also have had a brush with this problem.

It is sad but true that in the ISP industry, the only way to solve most of the customer bandwidth complaints on a properly configured ISP network is to throw money at the problem in the form of higher-bandwidth circuit connections. Larger ISPs can more easily afford to do this, particularly ISPs owned by telephone companies, which have an existing cash "cow" to draw on. Many smaller ISPs, without much money, specialize in niche markets, such as Web design, hardware sales, ISDN outdial, and consulting. These areas of specialization may be valuable to the prospective customer, but there is a greater chance that the smaller ISP may have restricted bandwidth. Remember that the value-added services, such as nameserving, may be valuable initially to the inexperienced customer, but as time passes, these services will become less important and bandwidth will become more important.

An ISP that has superior service and engineering (e.g., lots of bandwidth to the core) and has reasonably allocated bandwidth to its subscribers is happy to allow you to tour the facilities and talk to the engineers. It won't be afraid to offer service level agreements (SLAs) and such. Of course, such an ISP costs more than one that has inferior service. This kind of ISP probably restricts customer access to its facilities, disables ICMP router response to prevent its internal network from being mapped with network tracing tools, does not offer SLAs, and is unlikely to want the prospective customer to talk to other ISP customers.

## Shopper's Checklist

Businesses that connect to the Internet through higher-speed connections have to protect themselves when signing up for an ISP's business service. There are a few ways to do this.

**1.** Don't lock into an ISP contract for longer than a year. Regardless of the rate, this market simply changes too fast. If you must do so because of a deal that is simply too good to pass up, make sure the contract has trap doors that will let you out in case the ISP fails to deliver the promised services. Not that locking into the Telco circuit contract is a different matter: if your company connects to an ISP via a frame relay circuit, even if you quit using the ISP, you still need the frame circuit for the next ISP.

**2.** Control your own DNS by operating the primary DNS at your site, not the ISP's site. Some companies that do this have the ISP set up as a secondary.

**3.** Consider contracting any offsite Web hosting with a competitor of your ISP for backup redundancy. If something happens to your ISP, the offsite Web site will still exist. If something happens to the offsite, you can temporarily host it at your site. If you control your DNS, you can redirect Web queries to whatever server you please—you are not limited to your ISP's server.

**4.** Set up connectivity quality testing from the outset. Get a statement listing ten major well-connected FTP sites on the Internet, along with the average measured transfer speed for a 1MB sample file from those sites at given times. When the line is installed, verify that you are getting this, and periodically recheck it. Don't accept the excuse, "You cannot guarantee connectivity speeds to the Internet." Although this is true for single cases, it is not entirely true for an overall average sample. If the ISP balks, a poor substitute is a minimum bandwidth guarantee, but it's better than nothing. After all, ISPs do what their customers want. If all its customers are pushing it to maintain bandwidth, the ISP is going to think twice before overcommitting. If all the customers care about is pretty Web site graphics, why would the ISP knock itself out over bandwidth?

**5.** Detail in the contract what compensation you will receive for loss of connectivity (e.g., time, monetary credits).

**6.** Own and program your own router and firewall. Even if you have to contract out the router configuration, be sure to obtain a complete configuration printout and router passwords. Organizations using intermittent connections don't have to worry about the router because they are generally using PCs to autodial, but firewalling is always an issue.

**7.** Specify in the contract a minimum response time for queries to the ISP and the penalties that apply if the minimum isn't met. You're installing a mission-critical connection here, so the ISP should be providing 24/7 service.

**8.** Make sure the ISP can provide all services you want. If you want RealVideo offsite video serving services, don't accept the line, "We are going to install that within the next few months." They may have been "going to install it in the next few months" for a year by now.

**9.** Inquire about traffic shaping and prioritization. The current Cisco IOS lets a manager define different levels of importance for different types of traffic. For example, if a router receives a RealVideo packet and an FTP packet at the same time from the Ethernet, the router can be programmed to forward the FTP packet down the outgoing serial line before sending the RealVideo. For most businesses, this programming is useful only when done on the ISP side of the circuit because the incoming half of its circuit (i.e., traffic from the Internet) is what is full. However, prioritization may be valuable if the business is running Web servers or other servers that generate large amounts of outbound traffic.

## SECURITY AND FIREWALLING

Organizations that connect to the Internet have to deal with an unpleasant side effect of connection—they have to take reasonable precautions to prevent attacks on their internal networks. Some organizations solve this problem by having simple connections to the Internet to maintain a presence or get e-mail while keeping their interior production network separate from the Internet. An intelligence agency, such as the National Security Association, is one type of organization that maintains a separate physical network. For most organizations, however, the benefits of connecting to the Internet far outweigh the risks of network attack. The vast majority of attacks stem from physical and employee security problems. It is much more likely that a smash-and-grab thief will back up a truck to an office building in the middle of the night, break in, and steal a couple PCs. A crooked employee might walk in on a Saturday afternoon and make off with a few systems. If these PCs happen to be the main network servers, such thefts dwarf any possible network security issues.

Good network security has several components.

- Border filtering, set up by access lists on the external gateway router.
- Setup and operation of a demilitarized zone (DMZ) between the external gateway router and the firewall. This is where all hosts go that must offer services to the outside.
- Securing (hardening) all hosts in the DMZ.
- Securing the physical environment of the host.

The organization may want to consider network security on inside hosts as well. If the organization is large, has a lot of sensitive data on its network (e.g., medical records or credit card numbers), and many opportunities for unsupervised network access, inside hosts may need to be hardened. This costs a lot in time and effort, however, and many businesses in this situation designate a certain portion of the interior network as sensitive. The sensitive net is then isolated and the hosts on it are hardened while the rest of the net is allowed to be open. For example, a fileserver used by the IT department as a repository for device drivers for inside hardware would be considered noncritical, but a fileserver used for personnel records would be hardened.

## Packet Filtering and ipfw

The first step in securing an organization's network is to install packet filtering on the router or host used as the external gateway, or border, to the Internet (Figure 5.3). If a Cisco router is used, this is done by installing access lists on the router. If a FreeBSD system is the connection point (e.g., if the computer is used as a dial-on-demand PPP router), the `ipfw` packet-filtering program can be used. This filtering goes between the outside (Internet) and the DMZ network; it helps to protect the hosts that must offer services to the outside. A second set of filters is needed between the DMZ and the inside network.

Packet filtering works by allowing or blocking packets to destination hosts based on a list of entries (or holes) that the administrator sets up. The criteria can be specific IP numbers, specific service port numbers, or a combination. When an incoming packet is received by the list, the router or host starts comparing it to every entry. When the packet matches an entry, it is dropped or passed, depending on the statement, and entry processing stops on that packet. If no entry matches, the packet is dropped. Typically only some incoming packets are passed through the filter. Outgoing packets (originating from the internal network) are usually all allowed out.

Lists of entries can be set up by either allowing everything that is not specifically blocked or by denying everything that isn't specifically allowed. Usually, the first kind of access list is used on internal routers in large organizations to block troublesome protocols or network problems. A very common implementation is to block excessive Novell NetWare IPX or WinNT broadcast advertisements. These are commonly used on the "in" side of the router—the interface facing toward the internal network. Minimal versions of these access lists are also useful for blocking would-be spam relayers. This type of list is typically organized with the most specific statements at the beginning, followed by more general statements, and ending with a statement that allows everything.

*An access list that denies everything not specifically allowed is the standard kind of access list used on an Internet gateway router or gateway host. It is*

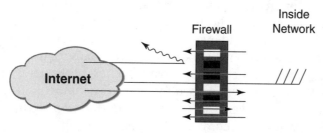

**Figure 5.3**  Packet filtering

typically organized with the most general statements at the top, followed by more specific statements, and ending with a statement that denies everything.

With either type of access list, the administrator typically organizes it so that most legitimate packets are passed depending on the results of the first few rules. This helps to keep system performance from being affected by the access list.

### Packet Filtering in a Simple Routed Network

When an internal network uses legal IP numbers, specific hosts are identified by the administrator as being allowed to provide services to the Internet, and holes are created for these hosts. For example, a specific host is identified as the organization's external Web server, so a hole is created for this host's IP number for incoming packets, with a destination port number of 80. Suppose there is a host named `www.fred.com` with an IP number of 199.5.4.3. Using a Cisco, the rule applied to the *in* interface on the external serial connection is

```
access-list 101 permit tcp any host 199.5.4.3 eq www
```

Access lists on a Cisco are entered by running the `config` command. Using `ipfw` on FreeBSD, the rule applied to the `ipfw` list is

```
ipfw add 120 allow tcp from any to 199.5.4.3 80.
```

The `ipfw` rules are entered into FreeBSD by modifying the `/etc/rc.firewall` file.

The biggest problem with this kind of setup is that if the host with the hole is compromised, the attacker can use the host as a place from which to attack any other host on the internal network. The attacker does this by spawning a subshell on the host or uploading a worm or virus to the host.

### DMZ Networks

A DMZ network prevents the problem of an attacker using a compromised host as a jumping-off point. With a DMZ net, the external gateway router (or border router) has an access list installed on it and its Ethernet interface is connected to a small network (the DMZ) that is then connected to the organization's internal firewall, usually a network address translation (NAT). Hosts that are to provide services to the Internet are located on the DMZ net, which puts them in front of the firewall (Figure 5.4). Hosts behind the firewall (the main internal network) do not provide services to the Internet. If an attacker makes it past the external gateway access list and compromises a host providing services to the Internet, he or she cannot use the host to attack inside hosts because the compromised host is still outside the firewall.

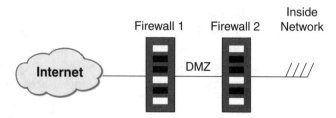

**Figure 5.4** The DMZ network setup

> **NOTE**   With a Cisco or FreeBSD router containing multiple Ethernet interfaces, the DMZ need not be physically between the outside and inside; it can be located on the separate Ethernet interface.

A DMZ network is not foolproof because some services need access to the internal, protected network while remaining accessible by the Internet. The most common example is e-mail, specifically SMTP. E-mail servers must be available to hosts that send them mail from the Internet. Therefore, they must be run on a host that has a legal IP number reachable from the Internet (i.e., within the DMZ). If the organization is small and can force all users to use a mail client, such as a POP3 client, the mailserver can be located on a separate host in the DMZ. This works because the mailserver initiates e-mail connections only to hosts on the Internet. If the organization is larger and runs mailservers on its internal network (e.g., multiple sites or many multiple subnets), the mailserver must also be able to initiate e-mail connections to internal mailservers in order to transfer mail to them. In this case there are only two alternatives: (1) run the mailserver on the firewall itself, or (2) using a NAT, make internal mailservers visible to a master mailserver in the DMZ.

### Domain Name System on DMZ Networks

The DNS is another server that is often run on the internal firewall. If the internal network is RFC-unassigned and isolated behind an http proxy, the organization may want to use DNS to name hosts on the internal network. In this case the DNS must be accessible by internal hosts for network applications that don't use the http proxy. Although it is quite possible to run an isolated server on the internal network for inside hosts only, to do this you must run two separate DNSs: one inside for inside queries, and one outside for outside queries. In addition, http queries for inside hosts on the RFC-unassigned net made through the http proxy will fail because the http proxy must query the outside

DNS to resolve external hostnames. It is usually much easier simply to run a DNS on the http proxy that can be used to resolve names for both inside and outside networks. Directives should then be put in the nameserver files to prevent queries originating externally from resolving internal hosts. In addition, any client Web browsers should be configured so that they use only the proxy server to contact hosts exterior to the network; interior hosts should not be contacted via the proxy. If transparent proxying (NAT) is used, the DNS can be located on a separate machine in the DMZ instead of on the firewall, without any of the fuss associated with a proxy server.

### Securing the Gateway

Because the external gateway router implements the external access lists, it must itself be secure. All services that are not absolutely essential for its operation must have outside access blocked. Some services that should be blocked from outside access are SNMP, Telnet, TFTP, Syslog, and simple services, such as echo. Additionally, routing protocols should be exchanged only with other, designated *safe* routing hosts.

Besides these TCP services, the organization may also consider blocking some Internet Control Message Protocol (ICMP), such as traceroute and Ping. Do this only after careful consideration of the issues. Often, indiscriminate ICMP blocking can create problems with ISPs that monitor link status and with Maximum Transmission Unit (MTU) path discovery, which is part of the TCP/IP defined in RFC1191.

The `ipfw` program can be used to set up these blocks on FreeBSD, and access lists can be used to set them up on a Cisco router.

Besides blocking access from the Internet to these services, access to the router should also be restricted to the firewall itself. No other hosts in the DMZ should have Telnet or other access to the router because if an attacker can compromise a host in the DMZ, he or she can also access the router.

### Securing the Inside Firewall

Between the DMZ and the real internal network is the main firewall. Securing this from attack is particularly important. After the external router, an attacker would try to get on any service available on the firewall itself. All services should be blocked from access by external hosts or hosts located in the DMZ.

Blocking service access by external hosts is done with the access list that is run on the external router. Blocking service access from hosts in the DMZ is done with an access list on the firewall itself. As an alternative to service blocks, all unneeded services on the firewall can be disabled. This is known as *hardening* the host. Edit the /etc/inetd.conf file under FreeBSD and comment out all service entries not absolutely required; then send a HUP signal to inetd. FTP, Telnet, shell, login, finger, comsat, and ntalkd could be commented out, which would prevent all network access to these programs and force all user access to the firewall host to be done at its console.

Many people also completely disable inetd on a hardened host, and use daemons, such as sshd, that run continuously to provide encrypted external services.

## Ipfw Access List Example

To use the ipfw program the FreeBSD kernel must be recompiled, as discussed in Chapter 3, Installation Phase 4. FreeBSD comes with several default firewall templates (in /etc/rc.firewall), and for most sites, a simple template can be used to set up a quick filter. Such a template is given in Exhibit 5.1, with an explanation of each line so that administrators can modify it to suit their network.

Use the following steps to modify the simple firewall template. Note that the ipfw templates supplied with each version vary greatly.

1. Recompile the kernel with the options IPFIREWALL line.
2. After the kernel has been installed and before the system is rebooted, make these modifications.
   a. Copy /etc/rc.firewall to /etc/rc.firewall.backup
   b. Modify /etc/rc.conf and change the following options
      firewall_enable="YES"
      firewall_type="simple"
      firewall_quiet="NO"
   c. For FreeBSD 2.2.6, modify /etc/rc.firewall starting at line 119 and ending at line 172 (see Exhibit 5.1). Later versions do not use the same line numbers.
3. Reboot the system and test.

## Cisco Router Setup

Cisco makes the recommended and most popular router to use for a *leaf-node* border router on a leased line. Generally, when an ISP or Cisco reseller sets up a router for an Internet connection, its primary concentration is on setting the leased line parameters and internal IP numbers properly so the line comes up. Once that is done and the Ethernet interface is pingable from the ISP, as far as they are concerned the router configuration and setup are complete. Any further configuration is the problem of the organization that owns the router.

An ISP or reseller can be asked to input a firewall access list, but this is something that the administrator of the organization's network should be doing. If hosts are set up, torn down, or modified in the DMZ, the firewall access list on the router must be changed. This may occur months or years after the ISP or consultant has

### Exhibit 5.1  Simple template `ipfw` rules and an explanation of how they operate

```
# set these to your outside interface network and netmask and ip
oif="ed0"
onet="192.168.4.0"
omask="255.255.255.0"
oip="192.168.4.17"
```

```
# set these to your inside interface network and netmask and ip
iif="ed1"
inet="192.168.3.0"
imask="255.255.255.0"
iip="192.168.3.17"
```

In this example `ipfw` is running on a host with two Ethernet interfaces, `ed0` and `ed1`. If you don't know the names of your Ethernet interfaces, you can run the `dmesg` command and look at its output. Ethernet interfaces are listed with their MAC addresses, such as the following example for a 3Com 3C503.

```
ed0 at 0x280-0x28f irq 9 maddr 0xd8000 msize 8192 on isa
ed0: address 02:60:8c:ae:69:75, type 3c503 (16 bit)
```

Usually, the person who has installed FreeBSD knows these names. `netstat -r` also lists the interface names.

The `onet` and `inet` network numbers are the *network* part of the TCP/IP number assigned to the interface—these are found by ANDing together the subnet mask and the TCP/IP number on the interface. The person in charge of numbering the TCP/IP network knows this number (e.g., nonsubnetted "Class C" network numbers have a zero in the rightmost decimal position).

The inside network in this template is from the RFC-unassigned number group. The template is for use on a system running NAT or a proxy.

If the system is acting as an external gateway between an asynchronous dialup connection to an ISP, typically the outside interface name is `ppp0`. In that case `ipfw` won't work properly if the ISP doesn't assign a static IP number on dialup.

```
# Stop spoofing
$fwcmd add deny all from ${inet}:${imask} to any in via ${oif}
$fwcmd add deny all from ${onet}:${omask} to any in via ${iif}
```

These rules are antispoofing rules. They prevent packets that appear to originate from inside the network and are received on the external interface from being forwarded inside. These rules work this way because it should be impossible for a normal packet that originates from the inside network to appear on the "in" side of the external interface unless it was spoofed. In a normal TCP/IP connection, packets that appear on the external interface originate externally, and packets that appear on the internal interface originate internally.

```
# Stop RFC1918 nets on the outside interface
$fwcmd add deny all from 192.168.0.0:255.255.0.0 to any via ${oif}
$fwcmd add deny all from 172.16.0.0:255.240.0.0 to any via ${oif}
$fwcmd add deny all from 10.0.0.0:255.0.0.0 to any via ${oif}
```

The code above represents a refinement of the antispoofing ruleset. If the inside network is running RFC-unassigned, the previous ruleset makes this particular ruleset unnecessary. However, if the interior network is running legal IP numbers, this may stop some types of spoofing attacks.

**Exhibit 5.1**  (*continued*)

```
# Allow TCP through if setup succeeded
$fwcmd add pass tcp from any to any established
```

This ruleset is at the heart of the TCP/IP communication channel. When an inside host initiates a connection to an external host, the return packets come back from that host with a flag set indicating that they are part of a connection initiated by the inside. This ruleset allows those packets to come back inside. This only works with the TCP protocol, not UDP.

```
# Allow setup of incoming email
$fwcmd add pass tcp from any to ${oip} 25 setup
```

This code allows access to inbound SMTP Internet mail. The Setup option helps to block some possible network-layer attacks.

```
# Allow access to our DNS
$fwcmd add pass tcp from any to ${oip} 53 setup
```

This code allows access to a nameserver that may be running on the firewall; it can be commented out if the system isn't running `named`.

```
# Allow access to our WWW
$fwcmd add pass tcp from any to ${oip} 80 setup
```

This code allows access to a Web server that is running on the firewall; it would normally be used only in a situation where the Web server had to be running on the firewall, such as if the firewall was plugged into the Internet via asynchronous dialup PPP. It is usually unsafe to run a Web server on a firewall, especially if the Web server has CGI on it. External Web servers should run on separate hosts in the DMZ.

```
# Reject&Log all setup of incoming connections from the outside
$fwcmd add deny log tcp from any to any in via ${oif} setup
```

This ruleset does two things: it triggers a log entry on SYN attacks, and it serves as the termination point for any service access attempts that weren't specifically allowed earlier.

```
# Allow setup of any other TCP connection
$fwcmd add pass tcp from any to any setup
```

This ruleset would normally allow everything, except that, coming after the previous ruleset, its main purpose is to allow outbound TCP traffic initiated from the inside.

```
# Allow DNS queries out in the world
$fwcmd add pass udp from any 53 to ${oip}
$fwcmd add pass udp from ${oip} to any 53
```

Since DNS queries are UDP, we need a specific ruleset for them. The previous ruleset only allows for TCP traffic.

```
# Allow NTP queries out in the world
$fwcmd add pass udp from any 123 to ${oip}
$fwcmd add pass udp from ${oip} to any 123
```

The same issue with DNS is present with NTP—it's UDP traffic—`# Everything else is denied as default.`

configured the router, and no notes will be left on the particular setup. Therefore, it is best if the network administrator takes responsibility for doing this early.

A number of ISPs have programs and promotions in which the ISP purchases and retains ownership of the routers used at the customer premises. For companies without much knowledge about router configuration, this can sometimes be a win-win situation. The ISP wins because its networking people can guarantee the consistency of their network, which greatly improves troubleshooting. The customer wins because it doesn't have to buy a router. The big problem with these deals, however, is that the customer may not be able to gain access to the router and so cannot use it for firewalling.

## Configure the Router as a Timeserver

Accurate timekeeping on the router is vital when monitoring hosts in the DMZ for crack attempts. If a cracker attempts to break into external hosts, it is much easier to figure out the attack plan when reviewing network server logs if the timestamps in the logs are all coordinated.

Also, many administrators run login script utilities that set host time when the user's computer is logged in to the master fileserver. If the organization has a dedicated Internet connection, one of the fringe benefits is access to the NTP, which provides highly accurate timekeeping. Since accurate time is available, the administrator might as well synchronize the major server clocks to network time on the Internet.

Note that Win95 and WinNT workstations don't need to use NTP to time-synchronize because Microsoft Networking has a provision for network time synchronization. Win95 and WinNT systems can synchronize to a master Windows NT Server with this command run in a command line: `net time \\SERVERNAME /SET /YES`. This command can be run from a batch file in a Win95 startup group, as an *at* job under Windows NT, or in the NT login script if the Windows workstation is logging into an NT domain. However, be aware that this command should be run only once. If you want to maintain continuous NTP time synchronization, run an NTP program on the Windows host.

On the NT server, the time must be synchronized to the router via NTP. A common way of doing this is to run the TimeServ utility that is part of the Windows NT Resource Kit Supplement 4. (NT ResKit Supplement 4 supersedes all previous supplements.) A Web page that explains how to configure TimeServ is located at `http://www.niceties.com/TimeServ.html`. The `net time` command can also synchronize from a FreeBSD server running Samba (see Chapter 7).

Using the set time in the login script is also very useful for installations concerned with Y2K compliance. Generally, most computer operating systems are

Y2K compliant, but a number of BIOSs are not insofar as they could not properly handle the transition from December 31, 1999, to January 1, 2000. As a result, older computers did not retain the correct date setting during reboots. Also, practically every PC made has a non-Y2K-compliant real-time clock (RTC) chip because the RTC chip stores the year with two digits only (the "19" or "20" is added by the BIOS code). By synchronizing the time to a master server that is synced to NTP, you can avoid losing the correct setting every time you reboot.

In addition to the Y2K concerns, many PC clocks drift a small amount, particularly when the BIOS battery ages. In a large network that is date sensitive, many machines may be off by as much as a day.

NTP, detailed in RFC1305, is a system set up to keep accurate time for all hosts on the Internet. In effect it is a distributed timekeeping system. A number of servers on the Internet are designated *stratum 1* servers; they have temperature-controlled atomic clocks connected to their serial ports. *Stratum 2* servers synchronize from the stratum 1 servers. Computers synchronizing from these sources are known as stratum 3 servers, and so on. If every computer on the Internet attempted to synchronize to stratum 1 servers, the network traffic—not to mention server load—would be significant because stratum 1 servers aren't always going to be within a few "hops" of the organization. NTP synchronization is also greatly helped when each synchronization interval has consistent round trip times, which is done by using NTP servers located as few hops away as possible. Typically, an organization connecting to the Internet sets its border router to synchronize from NTP time sources on the Internet that are very close to it, such as the router at the other end of the link to the ISP. Master servers within the organization then synchronize to the router.

Because maintaining synchronized time is particularly important for router management and logging, most ISPs participating with major providers have NTP running on all routers in their networks. An organization connected to the Internet can take advantage of this fact to keep accurate time on all its internal servers. The administrator sets up NTP timeserving on the gateway router, which is then slaved via NTP to other routers that the ISP owns. The gateway router then periodically queries the NTP servers it knows about, compares the results looking for obviously wrong time sources, and updates its clock. The administrator can then set up `cron` jobs that run `ntpdate` on FreeBSD servers (and a good many other systems in the organization), which slave off the gateway router. Under FreeBSD, the following entry in `/etc/crontab` can pull time from a router named `gateway.mydomain.com`.

```
10 * * * * root /usr/sbin/ntpdate -s gateway.mydomain.com
```

The FreeBSD server can also be set up as a NTP server to allow other machines in the internal network to slave their clocks from it. This is done with the `xntpd` program, which cannot be run concurrently with `ntpdate`. In addition to allowing other clients to obtain time from the FreeBSD server, this program also synchronizes the FreeBSD server with its NTP source. `Xntpd` is part of the base FreeBSD distribution, and a Web page on it is located at <u>http://www.ntp.org</u>. To run `xntpd` to synchronize to the PC RTC clock under FreeBSD, use the following `/etc/ntp.conf` file.

```
server 127.127.1.1 prefer
disable pll
```

You must also place these statements in `/etc/rc.conf` to enable `xntpd`:

```
ntpdate_flags="myispstimeserver.myispsdomain.com"
ntpdate_enable="YES"
xntpd_enable="YES"
```

`Xntpd` can also take time from an atomic clock connected to the serial port of the FreeBSD server. Some clocks get time broadcasts from the major radio broadcast time sources and can provide this via serial port. Of course, the PC internal clock can also be used as a time source, but it is not very accurate, although it may suffice to serve as a time source to synchronize time among servers. It is also possible to buy dedicated NTP servers that use global positioning satellite (GPS) signals to provide accurate time and date services. Avoid use of an internal Cisco router clock as a time source; router clocks are notoriously inaccurate.

The easiest way to determine which NTP servers to use is to ask the ISP if it is operating any stratum 1 NTP servers and to provide their IP numbers. Although public NTP servers exist on the Internet, they are extremely busy. If the ISP doesn't run a stratum 1 NTP server, it probably slaves its routers to at least one stratum 1 NTP server on the Internet. Most slave from several stratum 1 NTP servers.

Because network time is a security issue, NTP does have an authentication method that can be turned on; the ISP supplies any keys needed for this if NTP security on their routers is enabled.

The Cisco router's clock must be told what geographical location it is in for NTP to be any good. This can be done with the Cisco configuration commands. The following commands set the time zone to Pacific Standard Time with Daylight Savings.

```
clock timezone PST -8
clock summer-time PDT recurring
```

The router clock itself takes time to synchronize to the NTP time source. Before enabling NTP, set the router's clock to the closest current time with the `clock-set` command. For example, `clock set 22:10:10 23 june 1998` sets the clock to 10:10 PM, June 23, 1998.

If the ISP support person is unable to supply an NTP server IP number, it is a simple matter to figure out an appropriate one by using this method.

**1.** With a FreeBSD system plugged into the router, run several trace-routes to major FTP servers on the Internet, such as `ftp.uu.net` or `ftp.cdrom.com`. This quickly shows the IP numbers of the major routers that the ISP uses. Note the IP numbers of the routers that the traceroute passes through and where they are located in the ISP's router hierarchy. This is sometimes called *discovering the network.*

**2.** Now you need several routers that run NTP in the ISP and are at the same stratum level. Starting with the closest router IP number to your router, run the `ntptrace` command against it. Assuming that NTP is configured on this router, it traces back to a stratum 1 NTP server. Continue running `ntptrace` against the rest of the routers that your traceroute discovered that the ISP owns. `Ntptrace` prints their IP numbers and stratum levels.

**3.** If the router doesn't have NTP configured on it, run `ntptrace` against the next further hop router. Eventually, you run into a router that has NTP running on it, which allows a trace back to a stratum 1 NTP server.

**4.** After comparing the NTP traces it will become obvious how the ISP has internally set up NTP distribution within its network. The same stratum 1 NTP servers show up as the end result in a number of `ntptraces`. Because the ISP usually synchronizes router clocks against each other, most of their routers trace back to the same few stratum 1 NTP servers.

**5.** With this information it's possible to select the NTP servers that the gateway router will use. For a Cisco router to have a stable NTP configuration it should have a minimum of two NTP sources at the same stratum level. Cisco routers are somewhat protective of their internal clocks. If the router receives an NTP packet from its only NTP source saying that the router's clock is off, the router may decide that the external time source is insane, if the discrepancy is great enough, and refuse to maintain synchronization.

All NTP servers listed in the router must be from the same stratum level. The router ignores NTP time from any routers at lower stratum levels than the rest of the listed NTP sources. For even better accuracy, the NTP servers should trace back to different stratum 1 NTP servers.

**6.** From the group of NTP servers selected, run traceroutes to them and note the number of hops to the NTP sources. Find the source closest to your router (fewest hops away); this is your router's preferred NTP server.

Once the preferred NTP server IP number is located, the router can be slaved to it with the following configuration setting.

```
ntp server X.X.X.X source e0 prefer
```

The rest of the NTP servers that have been chosen can be added with the commands

```
ntp server X.X.X.X source e0
ntp server X.X.X.X source e0
ntp server X.X.X.X source e0
.
.
.
etc.
```

Run the `show ntp association detail` command. This displays a bunch of information on the NTP sources. Make sure that the keyword *sane* is in the output of each server and that the time and date are correct.

In any access lists in the router, the NTP port must be open to synchronize NTP, such as with the following statement.

```
access-list 101 permit udp any any eq ntp
```

### Miscellaneous Cisco Setup

When setting up a Cisco as the external gateway router, an administrator needs to do several things. Consult the router manual at http://www.cisco.com; first, however, review the following miscellaneous items.

- *Set up the first- and second-level passwords.* Do this in conjunction with the consultant or ISP, particularly if one of them will be responsible for the router management in the future. Before the person helping with the router setup leaves, make absolutely sure that you have both standard and enabled passwords for the router.

Cisco has a procedure for resetting lost passwords that involves using a serial terminal on the console port that is capable of sending a Break signal. Many PC terminal programs cannot do this, it's much easier to get the proper passwords to begin with. The procedure is different for different models of routers.

- *Set up DNS.* A simple command sets up DNS. If the DNS server IP number is 12.23.45.67, the line would be `ip name-server 12.23.45.67`.

- *Set up a `syslog` server (typically on the firewall).* For attack events on the router to be made known to the administrator, syslogging must be set up. Typically, the interior firewall server runs a `syslog` daemon that logs events to the administrator. Logging can occur via e-mail, console messages, or filters. For example, e-mail messages can also be sent to scripts that dial pager numbers.

Allowing external `syslog` messages to be accepted on the firewall is very dangerous; the firewall should never be configured to accept `syslog` messages from any host other than the external router. See the manual page for `syslogd` and `syslog.conf` for the exact syntax to use under FreeBSD. Depending on the version of `syslogd`, different command-line options must be used. For example, under FreeBSD 2.2.6 and later, `/etc/rc.conf` must be modified to specify the hosts allowed to send `syslog` messages. If the router's IP address is 192.168.1.1, `syslogd_flags="-a 192.168.1.1"`.

The `/etc/syslog.conf` file must also be modified. As an example, this `syslog.conf` line defines the default Cisco router facility to be logged to the `syslog` host's console: `local7.info    /dev/console`. Add this line to the `syslog.conf` file right after the `cron.*` line.

- *Set up syslogging.* If the selected `syslog` server host had an IP number of 192.168.1.1, logging on the router can be enabled with these commands:

```
logging 192.168.1.1
logging trap informational
service timestamps log datetime
```

Logging should be set to be informational or debugging to record access list violations. Access lists must be of the extended type to log. (See the Cisco documentation for the current range of access list numbers needed to designate the list as extended.) The default facility for logging on a Cisco router is `local7`. If this is changed on the router, it must also be changed on the `syslog` server.

It is advisable to block incoming `syslog` traffic from the Internet directed to either the gateway router or the interior firewall host. For example, an "in" access list on the serial interface for a gateway router numbered 192.168.1.1 and an interior firewall host numbered 192.168.1.2 might contain

```
access-list 101 deny udp any host 192.168.1.1 eq syslog
access list 101 deny udp any host 192.168.1.2 eq syslog
```

- *Set up traffic monitoring via SNMP.* It is very useful to turn on the SNMP service on the router, so that a management console located on the inside network may query traffic statistics from the router. Cisco routers have this service off by default. The following configuration example can be used to turn it on.

```
snmp-server community public RO
snmp-server community private RW
snmp-server location Organization Headquarters
snmp-server contact Administrators Name
```

It is also advisable to block external access to SNMP (port 161) with an access list entry. If it isn't blocked already, SNMP security is usually weak.

- *Flash router to firewall code.* If possible, flash the router to the "firewall" version of Cisco IOS and build a firewall access list specifically for this revision. As of this writing, the Firewall IOS Feature Set for an IP Only Cisco 2501 router costs approximately $1,200 retail. This is a bargain, considering the costs of standalone commercial firewalls, which offer no better security than Firewall

IOS and are considerably more complicated. If you're in an environment that requires a commercial firewall, the Cisco IOS FW may meet the requirements.

### *Cisco Access Lists*

Adding an access list to a Cisco router is simple. Typically, the access list installed is an "in" (incoming) list, which means that packets external to the router traveling into the router on the selected interface are matched against the access list. Generally, gateway routers (routers used to connect to the Internet) have an extensive, tight access list installed on the serial interface because this interface is usually connected to the ISP. They have a much smaller access list on the Ethernet interface, which is usually connected to the inside network.

Often, access lists on gateway routers that are managed by the ISP have lists built on the "out" interfaces. These lists are constructed inversely from those on the "in" interfaces, but they function identically. The advantage of "out" interface access lists is that a mistake in the access list does not accidentally lock the ISP out of the router.

An overview of Cisco access lists is available at `http://www.network computing.com/907/907ws1.html`. Documentation of Cisco access lists is also available online from Cisco. Even if you don't have a Cisco router, the lists are similar enough that the same ideas discussed in the Cisco documentation can be applied to `ipfw` rulesets running on the FreeBSD server. Go to the root of the Cisco Web site at `http://www.cisco.com` and select "Service & Support," then select "Cisco Documentation"; this gets you to the root of the IOS documentation CD. Select "Cisco IOS Software Configuration," then choose an IOS, the IOS Configuration Guides, and Command References. Select "Security Configuration Guide" and then "Traffic Filtering" to work down to the access list documentation. Another URL for the access list documentation is located at `http://www.cisco.com/univercd/cc/td/doc/cisintwk/ics/cs003.htm`.

An access list installed on the organization's router has one big drawback—it blocks packets only after they have traveled down the serial connection from the ISP. (This is also true of any firewall located on customer premises.) Thus, there are two things that an access list cannot do.

1. It cannot block denial-of-service attacks, such as smurf or ping-of-death attacks. These attacks work by flooding the serial connection to the point where legitimate traffic cannot travel on it.
2. It cannot prioritize traffic. For example, if the administrator wishes to prioritize traffic from the Internet so that incoming SMTP traffic is always passed down the serial connection ahead of RealAudio traffic,

it cannot be done at the customer site. This is true even though current Cisco IOS can prioritize and shape traffic. It *is* possible to shape outbound traffic from the customer site, for example, if the organization is running a busy Web server.

Both of these tasks can be done by the ISP on its router; ask about it when negotiating an Internet connection. Usually, smaller, local ISPs are more flexible about this; larger ISPs may have a policy against it. UUNET, for example, does not shape traffic or filter anything other than Ping packets and applies filters only during an attack on the customer.

To apply an access list numbered `101` to serial interface 1, the configuration command is

```
in s0
ip access-group 101 in
exit
```

When installing the access list on the serial interface, if the router is running IP-unnumbered on the serial connection (quite common), the list must be installed on the sub-interface (e.g., **s0.1**, **s0.2**).

**A Serial Interface Access List**   The following example is an access list applied to an external serial interface, which is running IP-Unnumbered. The Ethernet interface on the router has an IP number of `200.199.198.225` and is part of a subnetted Class C network with a network address of `200.199.198.224`. This production access list shows a number of tricks in use. Explanations of the lines are between each grouping.

```
access-list 101 permit tcp any any established
access-list 101 deny ip 200.199.198.0 0.0.0.224 0.0.0.0 255.255.255.224
access-list 101 permit icmp any any
```

The keyword *established* is used only for the TCP to indicate an established connection. A match occurs if the TCP datagram has the ACK or RST bits set, which indicates that the packet belongs to an existing connection. Thus, the first line is for the *return* packets of a TCP connection. The second line blocks *spoofed* IP packets. The third line allows all types of ICMP. Although ICMP can be blocked based on type, doing so may interfere with MTU path discovery and render the connection to the Internet useless.

```
access-list 101 permit udp any host 200.199.198.225 eq ntp
```

This line is required if the router is to synchronize its clock to NTP servers on the Internet.

```
access-list 101 permit tcp any host 200.199.198.226 eq smtp
access-list 101 permit tcp any host 200.199.198.226 eq domain
access-list 101 permit udp any host 200.199.198.226 eq domain
access-list 101 permit tcp any host 200.199.198.226 eq pop3
access-list 101 permit tcp any host 200.199.198.226 range 1024 4999
access-list 101 permit tcp any host 200.199.198.226 gt 30000
access-list 101 permit udp any host 200.199.198.226 gt 1023
```

The machine located at .226 is both a mailserver and nameserver, allowing incoming POP3 requests, SMTP, and DNS queries. It is also the interior firewall and has NAT running on it. The *permit* for the range of ports between 1,024 and 4,999 and for the ports greater than 30,000 allows active FTP, which does not open a return port under the established rule. The *greater than* permit for UDP ports above 1,023 is to allow return traffic for UDP-based applications, such as DNS queries against other nameservers. Return packets for TCP-based applications are covered by the *established* line earlier.

```
access-list 101 permit tcp any host 200.199.198.227 eq www
access-list 101 permit tcp any host 200.199.198.227 eq ftp
access-list 101 permit tcp any host 200.199.198.227 eq ftp-data
```

The machine at .227 is a combination Web and FTP server.

```
access-list 101 permit tcp any host 200.199.198.230 eq www
```

The machine at .230 is a Web server.

```
access-list 101 deny tcp any any eq ident
```

A number of mailservers automatically attempt to run ident before delivering an SMTP mail item; this line keeps these benign ident attempts out of the logs.

```
access-list 101 deny icmp any any log
access-list 101 deny tcp any any log
access-list 101 deny udp any any log
access-list 101 deny ip any any log
```

These four entries are *tripwires* protecting the router, mailserver, and Web servers listed above. The hosts are located in the external DMZ network. Crackers often attempt to Telnet or FTP into hosts they are trying to crack. The *log* keywords send notifications via syslog in the event that the router has to block these kinds of cracks.

**An Ethernet Interface Access List**   The following example is an access list applied to the inside Ethernet interface of a router.

```
access-list 102 deny    udp host 200.199.198.226 any eq netbios-ns
access-list 102 deny    udp host 200.199.198.226 any eq netbios-dgm
```

Because .226 is the outside end of a NAT, misguided Windows NT Servers on the inside network may sometimes attempt to broadcast WINS and other packets through the external gateway. These lines keep this kind of junk out of the logs.

```
access-list 102 deny udp host 200.199.198.232 host 200.199.198.255
access-list 102 deny udp host 200.199.198.233 host 200.199.198.255
access-list 102 deny udp host 200.199.198.236 host 200.199.198.255
```

The machines .232, .233, and .236 are Windows NT Servers located in the DMZ. These entries are broadcast blockers; NT servers and workstations all produce broadcast packets as a normal part of their browse handling. These entries keep this activity out of the logs.

```
access-list 102 permit udp host 200.199.198.232 any log
access-list 102 permit udp host 200.199.198.232 any log
access-list 102 permit udp host 200.199.198.232 any log
```

We are very interested in unicast UDP transmissions originating from the NT servers inside the DMZ—there shouldn't be any since these servers are not supposed to be filesharing. This rule is a way of looking for attack attempt traffic.

```
access-list 102 permit tcp host 200.199.198.226 any eq smtp
access-list 102 deny tcp any any eq smtp log
```

These lines allow the mailserver on the inside to send out e-mail and block any other server located in the DMZ from transmitting e-mail directly to the Internet. If these machines must be able to send mail, they should be configured to spool mail through the master mailserver. This primarily antispam configuration prevents any buggy and open SMTP mail implementations on machines in the DMZ from being hijacked by spammers. Since these rules force mail to be relayed through the master mailserver, that server can be spam-proofed much more easily.

```
access-list 102 permit tcp host 200.199.198.226 host 200.199.198.225
            eq telnet
access-list 102 deny tcp any host 200.199.198.225 eq telnet
```

This rule pair blocks all hosts in the DMZ from Telnetting into the router.

```
access-list 102 permit ip any any
```

This is the final catch-all rule that passes everything not already blocked.

### *Reflexive Cisco Access Lists and the IOS Firewall*

Application firewall vendors often say in their literature that packet-filtering firewalls are inherently unsafe and that *in some circumstances* packets can go through them. Of course, fear is a big motivator for buying firewalls. Additionally, at a large UNIX conference several years ago, a demonstration of filter cracking was shown that depended on the access list passing IP fragments with an offset of 1—fragments that have no use in normal TCP/IP other than cracking firewalls. No modern access list implementations pass these kinds of packets today. However, in recent years a number of denial-of-service crack attacks have been created to exploit a hole in the established rule, which allows the *return* packets of a TCP connection to come back inside, and under a normal access list, it is required. These attacks are known as *ACK flooding* or *RST attacks*. To remove the requirement for the established rule, Cisco began developing a new type of access list known as a *reflexive* access list. Reflexive lists dynamically configure TCP connection requests and allow the broad established rules to be removed. However, this kind of access filter is still limited because it cannot deal with applications that use port numbers that change during a session.

Because of the issues with applications, such as FTP, Cisco developed an addition to their router IOS called the *Firewall IOS*. This IOS contains filters that understand multichannel protocols. It is available only for some platforms, such as the 2500 series routers. Instructions on using the Firewall IOS are located at http://www.cisco.com/univercd/cc/td/doc/product/software/ios112/ios112p/firewall.htm.

Following is an example of a Cisco configuration that would be used on an IOS Firewall router.

```
!
ip inspect name myfw ftp timeout 3600
ip inspect name myfw http java-list 51 timeout 3600
ip inspect name myfw smtp timeout 3600
ip inspect name myfw udp timeout 15
ip inspect name myfw tcp timeout 3600
!
interface Ethernet0/0
ip address 12.43.45.67 255.0.0.0
ip inspect myfw in
!
access-list 51 deny 192.154.34.6
access-list 51 permit any
access-list 51 deny any
!
```

Note the mixture of regular non-IOS/FW access lists with the special inspection statements used with Firewall.

## The Security Attitude

It has been said that the price of peace is eternal vigilance, which means that trouble will come if the people and processes that prevent war become lax. This is as true of an Internet connection as it is in war. An organization may connect to the Internet, set up all the filtering and procedures needed to ensure its safety, and become impregnable. Six months later, however, a program may be developed and circulated on the Internet that exploits a weakness of the software the organization is using—and it gets cracked. It is simply impossible to produce software that is totally unexploitable, whether it's produced by the free software community or by a commercial developer. It is only really possible to produce software that is not exploitable by any currently known methods of exploitation or by currently available computer hardware.

New cracking tools have been developed and will continue to be developed. The rapidly increasing speed and power of computer hardware also makes some attack methods feasible that wouldn't be on slower hardware. In addition, the rapid entrance of commercial software organizations into the Internet market has released a flood of new Internet application programs. Most of these client and server pieces of software do not have the extensive history that the existing applications have and are fruitful territory for the cracker to operate in. To protect the organization, it is necessary to keep one step ahead of the cracking community.

## Security Tasks

Many larger companies with extensive assets and networks hire a person whose sole responsibility is to see to it that the company's network is as resistant as possible to unauthorized intrusion by a cracker. A small organization wouldn't have a network large enough to hire a separate person for this function, but it can still benefit if the administrator does some of the same things that a security officer would do. Some of the important tasks that the administrator can do are these.

■ Maintain current revisions of software on all servers and devices that are *exposed* to the Internet. This is a double-edged sword. On one hand, new versions are often the only means to patch security weaknesses, but on the other hand, security holes can be introduced in new software. Of course, an older version that is known to be insecure is always worse than a new version that might be insecure.

■ Take advantage of all security options on devices exposed to the Internet. They can range from simple things, such as adding passwords to the routers and all login accounts on external hosts, to upgrading router firmware to the Firewall IOS and rewriting access lists.

- Frequent the Usenet news groups that discuss security, and subscribe to the Internet mailing lists, such as the Firewalls list and the CERT notification list, that discuss cracks.

- Run cracking tools, such as SATAN, against the organization's network to become familiar with how crackers use these tools to break into networks.

- Maintain good password control. Password management is tricky and is something of a political issue. Passwords proliferate rapidly (it seems like practically every network device needs them) and many passwords, such as BIOS passwords, aren't used much. The unwary administrator who assigns different passwords to every device on the network ends up with devices having unknown passwords. A common trick is for the administrator to maintain a public administrative password and a private serviceman's password. The public administrative password goes onto the visible systems, such as the root user account on the main mailserver, and pressure from upper management and other do-gooders in the organization to share the password is high. The serviceman's password goes onto all other network devices, such as routers, printservers, data service units (DSUs), SNMP devices, network hubs, and phone systems to which general company employees don't need access. Having two passwords means that as people who have had access to the high-profile passwords leave the company and force a password change, the administrator only has to change a few systems. The service password should be buried in the general IS documentation; that way, if the administrator is killed in a car wreck or other misfortune, the critical systems in the organization won't be damaged by ignorant, well-meaning employees until a new, competent administrator can be hired.

Always consider the security implications of anything done on any part of the network that is in contact with the Internet. In security planning, a good question to ask is, "What can be done to wreck this system?" when new networking changes are made to the Internet connection. A good way to invite disaster is to look only for ways to make the system work. Crackers look for ways to make the system break, and they find them unless the administrator has thought of them first.

## PROXY SERVING AND IP ADDRESS TRANSLATION

Due to the possibility of forced renumbering, security considerations, and the shortage of IP numbers, most organizations that connect their internal networks to the Internet do not use routable IP numbers on their internal networks. Instead, they use older proxy servers or a newer idea of NAT, that is sometimes referred to as *transparent proxying*. Proxy servers and NATs are used for several reasons.

- They provide for IP number address conservation, which also allows the organization to easily switch ISP's without a renumber.
- They allow internal networks to use standard (classful) subnet masks instead of having to split up a legal subnet in tricky ways.
- They can provide firewalling, although packet filtering on the router can also provide this (better, in some cases).
- Caching proxies can, in some circumstances, save network bandwidth.

With a proxy server in use, the organization normally uses internal TCP/IP network numbers from the InterNIC-specified, RFC-unassigned IP number range per RFC1918 (Figure 5.5). Use of these number blocks doesn't require registration with IANA. Per the RFC, IANA has reserved the following three blocks of the IP address space for private internets:

10.0.0.0       10.255.255.255 (10/8 prefix)
172.16.0.0      172.31.255.255 (172.16/12 prefix)
192.168.0.0      192.168.255.255 (192.168/16 prefix)

These subnet numbers are not allowed to be routed on the Internet; thus, there will never be a situation in which any host that is accessible on the Internet is assigned an IP number from these ranges. Of course, this also makes it impossible for an organization using these numbers to use a simple router to connect to the Internet. Instead, organizations using these numbers internally must use a proxy server of some kind or use NAT.

It is possible to use internal legal subnet IP numbers with a proxy or NAT. This sometimes happens when an organization starts out with legal subnets and

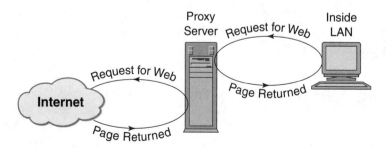

**Figure 5.5**  Routing via a proxy server

later decides to give them up and doesn't want to renumber. If another group on the Internet is later assigned the legal subnet that the proxying organization is using internally, its servers would normally be unreachable. Cisco has a special configuration for NAT on its routers that can get around this problem.

In the most typical Internet installation, the ISP assigns a small, legal set of IP numbers, such as an eighth of a Class C subnet (CIDR block notation /27), to the organization that wants to connect to the Internet. The IP numbers are used on the organization's gateway router and on a small network that exists between the gateway router and the organization's internal net. However, it is quite possible for a small organization that is using a low-speed Internet connection, such as an ISDN or multilink PPP modem, to use only a single legal IP number. In that case the FreeBSD server acts as the router and also runs the NAT or proxy right on the same server.

In these cases, if the organization is *really* cash-strapped, it might be able to use a standard individual dialup modem account with a dial-on-demand ISP account to provide Web surfing access only to its internal users. Naturally, ISPs in general attempt to detect and discourage this activity. Of course, throughput is limited to the speed of the modem. If four people surf the Internet at the same time, they are effectively getting a bandwidth of 7Kbps (28.8K divided by 4). In a small office, if it is rare that several people will surf simultaneously, it won't be an issue.

There are two general kinds of proxy servers: SOCKS5 and HTTP caching. It is quite possible to run both HTTP caching and a SOCKS5 proxy on the same server; NATs generally all work the same.

## SOCKS5 Proxies

SOCKS5 proxy servers were one of the first network schemes to use RFC-unassigned numbers. Because they are older than NAT they have a number of drawbacks compared to it, but since they are older they are much more widely used. I call this phenomenon the comfort factor. Proxy servers based on SOCKS5 handle most TCP/IPs, such as Web, news, Telnet, and FTP. With a SOCKS5 proxy server, a program known as *SocksCap* is run on the client machine. Different versions of SocksCap are available for different platforms, including WinNT. See the page at http://www.socks.nec.com/ for information on them.

SOCKS5 proxy servers operate by the TCP/IP client network stack, in this case SocksCap, encapsulating all network activity on the client that is directed to the Internet and sending it to the server. The server then performs the desired network action, such as fetching the Web page or establishing the Telnet connection, and then encapsulates the result and returns it to the client. The SOCKS5 protocol is used to communicate from the client to the server. This is purely a network proxy, it does not save a copy of requested data.

The FreeBSD SOCKS5 server is not available as a precompiled binary, but it is available in the Ports directory of the CD. During FreeBSD installation, the *Ports* option should be selected to get access to this software. Normally, all that is needed is to run `make` in its directory. The installer then FTPs the file needed, patches it, compiles it, and copies it to the appropriate directories. Unfortunately, the SOCKS5 port on FreeBSD 2.X was done with release 9 of the SOCKS5 server, which is no longer available, so this does not work. Instead, the current release of the SOCKS5 server (`SOCKS5-v1.0r10.tar.gz`) should be retrieved from the Internet at `http://www.socks.nec.com/cgi-bin/download.pl`. This server is currently sponsored by NEC (don't bother calling NEC about it because they won't know what you are talking about), and it has a noncommercial license restriction listed on the Web site.

The thrust of the restriction is that although a commercial enterprise may use the SOCKS5 server if it wishes, the server is restricted to internal business use only. (How they get away with labeling *internal business use* a noncommercial use is beyond me, but read the license and marvel.) Basically, this means that a business cannot download the server, compile it, and sell the compiled version or charge people for the use of the server. It is also safe to interpret this to mean that a person, such as a consultant, cannot charge for the service of downloading the server and compiling it for some other organization, which pretty much means that it cannot be included in other software for commercial sale. To put it succinctly, if an organization's administrator cannot figure out how to follow the relatively simple instructions in the server package, NEC would prefer that they buy a commercial server.

The `SocksCap` client program is also available from the NEC Web site. To use it with an operating server, the administrator downloads it, extracts it, and then copies the files to any convenient shared directory on the network for the clients to access. From the client, the administrator runs the setup program that installs the `SocksCap` client program (see Exhibits 5.2 and 5.3). Then, under the Win95 version, the administrator creates a profile for each network application that uses the Internet. Finally, the administrator creates a shortcut, which has the `SocksCap` program on the command line followed by the profile name. When the user clicks on the shortcut, this starts `SocksCap`, which then starts the Internet application, such as Telnet or a newsreader. If the administrator prefers, he or she can create `SocksCap` entries for the Web browsers on the clients instead of using an HTTP proxy; however the SOCKS5 server won't cache pages.

### Exhibit 5.2  Installing SOCKS5 under FreeBSD 3.4 and earlier

1. Make sure that the Ports directories are installed for SOCKS5. Check that the directory `/usr/ports/net/socks5` exists.

2. Using a Web browser, such as Lynx or Netscape, retrieve the `socks5-v1.0r10.tar.gz` package from http://www.socks.nec.com, and place it into `/usr/ports/distfiles`.

3. Go into the `/usr/ports/net/socks5` directory and copy `Makefile` to `Makefile.backup`. The Ports directory must have been installed on the FreeBSD system during installation.

4. Edit `Makefile` and change the DISTNAME to `socks5-v1.0.r10` and the PKGNAME to "socks5-1.0.10." Make WRKSRC point to `${WRKDIR}/socks5-v1.0.r10`.

5. Build the package by typing `make NO_CHECKSUM=yes`.

6. Install the package by typing `make NO_CHECKSUM=yes install`.

7. `cd` into the `work/socks5-v1.0r10/examples` directory and copy the `socks5.conf.dualhomed` file to `/etc/socks5.conf`.

8. Edit the `socks5.conf` file and change the route statement to the correct IP subnet number for the outside legal IP network.

9. Run the `/usr/local/bin/socks5` command, which should start the server. Do a `ps -ax` listing to verify that the server is running.

10. In the `/usr/local/etc/rc.d` directory, create the `socks5.sh` shell script with the following lines.
```
#!/bin/sh
[ -x /usr/local/bin/socks5 ] && /usr/local/bin/socks5 && echo -n
    ' socks5'
```

11. Install `SocksCap` on a client machine. Create a Telnet entry in it for the Windows Telnet program and an icon for it as described before. The defaults for `SocksCap` are the server IP number, port 1080, and the nobody user ID.

12. Test the server by running the Telnet program on a client with `SocksCap` loaded and Telnetting into a convenient host on the Internet.

## HTTP Proxies

HTTP proxy servers have an advantage over SOCKS5 proxies because they provide caching of frequently requested Web pages. The disadvantage is that they only support HTTP and not protocols such as Telnet. These proxy servers also may reduce the amount of traffic that the organization must pull from its Internet connection.

**Exhibit 5.3  Installing SOCKS5 under FreeBSD 3.5 and later**

1. Make sure that the Ports directories are installed for SOCKS5. Check that the directory `/usr/ports/net/socks5` exists.

2. Using a Web browser, such as Lynx or Netscape, retrieve the `socks5-v1.0r10.tar.gz` package from `http://www.socks.nec.com`, and place it into `/usr/ports/distfiles`.

3. Go into the `/usr/ports/net/socks5` directory and build the package by typing `make`.

4. Install the package by typing `make install`.

5. Change the working directory into the `work/socks5-v1.0r10/examples` directory and copy the `socks5.conf.dualhomed` file to `/etc/socks5.conf`.

6. Edit the `socks5.conf` file and change the route statement to the correct IP subnet number for the outside legal IP network.

7. Run the `/usr/local/bin/socks5` command, which should start the server. Do a `ps -ax` listing to verify that the server is running.

8. In the `/usr/local/etc/rc.d` directory, create the `socks5.sh` shell script with the following lines.
   ```
   #!/bin/sh
   [ -x /usr/local/bin/socks5 ] && /usr/local/bin/socks5 && echo -n
       ' socks5'
   ```

9. Install `SocksCap` on a client machine. Create a Telnet entry in it for the Windows Telnet program, and an icon for it. The defaults for `SocksCap` are the server IP number, port 1080, and user ID nobody.

10. Test the server by running the Telnet program on the client with `SocksCap` loaded and Telnetting into a convenient host on the Internet.

---

HTTP proxy servers operate by the TCP/IP application—in this case the Web browser—encapsulating all network activity on the client that is directed to the Internet and sending this activity to the server. The server performs the desired network action (e.g., fetching a Web page), encapsulates the result, and returns it to the client. Standard Web commands are used for the HTTP proxy server. Since the Web page is copied to a cache directory on the server, it is available for any later requests by other Web browsers that may want a copy of the page.

Under FreeBSD, the Squid proxy server is a popular implementation and is like the kind of server used in the Microsoft proxy server for WinNT. Since this server only supports HTTP, it is of little interest outside of Web browsers, so an equivalent to `SocksCap` is not used. Instead, Web browsers have direct HTTP proxy support compiled into the browser program.

To use FreeBSD as an HTTP proxy server, the Squid caching server is run on the machine. The Squid server is available from the FreeBSD CD-ROM as a precompiled server package. It is very easy to install, with one caveat: it should not be installed from the administration utility /stand/sysinstall. The installation spawns an editor to edit the squid.conf file, and /stand/ sysinstall hangs at this point. Instead, the Squid tgz file is copied directly to a staging area, and the pkg_add utility is run against it from the command line. Squid can also be built in the Ports directories.

Exhibit 5.4 lists the installation instructions for the HTTP proxy server; they assume that the administrator is starting with a FreeBSD 2.2.8 machine

**Exhibit 5.4  Installing Squid**

1. Mount the FreeBSD 2.2.8 CD-ROM onto the directory /cdrom with the mount -r -t cd9660 /dev/cd0a /cdrom command (assuming a SCSI CD-ROM).

2. Create the directory /usr/ports/distfiles. Copy the Squid package to it with the cp/cdrom/packages/All/squid-1.1.22.tgz/usr/ports/distfiles command. Alternatively, the package can be sent via FTP from ftp://ftp.cdrom.com/ pub/FreeBSD/ports/packages/All/squid-1.1.22.tgz.

3. Install the package with the pkg_add -v /usr/ports/distfiles/squid-1.1. 22.tgz command. Near the end of the installation, the installer spawns an editor to edit the /usr/local/etc/squid/squid.conf file. The editor is either Emacs or vi, depending on the setting of the EDITOR variable in your profile.

4. The squid.conf file is extensively documented, so a careful reading should be enough to figure out what variables you need to modify. Pay particular attention to the caching directories because the server creates and deletes a large number of files on them. Make sure there is adequate space on the filesystem to which these directories point. Leaving several gigabytes free is not too much; even better is an entirely separate hard drive. Smaller amounts work, but they don't utilize the cache as well. Note the http_port number, which you will need later.

5. The server installation program puts a startup file in /usr/local/etc/rc.d so that the next time the machine is rebooted, the server will start up. Before doing this, set the permissions on the server directory correctly with the chown -R nobody.nogroup/ usr/local/squid/ command followed by chmod -R 775 /usr/local/squid. Otherwise, the server emits numerous error messages on startup and won't work. Because this is where the HTTP cache will be, it should have many megabytes of free drive space.

6. Test the server from a client running Netscape or Microsoft Internet Explorer by checking the connect through proxy boxes under Options and enter the proxy server IP number (the internal number, not the external number) and the proxy port number listed in the http_port entry after rebooting the server.

that is directly connected to the Internet via PPP or a network card connected to a router, with DNS services available. Versions later than 2.2.8 work the same. It should be possible to ping an Internet name, such as `ftp.uu.net`, from this machine at this point. The machine should have an Ethernet card plugged into the internal network and assigned an IP number. Routing should *not* be turned on, and all operations are done from the console as the root user.

Use of HTTP caching proxy servers in a large organization can become chancy. On one hand, as more users make Web requests it becomes more likely that a duplicate request can be satisfied from the cache. On the other hand, as the volume of requests increases, the proxy server is more likely to be over-whelmed. It can become impossible to add enough hard drive and memory space to the proxy for it to operate efficiently. Eventually, the cache runs out of space and starts discarding, and as the discard rate rises the caching proxy can become no better than a straight wire connection. Worse, since every concur-rent connection creates an additional process on the proxy, each process must use the hard drive I/O. Once the drive channel is saturated, the caching proxy server becomes a bottleneck.

One way to speed up a pure caching proxy is to recompile the kernel with maxuser set to 100, turn off failsave, and mount the cache directory asynchro-nously. Turning off failsave results in corrupted files if the server crashes, but since the files are probably going to be in the cache they will just reload again. Raising maxusers raises the maximum number of open files.

## Network Address Translation

Network Address Translation is sometimes referred to as transparent proxying, IP address overloading, or IP masquerading (Figure 5.6). The principles of NAT are detailed in the informational RFC1631. NAT is the more advanced method of proxying RFC-unassigned IP address subnets behind legal subnets connected to the Internet. It can also be used to translate between two sets of legal IP numbers, but this can create special problems. NAT is much easier to administer than a proxy because it removes the requirement for dealing with icky proxy configuration on each client. NATs are also much faster and are eas-ily capable of handling network traffic for thousands of simultaneous users.

Simplistically, an NAT works by routing between a large *range* of IP num-bers to either a *single* IP number or a smaller range. In use, the large range is typically numbered from RFC1918 and is located on an organization's internal network. The single IP number or smaller range, by contrast, is a legal set of numbers and is located on the outside network. From the inside looking out, the machines can access any host on the Internet directly, whereas from outside it appears that all inbound and outbound TCP/IP traffic is originating from the

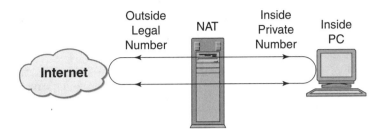

**Figure 5.6** Basics of NAT proxying

single valid IP number on the NAT, or a range of numbers. In essence, the NAT is a special kind of IP routing device.

An NAT operates by setting up an internal translation table of all the inside IP numbers that are sending packets through it. Next, it sets up a table of port numbers to use on the external address. When a packet from the inside is sent to the NAT to be delivered to a host outside, the NAT does several things. First, it makes an entry in the translation table of the source IP number and source port number, and then it replaces the source TCP/IP number of the packet with its external valid TCP/IP number. It assigns a specific port number to the outgoing packet, enters that into the translation table, and replaces the source port number with this.

When the response packet comes back to the NAT, it checks the destination port number in it. If this matches the specifically assigned source port number, the NAT checks to see which inside machine TCP/IP address number was assigned this port number. When it finds a match, it rewrites the destination port number and TCP/IP number with the original source address and port number used for the packet on the inside that initiated the connection. Then it transmits this packet to the inside host it is intended for. It maintains the translation table entries for as long as the connection is open.

Let's look at a routing example to see how a NAT modifies the process of routing. An administrator runs a Web server on the first machine, which has an IP number of 208.45.6.3. This system is located on a network with a router that connects it to the Internet. The router has two interfaces, the first connected to the hub that the machine is plugged into, with an IP number of 208.45.6.1. The second interface is connected to the administrator's ISP.

A user on a second machine points a Web browser to the Web server running on the first computer. The user's machine has an IP number of 192.168.1.8, and it is connected to a network behind an NAT plugged into a router that is plugged into an ISP. This router has an interface plugged into the hub to which the outside interface of the NAT is plugged, and the router interface has an IP number of

199.5.6.1 The NAT's interface connected to the router's hub is numbered 199.5.6.2, and the NAT's interface connected to the network that the internal machine is on is numbered 192.168.1.1

The Web browser on the user's machine causes the IP stack to start the process of transmitting a packet to machine 208.45.6.3. The IP stack first creates a *user return port* of 3456. This is used as a receptacle for the IP packets that come in response to the initial connection request. Then, the IP stack creates an outgoing packet with the following information.

Source port number: 3456
Destination port number: 80 (these are located in `/etc/services`)
Source IP number: 192.168.1.8
Destination IP number: 208.45.6.3

The IP stack on 192.168.1.8 then sends the packet to the default gateway. The network administrator has set up this gateway to be the NAT at 192.168.1.1. The NAT then rewrites the packet and sends out its other interface, 199.5.6.2, to the router at 199.5.6.1, which then forwards the packet through its connection to the ISP. The NAT rewrites the packet so that it has the following information:

Source port number: 9999 (assigned by the NAT)
Destination port number: 80 (these are located in `/etc/services`)
Source IP number: 199.5.6.2
Destination IP number: 208.45.6.3

The ISP the router is connected to then passes the packet to the ISP of the first machine on which the Web server is located. That ISP then passes the packet to the router located at 208.45.6.1, which forwards the packet to host 208.45.6.3. When the Web server on 208.45.6.3 gets the packet on port 80, it spins off a separate process that creates its own return port of 2323 and creates a connection response packet with the following information.

Source port number: 2323
Destination port number: 9999
Source IP number: 208.45.6.3
Destination IP number: 199.5.6.2

This Web server checks to see if 199.5.6.2 is local. It isn't local, so the Web server sends the packet to its default gateway—208.45.6.1—which sends it on to the ISP. The ISP eventually routes it back down to the router at 199.5.6.1, which forwards it to the NAT at 199.5.6.2. The NAT "sees" the incoming packet to port 9999 and checks its table to see if that port is in the translated IP number table. The port is in the IP number table, so the NAT rewrites the incoming packet with the following information.

Source port number: 2323
Destination port number: 3456
Source IP number: 208.45.6.3
Destination IP number: 192.168.1.8

Once the user's machine at 192.168.1.8 has the packet, it knows that a two-way connection has been established, and both systems can then begin transmitting data. The NAT transparently rewrites the source and destination port and IP numbers for each packet in the datastream between 192.168.1.8 and 208.45.6.3.

This is a very simplified example. Some communication protocols, such as FTP, negotiate port numbers in the protocol itself, not the packet header. Others, including some UDP applications such as Microsoft's WINS, use only a single port number or embed the source IP address in the data payload of the packet. NAT implementations for these TCP/IPs must use *helper applications* that reach into the protocol and pick out the appropriate port numbers.

NATs produce a very useful by-product—properly written, they make it very difficult for a cracker coming from the Internet to mount any kind of direct attack on any systems inside the organization's network. An intruder must obtain access to the NAT itself before attacking machines inside the organization. However, while the inside network may be protected, it is still necessary to implement packet filtering and other security measures on the NAT machine itself. It's also important to filter out nonessential protocols, such as the NetBIOS filesharing protocol, because if a host on the inside network establishes a TCP connection to a cracker's machine, that system can reach through the NAT via the open connection.

Under FreeBSD, NAT is implemented as a `daemon` program that is installed when the OS is installed. Because work is always being done on this program, more current versions can be obtained by anonymous FTP—and these should be obtained after the initial proofing is done with the supplied version. The FreeBSD user-mode PPP program also has an IP masquerading option that performs NAT. It can be turned on if the organization is using the FreeBSD server as a permanent dialup-to-Ethernet PPP router.

Chapter 4 covers setting up user-mode PPP. This topic is also covered thoroughly in the system manual pages for PPP, which should be selected during the FreeBSD install. In short, get PPP running first, and then make sure that the system is configured as a router (`/etc/sysconfig` or `/etc/rc.conf`). Next, run PPP with the `-nat` (`-alias` in earlier versions) switch to enable aliasing.

The FreeBSD NAT `daemon` program works with the IP Firewall package `ipfw`. It is independent of the interface, and it can be used with dialup PPP or with two or more network cards. Because the NAT daemon is a more general-purpose program, I'm including the instructions for setting up FreeBSD as an Ethernet NAT (see Exhibit 5.5). It is assumed that the FreeBSD machine is placed between the internal Ethernet network and a router, such as a Cisco, that is connected to an ISP.

> **NOTE**　Due to the continuing work of the cracker community, obscure holes are discovered in OSs every week. Everyone is probably familiar, by now, with `WinNuke`, a program used to crash Win95 and NT machines remotely over a network (for pointers to `WinNuke`, see <u>http://www.</u> <u>l0pht.com/</u>). FreeBSD, which is immune to these kinds of system-level TCP stack attacks, nevertheless has had its share of attention, and as a result many security fixes are included in each new release. Anyone running a firewall should plan on continuously upgrading it as new releases of the software appear.

**Exhibit 5.5　Instructions for installing the NAT daemon**

1. Start with a PC with two Ethernet cards. Inexpensive 10M NE2000 clone ISAs will work for this; they can be had for $20 per card from some dealers. Whichever card you use, if it's an ISA card it should use the "ed" network driver in FreeBSD; it is the oldest driver and has had enough time to have all the bugs shaken out.

   If you use ISA cards and an older, slower machine, such as a 486/66, do not run anything else on the system. I've clocked about a megabit per second through a 486/50 running NAT on two ISA cards, but this was with nothing else on the system. T1 lines run at 1.5M per second (for comparison). A faster system might use the fxp driver on PCI Ethernet cards.

   NAT can be run on FreeBSD 2.2.1 and later versions. There is a patch kit for use with the 2.1.x kernel, but this is all obsolete code and should be avoided for a fresh installation. FreeBSD version 2.2.8 installs `natd`, along with the rest of the superuser utilities, in `/usr/sbin/`. FreeBSD version 3.4 installs `natd` in `/sbin`.

2. Install the FreeBSD OS on the machine and assign an IP number from the inside IP range, typically RFC1918, to one of the interfaces. This IP number becomes the default gateway IP number for internal user computers that want to access the Internet through the NAT. Assign the *valid* IP number that your ISP has assigned to you on the interface connected to the router or other device connected to the Internet. For the following examples, 192.168.1.1 is the inside number used on the ed0 interface, and 34.56.3.2 is the outside valid number used on the ed1 interface.

3. The FreeBSD kernel must be recompiled with the options IPFIREWALL and IPDIVERT. The FreeBSD handbook in `usr/share/doc/handbook/handbook.html` contains instructions on how to do this (see also Chapter 3). The kernel may also need to be rebuilt to recognize additional network cards, depending on the type of cards chosen.

4. Make sure that both numbers are pingable from their respective networks. Turn on routing in the kernel by modifying the `/etc/rc.conf` or `/etc/sysconfig` file (depending on the FreeBSD version) with the statement `gateway_enable="YES"`.

5. If you are running an older version of FreeBSD, you may have to obtain the `natd` software via anonymous FTP from <u>`ftp://ftp.suutari.iki.fi/pub/natd/`</u> and use the `gunzip` program to put it in a convenient build directory, such as `/usr/ports/dist-files`. However, newer versions of FreeBSD (i.e., 3.X series and later) all include `natd` as part of the basic OS installation, and you can skip the next two steps.

6. For the older systems, `untar` the package with the `tar xf natd_1.12.tar` command. Change directory to the `natd_1.12` directory that this creates.

7. Follow the instructions in the README file to compile `natd`, then read the `natd` manual page (type `make`). If you don't install the manual pages, you can do this by changing to the `natd` directory and then running the `cat natd.8 | nroff -man | more` command.

8. Make sure the machine is configured as a gateway by the appropriate entries in `/etc/sysconfig` for FreeBSD 2.2.1 or `/etc/rc.conf` for 2.2.6 and later.

9. Copy the `natd` program into `/usr/local/sbin` and the `natd.cf.sample` file to `/usr/local/etc/natd.cf`. If you're using the system-installed `natd`, create a `natd.cf` file in `/etc` instead.

10. For FreeBSD versions before 3.X, in the `/usr/local/etc/rc.d` directory add the shell script
```
#!/bin/sh
[ -x /usr/local/sbin/natd ] && /usr/local/sbin/natd -config
      /usr/local/etc/natd.cf && echo -n ' natd'
```
For FreeBSD version 3.4 and later define the following variables in `/etc/rc.conf`:
```
natd_enable="YES"
natd_interface="ed0" (only use this if ed0 is your interface and
you don't define it in natd.cf)
natd_flags="-config /etc/natd.cf"
```

11. Modify the `/etc/rc.firewall` file and add the lines specified in the `natd` manual, that is:
```
/sbin/ipfw -f flush
/sbin/ipfw add divert natd all from any to any via ed0
/sbin/ipfw add pass all from any to any
```

12. Modify the `/usr/local/etc/natd.cf` file or `/etc/natd.cf` and make sure that the divert port number and interface name specified are the same as the one listed in `/etc/rc.firewall`.

13. Reboot the machine for changes to take effect.

Note that this describes a minimal configuration. Additional rules to `ipfw` would probably also be specified in `/etc/rc.firewall` to prevent attack packets from reaching the FreeBSD system itself, although the current FreeBSD kernel is resistant to these kinds of things. The additional rules can be set to allow inbound Telnet from inside but not outside. Also, don't forget to do the usual system protection precautions, such as turning off the `rcp`-based commands (like NFS) and any other services that are not required.

Keep in mind that most styles of attacks can be defeated simply by the use of RFC1918 numbers on the internal network, behind the `natd` translator.

Sample `/usr/local/etc/natd.cf` and `/etc/rc.firewall` files follow.

```
------natd.cf------
#
# Configuration file for natd.
#
#
# Logging to /var/log
#
log yes
#
# Incoming connections.
#
deny_incoming no
#
# Use sockets to avoid port clashes.
#
use_sockets no
#
# Avoid port changes if possible. Makes rlogin work
# in most cases.
#
same_ports yes
#
# Verbose mode. Enables dumping of packets and disables
# forking to background.
#
verbose no
#
# Divert port. Can be a name in /etc/services or numeric value.
#
port 32000
#
# Interface name or address being aliased. Either one,
# not both, is required.
#
# alias_address 34.56.3.2
interface ed0
#
# Alias unregistered addresses or all addresses.
#
```

```
unregistered_only no
#
# Configure permanent links. If you use hostnames instead
# of addresses here, be sure that nameserver works BEFORE
# natd is up—this is usually not the case. So either use
# numeric addresses or hosts that are in /etc/hosts.
#
# Map connections coming to port 30000 to Telnet in my_private_host.
# Remember to allow the connection /etc/rc.firewall also.
# Ted's machine WWW, FTP & telnet (ssh)
redirect_port    tcp 192.168.1.144:21 30002
redirect_port    tcp 192.168.1.144:80 30003
redirect_port    tcp 192.168.1.144:22 30004
#
# Make internal servers visible. Note we must also add the IP numbers
# .3, .4, .5 and .6 as virtual IP numbers to the external interface in
#     /etc/rc.conf
# if we are going to use the redirect_address command to make internal
# IP numbers visible.
#
redirect_address 192.168.1.72 34.56.3.3
redirect_address 192.168.1.16 34.56.3.4
redirect_address 192.168.1.10 34.56.3.5
redirect_address 192.168.1.206 34.56.3.6
#
------end of natd.cf------

------section of rc.firewall-----
.
.
.
/sbin/ipfw add 1000 pass all from 127.0.0.1 to 127.0.0.1
.
.
elif [ "${firewall_type}" = "nat" ]; then
        /sbin/ipfw add divert 32000 ip from any to any via
208.207.3.226
        /sbin/ipfw add pass ip from any to any
.
.
------end of section of rc.firewall------
```

# FREEBSD AND ROUTERS

In the early days of Internet connectivity, a corporation wanting to connect its internal network was expected to ask for an address range from the InterNIC, typically a Class C or several Class Cs. If the company was very large, it might receive a Class B or A address. The company would renumber its internal network to match the assigned range, which could be a huge project for a large company. Then, it would shop around for an ISP that would agree to route these addresses, which was accomplished by the ISP creating a routing entry for the subnet and broadcasting this onto the Internet. The result was that every host in the organization's network would be able to access or be accessed by all other machines on the Internet.

## Basic Routing

In the early 1990s, it became clear that this method of IP address assignment would exhaust all available IP numbers on the Internet within a few years. Worse, the core Internet routers couldn't possibly deal with the increasing number of route entries created by this connection method. This was due to the incredible speed at which organizations were connecting to the Internet. The former method of connection added every machine in a connected organization to the total number of reachable hosts on the Internet. To solve this, IPv6 was proposed, which works by simply making the IP address itself longer.

The biggest and most obvious problem with changing the IP number size was that it would require every IP stack on the Internet to be modified. This is practically impossible because many IP devices on the network are no longer supported by their manufacturers, many would require hardware upgrades because their code was in ROM, and the sheer difficulty of renumbering would have dwarfed the effort expended on the Y2K conversion programs.

In addition, many people—including myself—pointed out in various trade journals and other forums that many organizations that had connected years earlier to the Internet were extremely wasteful with their IP numbering. For example, some corporations with Class B addresses had taken to splitting these numbers up with a Class C subnet mask, and assigning whole Class C IP number subnets to serial links on their WAN lines. This took more than 250 addresses out of commission permanently for a link that needed only two IP numbers, if it was numbered at all.

The InterNIC finally realized that switching the entire Internet and all connected users to IPv6 in a short period was an engineer's pipe dream and began to look seriously into IP address reclamation. They took the following measures to reclaim IP addresses.

- The InterNIC parceled out blocks of IP addresses to major geographical address assignment groups—ARIN, RIPE, APNIC—and the U.S. military. These organizations were then given the authority to charge for IP number assignments and have started to do so, which creates an incentive to give back addresses to the InterNIC.

- Direct IP address assignment to end users and corporations ceased. Today, ISPs directly portion out subnets to organizations wanting to connect. This means that if an organization switches its ISP, it loses the addressing it has and must obtain new addresses.
- Cisco released an IOS that allowed the `IP Unnumbered` command, which removed the necessity of using IP numbers on routed serial lines.
- ISPs were encouraged to group together blocks of sequentially numbered IP address networks into CIDR blocks to decrease the core route table load. This is referred to as *classless routing*. Information on CIDR is located in RFC1519.
- End users and organizations wanting to connect to the Internet were encouraged to use RFC1918 (RFC-Unassigned) IP numbers on their internal networks and use either proxies or NATs to make the actual connection to the network. This practice also makes it easier to change ISPs, thereby helping to create competition among ISPs, which lowers prices.

These IP reclamation measures caused ISPs to make some changes.

- ISPs generally no longer assign static IP numbers to dialup customers unless the customers pay the hundreds of dollars that a business with a permanent connection would pay.
- ISPs typically split up their addressing into fractions and assign these to their customers. Most customers get subnets of 8 or 16 legal IP numbers.
- ISPs usually charge fees for excessive IP number consumption.

Because of these factors, pure, routed corporate networks on the Internet today are becoming rare, and few new installations of any size use them. Instead, proxy servers and NAT are becoming the norm. However, it is useful to understand how a routed connection operates, for internal use or for legacy networks.

## Routed Packet Movement

At the heart of TCP/IP packet routing is the concept of routability—the idea that a packet, once released from a machine, contains enough information to allow it to be redirected by external devices not under the control of the sender. To do this, TCP/IP packets all contain four important data fields: a source IP number, a destination IP number, a source port number, and a destination port number. Exhibit 5.6 shows a simplified example of how these data fields are used with a TCP connection between two machines. Note that some UDP applications work differently in that they use only a single port for both source and destination.

### Exhibit 5.6  Data fields for TCP connections

An administrator runs a Web server on one machine that has an IP number of 208.45.6.3. This system is located on a network that has a router connecting it to the Internet. The router has two interfaces: the first is connected to the hub that the machine is plugged into, with an IP number of 208.45.6.1; the second is connected to the administrator's ISP.

A user on a second machine runs a Web browser and types in the URL of the Web server running on the first computer. The second machine has an IP number of 199.5.6.8, and it is connected to a network with a router on it that is plugged into an ISP. This router has an interface plugged into the hub that the second machine is plugged into, and the interface has an IP number of 199.5.6.1.

The Web browser on the second machine causes the IP stack to start the process of transmitting a packet to Web server on machine 208.45.6.3. The IP stack first opens a *user return port*, which is a semirandomly selected port used as a receptacle for the IP packets that come in response to the initial connection request. For this example the return port is 3456. Thus, the IP stack creates an outgoing packet with the following information.

Source port number: 3456
Destination port number: 80 (located in `/etc./services`)
Source IP number: 199.5.6.8
Destination IP number: 208.45.6.3

The IP stack on 199.5.6.8 knows by comparing its subnet mask that 208.45.6.3 is not located on the same network, so it sends the packet to the default gateway, 199.5.6.1. The router at 199.5.6.1 forwards the packet through its connection to the ISP. This ISP passes the packet to the ISP for the first machine. That ISP passes the packet to the router located at 208.45.6.1, which forwards the packet to host 208.45.6.3.

When the Web server on 208.45.6.3 gets the packet on port 80, it spins off a separate process that creates its own return port and a connection response packet. In this example, the return port is 2323, thus a packet is created with the following information.

Source port number: 2323
Destination port number: 3456
Source IP number: 208.45.6.3
Destination IP number: 199.5.6.8

It also sets the *Established* bit in the TCP packet header. Since the Web server knows that 199.5.6.8 is not local, it sends the packet to the default gateway, 208.45.6.1. This sends the packet on to the ISP, which eventually routes it back down to the router at 199.5.6.1, which forwards it to 199.5.6.8.

Once 199.5.6.8 has the packet, it knows that a two-way connection has been established and that both systems have agreed on port numbers. Now the systems can begin transmitting data. But, how do the routers at 208.45.6.1 and 199.5.6.1 decide how and where to send packets? Through route tables.

## Routing Protocols

### *Routing Tables*

All TCP/IP stacks, whether located on a client machine or a router, use a route table. Under Win95, WinNT, or FreeBSD UNIX, to see what the route table looks like at a command-line prompt, issue the `netstat -r` command. On client machines, the route table basically has two routes. The first tells the stack where to send local subnet packets, which is always going to be the local interface. For example, if a client machine has the IP number 208.45.6.3, a packet with a destination address of 199.5.6.8 going to another machine is routed internally to the 208.45.6.3 interface on the client machine and then sent out to the network to the default gateway. The second route is the default route, which is set to the address of the default router, for example, 208.45.6.1. This route shows the destination for all nonlocal packets. For example, if the client transmits a packet with a destination address of 23.1.5.6, the route table causes this packet to be sent to the router at 208.45.6.1 via the 208.45.6.3 interface.

Route tables on routers are a little more complicated. On the large routers used in the Internet core or those with multiple interfaces, they can have hundreds to thousands of routes. With most *leaf node* organizations (those with only a single connection to the Internet), the router's route table doesn't need to be very complicated. All that is needed is a default route pointing to the ISP, which is always listed as a route to 0.0.0.0. The default router IP number 208.45.6.1 in the preceding example has a serial interface with the number 197.5.6.1; thus, the default route lists 0.0.0.0, reachable via the serial interface. The router's default route number differs from all other default route numbers on the other machines on the local net 208.45.6.0.

With an end-node router in the preceding scenario, the actual routing process is very simple compared to the work of assembling and disassembling the incoming and outgoing packets from each interface and encapsulating the packets in a serial line protocol. In effect, in either direction a router merely copies packets from one interface to the other.

### *Routing Information Protocol*

Route table propagation across networks is usually done automatically with the use of routing protocols. For example, RIP is a routing protocol that was in common use in corporate networks. RIP is not used as much anymore on local LANs, mainly because Windows Desktop clients cannot listen for route broadcasts and use default routes that are entered into their stacks. It is still used on some corporate WANs, although it is rapidly being replaced by the Open Shortest Path First (OSPF) routing protocol.

If RIP is to be used on an internal corporate WAN, administrators should be aware that by default the FreeBSD `routed` program supplies RIP version 1 advertisements. These advertisements cannot include classless subnet masks (e.g., `routed` cannot advertise 192.168.2.32/29). If the administrator is working with classless subnetting (i.e., subnetted class Cs) and RIP, it is necessary to put the keyword

```
ripv2
```

into the `/etc/gateways` file. This turns off RIP v1 advertisements. In addition, RIP v2 supports multicasting. If an administrator wants to use multicasting to supply route advertisements, he or she must create a route for the multicast net, using this command

```
route add 224.0.0.0 -netmask 0xf0000000 -interface ed0
```

This allows multicasting on the `ed0` network interface in the FreeBSD system.

The classless issue also affects static routes. By default, when issuing a `route add` command, the route mask is assumed to be a classful mask (i.e., 255.0.0.0, 255.255.0.0, or 255.255.255.0). To issue a classless route, such as a route to 200.54.3.16/29 via 45.6.7.8, the following syntax is used.

```
route add -net 200.54.3.16 45.6.7.8 -netmask 255.255.255.248
```

If the route is a *subnet-zero* route, the entire net should be specified or the results may be unexpected. For example, a route to 192.168.1.0/29 via 34.23.45.2 would be written as

```
route add -net 192.168.1.0 34.23.45.2 -netmask 255.255.255.248
```

## *BGP4/OSPF*

For more advanced and complex corporate WANs, the OSPF protocol is usually used. Multihomed ISPs generally use the Border Gateway Protocol (BGP) in conjunction with OSPF. Both protocols are supported by the `gated` program in the Port directories.

For extremely large routers running BGP4 with `gated`, earlier FreeBSD kernels should be compiled with the following options as minimal values.

```
options          NMBCLUSTERS=1024
options          VM_KMEM_SIZE=67108864
```

Note that this is no longer an issue with the FreeBSD 4.X kernels.

For a multihomed BGP connection, the FreeBSD router should have at least 128MB of system RAM and should be at minimum a 200Mhz system, preferably faster. On my own BGP router, the `gated` process running BGP consumes 32M of core RAM and the route tables themselves consume about 24MB.

The current *public* version of `gated` is 3.6; the version before it was 3.5.11. The public version is an ambitious rewrite, but it is not without bugs. In fact, when I attempted to upgrade from 3.5.11 to 3.6, with the identical configuration file, `gated` would not pass the internal BGP (iBGP) routes to my other iBGP routers.

In addition, there is a design disagreement between how `gated` implements BGP and how Cisco implements BGP. In `gated` versions all the way up through 3.5.11, iBGP/EBGP selection is made *before* Autonomous System (AS) path selection, with iBGP favored. In Cisco, AS path selection is made first. Although with `gated` this is the right thing to do if the BGP is being used internally only, it's the wrong way to do it for an ISP. The `table.c` file must be modified to fix this for BGP4 on `gated`. This issue is fixed in version 3.6, in which the `gated` developers changed `gated` to conform to Cisco's way, and AS path selection now has priority.

### *Media Conversion*

Most leaf node routers can perform other useful functions besides copying packets from one interface to another—they also perform a media conversion on the data.

FreeBSD supports four general kinds of network media: 10BaseT Ethernet, 100BaseT Ethernet, asynchronous serial connections, and synchronous serial connections. With each kind of media, TCP/IP packets are encoded differently, and the media is electrically different. For example, 100BaseT data is sent at a faster rate than 10BaseT, so the two networks cannot simply be plugged into each other. Synchronous data has a clock signal, whereas asynchronous data lacks one. Each medium is suited for different applications.

The vast majority of high-speed telephone communications lines run synchronous data so that the telephone company can easily multiplex the data together. The telephone network also has much more bandwidth than a large corporate network, besides being much vaster and covering a larger area. Since the telephone system took nearly a hundred years to build, it has tremendous backward compatibility. Many buildings today still are running with copper telephone cable feeds from a central office that are 30 to 60 years old. A router must be able to connect this old technology cabling to a modern network.

## Simple Routing with a PC

Although a dedicated hardware router is the most common type of router used at a customer end node, simply running FreeBSD on a PC can duplicate most routing functions. It is even possible to put an entire router on a disk. In an almost unbelievable feat of cramming, several people have created FreeRtr, which squeezes an entire PC PPP router onto a single 1.4MB disk. It is available at `http://www.rdrop.com/freertr/`. Of course, with such an arrangement it's pretty difficult to run Web or mail services on the server.

A newer version of this software, called PicoBSD, can be found at `http://people.freebsd.org/~picobsd/picobsd.html`. These *router-on-a-PC* BSD installations are drop-in replacements for the Linux versions of the same thing, at `http://www.linuxrouter.org/` and `http:0//www.zelow.no/floppyfw/`.

Although a FreeBSD server can run with a synchronous serial port plugged into telephone company equipment and the `gated` daemon running to provide BGP routing updates, the most common type of end-node PC router is made with a single modem and a single Ethernet interface. Typically, it has an Ethernet network adapter connected to the internal network, and a COM port plugged into a modem, which is dialed in to the ISP and running PPP. The COM port is considered the serial interface and the network card the Ethernet interface. The PC routes between both interfaces. The organization's legal IP subnet is assigned to the Ethernet interface and the machines connected to it, and the serial interface gets its IP number assigned by the dialup PPP server to which it is connected. For example, a PC running as a dialup router might have the PC's serial interface assigned to 192.168.1.1, and the IP number that is on the other end of the serial PPP link at the ISP is 192.168.1.2. The ISP may assign the organization a subnet number of 192.168.2.0. The organization then assigns the number 192.168.2.1 to the PC's Ethernet interface.

### Turning on Kernel IP Routing in Windows NT

Most PC TCP/IP stacks, such as the Win95 IP stack, cannot route IP traffic internally between multiple interfaces. Although both WinNT and FreeBSD can do it, they don't do it by default. With NT versions 3.51 and 4.0, a special registry key must be set to enable NT to be used as an Internet router between the network interface and the serial interface. This is diagrammed in the *Windows NT Resource Kit*. From the ResKit documentation, the key is

```
To \HKEY_LOCAL_MACHINE\System\CurrentControlSet\Services\RasArp\Parameters

add REG_DWORD DisableOtherSrcPackets set to 1
```

If the subnet IP number on the PPP interface must be in the assigned IP subnet, which is often done by the ISP to conserve IP numbers, an additional key is needed.

```
To \HKEY_LOCAL_MACHINE\System\CurrentControlSet\Services\RasMan\PPP\IPCP

add REG_DWORD PriorityBasedOnSubNetwork set to 1
```

In addition, under NT, IP Forwarding must be checked in the control panel. For a complete discussion, see the section "Installing a Simple Internet Router Using PPP" in the ResKit.

Besides turning on kernel routing in Windows NT, if the organization is using NT to route IP from Ethernet port to Ethernet port, it may also decide to use RIP as the routing protocol. RIP is included in NT 3.51 Service Pack 2 and above, and in NT 4.0. It is *not* in the Routing and Remote Access Service Pack update. Unfortunately, by default the RIP included in NT does not accept default route advertisements (routes of 0.0.0.0) and doesn't broadcast them, which is a requirement for connection to an ISP. The RIP can be changed by a registry parameter change documented in Microsoft Knowledge Base article Q169161. Two changes must be made: one to accept default route advertisements and another to rebroadcast them.

Additionally, the RIP included in the base NT 4 load is RIP version 1 only. To get RIP version 2 support you must run the Routing and Remote Access package on Windows NT 4. Win2K is supposed to correct this.

### *Turning on Kernel Routing in FreeBSD*
FreeBSD version 2.2.6 and later must have the `gateway_enable=` flag in `/etc/rc.conf` set to `yes` to enable IP routing between interfaces, whether they are PPP or Ethernet. It can be set in `sysinstall` or manually.

The administrator may also want to investigate alternate queuing schemes. Although a hardware router can be programmed to prioritize certain kinds of traffic, FreeBSD cannot. However, a package at http://www.csl.sony. co.jp/person/kjc/programs.html implements class-based queuing on FreeBSD2.X. It may be worth investigating, depending on the environment in which the routing server will be used. For FreeBSD 4.X, the `ipfw` packet-filtering firewall program implements a system facility known as `dummynet` to enable this the kernel must be recompiled (see the `man` page on `dummynet` and on `ipfw`).

It is important to understand, however, that unless heavy outbound traffic on the Internet connection is present, queuing won't help make better use of the bandwidth unless it's also implemented at the ISP.

RIP operates under FreeBSD and is managed by `routed`. If a FreeBSD system is used for routing and has multiple virtual IP numbers, the administrator may want to modify the `routed` configuration file to suppress advertisements of the virtual IP numbers.

### PPP Dialing Software

To set up the serial interface in WinNT, Remote Access Services (RAS) must be installed, which is done as part of the network installation in the control panel. The procedure is different under NT 3.51 and NT 4. RAS should be installed and tested before any registry keys are modified.

To set up the serial interface in FreeBSD, the `user ppp` software is used. For a complete discussion, as well as setting up FreeBSD as a router, see the `/usr/share/doc/handbook/handbook.html` pages. The pages may be read by the text-mode Lynx HTML reader, by Netscape or Mosaic running under the X Window System, or by a different browser running under a different machine connected to the FreeBSD machine with a network card. They are also available on the web at `http://www.freebsd.org`.

### Simple Routing Scenario Drawbacks

Setting up a simple routing scenario today is not recommended. Besides the previously mentioned issues with IP numbering, another problem with connecting the internal network to the Internet using a PC router is that it allows any host inside the network to be directly accessed from the Internet. This allows a cracker all kinds of opportunity to break into your machines. For example, if a Win95 machine with Microsoft file- and printsharing installed, a remote cracker can map the machine's hard drive to a drive letter and copy files. This is also true for the Windows NT workstation, using either Win95, WfW 3.11, or WinNT. It is also possible to Telnet into a port on a non-service-packed NT machine, press Enter a few times, and make the NT machine crash. Proxy servers and NAT can protect against these problems, which is the main reason they are used, although the IP numbering address conservation they provide is far more important to the rest of the Internet.

Using a PC running FreeBSD or other OS as a router has some other drawbacks as well. First and foremost, most higher-speed serial connections are synchronous connections. Hardware routers have synchronous serial ports on them, but PCs must have them added. Another big problem with using a PC as a router is reliability. Modern hardware routers have no moving parts except perhaps a fan, they have no hard drives, and they can withstand much greater physical shock and much wider temperature variations. In a large enterprise with WAN links, each router is configured the same with the same hardware and, as such, is much easier to manage. For these reasons, most larger organizations use a hardware router when connecting to the Internet, such as a Cisco 2501, 2610, 1600, or 1005, in conjunction with a NAT or proxy firewall. The firewall can be built on a FreeBSD system.

## The End-Node Hardware Routing Scenario

From an Internet-centric view, the core of the Internet is linked by large Cisco routers with many cards and numerous interfaces. The farther away from the core, the smaller the routers are, and the fewer connection points that exist at each router. The fringes of the network are where the customer organizational networks plug in; these are sometimes known as *leaf sites*.

Several years ago, it was common to find a leased circuit connected to a Cisco hardware router at a leaf site connected to the Internet. The router would have an Ethernet interface plugged in to the internal Ethernet network and a synchronous serial port plugged in to the leased high-cap telephone line running to the ISP. IP numbers on both interfaces were legal, reachable numbers. The organization's internal network would be connected through a firewall to a small hub, which was plugged into the Cisco router.

Today, organizations more often use digital subscriber lines (DSL) to connect to the Internet. Several DSL providers, such as Rhythms, offer DSL circuits with SLAs on them, the same as the more traditional Frame Relay or point-to-point circuits. In this case the leaf site generally has a DSL *modem* that has a port that connects to the DSL circuit and an Ethernet port. The leaf site is still connected to the ISP with a router, but the router consists of a device with two Ethernet ports: one connected to the DSL modem and the other connected to the organization's internal network.

Cisco designed the Cisco 1605 router for this setup. The 1605 router is two to three times the cost of a PC, however, and many other companies now produce two-Ethernet-port DSL routers, often in the $200 range. As a Cisco user and supporter for many years, I and many other Cisco users are very concerned with Cisco's lack of response to the competition. I used to recommend that leaf sites considering a permanent Internet connection use only Cisco routers, but no longer: the economic realities of DSL today have made it clear to me that Cisco may become a nonplayer in the leaf-node connectivity market.

I still recommend that leaf sites considering a permanent leased-line Internet connection, such as a T1, carefully consider the issues if FreeBSD is to be the primary gateway router. A FreeBSD PC can be directly connected to a T1 or Frame Relay circuit with a WaNIC or Evergreen Technologies synchronous serial card. The safer—but more expensive—approach is to use a Cisco hardware router for the connection to the ISP and place the FreeBSD servers behind the router. However, my current recommendation for organizations connected via DSL is to use a FreeBSD server as the router instead of using a less expensive two-Ethernet port router from a company such as 3Com.

Consider performance, reliability, compatibility, ease of troubleshooting, security, and maintenance when deciding on your organization's router and choosing between a PC-based or Cisco-based solution.

### Performance

A router with a serial connection and an Ethernet connection being used as a leaf-site router must perform several operations on each packet it handles. First, it checks the packet against any existing firewalling and antispoofing access lists. It must handle a media conversion of packets between the serial-level protocol encapsulation used and Ethernet, and it must create and manage statistical traffic-tracking information. Each operation is performed on every packet, and even though they require a tiny amount of time, they add up and introduce noticeable latency on connections through the router. This is unavoidable, but it pays to keep this time as short as possible. A PC server running as a router, mailserver, fileserver, and so on—even a server as efficient as a FreeBSD UNIX system—must also do other things and so may not have enough CPU power to avoid affecting routing performance. Designating the PC for routing only can alleviate the problem, but the temptation is to load the server down with lots of other tasks.

By contrast, a modern (i.e., *not* a 25xx series) Cisco router simply cannot perform functions other than those directly involved with routing management, so there is no temptation to add other tasks to the routing server. All the hardware in the Cisco router is designed for one thing—routing.

### Reliability

A PC is built as a general-purpose computing device. It contains a bus, peripheral I/O ports, a disk drive system, keyboard and video systems, and numerous other components that have little to do with the routing process. Each of these components adds complexity to the system. Although these components make the system very flexible, the additional complexity also introduces more potential problem areas.

A Cisco router contains only the network interfaces, a serial port, a CPU, and memory. There are not many hardware components that can fail.

### Compatibility

It is simply easier to get equipment from a single vendor to interoperate. With most Internet routers, the Ethernet interface is so basic and standardized that little can be misconfigured. This isn't the case with the synchronous serial connection because there are a number of low-level settings here. In particular, on point-to-point lines Cisco routers can use a proprietary link-level encoding that is more popular than the standard PPP. If the organization will eventually connect to multiple ISPs or multiple organization-owned sites, the routers will need to exchange routing information with each other and with the ISPs. Although routing protocols such as RIP are standardized, there are sometimes subtle differences in their implementation that are vendor dependent.

Since Cisco is the choice of router used in the Internet core, it should be the choice of router used to connect a serial line to that core. Cisco routers use an IOS. The company maintains a very conservative approach to managing IOSs and supports many older versions of IOS. Sometimes, unusual routing issues can be fixed with patched versions of IOS, and Cisco maintains a procedure to handle this.

### Ease of Troubleshooting
Although the Cisco IOS is unfamiliar to a newcomer, it is quickly learned by anyone who has command-line experience with UNIX or DOS command prompts. Many networking engineers are familiar with IOS, and fortunately the routing field is fairly clear of the scourge of *paper* certified Novell engineers (CNEs).[1]

### Security
Cisco's newer IOSs have excellent firewall packet-filtering capabilities, such as dynamic access lists. Because routers are almost always the first targets of crackers attempting to penetrate organizational networks, Cisco is extremely conscious of security issues. A properly configured Cisco router with current IOS is impossible to crack with currently known cracks.

### Maintenance
Because Cisco routers are remotely configured via Telnet, it is very easy for one person in a larger organization to manage a network of routers from a single point. Virtually all router maintenance activities, with the exception of adding memory, can be done remotely. Although UNIX does have strong remote access ability, some operations still must be done at the console.

Keep in mind that even if the organization is not using FreeBSD to perform the actual routing process, a FreeBSD server is still invaluable to use in conjunction with a Cisco router for several reasons. First and foremost, it is difficult to upgrade Cisco routers, such as the 1600 and 2500, that run the IOS from flash-ROM remotely through the serial port. The procedure involves booting

---

[1]A paper CNE is an individual who, despite having received certifications from a company such as Microsoft or Novell, is still unable to satisfactorily administer products from those companies.

the router into ROM, and many early Cisco ROMs don't understand things like subinterfaces, so the result is losing control of the router. With these units, one must have a TFTP server such as a FreeBSD system on the local Ethernet network. With such a TFTP server, the router configuration can be backed up, although TFTP itself is insecure and must be blocked from access by the general Internet. With ISPs in particular, the router configuration can represent years of work.

Second, with a FreeBSD system, SNMP can be run on the Cisco and on the FreeBSD system, and the FreeBSD server can do traffic monitoring of the Cisco. Third, if logging is enabled on the Cisco (e.g., an access list is installed to block intrusion probes from crackers), it's critical to send the log data to a syslog host, such as a FreeBSD server.

## Managing Your Cisco Router

An organization purchasing a Cisco needs to perform several management tasks with the router during its use: setting up and configuring, upgrading firmware, and monitoring security.

### Setup and Configuration

Typically, router setup is provided by the ISP that the organization connects to. ISPs often do the initial network configuration themselves. New router setup help can also be gotten from the dealer that sold the router. Additionally, if the organization also purchases a SmartNet contract with the router (highly recommended), Cisco engineers can assist in configuration and setup.

It is important to understand that due to time constraints and liability issues, practically all dealers and router consultants do not install any kind of firewalling configuration into the router unless prodded. Although there are consultants who provide exactly this service, any good router access list must have constant management. As machines are put up on the network and services on them changed, the list must be changed as well. It is very important for the network administrator to become thoroughly familiar with the security procedures and configurations on the router.

### Firmware Upgrading

The problem that causes more security holes than any other problem on the Internet is the failure of network managers to install new security patches and recommended upgrades.

A typical Cisco router, such as a 2501, has RAM, boot ROM, flash-ROM, and nonvolatile RAM (nvram). The RAM is used for work and array areas, the boot ROM for a basic IOS storage area, flash-ROM for the IOS code, and the `nvram` for configuration storage. When a Cisco router is turned on, it begins executing a bootstrap program in its boot ROM. This program almost immediately looks in an area of `nvram` for a configuration parameter. This parameter tells the router to boot either from the IOS burned into ROM or from an IOS image that was copied to flash-ROM. If the flash-ROM is damaged, the router can always boot from the older IOS image in the boot ROM.

Cisco maintains many IOS image files on `http://www.cisco.com` in a special subscription-only section of the Web server. Access to this location of the Web server requires a SmartNet service contract number or sponsorship from a Cisco dealer. When purchasing a new Cisco router from a value-added reseller (VAR), the network administrator should ask for a Cisco online access number sponsorship from the dealer. It should be clear that this sponsorship is a marketing tool that Cisco provides to its VARs to help them develop a better relationship with their customers; it is not intended to be a chargeable item. Only Cisco premium partners can issue these numbers. Many Cisco resellers are just regular partners, and some are nothing more than resellers and cannot set up customer sponsorships. This should be considered against any cost savings that may be obtained by purchasing the router from a mail-order dealer.

Network administrators who cannot get a Cisco dealer to sponsor them can purchase a minimum SmartNet service contract from Cisco to gain a contract number to allow them to access IOS image files. This is strongly recommended.

At one time Cisco sold routers to a number of the major hub and MUX manufacturers, but they no longer do this. Cisco router cards sometimes become available on the seconds market for hubs such as the Cabletron MMAC series or some Synoptics hubs. These router-on-a-hub cards often use specially modified Cisco IOS and cannot run the more modern IOS versions that have firewalling and traffic prioritization capabilities. They may be useful to make the physical connection, but a FreeBSD system with firewalling must be installed between these routers and the rest of the internal network.

IOS images are uploaded to the router via TFTP. It is easy to set up a FreeBSD server to act as a TFTP server, and the router configuration can also be backed up to the TFTP server. However, the FreeBSD server cannot be running `natd` because it interferes with TFTP. (The `natd` daemon should be disabled for the few moments needed to receive the router configuration via TFTP.)

### Security Monitoring
A router administrator should follow and be informed of newly discovered security threats. Periodically, as security threats are located in IOS, Cisco releases upgraded IOS firmware with the hole repaired. Cisco also releases

recommendations on how to modify router configurations to block security attacks. The router is usually one of the first targets of network security attacks.

The router should also be programmed for logging, with `syslog`. The administrator can configure a FreeBSD system to accept `syslog` entries from the router. This is needed because the router retains only a small number of the log entries it generates; these must be captured to a hard drive in a system running a `syslog` daemon program.

# Web Serving

One of the more popular reasons for running FreeBSD or other open-source UNIX software is to use it as a platform for a Web (HTTP) server. UNIX provides a rich set of scripting tools and programming languages that can be used to custom-build a Web server that is carefully tailored to solve a specific problem. FreeBSD is a particularly good platform as it is exceptionally reliable and stable, with a wealth of prebuilt tools in its Ports collection.

Since entire books have been written on the topic of running a Web server on a UNIX system, I am not attempting to describe all that can be done on a FreeBSD server. Instead, this chapter covers the basics of setting up a Web server on FreeBSD and creating HTML on a FreeBSD system that the Web server can publish.

## INTERNETS AND INTRANETS

Ask most people what the Internet is all about and you will get a single answer—the World Wide Web. The Internet itself is a global TCP/IP network involved in virtually all communication systems in the world. But the Web is not a single monolithic scheme, and Web servers can be classified by a wide variety of criteria. The two most common classification terms are internet and intranet. An *intranet* is a collection of *internal* Web servers and browsers—in short, servers that are available only on an organization's private network (i.e., behind a firewall). In contrast, *internet* often refers to *external* Web servers, or, more specifically, *externally accessible* Web servers. Under FreeBSD, both servers are set up and configured the same way.

The HTTP network protocol itself is standardized by the World Wide Web Consortium (W3C), located at `http://www.w3c.org/`. The major Web browser software vendors, Microsoft and Netscape, have each added incompatible proprietary extensions to the standard.

## WEB SERVER HISTORY AND OPERATION

Most people agree that the Web was started by Tim Berners-Lee, who took many ideas from other hypertext documentation management systems, such as Gopher, and numerous PC and Macintosh systems. Two major Open Source Web servers touched off development on all other Web servers that followed them: the Conseil Européen pour la Recherché Nucleaire (CERN) and the National Center for Supercomputing Applications (NCSA) servers. The first server developed was the CERN server in 1991. Its source is publicly usable, hosted by W3C. It can be built in the Ports section of FreeBSD under `/usr/ports/www/w3c-httpd`. CERN (`http://www.cern.ch`) was followed by the NCSA HTTPD server, whose last release is located at `ftp://ftp.ncsa.uiuc.edu/Web/httpd/Unix/ncsa_httpd/httpd_1.5.2a/`. Its Web site is `http://hoohoo.ncsa.uiuc.edu/`. NCSA also produced the Mosaic Web browser, located at `http://www.ncsa.uiuc.edu/SDG/Software/Mosaic/`. Neither server has had serious development effort for years. Although both can be compiled and installed under FreeBSD, the major attention today is focused on the Apache Web Server.

### The Apache Web Server

The Apache Web Server (`http://www.apache.org/`) is the most popular Web server on the Internet. Apache is used by more than 55 percent of all Web servers operating on the Internet today, according to a survey by Netcraft, located at `http://www.netcraft.com/Survey/`.[1] Apache originated as a set of patches to the NCSA server, its name originating from APACHyServer. Apache originated under UNIX, but a port for it to Windows NT 4 is available. It was so popular that, in June 1998, IBM announced that Apache would ship as the standard server in IBM's WebSphere product—`http://www-4.ibm.com/software/webservers/news.html`.

---

[1]By extension, since Apache is unstable under Windows NT, these survey results likely indicate that the majority of all Web servers on the Internet run under UNIX.

Apache version 1.3 can be built in the `/usr/ports/www/apache13` directory. The current version, available from their site (http://www.apache.org/) is version 1.3.14. The version in the Ports directory on FreeBSD 4.1 is 1.3.12. A port for an SSL version of Apache using SSLeay is available in the `/usr/ports/www/apache13-ssl` directory. More information on running Apache as an SSL server is available at http://www.cs.tamu.edu/helpdocs/ssl/.

Running an SSL server with an *authorized* certificate is kind of political among some people. Basically, SSL was developed for Web servers and browsers as a means of encrypting information sent between the browser and the server. It was assumed that a cracker would have access to the wire going between the Web browser and the Web server and thus be able to run a packet sniffer that would allow capturing of *cleartext* data transmitted between browser and server. This is despite the fact that this kind of environment exists practically nowhere except for a few specialized academic areas, such as dormitories, where switching Ethernet hubs are not employed and malevolent intruders have access to the Ether.

The vast majority of Web users access Web servers either from protected environments, such as corporate networks, where the possibility of a coworker running a packet sniffer is extremely remote, or from dialup lines, in which it is impossible to insert a sniffer. Although it is possible to break into an ISP's router, especially if it uses a UNIX system as a router, the odds of it happening are very small. Additionally, the enormous amount of data the attacker would have to sift just to get credit card information makes it far easier to obtain credit card numbers from restaurant dumpsters and other places. As a result, as e-commerce sites that run SSL have spread, many people now use self-signed certificates on their SSL servers. Some don't even run SSL at all on their credit-card-accepting Web sites.

SSL implementations all depend on a certificate authority, which is supposed to be an unbiased third party that issues certificates. The certificates go into the Web server and basically guarantee to the end users that the Web site they are accessing is indeed what it says it is. If it is not, an error message comes up on the browser saying that the site's certificate is untrusted or missing, and the browser user must *accept* it to complete the transaction. In fact, if a site is running an untrusted certificate and the user operating the browser accepts the certificate, the data transmitted between server and browser is encrypted to the point that even if a cracker did have sniffer access, it would be practically impossible to extract any data from the encrypted transmission.

So, the only thing that a trusted certificate gives is assurance to the end user that he or she is accessing a legitimate site; it is no better than an untrusted certificate with respect to encrypting data. As a result, an increasing number of sites have decided against paying a certificate authority (CA) $300 per year for doing nothing more than any other certificate can do to encrypt data. Naturally, the people who make money issuing certificates do not like this, and they have made many long and technically involved arguments against becoming your own certificate authority. Nonetheless, the number of sites accepting credit card numbers without any SSL, or with free certificates issued by themselves, continues to rise. Each site must decide whether to become its own CA or not. I have worked with customers that ran credit-card-accepting Web sites that had no SSL, had SSL with their own certificates, and had SSL with authorized VeriSign certificates. All of them had reasons for setting up their servers the way they did, and I've never heard that any of them have had a problem with a stolen credit card number. My conclusion is that any network theft of credit cards is most likely targeted at sites that take hundreds to thousands of credit card numbers a day, and the attacker is more likely to compromise the Web site itself than attempt to tap the traffic flow to and from the site.

As of this writing I have not heard one reason to claim that an SSL certificate issued by VeriSign is any better than one issued by the company setting up the Web site. Given a choice between sending $300 to VeriSign and investing that $300 in setting up an SSL server, I'd recommend that the Web site operator spend the money on setting up an SSL server.

A version of Apache 1.3.12 specifically created for use with Microsoft FrontPage extensions is available on FreeBSD 4.X in ports at `/usr/ports/www/apache13-fp`. It uses the Microsoft file available at `ftp://ftp.microsoft.com/products/frontpage/fp40.bsdi.tar.Z` built for BSDi UNIX. Microsoft now directly supports FrontPage extensions on Apache 1.3.12 on FreeBSD 3.3. Please refer to the appropriate MS documentation and to Microsoft technical support for additional assistance with and information about FrontPage.

Installing Apache under FreeBSD is simple enough: change the directory to the appropriate Ports directory for the server desired, run `make` and then `make install`. The server is installed in `/usr/local/www`. You may need to run `make` with the `NO_CHECKSUM=YES` option to get this built.

If the FrontPage port is installed, the FrontPage extensions are installed in `/usr/local/frontpage`. The FrontPage server administrator's login is `fpadmin`. Use a good password when asked to provide a password for it. Select the `apache-fp` port for the type of Web server and create any subwebs desired. End with Ctrl-D, and then answer `no` to any virtual webs.

If multiple virtual webs will be run on the system, don't create the root web; instead, create only subwebs under `www`. For example, create the root web as `www/somedirectory` and the other virtual webs as `www/virtualserver` directory. This is because if you just install the root web in the root Web server directory, FrontPage takes all subdirectories under the root web directory for use by the root web.

For each virtual server that needs FrontPage extensions, issue a command such as the following.

```
cd /usr/local/frontpage/version4.0/bin
./fpsrvadm.exe -o install -t apache-fp -s
/usr/local/apache/conf/httpd.conf -p 80 -m www.somedomainname.com
```

Then enter the username and password used to access the directory on the server the virtual site is using.

FrontPage may also require a kernel recompile to change some of the default virtual memory limits. For example, the following kernel parameter changes may help this.

```
options      "MAXDSIZ=536870912"   #Maximum Data Segment size = 512MB
options      "DFLDSIZ=268435456"   #Default Data Segment size = 256MB
```

Although these changes give enough virtual memory for heavy FrontPage use, the swap space must also be expanded.

Some other tips on speeding up Apache are to make sure that DNS and `ident` lookups are turned off in the Apache `config` files and that the `listen()` queue is set large enough. This is done with the `sysctl -w kern.somaxconn=XXX` command. A value of 128 is normal and should work for most servers; very heavily loaded servers may want to raise it.

The instructions shown in Exhibit 6.1 make a minimal Web server setup on a FreeBSD system act as a document-serving system to serve the FAQ and handbook pages.

Several tools can be used to redo wholesale copies of the Web site, thereby allowing the Webmaster time to pick through the HTML and learn new HTML techniques. One of these is the GNU's `wget`. Another is `webzip`, available from http://www.spidersoft.com.

MS Access Limited SQL databases are also available for FreeBSD to use as a back-end for an Apache Server. For example, the UNIX SQL database engine MySQL supports ODBC connectivity; there's even a Win95/NT client available that works with MS Access and so on. It is available in the `/usr/ports/databases/mysql322-server` section of the Ports directories. Another popular database is PostgreSQL; in ports at `/usr/ports/databases/postgresql`, see the Web site http://www.postgresql.org. The new

### Exhibit 6.1  Apache QuickStart

1. Run `/stand/sysinstall`. Go into "Install additional distribution sets," and then make sure that the "doc" set is installed. This shows up in `/usr/share/doc/` in the handbook and FAQ directories.

2. Select the Apache Server from the prepackaged software on the CD and install it.

3. Even better, if you have a CD-ROM set, place CD 2 in the CD drive, and mount it on `/cdrom`, and then recursively copy the `/cdrom/www` directory over to `/usr/local/www/data`. Then you can delete `/usr/share/doc/FAQ` and `/usr/share/doc/handbook`, which are now redundant.

4. The default install of Apache places four sample files in `/usr/local/etc/apache`. Copy these to `access.conf`, `httpd.conf`, `mime.types`, and `srm.conf`, respectively.

5. The `access.conf`, `srm.conf`, and `mime.types` can be left alone. Edit the `httpd.conf` file and add your username under the ServerAdmin directive.

6. Restart the FreeBSD server to make sure that the Apache `autostart` file is properly executed and the server starts up on boot. If it doesn't, or it has a very long timeout, make sure that `/etc/resolv.conf` has a valid nameserver entered into it.

7. Run a Web browser and type in the URL of the server you just restarted. A duplicate of the FreeBSD Web site should appear.

---

Informix SE for Linux SQL database has also been loaded on FreeBSD under the Linux emulation.

Apache also supports security on pages. Access can be restricted by use of `.htaccess` files in the server directory. These can define passwords for the pages by placing the encrypted password in the file.

It is also quite easy to field a search engine under FreeBSD; <u>http://www.htdig.org/</u> has code for a search engine available for free under the GNU license.

It is also possible to add the free Excite search engine (version 1.1.1) that can be found at <u>http://www.excite.com/navigate/download.cgi</u>. To install it, the binary version of Perl included in the `Architext.tar.z` file must be replaced by the Perl version 4 binary before the install script is run. This binary is supplied as the default Perl version in FreeBSD up through version 2.2.8. It must be built by hand in FreeBSD version 3.4, or Perl version 5 can be tried.

Large Apache installations may have to make some other changes as well. When many HTTP processes are running, the limits placed on the server user ID must be raised, and the kernel may also need to be recompiled to increase MAX-FILES and CHILD_OPEN_MAX definitions. To increase the user ID limits, edit the `/etc/login.conf` file and modify the entry under the appropriate login class (probably default). Set the `:openfiles-cur=` higher, and then save and run `/usr/bin/cap_mkdb/etc/login.conf` to update the database.

## External Web Publishing Considerations

Security is one of the major issues an organization faces when setting up an external Internet Web server. Web servers are very visible and are often managed by inexperienced administrators. The most common break-in point on a Web server is insecure CGI programs, such as shell scripts. Many older Web servers were distributed with example CGI scripts that were later found to be insecure. There has also been a tremendous increase in the number of free CGI scripts that can be retrieved from the Internet. Some of these, such as Form-Mail, have many thousands of users and have been extensively tested for security. Other CGI programs may be the efforts of individual programmers who have done little security checking.

One way of protecting the Web server is to wrap the CGI scripts in another script that checks for security holes. CGIWrap, located at `http://www.unixtools.org/cgiwrap/`, is one CGI script that does this.

Many sites specialize in categorizing CGI programs. One of these sites, `http://www.cgi-resources.com/`, contains a large index to documentation and many hundreds of CGI scripts. Another site, `http://perlsearch.hypermart.net/`, specializes in Perl and CGI programming.

The Perl scripting program is often used in CGI and is probably the most popular program for making CGI scripts. FreeBSD versions through 2.2.8 use Perl version 4 as the default Perl, located at `/usr/bin/perl`. Later versions of FreeBSD use Perl 5. Perl version 5 can be installed on older FreeBSD systems from the prepackaged binary software; it is normally placed at `/usr/local/bin/perl5`. The fact that the older version of Perl is used as the default in FreeBSD 2.2.8 is no reason that Perl CGI shell scripts should be restricted to this version. Use Perl version 5 for CGI scripting on the Web server.

## Internal Web Publishing Considerations

Perhaps the most important issue connected with setting up an internal Web server (an intranet server) is making it easy for end users who access the server to publish documents on it. External Web servers usually are looked on as money-making opportunities for the organization and as such usually have a dedicated person to pay attention to them. Internal servers, on the other hand, may have an administrator assigned to keep an eye on them, but beyond that, are more of a free-for-all.

Apache can be set up on FreeBSD to support Microsoft FrontPage, for those who wish to use it. However, FrontPage can cost a lot of money to deploy across the enterprise, and many people may not care for its Microsoft-centric view of the world. FrontPage is also by no means a standards-based program.

As an alternative, publishing to the Web server can be done with Netscape Navigator Gold using the PUT method. The Microsoft Web browser also has an add-in that is purported to allow PUT. PUT has been standardized by many browsers and servers. Apache can be loaded on FreeBSD to support PUT, and an excellent how-to article is located at `http://www.apacheweek.com/features/put`. Basically, a CGI script is written for the PUTting operation, and defined in `srm.conf` with the following line:

```
Script PUT /cgi-bin/put
```

> **NOTE**  As the article mentions, PUT scripts are extremely insecure and should be run with caution on Web servers that are accessible to the Internet, such as the PUT script the article references—`http://www.w3.org/Amaya/User/PutCern.html`. Another example of a PUT script is located at `http://www.palmira.net/apache/put_perl.html`. A PUT script is also listed in The Apache/Perl Module List, which is part of the Comprehensive Perl Archive Network (CPAN) located at `http://perl.apache.org/src/apache-modlist.html`. The master index to CPAN is located at `http://www.perl.com/CPAN-local/CPAN.html`. A compiled C program that can be linked into the Apache Server is documented at `http://hpwww.ec-lyon.fr/~vincent/apache/mod_put.html`.

## The Web Browser

Today, very little can be said about a Web browser other than "Is it going to be Netscape or Microsoft Explorer?" Both browsers are freely available and have no problems accessing pages from Apache. If the client is FreeBSD, the question actually becomes, "Which version of Netscape do we use?"

One point about Netscape that deserves mention is that there is a native FreeBSD version of Netscape Navigator that can run under X Window on FreeBSD. This can be installed from the Ports directories. It is interesting also to note that on the Microsoft side of the fence, one of the two chief UNIX developers who developed the Solaris version of MS Internet Explorer is also a Linux devotee. Microsoft hasn't released a Linux version of MS Internet Explorer, but it would not be surprising if a Linux version of MS Explorer was tucked away in some hidden office in Redmond.

There are some other browsers worth mentioning—Mosaic (the original Web browser) and Lynx. Mosaic is also in the Ports directories but there is little point in compiling it unless the administrator has Motif loaded on the FreeBSD server. Lynx is entirely a text-mode browser and is very useful to have. It is located in the Ports directory in /usr/ports/www/lynx. There are also a host of niche browsers, such as Emacs/WE, at http://www.cs. indiana.edu/elisp/w3/docs.html, and the Opera browser.

## Editors

HTML is written in ASCII text format, and although there are many text editors that can be compiled on FreeBSD, most people use just four of them. Three of these are visual editors and require proper TERM configuration.

Word wrap is an important setting within the editor. When word wrap is enabled, the editor acts much like a word processor: it wraps text around to the next line, which is *not* the same as word wrap implemented in a terminal emulation. The text is saved as a series of lines. It is very important when editing UNIX configuration files that *word wrap be set to Off*. If word wrap is turned on and a UNIX configuration file is edited, undesirable hard returns are inserted in the file, and *the file may be destroyed!* Typically, word wrap is enabled by the user only if the editor is used for a task such as composing e-mail. Wrapped words are unwrapped by the WWW server when it sends out the HTML.

Be careful when attempting to edit UNIX configuration files on exported directories that are mounted on Windows hosts. DOS and Windows text editors insert an additional carriage return character when saving text files. These characters can be removed with this command:

```
cat filename |tr -d '\015' > fixedfilename
```

Another problem to watch for is tabs. Many UNIX configuration files require tabs, and many Windows and DOS text editors replace them with spaces, which wrecks the configuration file. In general, avoid using Windows and DOS text editors on UNIX text files.

The caret notation (e.g., ^b) means to hold down the Control key and type the character (Ctrl-B). The \ (backslash) notation in a configuration file generally means *escaped newline*, indicating that the following text line is a part of the previous one.

### Ed

The ed editor is the lowest common denominator editor on the system. It is very important for only one reason: ed is the only editor that can be run if the system crashes and rebuilding procedures need to be run or if the system is booted into single-user mode with the -s command. The other editors all depend on shared libraries that won't be accessible if only the root partition is mounted.

Because ed is such a painful editor to use, only the most hopelessly committed UNIX wizard is going to remember its commands. The FreeBSD administrator is wise to make a printout of the system manual pages for ed and put it in a safe place (perhaps inside the case of the computer), hoping never to have to use it. An example of how to use ed is in Chapter 4 in the Breaking Root section.

### Ee

The ee editor was written by Hugh Mahon as a simple, easy-to-use editor for all normal UNIX system editing tasks. It is much like the DOS EDIT editor supplied with DOS 5 and later. It is the default system editor used by the /stand/sysinstall FreeBSD system installation program.

Word wrap in the ee editor is turned on by default. Before you edit complex configuration files, turn it off by setting "Margins observed" to Off and "Auto-paragraph format" to Off.

The editor is started with the ee command, which displays a window at the top of the screen with editing commands. Other commands can be accessed by pressing the Escape key.

### Emacs

The Emacs editor was intended as the ultimate programmer's UNIX editor. Like the ed editor, it is old and started with a version written very early in UNIX's life. LISP programmers like it because its commands are written in LISP. Many C programmers like its *kitchen-sink* approach (i.e., users can read e-mail and do other tasks while in Emacs). In fact, the approach used by Lotus Notes—an all-in-one computing workspace—was copied from Emacs.

In Emacs documentation the control symbol ^ is replaced with the notation c-. Emacs has extensive online documentation that is accessible from the editor by Ctrl-h, t. Exiting is done by Ctrl-X, Ctrl-C. Emacs documentation is available in TeX files and can be printed on a PostScript printer with the appropriate software.

Emacs depends heavily on the META and Control keys. The META key is mapped to the Escape key. Emacs shows lines longer than 80 columns with a "\" at the end of the line to indicate a wraparound. Emacs responds to terminal resizing commands on the fly for Telnet and Xterm clients that support this.

Emacs also has graphical code in it: if it is run under the X Window System, it uses a graphical menu set.

### Vi

The vi editor (vi being short for visual editor) is the antithesis of Emacs. Generally, people who like vi don't like Emacs, and vice versa. Like Emacs, vi is a full-screen editor. vi gained rapid popularity in the early days of UNIX because it makes excellent use of the *terminal movement commands* implemented in most terminals. This made it possible to rapidly edit files on UNIX systems, even at extremely slow connection speeds of 300 baud! It can still come in handy in today's modern WAN links, in which organizations have links that stretch for many hops.

Vi has much documentation on the Internet; some links to it follow.

http://www.networkcomputing.com/unixworld/tutorial/009/009.html
 (A nine-part tutorial run in UNIXWorld online.)
http://ecn.www.ecn.purdue.edu/ECN/Documents/VI/
http://www.edu.physics.uch.gr/~danalis/manuals/vi/faq_frames.html
http://www.thomer.com/thomer/vi/vi.html
http://www.oac.uci.edu/indiv/gdh/vi/vi.tut.txt

There is also a nice tutorial for the vi editor located at ftp://ftp.uu.net/pub/text-processing/vi/docs/vilearn.tar.Z.

## Windows Web Publishing Tools

Many Windows (as well as Macintosh and other OS's) Web publishing tools are available for creating documents in HTML. However, once HTML file is created, how is it transferred to the fileserver? For externally hosted Web servers, FTP is the only option. This means that the Web designer has to save the file to his or her local hard drive and run a separate FTP application to transfer it to the server. The FTP application takes care of the ASCII carriage return/linefeed translation (CRLF), if any is necessary.

For internal servers, FreeBSD can be set up with the Samba software to share out parts of its hard drives so that Windows clients can map the Web publishing directories to drive letters on the desktop. The HTML file can then be saved directly in the Web directory from the HTML editing tool. The only problem is the ASCII newline translation. Fortunately, Apache ignores the additional carriage return character present in HTML pages saved to the server this way.

## Minimalist Web Publishing Tools

Although graphical Web publishing tools and editors abound, many people forget that HTML was created specifically so that it could be written by hand with an ordinary text editor. HTML was never intended to require huge, expensive, fancy editors. Sadly, when most end users are asked to publish something to the Web, they run away in fear unless the editor practically does everything for them. If they are putting up only a plain text document, that really doesn't matter. Never forget, however, that using a graphical editor limits your Web pages to the graphical editor programmer's idea of how a Web page should look.

Graphical editors have another problem: many generate HTML that looks horrible, is not indented, has no embedded comments, and is very difficult to read. This is due to the free-form nature of HTML and the fact that the editor's output is the lowest thing on the priority list. Also, many editor vendors have a stake in keeping the end user locked into using their tools, and a graphical editor is about the only thing that can deal with the poor HTML that these tools generate.

Most experienced Webmasters understand this. Although they may use "Save as HTML" for the initial preparatory work on a Web page, the real editing is done with a sparse text editor using a cheat sheet. One example of a cheat sheet is "The Bare Bones Guide to HTML" located at `http://werbach.com/`.

Another great thing about using a minimalist tool is that it allows the Webmaster to use good style in designing the Web page. Style examples can be found at

```
http://www.ology.org/tilt/cgh/
http://www.sun.com/styleguide/tables/Welcome.html
http://www.ncsa.uiuc.edu/edu/trg/styleguide/
http://www.hypernews.org/HyperNews/get/www/html/guides.html
```

## vi HTML Tool

The following post appeared on the Usenet newsgroup `comp.unix.freebsd.misc` listing a macro file that can be used with the vi editor to assist in editing HTML. It can be expanded to a much larger macro file for vi.

```
Newsgroups: comp.unix.bsd.freebsd.misc
Subject: Re: HTML Editors for BSD?
Date: 2 Jan 1997 22:50:05 GMT
```

```
Message-ID: <5ahe2t$3ac@rabbit.augusta.de>
References: <32C7A9A4.446B9B3D@freenet.mb.ca>

> Are their any HTML editors out for FreeBSD or XFree86.  I am NOT looking
> for A WYSIWYG interface.  Just a plain text interface would suit me
> fanncy.  thnks

here is a very handy .exrc, I found it but didn't remember who wrote
it, sorry ...

For example, you start vi, go in INSERT-Mode, type br Ctrl-M and get <BR>

"
"  this is an initialisation file for vi.  put it in you home
"  directory and call it '.exrc'
"  set noautoindent beautify noexrc ignorecase ruler showmode
"
"
"                          HTML - Editor
"
"  ab .... Abbreviations.   (to be used in insert mode with Ctrl-M)
"
"  if   xy  produces <XY>,
"       nxy  produces </XY>
"  ab pg <!DOCTYPE HTML PUBLIC "-//W3C//DTD HTML 3.2//EN">
<HTML>
<HEAD>
 <TITLE>#</TITLE>
 <META NAME="Author" CONTENT="shanee@rabbit.augusta.de">
 <META HTTP-EQUIV="Erstellt" CONTENT="#">
 <META NAME="KeyWords" CONTENT="#">
</HEAD>
<BODY>

</BODY>
</HTML>
ab br <BR>
ab hr <HR>
ab pp <P>
ab ht <HTML>
ab nht </HTML>
ab hd <HEAD>
ab nhd </HEAD>
ab ti <TITLE>
ab nti </TITLE>
ab bd <BODY>
ab nbd </BODY>
ab em <EM>
ab nem </EM>
ab str <STRONG>
ab nstr </STRONG>
ab pre <PRE>
```

```
ab npre </PRE>
ab ul <UL>
ab nul </UL>
ab ol <OL>
ab nol </OL>
ab li <LI>
ab dl <DL>
ab ndl </DL>
ab dt <DT>
ab dd <DD>
ab adr <ADDRESS>
ab nadr </ADDRESS>
ab h1 <H1>
ab nh1 </H1>
ab h2 <H2>
ab nh2 </H2>
ab h3 <H3>
ab nh3 </H3>
ab h4 <H4>
ab nh4 </H4>
ab h5 <H5>
ab nh5 </H5>
ab h6 <H6>
ab nh6 </H6>
ab ig <IMG SRC="#">
ab fr <FORM ACTION="#" METHOD="#">
ab nfr </FORM>
"
"   map .... Macros.    (to be used in command mode)
"
"  ctrl-x ctrl-l : the line under the cursur ends up as the text for
"                  a hyperlink, the cursor is places on the HREF, to let
"                  you insert the URL.
"
map _
 o</A>__kO">__I<A HREF="
"
"  ctrl-x ctrl-w : the word under the cursur ends up as the text for
"                  a hyperlink, the cursor is places on the HREF, to let
"                  you insert the URL. (this only works with the cursor
"                  at the *end* of the word)
"
map __ a</A>_bbbi<A HREF="#">_F#s
"
"  ctrl-x number : the line under the cursur is turned into a Heading
"                  ctrl-x 1  --->   H1  biggest Heading
"                  ctrl-x 2  --->   H2  next smaller Heading
"
map _1 I<H1>_A</H1>_j
map _2 I<H2>_A</H2>_j
map _3 I<H3>_A</H3>_j
map _4 I<H4>_A</H4>_j
```

```
map _5 I<H5>_A</H5>_j
map _6 I<H6>_A</H6>_j
"
"


_
Greeting, Andy
                                                           running FreeBSD-current
------------------------------------------------------------------------
```

# Fileserving with Samba

A major benefit of using the FreeBSD UNIX system in the corporation is its ability to *share out* hard drive space for use by Windows fileserving clients. Historically, UNIX has always used *Network File System* (NFS) protocols for this function, and it is certainly possible to load NFS on a Windows client. However, adding NFS to each Windows client is costly and adds an administrative burden on the client, compared to a network of Windows clients and NT Servers. Rather than loading NFS on Windows clients, an increasing number of administrators are loading Windows Networking on the UNIX server system. This is done by installing and configuring Samba software.

This chapter covers Samba installation and configuration, along with SMB client setup specifics. I also discuss the FreeBSD filesystem here because in a Samba server, the UNIX filesystem is where served files are actually written.

## THE FREEBSD FILESYSTEM

The filesystem is one of the basic components of UNIX. The FreeBSD filesystem begins with the concept of the *root directory*. The root is unique, and every other directory in the filesystem is a subdirectory somewhere under the root directory. This is true no matter how many physical hard drives are attached to the UNIX system—under UNIX, the physical hard drives do not affect the layout of the filesystem. A UNIX system can have the identical directory structure whether it has one drive or 100 drives. This concept gives tremendous flexibility to the system. Unlike any of the Microsoft OSs, drives are not assigned a drive letter. Instead, hard drives are *mounted* on *mountpoints* (usually subdirectories) in the filesystem, which can be located almost anywhere in the filesystem. This is roughly analogous to the concept of adding physical hard drives to make the volume in a NetWare server larger.

Although UNIX systems have a filesystem hierarchy that varies somewhat between systems and versions, several generalizations can be made. Practically all have the /usr, /bin, /etc, /usr/bin, and /usr/lib directories. The /home directory is usually in either /home or /usr/home, often depending on whether or not the system has the home directories located on a second drive. Many UNIX systems have a manual page named hier that covers the filesystem hierarchy for that UNIX. This manual page explains the purpose of each of the major first-level subdirectories under the root directory.

UNIX uses *inodes* to store files on, which are roughly analogous to the clusters used in the file allocation table (FAT) and high-performance NT filesystems. UNIX divides the drive using partitions in which the inode table and inodes are created. These partitions are *not* the same thing as the partitions used in DOS and Windows. Partitions on the drive can be named a, b, c, d, through h. In a special UNIX partition, called the *swap partition*, the system does its swapping. UNIX also has a repair program, fsck, that is roughly analogous to the chkdsk program in DOS.

The physical hard drives in the system are represented by special files in the filesystem known as *device files*. These files exist in the /dev directory. When a program running under the operating system attempts to open or read or write to these files, instead of affecting the file, the UNIX kernel directs the data transfer through the *device drivers* compiled into the kernel. Every UNIX system uses a different naming scheme for its devices.

## Device Files

When the FreeBSD UNIX system is booted, it attempts to load all device drivers that are compiled into the kernel. When the driver loads properly, it lists the discovered hardware and I/O, memory, and port assignments during kernel boot. The system manual pages for the drivers have a list of all device files that are used to *access* the drivers. The device files are *not* part of the drivers. Usually, when UNIX is first installed, it generates a default set of device files for the most commonly used devices. Some of the more esoteric hardware does not have device files created; the MAKEDEV script is used to create them. The system manual pages for each device driver lists the device files that are used to access the device.

The following list shows how to add joystick device files to the system.

1. The superuser plugs a joystick into either the joystick port on the mother-board or on an add-in card, such as a sound card.

2. The FreeBSD kernel is recompiled to add the joystick driver.

3. The system is rebooted, and /var/log/messages is inspected to ensure that the hardware was detected. The joystick driver detection message is
   ```
   Nov 12 16:18:33 thesysname /kernel: joy0 at 0x201 on isa
   Nov 12 16:18:33 thesysname /kernel: joy0: joystick
   ```

4. The superuser executes ./MAKEDEV joy in the /dev directory.

5. The /dev/joy0 and /dev/joy1 device files are created and the joystick is ready for use.

FreeBSD represents hard drives with different device files depending on what type that they are. Device files for SCSI drives are represented by sd or da (depending on the FreeBSD version), followed by a number indicating which physical drive it is. For example, under FreeBSD 2.X, /dev/sd0 is the device file for the first SCSI drive and /dev/sd1 is the second. The 0 and 1 are not directly related to the SCSI identifiers, they just indicate a separation of drives. Integrated Drive Electronics (IDE) drives are represented by wd, for example, /dev/wd0 is the device filename of the first IDE disk, and /dev/wd1 is the second.

FreeBSD uses the term *slice* to represent DOS-style partitions, which are indicated by the letter s followed by a number. For example under version 2.X, /dev/wd0s1 is the first slice on IDE drive 0, and /dev/sd2s3 is the third slice on SCSI drive 2 (the third physical SCSI drive). The UNIX partition name follows the slice. So, /dev/wd0s2e would indicate drive 0, slice 2 (DOS partition), and UNIX partition e within the DOS-style partition. These names are also used in the /etc/fstab file, which tells the OS where all drives are mounted.

Here is a sample fstab file in a small FreeBSD 2.X system. This system has a single 500MB ESDI hard drive.

| # Device | Mountpoint | FStype | Options | Dump | Pass# |
|----------|-----------|--------|---------|------|-------|
| /dev/wd0s1b | none | swap | sw | 0 | 0 |
| /dev/wd0a | / | ufs | rw | 1 | 1 |
| /dev/wd0s1f | /usr | ufs | rw | 1 | 1 |
| /dev/wd0s1e | /var | ufs | rw | 1 | 1 |
| proc | /proc | procfs | rw | 0 | 0 |
| /dev/cd0a | /cdrom | cd9660 | ro,noauto | 0 | 0 |

In this system, the ESDI drive was set up with the entire drive devoted to FreeBSD, thus the slice number doesn't have any meaning and is always 1. (The slice number is actually omitted from partition a.) Within this slice, there are four UNIX partitions: a, b, f, and e. Partition a is always used for the root filesystem /. Partition b is always used for the swap partition. Swap partitions aren't mounted, thus the mountpoint is "none." Partition c doesn't exist because in UNIX partition c is a symbolic partition name used to indicate the entire drive. Partition e is mounted on the /var directory. Partition f is mounted on the /usr directory. The CD-ROM drive that is attached to the system is mounted on /cdrom.

Typical UNIX workstation systems have only one drive. These mount with the bulk of the space on /usr and place the home directories in /usr/home. Sometimes administrators put a second drive in the workstation to allow each home directory to be on its own drive, putting the drive at /home and the home directories under it. Server systems with three drives can put one drive on /usr, one on / and /var, and the third on /home. Systems with four drives might put /home on one drive, root, var on a second, /usr on a third, and /usr/local on a fourth.

## Soft Links

If the administrator who sets up the UNIX server has all the drives the system will ever need available in the beginning and knows how much data will be stored in the various directories, life is good. He or she can make a very good set of decisions on how best to allocate partition space on the various drives and where to mount them. Of course, life is never this easy: servers grow and need new drives, users install huge packages in unexpected locations, drives get cheaper, and so on. As a result, adding a drive to a UNIX system later often changes a number of paths. To get around this, UNIX has a provision known as *soft linking*.

Soft links are created with the command ln -s and are used as *forwarding addresses* for files and directories. For example, suppose the example system presented under Device Files, earlier in this chapter, needs an additional hard drive added because the home directories are out of space. If the home directory is located in /home, the directory structure can be backed up (often with tar) and moved out of harm's way. The drive can then be mounted directly on /home, and the home directories restored to it. The fstab file would now appear as follows.

```
# Device         Mountpoint    FStype    Options    Dump    Pass#
/dev/wd0s1b      none          swap      sw         0       0
/dev/wd0a        /             ufs       rw         1       1
/dev/wd0s1f      /usr          ufs       rw         1       1
/dev/wd0s1e      /var          ufs       rw         1       1
/dev/wd1s1a      /home         ufs       rw         1       1
proc             /proc         procfs    rw         0       0
/dev/cd0a        /cdrom        cd9660    ro,noauto  0       0
```

Suppose the home directories were physically located in /usr/home instead of /home. The drive could then be mounted as follows.

```
# Device        Mountpoint    FStype    Options    Dump    Pass#
/dev/wd0s1b     none          swap      sw         0       0
/dev/wd0a       /             ufs       rw         1       1
/dev/wd0s1f     /usr          ufs       rw         1       1
/dev/wd0s1e     /var          ufs       rw         1       1
/dev/wd1s1a     /usr/home     ufs       rw         1       1
proc            /proc         procfs    rw         0       0
/dev/cd0a       /cdrom        cd9660    ro,noauto  0       0
```

One problem with this solution is that when a number of drives are added to the system, if the system blows up and must be restored from tape, things can get very messy. The person doing the restoring might not remember how the system was put together, guess at where drives were mounted, and then do the restore and overflow filesystems. Many UNIX systems built with drives scattered willy-nilly across their filesystems can be a headache for the administrator.

For this reason, superusers often like to mount any external drives in directories off the root, such as /disk1, /disk2, /disk3, and so on. Soft links are used to make it *appear* that the drives are somewhere else. For example, assume a drive mounted on /disk2 with the fstab file line

```
/dev/wd1s1a     /disk2      ufs      rw            1          1
```

The space actually needs to go to /usr/home, so the superuser changes to the /usr directory and creates a soft link with the ln -s /disk2 home command. Doing an ls -l of /usr shows the following.

```
$ ls -l
total 26
drwxr-xr-x   2 bin    bin     5632 Sep 11 19:57 bin
drwxr-xr-x   3 bin    bin     1024 Sep 11 19:13 games
lrwxrwxrwx   1 root   staff      4 Nov 13 23:26 home -> /disk2
drwxr-xr-x  24 bin    bin     2560 Sep 11 19:57 include
drwxr-xr-x   3 bin    bin     3072 Sep 11 19:57 lib
drwxr-xr-x   6 bin    bin      512 Sep 11 19:07 libdata
drwxr-xr-x   5 bin    bin     1024 Sep 11 19:08 libexec
drwxr-xr-x  11 root   wheel    512 Oct 21 22:42 local
drwxrwxr-x   2 root   wheel    512 Nov 13 07:28 mail
drwxr-xr-x   2 bin    bin      512 Sep 11 19:08 mdec
drwxr-xr-x   2 bin    bin      512 Sep 11 20:01 obj
drwxr-xr-x   2 bin    bin     3072 Sep 11 19:09 sbin
drwxr-xr-x  25 bin    bin      512 May 20 03:56 share
drwxr-xr-x  19 bin    bin      512 Sep 11 19:58 src
drwxr-xr-x   4 root   wheel    512 Oct 21 22:49 tmp
$
```

## Hard Links

Hard links are also available under the UNIX OS. These are restricted from spanning filesystems and so aren't used as pointers in the same way that soft links are. Instead, hard links are used with polymorphic programs. These programs operate differently, depending on what name they are called. For example, the `compress` program is a bit like PKZIP in that it compresses files. However, instead of uncompressing them with a different program, it uses the same program by calling it with the name `uncompress`. A hard link is created from the filename `compress` that creates a second filename, `uncompress`. When the program is run, it checks to see what name it was called under and then follows that mode of operation.

## SAMBA SYSTEM OVERVIEW

The Samba system, named after the Server Messaging Block (SMB) networking protocol on which it is based, was developed to allow UNIX servers to fileserve and printserve to Microsoft Networking and IBM LanManager network clients. It was written by Andrew Tridgell and is maintained and extended by a large number of volunteer programmers on the Internet. The central Samba Web page is located at http://www.samba.org/, and new versions of the software are made available there.

Samba allows FreeBSD to serve file and printer resources to DOS, Win31, WfW, Win95/98, WinNT, and Win2K. It can also serve file and printer resources to OS/2 Warp Connect and to later versions of OS/2 with networking support. Samba requires that clients have a TCP/IP stack loaded with appropriate network client software. WfW 3.11, Win95/98, NT, and Win2K all contain the client software; Win31 and DOS do not. Suitable clients for Win31 and DOS can be downloaded from Microsoft or obtained from the Windows NT Server CD-ROM. The WfW network client must use the TCP/IP available from Microsoft.

In effect, Samba makes a UNIX system look like any other Windows NT Server running TCP/IP. Windows systems can browse and map drives on the UNIX server running Samba.

Samba does *not* participate fully in the Windows NT PDC or BDC system. A Samba system cannot currently be used as a BDC because the mechanism that Microsoft uses to replicate from a PDC to a BDC is proprietary and undocumented. An NT server cannot be used as a BDC to a Samba PDC for the same reasons. A Samba server *can*, however, be used as a PDC. As of this writing, use of Samba as a PDC is still experimental.

Administrators unfamiliar with Microsoft Networking and running small NT networks with a single NT server may wonder what the fuss is over an NT domain controller. The truth is that there is absolutely no technical reason that a single NT server on a network of Windows clients must be installed as a PDC. A PDC does allow a complete NT workstation network to be set up in such a way that users are locked out of changing settings on their NT workstations. This doesn't work if the network is anything other than NT workstation, such as Win95/98, but it is easy to see why larger corporate networks implement this functionality.

With the release of Win2K and Active Directory, Microsoft is moving toward the destruction of the primary and secondary domain controller model with Windows. This cannot be anything other than good because NT domain networking has many technical problems on larger distributed TCP/IP networks. As more specifications are released on Active Directory by Microsoft, newer versions of Samba are expected to incorporate these enhancements. The current version of Samba, version 2.0.7, is compatible with Win2K, except that a Samba server cannot act as a PDC for Win2K clients. Samba version 3 will be able to act as a PDC.

For NT networks that are set up in the domain model, a FreeBSD system running Samba can be configured to use the NT PDC as the password server. This is similar to the functionality that a regular NT server has in a controlled domain when it is "joined" to the domain.

Kerberos security will be important to watch as Active Directory unfolds under Win2K. The Microsoft Kerberos standard is slightly different from everyone else's right now, and so Kerberos cannot be used for authentication. Microsoft has stated that it will release documentation on its implementation in the future; in a year or so we may see Kerberos authentication in Samba.

## THE SMB AND NETBIOS PROTOCOLS

The SMB network protocol is the basis of the Microsoft Networking client present in all Microsoft Windows OSs that include networking. It was originally specified in *Microsoft Networks/OpenNet-File Sharing Protocol*, written by Microsoft and Intel in 1987. At the time, Microsoft was working on LanManager for OS/2 in conjunction with IBM. In fact, at COMDEX in 1990, Microsoft CEO Bill Gates stated that "OS/2 was going to be the most important operating system of the nineties," which turned out to be wrong.

Unfortunately for Microsoft, LanManager never received much market share, and it wasn't until five years later, when Novell stumbled, that Microsoft had an opportunity. By then, LanManager had been sold to IBM and renamed

LanServer, but it still contained the basic SMB networking design. Microsoft had taken the fundamental ideas and some code of LanServer and rebuilt it into Windows NT using the same SMB networking.

SMB uses the NetBIOS networking interface developed in 1984 by IBM and Sytek, Inc., which later merged into Hughes LAN Systems, Inc. SMB-on-NetBIOS has been implemented on NetBIOS Extended User Interface (NetBEUI), on IPX (by Microsoft), and on TCP/IP using the RFC1001 and RFC1002 NetBIOS-over-TCP/IP standards. Microsoft is attempting to make SMB a standard on the Internet by renaming it the Common Internet File System (CIFS) protocol and has made documentation available at `http://msdn.microsoft.com/workshop/networking/cifs/default.asp`. There is also a Microsoft Knowledge Base article, Q199072, which lists other Microsoft resources on CIFS.

In December 1997, Microsoft submitted what documentation it had on its SMB implementation to IETF as a draft. The work received poor reviews because many areas were either glossed over or completely unspecified. Since then, engineers on the CIFS mailing list have attempted to narrow and sharply define the standard that someday may be specific enough to use as an IETF RFC. Fortunately, the wide proliferation of multiple versions of Windows has in effect blocked further fundamental shifts in SMB implementation and thus stabilized the protocol.

NetBIOS has the basic characteristic that every computer in the network must be given a *machine name* to differentiate itself from others in the network. These names *must* be unique. In Microsoft Networking, computers in a NetBIOS are organized into *domains* or *workgroups*. The domain or workgroup names must also be different from other domains, workgroups, or machine names on the network.

The NetBIOS name is *not* the same thing as the machine DNS name. For example, a machine named `www.microsoft.com` in the DNS can easily carry a NetBIOS name of "OUTSIDE1." NetBIOS has a similar facility called NetBIOS Name Service (NBNS).

Typically, in mixed UNIX and NetBIOS networks, a number of conventions are followed. Whereas UNIX Fully Qualified Hostnames (FQNs) can be as long as 256 characters, because NetBIOS names are limited to a maximum of 15 characters, the computer's *host part* of its DNS name is generally set to be the same length and name as the NetBIOS name. Often, the hostname is set to the name of the user who is assigned to a computer. Additionally, although NetBIOS names can use the characters ! # $ % " & ( ) ^ _ ' { }, usually in TCP/IP networks, administrators follow the DNS convention and restrict computer names to those created with letters A to Z and numbers zero to nine and dashes rather than *underscores*.

If the host is going to be listed with the *same name* in both DNS and NBNS, it is *very important* that it resolve to the *same IP number* in both systems. For example, IP number 123.45.6.7 could resolve to a DNS hostname of sam.domain.com and its NBNS name could resolve to either SAM or FRED. If IP number 123.45.6.7 had an NBNS name of FRED and the DNS listed a separate fred.domain.com at a different IP number of 123.45.6.3, this could create problems on the NetBIOS network.

Another convention generally followed in NetBIOS networks and practically never broken in UNIX networks is to limit the username to a maximum of eight characters. Although Microsoft networking NetBIOS clients allow usernames of up to 20 characters, created with oddball characters, administrators usually limit usernames to eight characters, letters to A through Z, and numbers to zero through nine. FreeBSD, in particular, allows usernames longer than eight characters if the proper definition is made and the entire UNIX system is recompiled. (Current versions permit longer usernames without a recompile.) A username longer than eight characters is strongly advised against because every other UNIX system that is dealt with must be modified. A large number of existing UNIX software programs assume a maximum of eight-character usernames—just about all UNIX programs not supplied with FreeBSD won't work right with eight-character usernames.

One last convention is share names. Earlier versions of NetBIOS on DOS and Win31 could not view shares that had odd characters, such as spaces. Administrators setting up Samba servers should avoid creating share names that contain spaces or other nonstandard characters.

## MICROSOFT NETWORKING CLIENT INSTALLATIONS

Before discussing SMB and NetBIOS server networking implementation, it is useful to understand their client implementation. A functioning client is necessary to troubleshoot the Samba installation that is covered later in this chapter.

The following sections detail how to load the Microsoft Networking client and TCP/IP on DOS and Windows OS. These are here as a convenience for the few people who run them. All NetBIOS clients should be in place and operating before the Samba software is loaded on the FreeBSD system.

## DOS

To load MS Networking client on DOS, follow the instructions in Exhibit 7.1.

## Exhibit 7.1  Loading MS Networking client onto a DOS system

1. Get a machine name, workgroup name, primary user's username, and TCP/IP network number for the computer. Often, administrators name the machines after the people assigned to use them.

2. Obtain the Adapter Files Driver diskette for the network adapter in the computer; this can often be downloaded from the manufacturer. Search the driver files diskette for an \NDIS or \LANMAN.DOS directory, and locate the NDIS DOS driver. For example, the 3Com 3C5x9 series of adapter cards uses a driver disk with an \NDIS2\DOS directory and the ELNK3.DOS network card device driver located in this directory.

   Don't be surprised if some of the cheaper network adapter cards lack these files; they are rarely used under modern Windows OSs. Fortunately, there is a collection of some NDIS drivers in the DOS client files, so step 2 may be skipped for some adapter cards.

3. Using the network card adapter software configuration program from the adapter files driver disk or from jumper settings on the card, determine the port, interrupt, and memory location settings for the adapter card. Plug-and-play PCI and the Personal Computer Memory Card International Association (PCMCIA) network cards may not have these settings available.

4. Obtain the Microsoft Networking DOS client diskette files DSK3-1.EXE and DSK3-2.EXE from the following URL: ftp://ftp.microsoft.com/bussys/Clients/MSCLIENT. Place them in separate temporary directories. These files are also obtainable from the Windows NT Server CD-ROM.

5. Run each file in separate empty directories under DOS. They will expand into a set of files. Copy these files to separate disks. The files in DSK3-1 should be copied onto disk 1, and the files from DSK-2 should be placed on disk 2.

6. Start with a clean DOS system (i.e., PC-DOS, MS-DOS, or DR-DOS/OpenDOS and autoexec.bat and config.sys files that are clear of any terminate and stay residents (TSRs). If Win31 is to run on top of the Microsoft Networking client, it should be installed.

7. Insert disk 1 and run SETUP. The setup program is *not* rodent-driven; use the Tab, Space-bar, and Arrow keys to move around and select items. Press Enter at the setup screen.

8. At the next screen, keep the default of C:\NET, and press Enter.

9. At the next screen select an adapter file from the network cards listed or "*Network Adapter not shown on list below." If you select an unknown card, the setup program requires the adapter driver disk and attempts to read the DOS NDIS driver from it. Often, this fails even when perfectly legitimate and usable DOS driver files exist. It may be necessary to rerun the installation program and select a similar adapter from the included list, modifying the DOS client files by hand after setup is complete (see *Note* on page 226).*

10. Press Enter twice to get past the "Optimizing performance" prompt.

11. Type in the username and press Enter.

12. The next screen is the main setup parameter selection screen. Arrow to "Change Names" and press Enter.

13. The Change Names screen allows the administrator to change the workgroup and computer names. Make the user and computer names the same, and the domain and workgroup names the same. Arrow down to "The listed names are correct" and press Enter.

14. At the main screen, arrow up to "Change Setup options" and press Enter.

15. Arrow up to "Change Redir options." If you're not using Win31, change it to "Use the Basic Redirector"; *otherwise*, leave it at "Use Full Redirector," and press Enter at "The listed options are correct" to get back to the main screen.

16. Arrow up to "Change Network Configuration" and press Enter.

17. Press Tab a few times. The adapters and protocols boxes are highlighted. Highlight the top Adapter box and make sure the adapter card is highlighted, then tab to highlight the bottom box and arrow up to "Change Settings" and press Enter.

18. Enter any resource addresses here, such as port, interrupt, or memory locations, and press Enter at "The listed options are correct."

19. In the bottom window arrow up to "Add Protocol" and press Enter.

20. Highlight "Microsoft TCP/IP" and press Enter.

21. Tab to highlight the top Adapter window and arrow to highlight the "NWLink IPX Compatible Transport." Tab to highlight the bottom window.

22. Arrow to "Remove" and press Enter to remove IPX.

23. Tab to highlight the adapter window and highlight the Microsoft TCP/IP. Tab to the bottom window, arrow to "Change Settings," and press Enter.

24. Arrow to the IP Address and enter the IP number, the IP Subnet Mask, and the mask. Do not put periods between the numbers. Enter the default gateway IP numbers. Set Disable Automatic Configuration to "1" to disable DHCP. Arrow to "The Listed options are correct" and press Enter.

25. Arrow to "Network configuration is correct" and press Enter.

26. Arrow to "The listed options are correct" and press Enter.

27. Setup may ask for the OEM driver disk. Insert disk 2. Insert disk 1 when prompted and press Enter.

28. Setup copies the files needed and modifies the `autoexec.bat` and `config.sys` files. The program then quits. The completed setup program makes the following entries in the `config.sys`

```
LASTDRIVE=Z
DEVICE=C:\NET\IFSHLP.SYS
```

and makes the following changes in `autoexec.bat`

```
C:\NET\NET initialize
PATH=C:\NET;
C:\NET\netbind.com
C:\NET\umb.com
C:\NET\tcptsr.exe
C:\NET\tinyrfc.exe
C:\NET\nmtsr.exe
C:\NET\emsbfr.exe
C:\NET\net start
```

**Exhibit 7.1** (*continued*)

29. If the network adapter driver must be manually entered, do the following.

   a. Copy the DOS NDIS driver to the `C:\NET` directory (e.g., `ELNK3.DOS`).
   b. Modify the `C:\NET\PROTOCOL.INI` file to change "`DriverName=`" and other lines to reflect the logical in-memory device driver name to be loaded by the network card. Often, sample `PROTOCOL.INI` files on the adapter driver disk have the logical driver name.
   c. Modify the `C:\NET\SYSTEM.INI` file and change the `netcard=` line in the [network drivers] section to point to the filename of the DOS NDIS network adapter card driver.

30. Reboot the machine and make sure that all drivers load. Common reasons that drivers don't load are port and interrupt conflicts or attempting to load drivers high that cannot be loaded high. Typically, the DOS client hangs rather than emitting an error message.

*Note:* This is particularly true of PCMCIA cards. Many of these cards require DOS card services to be loaded to load their DOS NDIS drivers at all. Some, such as the 3Com 10Mbt PC card, use a so-called point enabler in the driver that is activated if card services aren't available and allows the card to be used.

## Windows 3.1

Win31 does *not* contain any TCP/IP NetBIOS networking software. Instead, the DOS Microsoft Networking client is run (listed in the previous section) and Win31 runs on top of it. Win31 *must* use the Enhanced or Full installation of the DOS redirector. *Win31 will not properly load Windows Networking on the basic redirector!* To load the Windows section of the client, follow the steps in Exhibit 7.2.

### Exhibit 7.2  Loading MS Networking client onto Win31

1. Install the DOS client per the instructions listed in the previous section.
2. Double-click Main, Windows Setup.
3. Click Options, Change System Settings.
4. Click the down arrow next to Network. Select Microsoft LanManager (version 2.1 Enhanced) and click OK.
5. Restart Windows.

This process makes three changes under Win31.

- It installs a network icon in the control panel.
- It enables the Network Connection button under the Connect button in Printers.
- It enables a Network Connections menu item in the file manager.

Unfortunately, this client is not as full-featured as the WfW client, and there is no graphical browse utility. The user must run NET VIEW \\SERVER-NAME in a DOS window to see a list of shares. In the graphical File and Printer connection boxes, the full UNC name must be typed (e.g., \\SERVER1\ PRINTER1).

## Windows for Workgroups 3.11

WfW was released in two versions, 3.1 and 3.11. Microsoft didn't include TCP/IP with either version but did release TCP/IP for WfW 3.11 later.

Among 16-bit Windows clients, which are usually required for older hardware, WfW 3.11 is the preferred client to use to access a Samba server running under FreeBSD. WfW 3.11 *requires* an 80386 computer or better; it cannot load networking on a 286.

Microsoft released three versions of TCP/IP for WfW: the original version, version A, and version B. Copies of the original version files are getting rare and shouldn't be used in any case. Version B corrects a number of bugs in the protocol implementation. The files are available on the Windows NT CD-ROM, and from Microsoft at ftp://ftp.microsoft.com/Softlib/ MSLFILES/TCP32B.EXE.

The TCP32B.EXE file contains a winsock.dll that allows only TCP/IP applications to send and receive TCP/IP packets through the network adapter. It does *not* contain any kind of dialup support for remote TCP/IP access. Microsoft includes a winsock.dll for 16-bit Windows, as part of its Internet Explorer for Win31 and WfW 3.11, that many 16-bit Windows TCP/IP applications run on. Unfortunately, this stack is completely incompatible with WfW 3.11's networking and cannot be used to provide simultaneous TCP/IP dialup support and network adapter support. However, it is possible to set up a selection menu in config.sys and autoexec.bat that would allow a user to select either the network adapter or the dialup TCP/IP stack.

If dual network adapter and dialup support is required under WfW 3.11, this can be accomplished with the dialup TCP/IP stack available from Shiva, intended for use with their LanRover dialup server product. This stack is properly implemented in the NDIS stack of WfW 3.11, but it is somewhat kludgy. Users needing simultaneous network adapter and dialup TCP/IP support on the same machine are well advised to upgrade to Win95 or later.

WfW 3.11's network stack can be set up to work with a 16-bit NDIS driver for the network adapter card or an NDIS-on-top-of-ODI driver for concurrent use with Novell NetWare's IPX protocol. The TCP/IP for WfW 3.11 protocol has no trouble running on either of these stacks. TCP/IP does require 32-bit NDIS3-level network adapter drivers for the network card. Some network adapters lack these drivers, and in that case the Novell ODI driver plus the NDIS-to-ODI shim can be used even if no Novell network is present: simply remove references to NETX or VLMs in the `autoexec.bat`, and don't load Novell Network shell support in WfW 3.11.

Administrators who are not experienced with loading TCP/IP under WfW 3.11 are advised to familiarize themselves with the 150-page *Microsoft Workgroup Add-On for Windows* user manual that is shipped standard with every copy of WfW 3.11. Unlike the later Windows OSs, such as Win95, when Microsoft released WfW 3.11, it was still including a comprehensive user's manual with its OS software. The administrator in this situation should install the Microsoft Networking IPX-compatible protocol and become familiar with Microsoft Networking under WfW 3.11 before attempting to install TCP/IP. To install Microsoft WfW TCP/IP, follow the steps in Exhibit 7.3.

> **NOTE**   TCP/IP does *not* install DOS networking support, except in a DOS window under WfW 3.11 When the system is booted and goes to DOS, no networking is available until Windows is run.

Much like Win31 networking, WfW TCP/IP adds both printer networking support and file manager networking support. However, unlike the Win31 support, the file and print networking support is advanced enough to allow users to browse the network for the resources they wish to connect to.

## Windows 95

When Microsoft released Win95, it included code from WfW, DOS, and Windows NT. As a result, Win95 comes complete with 32-bit networking code that supports a large number of network adapter cards, as well as dialup networking. Dialup networking allows a Win95 system to establish a PPP or a Serial Line Internet Protocol (SLIP) connection to a remote host and fully participate on the network as if it was there. Drives and printers can be mapped over a dialup connection, in addition to the use of more common remote network applications such as Web browsing. The only major difference between a TCP/IP dialup networking connection and a LAN connection is that Network Neighborhood is not available in the dialup connection *unless* the Windows network is part of a domain and a WINS server is present. If a FreeBSD server is set up as a PPP dialup server for Windows clients, it should enable the `MS-WINS` option in the PPP daemon if a WINS server is present and hand out an NBNS IP number during the IP number negotiation.

**Exhibit 7.3  Loading the MS WfW TCP/IP**

1.  Copy the `TCP32B.EXE` file to a temporary directory and run it. This extracts the installation files.

2.  On a running WfW 3.11 system, double-click the Network Program Group to open it.

3.  In the group, double-click the Network Setup icon, which opens the Network Settings window.

4.  Click the Networks button, and check the Install Microsoft Windows Network box. You don't have to check any additional buttons if you don't need them.

5.  Click OK to go back to the Settings window, then click the Sharing button.

6.  Unless you know that you require these, uncheck both of the "I want to give others access to my . . ." buttons.

7.  Click OK to go back to the Settings window, and then click the Drivers button.

8.  Make sure an adapter card is listed; if not, click Add Adapter. Install the appropriate driver and set it to the correct port and interrupt settings if required. Select either from the list of included drivers or an adapter driver disk with the Unlisted setting.

9.  At the Drivers window, click the Add Protocol button.

10. Select "Unlisted or Updated Protocol" and click OK.

11. Type in the drive and directory in which the `TCP32B.EXE`-extracted files are located and click OK.

12. Select Microsoft TCP/IP-32 3.11b and click OK.

13. A window should open asking for the IP Address and Subnet mask; fill these out and click the DNS button, and then fill that out and click OK to close the windows. If that window does not open, highlight TCP/IP in the drivers window and click Setup.

14. Click OK to close all the windows, and then restart the computer.

Installation of TCP/IP under Win95 is done with the Network settings in the control panel. The OS loads additional files from the Win95 `*.cab` files. A common trick is to create a directory named `cabs` under the `C:\windows` directory and copy all the files from the `\win95` directory on the Win95 CD-ROM to it. When components are later added or removed from the OS, the `*.cab` files will be easily available.

Win95 is one of the first plug-and-play OSs and has an automatic hardware detection system. This system automatically senses many kinds of hardware during installation, including network adapters. If a network adapter is probed, Win95 initiates networking installation. Even after installation, if a PCI network card or an ISA network card that meets the plug-and-play specification is inserted, on the next boot, Win95 recognizes the network hardware and initiates networking installation.

When networking installation is initiated on Win95, the OS defaults to selecting the IPX-compatible network protocol and the NetBEUI networking protocol. This is done because either protocol is suitable for a small network and Microsoft wants to make networking simple for a small office that does not have a dedicated networking specialist. The low-end HP JetDirect network print server card and standalone print servers also support IPX, as do the low-end Intel NetPort printservers. By installing IPX, Microsoft saves itself a lot of tech-support calls. Of course, IPX and NetBEUI are not suitable for an Enterprise network and cannot be used to access UNIX servers.

To install TCP/IP on a Win95 system, follow the steps in Exhibit 7.4.

### Exhibit 7.4  Installing TCP/IP on Win95 systems

**New network installations**

1. Insert the network card into the Win95 system if one isn't there already.

2. Boot the system and escape the boot process into DOS (i.e., press Ctrl-F8 and answer no to all questions).

3. Insert the adapter driver disk that came with the network card and run its diagnostic utility. (Some of the less expensive PCI network cards* may not have such a utility.)

4. Using the diagnostic utility, determine the resources used by the card.

5. If the card resources must be modified to prevent a conflict, do that now. Then reboot the system into Win95.

6. When the system comes up it autodetects the network card and starts the networking installer. If this doesn't happen, click Start-Settings-Control Panel and double-click the Network icon to start the installer.

7. The installer determines resources for the card automatically. If it doesn't, enter the network adapter resources.

8. Click through the rest of the installer and add TCP/IP according to the directions in this exhibit's next section. Then restart the system.

**Existing Win95 networking installations**

1. Click Start-Settings-Control Panel and double-click the System icon to open it.

2. Click the Device Manager tab and click on the Plus sign to expand the Network Adapters icon. Make sure the network adapter is listed without an ! in a yellow circle or other indication that the card is inoperative. Click Cancel to close the window. If the network card isn't listed or is listed with an error, follow the steps in the previous section for a new installation.

3. Click Start-Settings-Control Panel and double-click the Network icon to open the Network window.

4. The adapter card is listed, along with any clients or protocols installed.

5. Remove any unneeded protocols and clients.

6. Click Add, highlight Protocol, and click Add, select Microsoft, and select TCP/IP. Click OK.

7. In the Network window, click Add, select Client, click Add, select Microsoft, and then click Client for Microsoft Networks (this may already have been added in the Network window).

8. In the Network window, click TCP/IP, and then click Properties.

9. Fill out the IP number (unless using a DHCP server). Click through the rest of the tabs, and fill out any other numbering needed.

10. Click OK twice, and then shut down and reboot the system.

### Laptop installations

All laptop PCMCIA network adapters are autosensing in Win95. Inserting the PCMCIA network adapter into a running system makes the system prompt for the adapter driver disk, which should then start the Network installer.

PCMCIA network cards come in 16-bit versions and 32-bit CardBus versions. The CardBus versions are preferable, but many laptops don't have CardBus PCMCIA slots. Check the laptop documentation before purchase.

---

*Note:* Desktop system network cards come in the following versions.

- ISA network cards that are not plug-and-play and use jumpers to set resources. Some of these may not have a diagnostic utility; use a card layout diagram and look at the jumper positions to determine resources. The Western Digital 8013 is an example.
- ISA network cards that are not plug-and-play and use a configuration program to change resources and program them into the card's Electrically Erasable Programmable Read-Only Memory (EEPROM). The Intel EtherExpress 16, 3Com 3C507, later models of Western Digital 8013, and early models of the SMC 8013 cards are examples.
- ISA network cards that can be switched into plug-and-play mode with a configuration program or are programmed by utility. The Intel EtherExpress Pro is an example.
- ISA network cards that are completely plug and play and cannot have resources set automatically by a utility, such as the Compex NE2000 clone adapter card.
- Completely plug-and-play PCI cards that cannot have resources modified by a configuration utility.

# Windows 98

Win98 networking installation is functionally identical to Win95. Active Desktop represents the most fundamental change between Win98 and Win95. Another difference between them concerns SMB/NetBIOS: by default, Win98 uses encrypted passwords to access Microsoft Networking resources. This is discussed later in this chapter in the Encrypted Passwords section.

## Windows Millennium

Windows ME is the next generation of OS from Microsoft in the Win95/98 family and is virtually identical to Win98 from a TCP/IP SMB/LAN networking perspective.

## Windows NT

Installing TCP/IP networking under Windows NT Workstation or Server is somewhat complex. The Windows NT Resource Kit contains installation instructions for NT networking and should be obtained. The Resource Kit is the "missing" documentation that Microsoft used to provide with older versions of Windows NT.

Typically, the networking installer is automatically started during Windows NT installation. The administrator can attempt to autodetect the network adapter card, but most mainstream ISA network cards and many PCI ones are detected and the drivers automatically installed. The Windows NT CD-ROM contains a third-party device driver library with many network card drivers. Alternatively, if the network card is not in the NT database of cards, or if it is, but the administrator wants to use a more current device driver, the adapter driver disk can be inserted and the adapter card driver installed from that.

When the adapter card driver is installed, the NT network installer program automatically selects the IPX and TCP/IP. The administrator can uncheck the IPX protocol and complete the networking installation.

If the networking installer is skipped during initial NT installation (because, for example, a network adapter card isn't inserted in the system), it can be activated by double-clicking the Network icon in the NT control panel.

Several caveats apply to Windows NT Networking installation.

- Windows NT version 4.0 and under is not plug-and-play by default. A plug-and-play manager for NT is on the NT CD-ROM and can be installed if required; this is most commonly done for ISA plug-and-play soundcards that are installed under Windows NT. Refer to the documentation supplied with the network card to determine if it is required. Most PCI network cards do not require it, but ISA plug-and-play network cards may; however, it is preferable to place the ISA card into non-plug-and-play mode with its DOS configuration program before use under Windows NT.
- Use the Microsoft-supplied network card drivers for NE2000 clone network cards. The NE2000 was an ISA network adapter; PCI "clone NE2000" adapters are not real NE2000 clones. Many clone NE2000 card

manufacturers supply NT drivers, but the Microsoft-supplied driver has been fully tested under NT.

- Unless you plan to manage user accounts through the Microsoft NT domains system, do not set up any NT servers as PDCs or BDCs. The NT domains system mentioned in the Microsoft documentation has nothing whatsoever to do with the TCP/IP DNS. The Microsoft domains system is intended as a security control system for a network of Windows systems.

## The NET Command and Logins under Samba

In addition to the graphical networking utilities included with the various Windows Microsoft Networking clients, all versions of Microsoft Networking support access with the NET command in a DOS window.

The NET command is in many cases much more powerful than the graphical utilities and is particularly suited for batch-processing applications. For example, many administrators who are familiar with Novell but new to Microsoft Networking discover that Microsoft Networking clients do not execute any kind of login script when logging into the network, unless the Microsoft Network is configured in the NT domain model, with full domain controllers. Many smaller offices may not want to go through the hassle of setting up an NT domain. An NT domain requires a reinstallation of Windows NT on the server if the NT Server was not set up originally as a domain controller and you want to change it into one.

FreeBSD running Samba can also be set up to support NT domain-style login scripts and user profiles; this is detailed in the file DOMAIN.txt that comes with the Samba software. However, domain-style login support is still being worked on; also, it depends on access to the server via network browsing. If there are multiple subnets on the network, the master login Samba server must also be configured as a WINS server, and the clients on the remote subnets must have the WINS IP number added to their configurations.

To avoid the hassle of domain-style logins, it is possible to create a LOGIN.BAT file somewhere on the NT server or UNIX Samba server on a share accessible to all users; it will contain a series of NET commands that map various drive letters and printer ports to shares. This file can then be run on system startup under any of the clients to set up a common drive letter and printer port mapping.

The example that follows Exhibit 7.5 shows how a centralized login script can be implemented with only a Samba server on the network using the NET command. This idea is usable for both WfW and Win95 clients.

## Exhibit 7.5   Central login script client setup

### DOS or Win31 client

Add the following in the `autoexec.bat` file, after the `NET START` command.

```
net use F: \\FBSDSERVER\LOGIN
call F:login.bat
```

### Windows for Workgroups 3.11 client

In the file manager, click Disk, Connect Network Drive, and select F. Select a path of
`\\FBSDSERVER\LOGIN`, and check the Reconnect at Startup box.

Create the program icon LOGIN, with a command line of `call F:login.bat` in the
Startup program group in the program manager.

### Win95 client

1. Right-click on Network Neighborhood and select Map Network Drive.

2. Change the drive to `F:` and the share to `\\FBSDSERVER\LOGIN`. Make sure the Reconnect at login box is checked.

3. Click Start-Settings-Taskbar. Click the Start Menu Programs tab and then the Advanced button.

4. In the Exploring window, open the Programs folder and click Startup.

5. Click File-New-Shortcut.

6. Type in the command line **call F:login.bat** and click Next.

7. Type in **LOGIN** for the name and click Next.

8. Select an icon and click Finish. This creates the LOGIN icon in the Contents of Startup window.

9. Right-click the LOGIN icon and click Properties.

10. Click the Program tab and check the Close on exit box.

11. Click OK, then close the Exploring window. Click OK on the Taskbar Properties window.

---

Server name: FBSDSERVER
Public login sharename: LOGIN
Contents of LOGIN.BAT:

```
echo off
REM
REM The following maps some drive letters, sets the time, and runs the
REM McAfee DOS AntiVirus scanner located at ftp.mcafee.com
REM
REM This File works fine under Win95 because Win95 does not make
REM connections made with NET USE persistent. WfW and the DOS client
REM do, however, and a cleaner solution would be to have two separate
REM login files, one for DOS/WfW, the other for Win95. The DOS/WfW login
REM file would use the command NET USE X: \\servername\share /persistent:no
```

```
REM and get rid of the /delete statements, which are a hack needed for
REM Win95 since its NET command doesn't support the /persistent option.
REM The following clears any old persistent connections.
net use g: /delete
net use h: /delete
net use lpt1: /delete
net use g: \\FBSDSERVER\FIRSTSHARE
net use h: \\FBSDSERVER\SECONDSHARE
net use LPT1: \\FBSDSERVER\FIRSTPRINTER
net time \\FBSDSERVER /SET
g:\scan c: /boot /nomem
exit
```

There are numerous other things the NET command can do. NET DIAG/ STATUS can give some information about the local workstation. NET VIEW\\ SERVERNAME lists the shares available on the specified server. NET VIEW only lists shares of a server that uses legal sharenames (i.e., sharenames without spaces in them). NET USE can connect to Samba servers that are *not* browsable but are listed in the LMHOSTS file. This is discussed more fully under Network Browsing Issues, later in this chapter.

## Other Microsoft Networking Client Tools

Other client tools are available. All versions of the client contain ping, and the WfW 3.11 and Win95 clients also contain netstat, nbtstat, and netwatch. In addition, WfW contains a program on disk 8 called admincfg, which can be expanded into the c:\windows directory and used to set a number of password options. The graphical clients also have password-changing tools that can be used to change the password on the Samba server. The NT Resource kit has some NetBIOS tools, such as a Browse Master determination utility.

## NETWORK BROWSING ISSUES

SMB clients connect to servers based on the user sending a servername and sharename pair to the client software. Sometimes this is done by the user typing the name pair into the client software. For example, the Map menu item in Win95 can accept a Universal Naming Convention (UNC) name such as \\servername\sharename. Other times this is done by the user requesting a server list from NET VIEW, or via the Connect Network Drive menu item in the NT file manager, or via the Network Neighborhood icon in Win95/98/NT/2K.

The process by which the SMB client gathers servernames to display to the user is known as network browsing (see Figure 7.1).

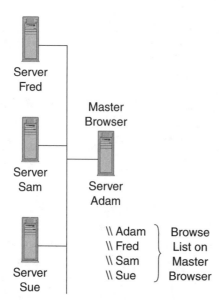

**Figure 7.1**  Browsing setups

## What Is Network Browsing?

*Network browsing* is an automatic mechanism that is negotiated between all NetBIOS systems on the local network. In a simple system, machines send out TCP/IP broadcast announcements when they are first brought up on the network and in response to query packets. A specific system on the network acts as a master browser, collecting these packets and building a browse list. Periodically, all machines on the network hold an election, and the system with the most free resources wins and becomes the master browser. Since it is advantageous to have the official servers in the network become and remain master browsers, Samba has a mechanism that can be enabled to weight the election in its favor if desired.

If the network is set up as an NT domain network, Samba should be configured to give up master browser participation—in NT domain networks the PDCs and BDCs must also be master browsers.

When a client needs to supply a list of servers to the user, it queries the master browser, which returns the list of current servers to the client. The entire system is set up this way to reduce the amount of broadcast traffic on the network.

## What Is NetBIOS Nameserving?

NetBIOS nameserving, also referred to as WINS, is similar to browsing. In an NBNS system, a single machine is statically designated by the administrator as the NBNS or WINS server, and clients have this system's IP number configured into their TCP/IP stacks. The configuration can either be static or assigned via PPP or DHCP. The WINS server listens to broadcast packets from servers that come up on the network and adds them to the list returned to the clients.

The advantage of NBNS or WINS is that clients and servers can be remotely located on different subnets. Each separate subnet is supposed to have a separate WINS server that listens to broadcasts on that subnet. The Microsoft WINS servers all replicate between each other.

NBNS or WINS is documented in the NetBIOS RFCs, but the replication between WINS servers is not standardized. Each vendor implements replication in its own way.

A Samba server can be set up as a WINS server, but it *cannot* replicate between Microsoft WINS servers at the present time.

## Broadcast Forwarding

Normally, TCP/IP broadcast traffic is not forwarded between subnets because TCP/IP was originally designed for long-haul networks, where packet traffic was much more expensive. It made little sense to stuff the line with broadcast traffic that could be engineered around—better to leave the line for data transmission. Today, it would be ludicrous to design routers to forward IP broadcasts by default. If every router on the Internet did that, the Internet would be clogged with broadcast traffic.

In contrast, the IPX protocol designed by Novell does default to broadcast forwarding. Although this is fine for small networks, it causes huge problems in larger corporate networks. Thus, NDS was devised, although it doesn't cut down all IPX broadcast traffic.

In a smaller corporate network of a few subnets connected with a LAN router, it may be advantageous to turn on broadcast forwarding if the router supports it. It is also possible to set Samba servers on remote subnets to forward their announcements to specific servers via unicast traffic.

Because of the problems in larger nets with forwarding broadcasts, the best solution is to set up a central Samba server as a Domain Browse Master and a WINS server. Then, either have Samba servers running as replicated master browsers in each subnet, or configure all of the clients with the WINS server IP number. This is discussed in the BROWSING.TXT document supplied with Samba.

## INSTALLING THE SAMBA SOFTWARE

Samba software is available as a precompiled binary in the Packages section of FreeBSD. It can be compiled and installed from the Ports section, or it may be downloaded from the central Samba Web site and compiled and installed from there. It is strongly recommended on any production server that current software be downloaded, compiled, and installed rather than using the precompiled Samba software.

If Win2K clients are in use on the network, the *minimum* version of Samba that can be run is 2.0.7—do *not* run any lower version! The simplest way of doing this is to use the Ports directory. The instructions for FreeBSD 4.0 and Samba 2.0.7 in Exhibit 7.6 give this method. FreeBSD 4.0 does not supply Samba 2.0.7 in the Ports area (FreeBSD 4.1 does). Instead, 2.0.6 was used, so a few modifications must be made.

### Exhibit 7.6  Installing Samba software

1. As root, change directory into `/usr/ports/net/samba`. Edit the `Makefile` and change the version number of `DISTNAME` from 2.0.6 to 2.0.7.

2. Change into the `patches` subdirectory and move patchfiles `patch-ab`, `patch-ac`, `patch-ag`, `patch-ai`, and `patch-bb` above to the parent directory.

3. Run the `make NO_CHECKSUM=yes` command.

4. Create the directory `/usr/local/swat`.

5. Run the `make NO_CHECKSUM=yes install` command. This terminates with the error about inappropriate file type, which can be ignored because the program has been installed. FreeBSD 4.1 should have this all fixed.

6. Customize `/usr/local/etc/rc.d/samba.sh.sample` if needed, and rename `samba.sh`.

7. The default `samba.sh` runs `smbd` permanently as a daemon. Alternatively, it can be run by `inetd` by uncommenting the # mark in `/etc/inetd.conf` in front of the `smbd` entry and commenting `smbd` out in `samba.sh`. The `nmbd` program should always be run continuously from the `samba.sh` script.

8. The last thing to do is modify the `smb.conf` file to create the Samba shares and to set the server defaults. Start by reading the system manual page on `smb.conf` (type in **man smb.conf**). Rename `/usr/local/etc/smb.conf.default` to `/usr/local/etc/smb.conf` and edit it to create the shares.

The administrator may also be interested in installing `tcp-dump`, an SMB extension to the regular `tcpdump` program, available from <u>ftp://samba.</u> <u>anu.edu.au/pub/samba/tcpdump-smb/tcpdump-3.2.1-smb-</u> <u>src.tar.gz</u>.

## Modifying the smb.conf File

The `smb.conf` file is located in `/usr/local/etc` and needs to be modified for the system. Although the `swat` Web interface can be used to do this, it is good to be familiar with how to create the file manually. A `default` file named `smb.conf.default` is located in this directory and should be modified and renamed to `smb.conf`. This file is very well commented. Parts of it are shown in Exhibit 7.7 without the comments about the file, but with some additional explanations interspersed.

### Exhibit 7.7  Excerpts from the `smb.conf.default` file

[global]

*SMB definitions can be grouped together with [] (brackets). The* global *keyword means everything following is applicable to all other groups in addition to the individual group definitions. Typically, the other group names are names of shares or printer shares.*

workgroup = MYGROUP

*In default Win95, WfW 3.11, and WinNT, the name of the workgroup is set to* workgroup *by the installation program. Usually, administrators change this to their organizational name.*

server string = Samba Server

*The text here appears in the far right column on NT and some Win95 browse lists, and in* net view *commands.*

load printers = yes

*With this command Samba searches* /etc/printcap *and exports all printers defined in it as shares, without needing to create special group definitions for each printer share. In most Samba installations, the administrator redefines the printers anyway to provide information such as printer driver information that is not present in* /etc/printcap, *so this option has questionable value.*

printing = bsd

*This should always be set to "bsd" on FreeBSD.*

print command = lpr -r -s -P %p %s

***This command should be present in** all **FreeBSD installations.** The* lpr *program has an internal size limitation for printer files: it truncates any printer files it thinks are too large, thereby wrecking the file. The* -s *option prevents this from happening.*

security = user

*Blindly setting user security may cause trouble in some WinNT workstation environments, leaving NT clients unable to connect to the Samba server. Use the information in the following list as a guide.*

**Exhibit 7.7**  (*continued*)

- *If the Windows network is an NT domain, with clients logging in to the domain and all clients on the Samba UNIX server defined in the domain, use server-level security and define the password server in the config file pointing to the NT domain controller.*
- *If the Windows network has multiple NT domains, with some clients logging in to them and others not, and some users not defined in the domain defined on the UNIX Samba server, use share-level security. Also use this if NT clients are present but are logging in to themselves instead of in to the domain. This situation should be avoided: if you run a network of Windows clients, either run a domain or don't. Don't fall into the trap of running some hybrid domain-yet-not-a-domain network; either put all clients into an NT domain and make them all log in to the domain, or dispense with the domain controller entirely and run in workgroup security only. Windows networks that attempt to mix workgroups and domains are extremely troublesome to manage, even if every single server and client on the network is a Microsoft product.*
- *If the Windows network is a* workgroup *network without an NT domain controller present and all Win95 systems, use user-level security. If NT workstations are present and access to the server results in problems, use share-level security—or run encrypted passwords and use user-level security. In any case, encrypted passwords are recommended whenever feasible. User-level plus unencrypted (cleartext) passwords will prevent the automatic reconnection feature of NT, as well as making NT refuse to browse the server.\**

```
encrypt passwords = yes
```

*This should be set to yes if the Samba server has encrypted password support compiled in it and is maintaining user passwords. It should also be set to yes if the Samba server is in an NT domain and is using the PDC as the password server.*

```
local master = no
```

*Set this to yes only if the Samba server is not on a network with an NT domain on it and the Samba server is the most powerful server on the network.*

```
domain master = yes
```

*Only set this to yes if there are no NT servers on the network.*

```
preferred master = no
```

*Never set this to yes if the Samba server is on a network with an NT domain running on it. On an NT domain network, the PDC must always be the master browser; setting this keyword to no ensures it.*

```
domain controller = <NT-Domain-Controller-SMBName>
```

*Only set this if all clients are logging in to an NT domain on the network.*

```
domain logons = yes
logon script = %m.bat
logon script = %U.bat
logon path = \\%L\Profiles\%U
```

*These entries are all part of login scripting for Windows clients.*

```
wins support = yes
```

*Never set this unless there are no NT domains on the network. If there is an NT domain, make the PDC the WINS server, not the Samba server.*

```
dns proxy = no
```
*Set this to yes. Set it to no only if there are NT servers with NetBIOS names that are not the same as the host portion of their DNS name—something that normally should be avoided.*

```
# Samba performance workaround:
# If you have performance problem, please test these parameters.
```
*Avoid setting workarounds unless needed. A commonly required workaround for FreeBSD is setting* `socket options = TCP_NODELAY`*—often used if large file copies to and from the Samba server result in slowness and hard drive thrashing.*

```
[homes]
```
*Another special group keyword,* homes, *is used if user home directories exist on the Samba server (i.e., users can Telnet into their home directories and get a shell prompt). On Windows networks with a Samba UNIX server acting as the primary fileserver, it is usually advisable to keep users from Telnetting into the fileserver if possible.*

```
[netlogon]
```
*Use this share definition only if the login scripting is set up and no NT domains are on the network.*

```
[printers]
   comment = All Printers
   path = /usr/spool/samba
   browseable = no
# Set public = yes to allow user 'guest account' to print
   guest ok = no
   writable = no
   printable = yes
```
*The* printers *keyword is another special group keyword used to apply settings to all printers. It works hand in hand with the* load printers *definition in the global section. Usually, this is not used in a Windows environment because the administrator defines printers separately so that printer drivers can be defined.*

```
[nec-raw]
comment = Main PostScript printer
printer driver = NEC SilentWriter 95
printable = yes
```
*This is an example of a printer defined in* /etc/printcap *having the Windows printer driver automatic loading definition applied. The string of text after* printer driver = *must exactly match the name of the driver defined in Windows to activate the automatic driver-loading feature of Windows.*

---

*See Encrypted Passwords section, later in this chapter, for additional information.

## Filesharing from the Samba Server

Since the DOS and Windows filesystem is somewhat different than the UNIX server layout and in many cases there is no direct mapping between concepts, the administrator has the choice of the following two general approaches when setting up Samba server shares. Each approach has a different philosophy.

- The UNIX filesystem, including user home directories, can be regarded much like a *system* partition is regarded under Windows NT and can be set as inaccessible to Samba share users. In this instance, users have no shell access to the UNIX system. The idea here is that all share space on hard drives the FreeBSD system has set aside for this activity.
- Samba can be regarded as an adjunct to regular shell access to the UNIX fileserver, and UNIX user home directories can be accessible from either the shell prompt or the Samba share.

The first approach is frequently selected when the users are all Windows users, such as in a corporate setting. It has a number of advantages. To start with, filesystem security on the server can be made quite lax: after all, if no users have shell access, the administrator doesn't have to worry that a user may attempt to break root. Second, most Windows client users have no interest in the shell anyway, and all they are looking for in a network server is a place to transfer and share files among themselves.

If this approach is used, it is advisable to use multiple hard drives in the fileserver. For example, a 2GB system hard drive might be used for the entire FreeBSD system. Then, multiple 9GB drives might be mounted on an arbitrary root directory structure, such as the following.

- /pubnet—Drive 1, root mountpoint
- /pubnet/users—Drive 2, home directory for users
- /pubnet/sales—Drive 3, all sales files
- /pubnet/admin—Drive 4, all administration files
- /pubnet/marketing—Drive 5, all marketing files

All these drives would be shared out under a single [PUBNET] share from the FreeBSD Samba server, perhaps mapped to a single hard drive letter on the Windows clients. This approach also illustrates the advantage of using FreeBSD UNIX for fileserving instead of WinNT: under an NT server each separate drive requires a different drive letter, thereby dictating a unique sharename on the network and requiring separate hard drive letter mapping at the client.

Under this method, backups are also greatly simplified. If the largest single drive is 9GB, for example, a 5 to 10GB DAT drive using the dump command should be able to back up the server adequately, perhaps with a single tape for each hard drive.

The second approach is usually selected when the users also access the FreeBSD UNIX server with shell prompts. In this case, the filesystem might be organized like this.

- `/`, `/var`, `/tmp`, `/bin`, `/sbin`, etc.—Drive 1, root system
- `/usr`—Drive 2, main location for system binaries, etc.
- `/usr/home/ag`—Drive 3, user home directories for usernames starting with A through G
- `/usr/home/hq`—Drive 4, user home directories for usernames starting with H through Q
- `/usr/home/rz`—Drive 5, user home directories for usernames starting with R through Z
- `/usr/home/etc`—Drive 6, additional directories for departments (e.g., sales, marketing)

With this organization, the drive space is spread evenly across the file-server. Notice that the main emphasis is on having users share files in their home directories. The FreeBSD server exports the `/usr/home` mountpoint as a single share and, using the Automatic Home directory export functionality, it exports individual users' home directories as shares. The second approach allows maximum convenience for users who spend as much time with the shell prompt on the FreeBSD server as they do with fileserving access. However, it can make it more difficult to back up the server and restore it in the event of a hard drive crash.

## DOS and Windows-to-UNIX Permissions

UNIX systems, like FreeBSD, base their filesystem security on the concept of ownership. Since DOS and Windows clients lack the ability to run as a multi-user OS, their filesystem security has a different basis. As a result, there is not a direct one-to-one mapping between filesystem security under DOS and Windows and under UNIX. Some of the key differences follow.

- *File ownership.* Users on UNIX systems can apply different ownership to files, for example, a user can run the `chown` command and transfer ownership of a file he or she has created to someone else. DOS and Windows do not have this because they are single-user systems. Windows NT does contain ownership, but only on the NT File System (NTFS). The de facto standard is that the DOS or Windows client logs in with a particular username and password, and all files created on the UNIX filesystem by the Samba server are owned by the username used to validate over the network. This is very important if the files are created on the UNIX system by another user and then accessed by Samba; the Samba user may not have rights to the files nor any way to change permissions on them.

- *Group ownership.* The administrator on the UNIX system can create groups and place users in them, but users also all start out with a default group. Files created by users in a group carry the group ownership. DOS and Windows do not have a similar functionality. Windows NT does, but there is no mechanism to designate a group ownership over the network to a Samba server. Therefore, files created on the Samba server carry the default group ownership listed in /etc/passwd of the user who created them.

- *Permission bits.* UNIX can apply different types of permissions to the file—user, group, and everyone permission bits. Files can be marked executable, read-only, or write-only. DOS and Windows do not have separate executable permissions on files; instead, they use extensions such as .com and .exe to designate file types. UNIX create permissions are controlled by a mask, which is set in the smb.conf file with the command create mask = XXXX.

- *Allowed operations.* Under DOS and Windows, a readonly file cannot be deleted; it must be changed to readwrite with the attrib command first. Under UNIX, a readonly file can be deleted without changing permissions first. The smb.conf file also has the parameter delete readonly, which deletes a readonly file. Under DOS and Windows, anyone can change a file timestamp, whereas under UNIX, only root or the owner can change a timestamp. The SMB parameter dos filetimes is used for this purpose.

- *Other bits.* DOS and Windows both support the idea of an archive bit as well as a hidden bit, but UNIX has no parallel.

- *Filenames.* UNIX uses some filenames that are not allowed under DOS and Windows. The 8.3 filename (8 characters, 3 extension characters) limitation of DOS is one difference, and UNIX can have more deeply nested subdirectories than DOS. Although UNIX can have filenames containing spaces, this breaks many UNIX utilities.

- *Case sensitivity.* Under UNIX, filenames are case sensitive; for example, AfiLEnaME is a completely different file than AfilenAME. Under DOS and Windows, filenames are case insensitive.

- *Locking.* DOS supports different types of locks on files. In general, UNIX doesn't honor many of these kinds of locks, but Samba can be configured to use special files in a lock directory to support the additional locking modes that DOS and Windows clients may use. Although this may allow multiple DOS and Windows programs that manage file locks to be served from a UNIX server, it won't help anyone trying to share locked files between a DOS or Windows client and a UNIX client.

- *Linking.* UNIX supports both hard and soft links, but DOS and Windows have no counterparts. The Win95 and NT 4.0 *shortcuts* are a first halting step toward file linking, but there is no way to communicate this linking back to the Samba server.

> **NOTE**    Locking can be a big issue if the administrator is attempting to run *network-aware* DOS or Windows programs, such as an accounting program that allows multiple users to access shared data files. The design of these programs is more than 10 years old and originated mainly in the Novell environment. Good modern practice in multiuser applications calls for *client-server* design, in which clients do not have direct access to shared data files. Older programs, such as the network version of the ACT! contact manager, are very dangerous—a single user can destroy or delete data files by accident or intent. ACT! would require the full DOS or Windows locking modes to be available. In contrast, a contact manager of true client-server design might use SQLnet to contact an Oracle database running on the FreeBSD fileserver, and the data files are fully protected against problems originating on the client.

## Running Microsoft Access on Samba

One of the big differences between NT servers and UNIX is that NT servers have a rich set of file-locking commands built into the networking protocol. Although Samba tries to honor locking between the UNIX filesystem and DOS, many locking types available under the NT server aren't part of UNIX. Samba handles these kinds of lock requests internally.

This difference comes into play when running a Microsoft Access shared database. MS Access has always been regarded as the litmus test of compatibility testing. Access has a horrible and ugly internal structure for handling shared locking across the network; if the server software can handle this, it can handle all types of DOS locking.

To successfully run a Samba server with a shared MS Access database on it, the following must be done.

- The subdirectory in which the MS Access `*.mdb` file is located must be mode 777 (i.e., world-readable).
- The Access `*.mdb` file must be group-writable, and all users must be put into the FreeBSD group that has group ownership on the file.
- The MS Access clients *cannot* open the database with "Exclusive Access" checked.

- The following entries should be made in the `smb.conf` file for the share that the Access `*.mdb` file will be available on.

```
[ashare]
        comment = A share for Access
        path = /export/accessdata
        writeable = Yes
        create mask = 0774
        oplocks = No
        share modes = No
```

## ENCRYPTED PASSWORDS

The Microsoft Networking DOS client, the WfW client, all Win95 versions, and all Windows NT 4.0 versions support unencrypted passwords out of the box. In other words, the clients query the server to see if it supports encryption, and if not, the clients use unencrypted passwords.

Windows NT 4.0 Service Pack 3, Win98, and a patch to Win95 turn off this capability: if the server doesn't support encrypted passwords, the clients refuse to connect, with an "Access denied" message, even if the username and password are correct.

The Win95 patch that breaks unencrypted passwords is detailed in the MS Support Online article Q140558. The patch is located at http://support.microsoft.com/download/support/mslfiles/Vrdrupd.exe.

For various reasons the precompiled Samba software distributed with FreeBSD has encryption disabled by default. To support encryption, the Samba server must be recompiled, which is one reason I recommend downloading the latest version of Samba and compiling it. If no Windows NT Server domain controller is present, a complicated procedure needs to be run to move UNIX usernames to Samba encrypted names. This procedure is detailed in the `ENCRYPTION.txt` file distributed with Samba.

Because of the way that encrypted passwords work in Microsoft Networking, the Samba server never knows the cleartext version of the user's password. In addition, the Microsoft encryption mechanism is not DES or MD5 compatible, so the UNIX `/etc/password` file cannot be used to store user passwords. As a result, a UNIX system running Samba must use an additional password file storing only encrypted Samba passwords if the system doesn't use a password server, such as an NT domain controller.

The Samba password file can be built by the administrator when the user accounts on the FreeBSD server are created. Once created, the passwords can be changed by Windows clients with the Passwords icon in the control panel.

Regular UNIX password-changing tools, such as `popasswd` or the `passwd` command run at the UNIX prompt, do *not* change the Samba encrypted password. Samba supplies a program, `smbpasswd`, which when run at the command prompt, can change both the UNIX password and the Samba encrypted password.

It is quite likely that the administrator may prefer to use the precompiled Samba or may not wish to go through the additional steps of turning on Samba encryption. In that case, if only a few clients on a network such as Win98 require encrypted passwords, the clients can easily be modified to go back to the old behavior—supporting unencrypted passwords. For Win98 and the patched Win95, Microsoft Support Online article Q187228 details this procedure. To enable plain-text passwords, follow these steps.

1. Start `Regedit.exe`.
2. Locate the following key in the registry:

   `HKLM\System\CurrentControlSet\Services\VxD\VNETSUP`
3. If you have Win95, you must highlight VNETSUP. Click Edit-New-DWORD value and type in **EnablePlainTextPassword**.
4. Highlight the `EnablePlainTextPassword` value and click Edit-Modify. Change the data value for `EnablePlainTextPassword` to `1`.
5. Restart your computer.

If modifying the registry makes you uncomfortable, an alternate procedure can be used if the Win98 CD-ROM is available. This procedure is detailed in the `Tools\Mtsutil\Mtsutils.txt` file.

For Windows NT 4.0 Service Pack 3, the `readme.txt` discusses how to support unencrypted passwords and refers to MS Support Online article Q166730.

1. Run Registry Editor (`Regedt32.exe`).
2. From the `HKEY_LOCAL_MACHINE` subtree, go to

   `\SYSTEM\CurrentControlSet\Services\Rdr\Parameters`.
3. Click Add Value on the Edit menu.
4. Add the following.
   ```
   Value Name: EnablePlainTextPassword
   Data Type: REG_DWORD
   Data: 1
   ```
5. Click OK and then quit Registry Editor.
6. Shut down and restart Windows NT.

Whether or not to require encrypted passwords is subject to much emotional debate. Those in favor claim that people running password sniffers on the local network can obtain passwords and break user accounts. This argument has been used against Microsoft in various anti-Windows NT encryption, publicity campaigns. Before rushing into requiring wire encryption, consider the following.

- *Is the network secure?* A college dormitory filled with students sharing a single flat network is far more likely to harbor someone who's running password sniffers. In a controlled corporate network of less than a hundred people, most of whom can barely turn on their Windows systems, even with little security on the fileservers, this is very unlikely to happen.

- *Is the network switched?* A creaky, old college network hub run on a shoestring budget is most likely to be completely flat. Thus, a single unicast packet is going to be available for inspection on every single port in the network. A modern corporate network, however, in which every port goes back to a 10BaseT switched hub, is completely different. In this network, unicast packets are normally available only at the source and destination MAC addresses and the hub.

- *How much work is involved?* To me, it has always boiled down to which is more complicated to change. On a large Win98 network, the administrator will want to avoid having to go to every system and install a registry hack; it may be easier to support encrypted passwords at the Samba server. On a small network, by contrast, it may be simpler to turn on unencrypted passwords at the clients.

Being conscious of the kind of network you have and the kinds of users on it is the best security.

# Printserving

Printserving is a complicated topic. There are many different software interfaces to printers, as well as a wide variety of printer hardware interfaces. This chapter covers the basics of setting up a print queue, using Samba to print, and administering print queues and connections.

## PC PRINTING HISTORY

In the early days of the personal computer, printing was simple. The PC owner bought a cheap printer, usually a dot matrix that barely supported ASCII, and plugged it into the computer with a parallel cable. Applications would either work with the printer or not, and most of them did because all they could do was output DOS or ASCII text. The few software applications that supported graphics generally could output only on specific makes and models of printers. Shared *network* printing, if it existed, was usually done by some type of serial port switchbox.

This was the general state of affairs with the PC until the Windows operating system was released. All at once, application programmers were finally free of the restrictions of worrying about how some printer manufacturer would change printer control codes. Graphics printing, in the form of fonts and images, was added to most applications, and demand for it rapidly increased across the corporation. Large, high-capacity laser printers designed for office printing appeared on the scene. Printing went from 150 to 300 to 600dpi for the common desktop laser printer.

Today organizational network printing is complex, and printers themselves are more complicated. Most organizations find that sharing a few high-quality laser printers is much more cost effective than buying many cheaper dot-matrix units. Good network printserving is a necessity, and it can be very well provided by the FreeBSD UNIX system.

## PRINTER COMMUNICATION PROTOCOLS AND HARDWARE

Printers that don't use proprietary vendor codes communicate with computers using one or more of three major printing protocols. The communication is done over a hardware cable that can be a parallel connection (printer port) or a serial connection (COM port).

### ASCII Printing Protocol

The ASCII protocol is the simplest protocol used, as well as the oldest. ASCII is also used to represent text files internally in the DOS, UNIX, and Windows operating systems. Therefore, data taken from a text file or a directory listing generally requires little preparation before being sent to the printer other than a newline-to-carriage return/linefeed conversion for UNIX. Printers usually follow the DOS text file convention of requiring an explicit carriage return character followed by a linefeed character at the end of a line of text. Since UNIX uses only the linefeed character to terminate text, an additional carriage return character must be added to the end of each line in raw text print output; otherwise, text prints in a *stairstep* output. (Some printers have hardware or software switches to do the conversion.)

### PostScript Printing Protocol

Adobe introduced the PostScript language in 1985; it is used to enable the printout of high-quality graphics and styled font text. PostScript is now the de facto print standard in the UNIX community and the only print standard in the Macintosh community. Numerous UNIX utilities exist to *beautify* and enhance text printing with PostScript. PostScript can be used to download font files into a printer as well as the data to be printed. PostScript commands can be sent to instruct the printer CPU to image, rotate, and scale complex graphics and images, thus freeing the host CPU. Scaling is particularly important with fonts since the document with the font has been produced on a computer screen with far lower resolution than the printer. For example, a $1,024 \times 768$ computer screen on a 17-inch monitor allows for a resolution of approximately 82dpi, but a modern desktop printer prints at a resolution of 600dpi. Therefore, a font must be scaled at least seven times larger for WYSIWYG output.

PostScript printers generally come with a number of resident fonts. For example, the NEC Silentwriter 95 contains Courier, Helvetica, ITC Avant Garde, Gothic Book, ITC Bookman Light, New Century Schoolbook Roman, Palatino Roman, Times Roman, and several symbol fonts. These are stored in ROM in the printer. When a page prints from a Windows client that contains a font not in the printer, a font substitution table is used. If no substitute can be made, Courier is usually used. The user should be conscious of this when creating documents—documents with fonts not listed in the substitution table may cause other users problems when printing. Avoid use of strange fonts for documents that will be widely distributed.

The user program can choose to download different fonts as outline fonts to the PostScript printer if desired. Fonts that are commonly used by a user are often downloaded to PostScript printers that are connected directly to the user's computer; the fonts are then available for successive print jobs until the printer is turned off. When PostScript printers are networked, clients must download any fonts desired *with each print job*. Since jobs come from different clients, clients cannot assume that downloaded fonts are still in the printer.

PostScript print jobs also contain a header that is sent describing the page layout, among other things. On a shared network printer, this header must also be downloaded with each print job. Although some PostScript drivers allow downloading of the header only once, this usually requires a bidirectional serial connection to the printer instead of a unidirectional parallel connection.

PostScript print jobs can be sent either as binary data or as ASCII. The main advantage of binary data transmission is that it is faster. However, not all Post-Script printers support it, and fonts generally cannot be downloaded in binary. When FreeBSD is used as a printserver, ASCII PostScript printing should be selected on the clients; this is the default with most PostScript drivers.

The Adobe company licenses PostScript interpreters as well as resident fonts to printer manufacturers, and extracts a hefty license fee from any printer manufacturer who wants to use them in its printer. This presents both a benefit and a problem to the end user. Although a single company holding control over a standard can guarantee compliance, it does significantly raise the cost of the printer. As a result, PostScript has not met with much success in lower-end laser and inkjet Windows printing market, despite the fact that Adobe distributes PostScript software operating system drivers for free.

One issue that is a concern when networking PostScript printers is the selection of banner page (also known as header page or *burst page*) printing. UNIX shared printing began with ASCII line printers, and since UNIX is a multiuser system, often many different user print jobs would pile up in the printer output hopper. To separate these jobs the UNIX printing system programs support banner page printing if the client program that submits jobs asks for them. These pages print at the beginning or end of every print job and contain the username, submittal date, and so on. By default, most clients, whether remote (e.g., a Windows LPR client) or local (e.g., the `/usr/bin/lpr` program) trigger a banner page to be printed. One problem is that some PostScript printers abort the entire job if they get unformatted ASCII text instead of PostScript. (In general, PostScript printers compatible with Hewlett-Packard Printer Control Language [HPPCL] handle banners without problems.) Banner printing should be disabled for any printers with this problem unless PostScript banner page printing is set up on the server.

## HPPCL Printing Protocol

The Hewlett-Packard (HP) company currently holds the largest market share of desktop inkjet and office laser printers. Back when Windows was released, HP decided to expand into the desktop laser jet market with the first LaserJet series of printers. At the time there was much pressure on Microsoft to use Adobe Type Manager for scalable fonts within Windows and to print PostScript to higher-end printers. Microsoft decided against doing this and used a technically inferior font standard, Truetype. They thought it was unlikely that the user would download fonts to the printer since desktop publishing was not being done on PCs at the time. Instead, users would rasterize the entire page to the printer using whatever proprietary graphics printer codes the selected printer needed. HP devised HPPCL for their LaserJets and made PostScript an add-on. The current revision of HPPCL allows for many of the same scaling and font download commands that PostScript does. HP laser jet printers that support PostScript can be distinguished by the letter "M" in the model number. (M is for Macintosh, because Macintosh requires PostScript to print.) For example, the HP 6MP has PostScript; the 6P doesn't.

HPPCL has almost no support in the UNIX applications market, and it is very unlikely that any will appear soon. One big reason is the development of the free *Ghostscript* PostScript interpreter. `Ghostscript` can take a PostScript input stream and print it on a PCL printer under UNIX. Another reason is the UNIX community's dislike of reinventing the wheel. HPPCL has no advantage over PostScript, and in many ways there are fewer problems with PostScript. Considering that PostScript can be added to a printer, either by hardware or use of `Ghostscript`, what is the point of exchanging an existing working solution for a slightly technically inferior one? Over the life of the printer, taking into account the costs of toner, paper, and maintenance, the initial higher cost of PostScript support is infinitesimal.

## NETWORK PRINTING BASICS

The most common network printing implementation is a printserver accepting print jobs from clients tied to the server via a network cable.

### Printservers

The term *printserver* is one of those networking terms, like *packet,* that has been carelessly tossed around until its meaning has become somewhat confusing and blurred. To be specific, a printserver is simply a program that arbitrates print data from multiple clients for a single printer. Printservers can be implemented by one of four methods described in the following sections.

#### Printserver on a Fileserver
A printer can be physically cabled to the PC running the NOS (Figure 8.1). Print jobs are submitted by clients to the printserver software on the fileserver, which sends them down the parallel or serial cable to the printer. The printer must be physically close to the fileserver. This kind of printserving is popular in smaller workgroup networks in smaller offices.

#### Printserver on a Separate PC
It is possible to run a printserver program on a cheap PC that is located next to the printer and plugged into it via parallel cable (Figure 8.2). This program simply acts as a pass-through program, taking network packets from the network interface and passing them to the printer. This kind of server doesn't allow any manipulation of print jobs; jobs usually come from a central file server, where jobs are controlled.

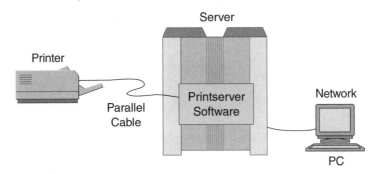

**Figure 8.1** Printserver on a fileserver

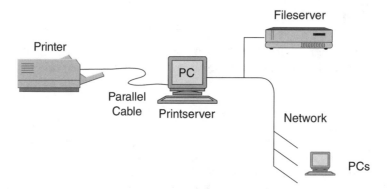

**Figure 8.2**  Printserver on a separate PC

### Printserver on a Separate Hardware Box

A printserver on a separate hardware box is exemplified by network devices such as the Intel Netport, the HP JetDirect Ex, the Osicom/DPI NETPrint, and the Lexmark MarkNet (Figure 8.3). Basically, these are plastic boxes with an Ethernet connection on one side and a parallel port on the other. Like a printserver on a PC, these devices don't allow remote job manipulation and merely pass packets from the network down the parallel port to the printer.

### Printserver in the Printer

The HP JetDirect Internal is the best known printserver of this type (Figure 8.4). It is inserted into a slot in the printer case, and it works identically to the external JetDirect units.

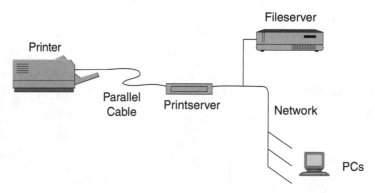

**Figure 8.3**  Printserver on a hardware box

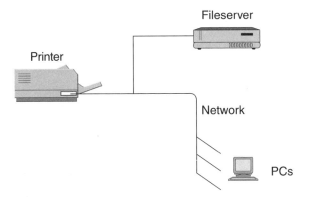

**Figure 8.4** Printserver in the printer

## Print Spools

Print spooling is an integral part of network printing. Since the PC can spit out data much faster than the printer can accept it, the data must be buffered in a spool at some location. In addition, because many clients share printers, when clients send print jobs at the same time, jobs must be placed in a queue so that one can be printed after the other.

### Logical Location of the Print Spool

Print spooling can be implemented at one of three locations (see Figure 8.5).

**1.** *The client.* Clients can be required to spool their own print jobs on their own disks. For example, when a Windows client application generates a print job, the job must be placed on the local client's hard drive. Once the remote printserver is free to accept the job, it signals the client to start sending the job a bit at a time. Client spooling is popular in peer-to-peer networks with no defined central fileserver. However, it is impossible for a central administrator to perform advanced print job management tasks, such as moving a particular print job ahead of another or deleting jobs.

**2.** *The printserver.* If each printer on the network is allocated its own combination print spooler–printserver, jobs can stack at the printer. Many of the larger printers with internal printservers have internal hard drives for this purpose. Although this enables basic job management, it still restricts the ability to move jobs from one printer to another.

**3.** *A central print spooler on a fileserver.* Print jobs are received from all clients on the network in the spool and then dispatched to the appropriate

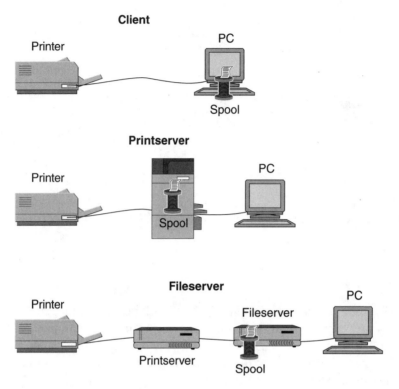

**Figure 8.5**  Print spool locations

printer. This scheme is the best for locations with several busy printers and many clients. Administration is extremely simple because all print jobs are spooled on a central server, which is particularly important in bigger organizations. Many large organizations have standardized on PostScript printing for all printing; in the event that a particular printer fails and is offline, incoming PostScript print jobs can be rerouted automatically to another printer. Since all printers and clients are using PostScript, clients don't need to be reconfigured when this happens. Print jobs appear the same whether printed on a four-page-per-minute NEC Silentwriter 95 or a 24-page-per-minute HP LaserJet 5SiMX if both printers are defined in the client as PostScript printers.

FreeBSD is an excellent platform to implement centralized printserving and print spooling. The rest of this chapter concentrates on the centralized print spooler model. Note that PostScript printing is not a requirement for this model—the HPPCL protocol can be the standard print protocol as well. For transparent printing between printers with HPPCL, however, the printer models must be similar.

### Physical Location of the Print Spool

In some companies, the central fileserver is often placed in a closet, locked away. Printers, on the other hand, are best located in high-traffic areas for ease of use. Network printing works best when the printers are evenly distributed throughout the organization. Attempting to place all the major printers in one location, as technically advantageous as it may seem, merely provokes users to request smaller printers that are more convenient for a quick print job. The administrator may end up with a data center full of nice, expensive printers that are never used while the smaller personal laser printers scattered throughout the plant bear most of the printing load.

The big problem with this situation is that scattering printers throughout the organization makes it difficult to use the three possible parallel ports on the fileserver due to parallel port distance limitations. Although high-speed serial ports may extend that distance, not many printers have good serial ports on them. This is where the hardware network printserver devices can come into play. I prefer using these devices because they are much cheaper and more reliable than a standalone PC running printserver software. For example, Castelle (http://www.castelle.com) sells the LANpress 1P/10BT printserver for about $170. Using these devices, a FreeBSD UNIX server can have dozens of print spools accepting print jobs and then route them back out over the network to these remote printserver boxes. If these kinds of hardware servers are used, they must support the Line Printer Daemon (LPD) print protocol.

With a scheme like this, it is important to have enough disk space on the spool to handle the print jobs. A single large PowerPoint presentation PostScript print job containing many graphics may be over 100MB. When many such jobs stack up in the print spool waiting to print, the print spooler should have several gigabytes of free disk space available.

### Network Printing to Remote Spools

Although several proprietary network printing protocols, such as Banyan Vines and NetWare, are tied to proprietary protocols, FreeBSD UNIX can use two TCP/IP network printing protocols to print to remote print spools. The two print protocols available on TCP/IP with FreeBSD are the open LPD protocol and the NetBIOS-over-TCP/IP Server Messaging Block (SMB) print protocol first defined by Intel and Microsoft and later used by IBM and Microsoft.

The LPD protocol is defined in RFC1179. This network protocol is the standard print protocol used on all UNIX systems. LPD client implementations exist for all Windows operating systems and DOS. Microsoft has written LPD for the Windows NT versions; the other Windows operating system implementations are provided by third parties.

The Microsoft Networking network protocol that runs on top of SMB can use NetBIOS over TCP/IP, as defined in RFC1001 and RFC1002. This protocol has a specification for printing that is the same print protocol used to send print jobs to NT server by Microsoft clients. To implement this protocol on FreeBSD requires the installation of the Samba client suite of programs discussed in Chapter 7.

## SETTING UP LINE PRINTER REMOTE ON WINDOWS CLIENTS

The program clients use to print via LPD is the Line Printer Remote, or LPR, program. The following instructions cover enabling this program on Windows clients.

### Windows 3.1 and Windows for Workgroups 3.11

Several commercial TCP/IP stacks are available for Win31 that provide LPR client programs, in addition to the basic TCP/IP protocol, to Win31. WfW has TCP/IP networking available for free from Microsoft, but it doesn't include an LPR client. Unfortunately, I have not come across a freeware implementation of a 16-bit Windows LPR client, so with the following instructions I use the shareware program WLPRSPL, available from `http://www.winsite.com/info/pc/win3/winsock/wlprs41.zip`. This program must be active during client printing and is usually placed in the Startup group.

Organizations that want to use UNIX as a printserver to a group of Win31 clients without using a commercial or shareware LPR program have another option. The Microsoft Networking client for DOS used underneath Win31 contains SMB-based printing, which is covered later in this chapter. DOS networking client setup and use are covered in Chapter 2 and Chapter 7.

If LPR-based client printing is desired and the organization doesn't want to upgrade to Win95 (which has several LPR clients), the following instructions can be used. WLPRSPL needs a Winsock under Windows 3.1, so for the example, I explain the setup of the Novell 16-bit TCP/IP client. The stack can be FTPed from Novell and is easy to integrate into sites that already use the 16-bit NetWare networking client, usually NW 3.11 and 3.12. In most cases, however, sites that use NetWare plus Win31 are probably best off printing through the NetWare server and then loading an LPR spooler as a Netware Loadable Module (NLM) to send the job over to FreeBSD.

As an alternate, the Microsoft Networking DOS 16-bit TCP/IP client under Win31 contains a Winsock, as does Microsoft TCP/IP for WfW. The target machine used here is a Compaq Deskpro 386/33 with 12MB of RAM with an operating version of Windows 3.1, and a 3Com 3C579 EISA network card. The instructions assume an LPR printserver on the network, named `mainprinter.ayedomain.com`, with a print queue named `RAW` (see Exhibits 8.1 and 8.2).

Use the installation instructions in Exhibit 8.1 for a quick and dirty TCP/IP Winsock for Win31 systems. Administrators who already have the Novell IPX client installed should skip those steps.

### Exhibit 8.1  Installing the Novell TCP/IP Winsock client

1. Make sure that the machine has enough environment space (2,048 bytes or more) by adding the following line to the `config.sys` file and rebooting.
   `SHELL=C:\COMMAND.COM /E:2048 /P`

2. Obtain the `TCP16.EXE` file from <u>ftp3.novell.com/pub/updates/eol/nweol/</u> <u>tcp16.exe</u>.

3. Obtain the Network Adapter support diskette for the network card in your machine. This should be supplied with the card or available via FTP from the network adapter manufacturer's FTP site.

4. Now you need the file `LSL.COM`, which is available on some Network Adapter Driver diskettes. It used to be available from the `VLM121_2.EXE` file from Novell, but unfortunately, this file is no longer publicly accessible from Novell.

5. If you have `vlm121_2.exe` in a temporary directory, run it. This will extract a number of files.

6. One of the files extracted is `LSL.CO_`. Extract this file with the command `nwunpack lsl.co_`.

7. Create the directory `c:\nwclient`. Then, copy `lsl.com` from the temporary directory into the directory.

8. Obtain and install the printer driver for the model of printer that you will be spooling to, and point it to `LPT1:`. Win31 and WfW 3.11 have an incomplete printer driver list, so if you need a driver, Microsoft has many Win16 printer drivers on their FTP site. A list is available at <u>ftp://ftp.microsoft.com/Softlib/index.txt</u>. In addition, if you are installing a PostScript printer driver for a printer supplied in Win31, it may be necessary to patch the driver. The Microsoft PostScript driver supplied in Win31 is version 3.5. (The patch named `PSCRIP.EXE`, which brought the PostScript driver to version 3.58, is no longer publicly available.) WfW already uses the more recent PostScript driver, as does Win31 version A. Installing the Adobe PostScript driver for Win31 is also an option (see <u>http://www.adobe.com/support/downloads/pdrvwin.htm</u> for the version 3.1.2 Win31 PostScript driver).

**Exhibit 8.1** *(continued)*

9. Look on the network adapter driver disk for the subdirectory `nwclient`, and then look for the ODI driver with the adapter card. For example, on the 3Com 3C509/3C579 adapter driver disk, the driver and location are `\NWCLIENT\3C5X9.COM`. Copy this driver to the `c:\nwclient` directory.

10. Create a file called `NET.CFG` in the `c:\nwclient` directory. Often, the network card adapter driver diskette has a template for this file in the same location as the ODI driver. This template can be modified, as can the following example.

```
LINK SUPPORT
    BUFFERS 4 1600
    MEMPOOL 8192

    LINK DRIVER 3C5X9
    ; PORT 300 (these are optional if needed by card uncomment)
    ; INT 10 (optional; uncomment, and modify if needed)
```

11. Attempt to load the network card driver. First, load `lsl`, and then load the ODI driver. With the 3Com card the commands are

```
lsl
3c5x9
```

If the driver properly loads, it will list the hardware port and interrupt settings for the network adapter. If it has loaded properly, unload the drivers in reverse order with the `/u` command.

```
3c5x9 /u
lsl /u
```

12. Go to the temporary directory that contains the `tcp16.exe` file and extract it by running the program.

13. Run the install batch file by typing `installr`. It should list "New Installation detected." It will then copy a number of files into `nwclient`, add some commented-out sections to `net.cfg`, and call "edit" on `net.cfg`.

14. Read the editing instructions and make the appropriate entries. The sample `net.cfg` file from above would look like this.

```
LINK SUPPORT
    BUFFERS 4 1600
    MEMPOOL 8192
LINK DRIVER 3C5X9
    FRAME ETHERNET_II
    Protocol TCPIP
PATH TCP_CFG c:\nwclient
    ip_address 192.168.1.54 LAN_NET
    ip_netmask 255.255.255.0 LAN_NET
    ip_router 192.168.1.1 LAN_NET
    Bind 3C5X9 #1 Ethernet_II LAN_NET
```

Save and exit. The Installer should list "TCP16 installation completed."

15. Reload the client with the following commands.

```
lsl
3c5x9
tcpip
```

The TCP/IP driver should list the IP numbers and other information.

16. Optionally, either create a HOSTS file, or a RESOLV.CFG file (pointing to a nameserver), in c:\nwclient. Check to see that this is operating properly by pinging a hostname.

17. Add the c:\nwclient directory to the path, as well as the three startup commands in step 15 in autoexec.bat.

---

### Exhibit 8.2  Installation of the LPR client on 16-bit Windows with a Winsock installed

The following assumes a running Win31 installation with a Winsock or a running WfW installation with the 32-bit Microsoft TCP/IP protocol installed.

1. Install the printer driver desired. See step 8 of Exhibit 8.1.

2. Obtain and extract into a temporary directory the wlprs41.zip file from the location mentioned above.

3. Run setup.exe from the temporary directory containing the wlprs files.

4. In setup, accept the default directory, and check Yes to add to its own group. Click "Continue" when asked for group name, and check whatever choice you want when asked to copy the doc files.

5. Click No when asked to add the program to Startup.

6. On the UNIX FreeBSD print spooler, make sure that there is an entry in /etc/hosts.lpd or /etc/hosts.equiv for the client workstation, thereby allowing it to submit jobs.

7. Double-click the Windows LPR Spooler icon in the Windows LPR Spooler group that is opened. When it asks for a valid spool directory, select the c:\wlprspl directory that the program installed its files into.

8. When asked for a valid Queue Definition File, click OK to use the default filename. The program automatically creates a queue definition file.

9. The program opens up with its menu. Click Setup in the top menu, and then select "Define New Queue."

10. For a local spool filename, just use the name of the remote queue (RAW) to which the client will print.

11. For the remote printer name, use the same name as the remote queue (RAW) to which the client prints.

12. For the remote hostname, use the machine name of the FreeBSD print spooler, mainprinter.ayedomain.com.

13. For the Description, enter a description such as "3rd floor Marketing printer."

14. For the protocol, leave the default of BSD LPR/LPD selected.

15. Click on Queue Properties, and make sure that "Print unfiltered" is selected. If you're printing PostScript, then also click the Advanced options button. Make sure that "Remove trailing Ctrl-D" is *unchecked* and that "Remove Leading Ctrl-D" is *checked*. Also with PostScript, if the printer cannot print ASCII, uncheck the "Send header page" box. (PostScript header and banner pages are discussed later in this chapter.)

**Exhibit 8.2**　(*continued*)

16. Click OK. At the main menu of the program, click File and then "Control Panel/Printers" to bring up the Printers control panel of Windows.

17. Make sure that the "Use Print Manager" button is checked, and then highlight the printer driver and click the Connect button.

18. Scroll down to the `C:\WLPRSPL\RAW` entry for the spool that was built and highlight this. Click OK.

19. Minimize the Windows LPR Spooler. Copy the Windows LPR Spooler icon to the Startup group. Click "File/Properties" with the Windows LPR Spooler icon highlighted in the Startup group. Check the "Run Minimized" button.

20. Exit Windows, and when the "Save queue changes?" button comes up, click Yes.

21. Restart Windows, and make sure that the spooler starts up.

22. Open the Control Panel and look for a new yellow icon named "Set Username?" If you are running the Novell or other Winsock under Win31, click on this icon and put the username of the person using this computer into the space provided. If you are running WfW, this isn't necessary because Windows will supply the username.

22. If the spooler is not started properly in some installations, there may be a bug. If placing the icon in the Startup group doesn't actually start the spooler, the program name can be placed in the `run=` line of `win.ini`.

23. Try printing a print job from an application such as Notepad. If everything goes properly, clicking on the "Queues/Show remote printer status" in the Windows LPR menu should show the print job spooled and printing on the remote printserver.

## Installation of LPR Client on Windows 95/98

The `wlprspl` program also can be used under Windows 95, but as a 16-bit program, it is far from an optimal implementation on a 32-bit operating system. In addition, Win95 and its derivatives have fundamentally changed from Windows 3.1 in the printing subsystem. For these reasons I use a different LPR client program for Win95/98 LPR printing instructions. It is a full 32-bit print program, and it installs as a Windows 32-bit printer port monitor. The program is called ACITS LPR Remote Printing for Windows 95, and it is located at `http://shadowland.cc.utexas.edu/acitslpr.htm`.

ACITS stands for Academic Computing and Instructional Technologies Services. The ACITS LPR client includes software developed by the University of Texas at Austin and its contributors; it was written by Glenn K. Smith, a systems analyst with the Networking Services group at the university. The filename of the archive in the original program was `ACITSLPR95.EXE`, and, as of version 1.4, it was free for individuals or organizations to use for their internal printing needs. Since that time, it has gotten so popular that the university has taken over the program, incremented the version number (to get out from under the free license), and charges a \$35 per copy fee for commercial use for the newer versions. The older, free version can still be found on overseas FTP servers, such as `http://www.go.dlr.de/fresh/pc/src/winsock/acitslpr95.exe`.

It is likely that the cost of a shareware or commercial LPR program for Win95 plus the cost of Win95 itself will meet or exceed that of Win2K. As such, users wishing to print via LPR to FreeBSD UNIX systems will probably find it cheaper to simply upgrade to Windows NT Workstation or Win2K.

ACITS LPR and Win95 have a few printing idiosyncrasies. Most Win95 programs, such as Microsoft Word, expect print output to be spooled on the local hard drive and then metered out to a printer that is plugged into the parallel port. Network printing, on the other hand, assumes that print output will go directly from the application to the remote printserver. Under Win95, local ports have a setting under Properties, Details, Spool Settings labeled "Print directly to the printer." If this is checked, the application running on the desktop, such as Microsoft Word, does not create a little Printer icon with pages coming out of it or use some other means of showing the progress of the job as it is built. This can be very disconcerting to the user of a network printer, so this option should be checked only with printers plugged directly into the parallel port. Worse, if this is checked with ACITS, it can cause the job to abort if the remote print spooler momentarily goes offline.

Another local setting also should be changed. Generally with local ports, Win95 builds the first page in the spooler and then starts printing it while the rest of the pages spool. If ACITS starts printing the first page while the rest of the pages are building, timeouts at the network layer can sometimes cause very large jobs to abort. The entire job should be set to spool completely before the LPR client passes it to the UNIX spooler. This problem is partly the result of program design: because ACITS is implemented as a local printer port instead of being embedded into Win95 networking (and available in Network Neighborhood), the program acts like a local printer port in some ways.

The LPR program can be set to deselect banner or burst page printing if a PostScript printer that cannot support ASCII is used. The burst pages referred to here are *not* generated by the Windows machine. Use the instructions in Exhibit 8.3 to install.

### Exhibit 8.3  LPR client on Win95/98 installation instructions

1. Obtain the `ACITSLPR95.EXE` file and place it in a temporary directory, such as `c:\temp1`.

2. Close all running programs on the desktop. The computer *must* be rebooted at completion of installation or the program will not work.

3. Click Start, Run and type in `c:\temp1\acitslpr95`. Click Yes at the InstallShield prompt.

**Exhibit 8.3** (*continued*)

4. Click Next, then Yes. The program runs through some installation and then presents a Help screen that explains how to configure an LPR port.

5. After the Help screen closes, the program asks to reboot the system. Ensure that Yes is checked, and click Finish to reboot.

6. After the machine comes back up, install a Printer icon in the "Start, Settings, Printers" folder if one hasn't been created for the correct model of destination printer.

7. With the Printers folder open, right-click over the printer icon that needs to use the LPR program, and click on the Properties tab.

8. Under the Details tab, click the Add Port tab, then click Other.

9. Highlight the ACITS LPR Remote Printing line, and click OK.

10. The Add ACITS LPR screen opens. Type in the hostname of the UNIX system that the client spools through—`mainprinter.ayedomain.com`.

11. Type in the Printer/Queue name, and click OK. (Some versions have a "Verify Printer Information" button.) The LPR program then contacts the UNIX host and makes sure that the selected printer is available.*

12. If the printer is PostScript and cannot print ASCII, make sure that the "No banner page control flag" is checked to turn off banner pages. Accessible under Port settings, this flag is overridden if the `/etc/printcap` file specifies no banner pages.

13. Review how the "Send plain text control" flag is set. With this flag unchecked, the LPR code sent is L (i.e., print unfiltered), meaning that the `if` filter gets called with the `-c` option. This is equivalent to the local invocation of `/usr/bin/lpr -l`. With the flag checked, the code is F (formatted), meaning that the `if` filter gets called without the `-c` option. This is equivalent to the default invocation, `/usr/bin/lpr`. (This is also an issue under Windows NT, which retypes the print job to text if this flag is checked.) Some filters understand the `-c` flag, which is used to preserve control characters, so it should generally remain unchecked.

14. Leave the "Send data file before control file" box unchecked. This option is used only in rare mainframe spooling circumstances.

15. Click OK, and then click the Spool Settings button at the Properties page.

16. Make sure that the "Spool print jobs so program finishes printing faster" box is checked.

17. Make sure that "Start printing after last page is spooled" box is checked.

18. Make sure that "Disable bi-directional support for this printer" box is checked or greyed out.

19. Make sure that "Spool data format" is set to RAW. Some printer drivers present a choice of EMF or RAW, such as the Generic Text driver; in this case, select RAW.

20. Click OK and then OK again to close the Printer Properties. The printer icon now spools through FreeBSD.

---

*Note*: If this fails, the client machine name is probably not in `/etc/hosts.equiv` or `/etc/hosts.lpd` on the FreeBSD printserver. Most sites may simply decide to put a wildcard in `hosts.equiv` to allow printing, especially if DHCP is used, but many security-conscious sites may stick with individual entries in `hosts.lpd`.

## Installation of LPR Client on Windows NT

Unlike WfW and Win95 TCP/IP, Windows NT—both server and workstation—includes an LPR client as well as an LPD program that allows incoming print jobs to be printed from LPR clients, such as UNIX systems.

To install the LPR client and daemon program under Windows NT 3.51, use the following instructions. The TCP/IP protocol should be installed beforehand and you must be logged in to the NT system as Administrator. This can be done at any time after the NT system is installed, or during OS installation.

1. Double-click on Main, Control Panel, then Network Settings.
2. In the Installed Network Software window, Microsoft TCP/IP Printing should be listed as well as TCP/IP Protocol.
3. Click the Add Software button to get the Add Network Software dialog box.
4. Click the down arrow and select TCP/IP Protocol and related components. Click Continue.
5. Check the TCP/IP Network Printing Support box and click Continue. LPR printing is now installed. Follow the instructions to reboot to save changes.

To install the LPR client and daemon program under Windows NT 4, use the following instructions. The TCP/IP protocol should be installed beforehand and you must be logged in to the NT system as Administrator. This can be done at any time after the NT system is installed, or during OS installation.

1. Click on Start, Settings, Control Panel, and double-click on Network to open it.
2. Click on the Services tab. Microsoft TCP/IP Printing should be listed. If not, continue to steps 3 and 4.
3. Click Add, and then select Microsoft TCP/IP Printing and click OK.
4. Click Close. Follow the instructions to reboot to save changes.

> **NOTE**  Any NT Service Packs that were previously installed must be reapplied after these operations.

Once LPR printing has been installed, the Printer icon or icons must be created on the NT system so that applications can print. Since this printer driver does all job formatting before passing the printing to the FreeBSD printserver, the print queues specified should be raw queues on the FreeBSD system, which don't do any job formatting.

To install the printer icon in Print Manager and set it to send print jobs to the FreeBSD UNIX system, use the following instructions under NT 3.51. You must be logged in to the NT system as Administrator. This can be done at any time after the NT system is installed, or during OS installation.

1. Click on Main and open it. Then click on Print Manager to open it.
2. Click on Printer, Create Printer. Select the appropriate printer driver.
3. Click the down arrow under Print To and select Other.
4. In the Available Print Monitors window select LPR port and click OK.
5. Enter the hostname of the FreeBSD printserver and the name of the printer queue and click OK.
6. Click OK to close the Create Printer window. The Printer icon is created.

To install the Printer icon in Print Manager and set it to send print jobs to the FreeBSD UNIX system, use the following instructions under NT 4. You must be logged in to the NT system as Administrator. This can be done at any time after the NT system is installed, or during OS installation.

1. Click Start, Settings, Printers to open the printer folder.
2. Double-click Add Printer to start the wizard.
3. Select the My Computer radio button, *not* the Network Print Server button, and click Next. (The printer *is* a networked printer, but it is managed on the local NT system. Microsoft used confusing terminology here.)
4. Click Add Port and select LPR Port, and then click New Port.
5. Enter the hostname and print queue for FreeBSD printserver and click OK.
6. Click Next and select the correct printer driver. Continue until the printer is set up.

The LPR client in Windows NT allows DOS print jobs originating in DOS boxes to be routed to the central UNIX print spooler. This is an advantage over the Win95 and WfW LPR programs.

## Windows NT Registry Changes

Using the LPR daemon program under Windows NT presents one problem. If the NT server is used as an LPR/LPD "relay," for example, to pass jobs from clients to LPR print queues on a UNIX system, to pass jobs from LPR programs on UNIX terminating at NT print queues, or to pass jobs from AppleTalk clients to LPR printers, NT retypes the job if the type code is set to P (text). This can wreak havoc with PostScript files printed through HP LaserJet printers with internal MIO cards in them if the job originates from the `/usr/bin/lpr` program under UNIX, which assigns a P type code. The printserver card treats PostScript jobs as text, and instead of the print job, the raw PostScript codes print. This problem often manifests in the following way: `/usr/bin/lpr` is used to print a PostScript file from UNIX directly to the remote printer printserver, which works fine, but spooling it through NT causes problems.

A registry change that can override the NT server formatting behavior is detailed in Microsoft Knowledge Base article ID Q150930. With Windows NT 3.51 and 4.0 up to Service Pack 1, the change is global. Starting with NT 4.0 Service Pack 2, the change can be applied to specific print queues (see Knowledge Base article ID Q168457).

Under Windows NT 4.0, the change is shown in Exhibit 8.4.

### Exhibit 8.4  Changing the Windows NT Registry

**Windows NT 4.0**

1. Run the Registry Editor (`REGEDT32.EXE`).

2. From the `HKEY_LOCAL_MACHINE` subtree, go to the following key: `\SYSTEM\CurrentControlSet\Services\LPDSVC\Parameters`.

3. On the Edit menu, click Add Value.

4. Add the following.*
   ```
   Value Name: SimulatePassThrough
   Data Type: REG_DWORD
   Data: 1
   ```

**Windows NT 3.51**

1. Run the Registry Editor (`REGEDT32.EXE`).

2. From the `HKEY_LOCAL_MACHINE` subtree, go to the following key: `\SYSTEM\CurrentControlSet\Services\LPDSVC\Parameters`.

3. On the Edit menu, click Add Value.

4. Add the following.
   ```
   Value Name: SimulatePassThrough
   Data Type: REG_DWORD
   Data: 1
   ```

5. Create an LPD key at the same level as the LPDSVC key.

6. Click the LPDSVC Key, click Save Key from the Registry menu, and then save the file as `LPDSVC.KEY`.

7. Click the LPD key created in step 5.

8. Click Restore on the Registry menu, click the file created in step 6, and then click OK.

9. A warning message appears. Click OK and then quit the Registry Editor.

10. At a command prompt window, type `net stop lpdsvc`, then `net start lpdsvc`.

*Note*: The default value is 0, which tells LPD to assign data types according to the control commands.

## PRINTING POSTSCRIPT AND DOS COMMAND FILES

One problem with printing under Win31 and Win95 with the LPR methods discussed is the lack of a "raw" LPT1: device. This is annoying to the administrator who wants to print an occasional text file, such as a file full of printer control codes, without their being intercepted by the Windows printer driver. Of course this is also an issue with DOS programs, but a commercial site that runs significant DOS software and wants to print directly to UNIX with LPR really has only one option—to use a commercial TCP/IP stack containing a DOS LPR program.

Normally under Windows printing, virtually all graphical programs print through the Windows printer driver. This is true even of basic programs such as Notepad. For example, an administrator may have a DOS batch file named `filename.txt` containing the following line: `echo \033&k2G > lpt1:`. This batch file switches a HP LaserJet from CR-LF, MS-DOS text file printing into Newline termination UNIX text file printing. Otherwise, raw text printed from UNIX on the HP prints with a stairstep effect.

If the administrator opens this file with Notepad and prints it using a regular printer driver, such as an Epson LQ, the Windows printer driver encapsulates this print output into a series of printer-specific control codes that do things such as initialize the printer, install fonts, and so on. The printer won't interpret this output as control code input. Usually if the printer is locally attached, the user can force a "raw text print" of the file by opening a DOS window and running

```
copy filename.txt lpt1: /b
```

Since the LPR client program doesn't provide a DOS driver, it cannot reroute input from the LPT1: device ports. The solution is to use the Generic/Text Only printer driver in conjunction with Wordpad (under Win95); under Win31, use a different text editor. The Notepad editor supplied with Windows is unsuitable for this: it "helpfully" inserts a one-inch margin of space around all printed output, as well as the filename title. Wordpad supplied with Win95 can be set to use margins of zero, and it inserts no additions into the printed output. Make sure that banner pages are turned off and that the print type is set to RAW.

## CHECKING POSTSCRIPT PRINTER CAPABILITIES

Following is a PostScript command file that can be used to get a PostScript printer to output a number of useful pieces of information that are needed to set up a Printer icon under Windows properly. It was printed from Wordpad in Win95 through the Generic/Text Only printer driver with the following instructions.

1. Start, Run, type in `Wordpad` and press Enter.
2. File, Open testps.txt.
3. File, Page Setup, Printer, select Generic /Text Only, click Properties.
4. Click Device Options, select TTY custom, click OK.
5. Click OK, then set all four margins to 0; click OK.
6. Click File, Print, OK.

This file could also have been printed with `/usr/bin/lpr` on a UNIX command prompt. The file prints *Test Page* and some printer statistics below that, as follows.

```
% filename: testps.txt
% purpose: to verify proper host connection and function of PostScript
%          printers.
/buf 10 string def
/CM {
     save statusdict/product get (PostScript) anchorsearch
     exch pop {length 0 eq
             {1}{2}ifelse
          }
             {2}ifelse exch restore
     }bind def
/isCM {
          CM 1 ge
     }bind def
/Times-BoldItalic findfont 75 scalefont setfont
150 500 moveto
(Test Page) false charpath
     isCM{gsave 0.0 1.0 1.0 0.0 setcmykcolor fill grestore}if
2 setlinewidth stroke
/Times-Roman findfont 10 scalefont setfont
150 400 moveto
(Your PostScript printer is properly connected and operational.)show
150 380 moveto
(The border around the page indicates your printer's printable
     region.)show
{ vmreclaim } stopped pop
```

```
vmstatus exch sub exch pop
150 360 moveto
(Max Available Printer Virtual Memory (KB):)show
150 340 moveto
dup 1024 div truncate buf cvs show
150 320 moveto
(Calculated memory size used for PostScript printer icon
properties:)show
150 300 moveto
0.85 mul 1024 div truncate buf cvs show
150 280 moveto
(Printer Model:          )show
statusdict begin product show end
150 260 moveto
(PostScript Level:       )show
/languagelevel where
   {  languagelevel 3 string cvs show pop }
   {(1)   show }   ifelse
150 240 moveto
(PostScript Version: )show
statusdict begin
      version show (.)show
revision 40 string cvs show end
clippath stroke
showpage
```

## SETTING UP LPR/LPD ON FREEBSD

When a FreeBSD system is booted, it starts the LPD spooler control daemon program if the /etc/rc.conf file has lpd_enable="YES" set. If this is not set, attempts to print through and from the FreeBSD system will fail with an **lpr: connect: No such file or directory** error message.

The LPD program manages all incoming print jobs, whether they come in from the network or from local users on the UNIX system. It transfers print jobs to all locally attached parallel or serial printers, as well as defined remote printers. Several programs also are used to manipulate jobs in the print spools that LPD manages, as well as the user programs to submit them from the UNIX command prompt. All these programs use the /etc/printcap file, which is the master control file for the printing system.

Back when printing was mostly text, it was common to place printers on a serial connection that stretched for long distances. Often, 9,600bps was used because it could work reliably up to a block away, which allowed printers to be located almost anywhere on an office high-rise floor. Modern office print jobs, on the other hand, are generally graphics-laden and tend to be rather large.

These jobs would take hours to transfer over a slower 9,600bps serial printer connection. Today, most printers that are not connected to a remote hardware printserver box are connected directly to the server using parallel cables. All of the examples shown here use direct connections that are parallel connections.

The `printcap` configuration file, like most UNIX configuration files, indicates comment lines starting with a hash character. Lines without a hash character are meant to be part of a printer queue description line. Each printer queue description line starts with a symbolic name and ends with a newline. Since the description lines are often quite long, they are often written to span multiple lines by escaping intermediate newlines with the backslash (\) character. The `/etc/printcap` file, as supplied, defines a single printer queue, `lp`. The `lp` queue is the default queue. Most UNIX-supplied printing utilities send print output to this queue if no printer is specified by the user. It should be set to point to the most popular print queue with *local* UNIX print users (i.e., users who have shell accounts).

The layout of `/etc/printcap` is covered in the manual page, which is reached by running the `man printcap` command. The stock `/etc/printcap` file at the line defining the spool `lp` shows

```
#
lp|local line printer:\
        :lp=/dev/lpt0:sd=/var/spool/output/lpd:lf=/var/log/lpd-errs:
#
```

In this example the first line defines the names by which the printer is known and ends with an escaped newline. The next line defines the physical device, the PC parallel port, by `/dev/lpt0`; the directory in which the spool files are stored by `/var/spool/output/lpd`; and the `error log` file. Note that this particular `error log` file does not show all LPD errors, such as bad job submittals; it usually shows only the errors that originate within the printing system itself.

In general, the administrator creates two print queues for every printer that is connected to the FreeBSD machine. The first queue entry contains whatever additional capabilities UNIX shell users on the server require. The second is a raw queue that performs no print processing on the incoming print job. This queue is used by remote clients, such as Windows clients, that format their own jobs.

If the administrator is setting up the printer to allow incoming LPR jobs from network clients, such as other Windows or UNIX systems, those systems *must* be listed in `/etc/hosts.lpd`.

## Creating the Spools

Building new print spools is merely a matter of making an entry in the
`/etc/printcap` file, creating the spool directories, and setting the correct permissions on them. For example, the following additional line defines a Post-
Script printer named NEC (in addition to the `lp` definition).

```
#
lp|local line printer:\
     :lp=/dev/lpt0:sd=/var/spool/output/lpd:lf=/var/log/lpd-errs:
NEC|NEC Silentwriter 95 PostScript printer:\
     :lp=/dev/lpt0:sd=/var/spool/output/NEC:lf=/var/log/lpd-errs:
#
```

Because UNIX is case sensitive, NEC is different from nec in both the name
of the printer and the name of the Spool directory. With the print spooler LPD,
the Spool directories *must* be different from each other, or the spooler gets confused and doesn't print.

After the `/etc/printcap` is modified, the root user must create the `/var/`
`spool/output/NEC` directory and assign ownership of it to the `bin` user, assign
group ownership to `daemon`, and set permissions with the following commands.

```
su root
cd /var/spool/output
mkdir NEC
chown bin NEC
chrgrp daemon NEC
chmod 755 NEC
```

## Additional Spool Capabilities

Because modern print jobs, especially PostScript, can sometimes reach hundreds
of megabytes, the `sd` capability entry in the `/etc/printcap` file should always
point to a Spool directory on a filesystem that has enough space. The `/var` directory on a default FreeBSD installation is generally set to a fairly small amount,
which can easily overflow the spool. There are four ways to handle this problem.

1. During FreeBSD installation, if the administrator knows that a lot of print
   jobs are going to go through the spooler, `/var` should be set to a large
   amount of free space.
2. Modify the `sd` capability in the `/etc/printcap` file to point to a spool
   directory in a different, larger filesystem, such as `/usr/spool`.
3. Use soft links to point the `/var/spool/output` directory to directories
   on a larger filesystem.
4. Don't define a `/var` directory at all during FreeBSD installation; this
   would make the installer link `/var` to `/usr/var`.

In addition to spools, the following other capabilities are usually placed in a production `/etc/printcap` file.

- The entry `fo` prints a form feed when the printer is opened. It is handy for HPPCL (HP LaserJets) non-PostScript printers that are located behind electronic print-sharing devices. It can also be used for printers that accept input from multiple connections, such as a parallel port, serial port, and localtalk port. An example is an HP LaserJet with an MIO card in it plugged into both Ethernet and LocalTalk networks. It will clear any garbage out of the printer before the job is processed.

- The entry `mx` defines the maximum size of a print job, which is a must for modern print jobs that frequently grow far past the default print size of a megabyte. The original intent of this capability was to prevent errant programs from stuffing the spool with jobs so large that they would use up all paper in a printer. Graphics-heavy print jobs have made it impossible to depend on this kind of space limitation, so `mx` is usually set to zero, which turns it off.

- The entry `sh` suppresses printing of banner pages in case the printer cannot handle ASCII and the client mistakenly requests them.

- The entry `ct` denotes a TCP connection timeout. It is useful if the remote printserver doesn't close the connection properly.

> **NOTE** FreeBSD 2.2.5 contains a bug in the LPD system: as a workaround, the `ct` capability must be set very large (e.g., 3,600sec) or the appropriate patch must be installed and LPD recompiled. More recent versions of FreeBSD do not have this bug.

## Printing to Hardware Printserver Boxes or Remote Printservers

Hardware printserver boxes, such as the HP JetDirect internal and external cards, need some additional capabilities defined in the `/etc/printcap` entry: `rp`, for remote print spool, and `rm`, for remote machine name.

The `rm` capability is simply the DNS or `/etc/hosts` name of the IP number associated with the remote printserver device. Obviously, printserver devices, such as the HP JetDirect, must not use a dynamic TCP/IP network numbering assignment. If they get their numbering via DHCP, the IP number should be assigned from the static pool; it should always be the same IP number.

Determining the name used for `rp`, on the other hand, can be rather difficult. Here are some common names.

- *Windows NT Server:* Printer name of the Printer icon created in Print Manager.

- *FreeBSD:* Print queue name defined in `/etc/printcap`.

- *HP JetDirect:* Either the name TEXT or the name RAW. TEXT automatically converts incoming UNIX newline text to DOS-like CR/LF text that the printer can print. RAW should be used for PostScript and HPPCL printing.

- *HP JetDirect EX +3:* External, three-port version of the JetDirect. Use RAW1, RAW2, RAW3, TEXT1, TEXT2, or TEXT3, depending on the port desired.

- *Intel NetPort:* Use TEXT for UNIX text conversion printing, or use PASSTHRU for normal printing.

- *DPI:* Use PORT1 or PORT2, depending on which port the printer is plugged in to.

For other manufacturers' printservers, refer to the manuals supplied with those devices.

The following is an example `/etc/printcap` that redefines the default `lp` print queue to send print jobs to the first parallel port on a remote HP LaserJet plugged into a JetDirect EX +3 named `floor2hp4.biggy.com`.

```
#
lp|local line printer:\
    :rm=floor2hp4.biggy.com:rp=RAW1:\
    :sd=/var/spool/output/lpd:\
    :lf=/var/log/lpd-errs:
#
```

> **NOTE** The `rp` capability must be defined or the job goes to the default print queue on the remote host. If the remote device does not have a single print queue, such as another UNIX system, this causes problems. For example, if the remote device was a JetDirect EX +3 and `rp` was omitted, all queues defined would print out of the first parallel port.

## Filters

The last two important `/etc/printcap` capabilities concern print filters: `if` (input filter) and `of` (output filter). If defined, incoming print jobs are run through the filters that these entries point to for further processing.

Filters are the reason that the UNIX print spooling system is so much more powerful than any other commercial server operating system. Under FreeBSD, incoming print jobs are acted on by any filters specified in the `/etc/printcap` *no matter where they originate.* Incoming print jobs from remote Windows, Macintosh, NT, OS/2, or other clients can be intercepted and manipulated by any program specified as a filter. Want a PostScript printer? There's a filter that adds PostScript capability to a non-PostScript printer. Want to make a cheap Epson MX 80 dot-matrix printer emulate an expensive Okidata Microline dot-matrix printer for some archaic mainframe application? Write a filter that will rewrite the print codes to do it. Want custom-built banner pages? Use a filter. Many UNIX `/etc/printcap` filters on many Internet sites can do a variety of interesting and unique things. Someone may have already written a filter that does what you want!

### Types of Filters

Three types of filters can be defined in the `/etc/printcap` file. In this book all filter examples are for input filters.

**Input Filters**   Input filters are specified by the `if` capability. Every job that comes to the spool is acted on by any filter specified in the `if` entry for that spool. Virtually all filters that an administrator would use are specified here. These filters can be either shell scripts or compiled programs.

**Fixed Filters**   Fixed filters are specified by separate capabilities, such as `cf`, `df`, and `gf`. Mostly, these exist for historical reasons. Originally, the idea of LPD was that incoming jobs would be submitted with the type fields set to trigger whatever filter was desired. However, type codes are confusing and annoying to the user, who has to remember which option is needed to trigger which type. It is much easier to set up multiple queues with different names, and this is what most sites do these days. For example, originally a DVI fixed filter might be specified in a spool for `lp`, triggered by the `-d` option passed to LPR. Jobs without this option aren't acted on by the DVI filter. However, the same thing can be done by creating a queue named `lp` that doesn't have a DVI filter and a queue named `lpdvi` that has the DVI filter specified in the `if` capability. Users just need to remember which queue to print to instead of what option is needed for this or that program.

**Output Filters**   Output filters are specified by the `of` capability. Output filters are much more complicated than input filters and are hardly ever used in normal circumstances. They also generally require a compiled program somewhere, either directly specified or wrapped in a shell script, since they have to do their own signal handling.

## Printing Raw UNIX Text with a Filter

One of the first things that a new UNIX user discovers when plugging a standard LaserJet or impact printer into a UNIX system is the *stairstep* problem. The symptom is that the user dumps text to the printer, either through LPR or redirection (by catting it to the parallel device), and, instead of receiving the expected Courier 10-point printout, gets a page with a single line of text, or two lines of stairstepped text, and nothing else.

The problem is rooted in how printers and UNIX handle text files internally. Printers by and large follow the MS-DOS text file convention of requiring a carriage return and a linefeed at the end of every text line. This is a holdover from the early days when printers were mechanical devices, and the print head needed to return and the platen to advance to start a new line. UNIX uses only the linefeed character to terminate a text line. So, simply dumping raw text out the parallel port works on MS-DOS, but not on UNIX.

If the printer is a PostScript printer and doesn't support standard ASCII, then dumping UNIX text to it doesn't work. But then, neither would dumping MS-DOS text to it. (Raw text printing on PostScript printers is discussed later in this chapter.) Note also that if the printer is connected over the network to an HP JetDirect hardware printserver, internal or external, the TEXT queue on the hardware printserver automatically adds the extra carriage return character to the end of a text line.

If the printer is the garden-variety HP LaserJet, DeskJet, or impact printer, and under DOS the administrator is accustomed to printing raw text from the command line for directory listings, there are two ways to fix stairstep. The first is to send a command to the printer to make it print in *UNIX text file* mode, which makes the printer supply its own carriage return. This solution is ugly in a printer environment with UNIX and Windows machines attempting to share use of the same printer. Switching the printer to work with UNIX disrupts DOS/Windows raw text printouts.

The better solution is to use a simple filter that converts incoming text from UNIX style to DOS style. The following filter, posted on `questions@ freebsd.org`, and the sample `/etc/printcap` entry can be used to do this.

```
#!/bin/sh
# /usr/local/libexec/crlfilter
#
# simple parlor trick to add CR to LF for printer
# Every line of standard input is printed with CRLF
```

```
# attached.
#
awk '{printf "%s\r\n", $0}' -
```

An alternative filter posted using `sed` could be written as follows.

```
#!/bin/sh
# /usr/local/libexec/crlfilter
#
# Add CR to LF for printer
# Every line of standard input is printed with CRLF
# attached.
#
# Note, the ^M is a real ^M (^V^M if you're typing in vi)
#
sed 's/$/^M/' -
```

Here is an example of a filter that triggers the printer's automatic LF-to-CR/LF converter (this option is useful only on HP LaserJets that support this command).

```
#!/bin/sh
# Simply copies stdin to stdout. Ignores all filter
# arguments.
# Tells printer to treat LF as CR+LF. Writes a form feed
# character after printing job.
printf "\033&k2G" && cat && printf "\f" && exit 0
exit 2
```

The `/etc/printcap` file used to trigger the filter is

```
# /etc/printcap
# The trailer (tr) is used when the queue empties. I found that the
# form feed (\f) was required for the HP to print properly.
# Banners also need to be shut off.
#
lp|local line printer:\
    :lp=/dev/lpt0:sd=/var/spool/output/lpd:lf=/var/log/lpd-errs:
    :if=/usr/local/libexec/crlfilter:sh:tr=\f:mx#0:
#
```

## The pr Filter

Although most filters are built by scripts or programs and are added to the UNIX machine by the administrator, one filter that is supplied with the FreeBSD operating system is very useful for raw text files: the `pr` filter. It is most commonly used when printing from the UNIX command shell. The `pr` filter paginates and applies headers and footers to ASCII text files. It is automatically invoked with the `-p` option used with the LPR program at the UNIX command prompt.

The pr filter is special—it runs *in addition* to any input filters specified for the print queue in /etc/printcap *if* the user sets the option for a print job. This allows headers and pagination to be applied in addition to any special conversion, such as CR to LF that a specified input filter may apply.

## Printing PostScript Banner Pages with a Filter

Unfortunately, the canned banner page supplied in the LPD program prints only on a text-compatible printer. If the attached printer understands only PostScript and the administrator wants to print banner pages, it is possible to install a filter into the /etc/printcap file to do this.

The following filter is taken from the FreeBSD Handbook. I've slightly changed its invocation for a couple of reasons. First, some PostScript printers have difficulty when two print files are sent within the same print job or they lack the trailing Ctrl-D. Second, the handbook invocation uses the LPRPS program, which requires a serial connection to the printer.

The following filter shows another trick: calling LPR from within a filter program to spin off another print job. Unfortunately, the problem with using this trick is that the banner page always gets printed after the job. This is because the incoming job spools first, and then FreeBSD runs the filter against it, so the banner page generated by the filter always spools behind the existing job.

There are two scripts; both should be put in the /usr/local/libexec directory, and the modes should be set to executable. The printcap also must be modified to create the nonbanner and banner versions of the print queue. Following the scripts is the /etc/printcap file showing how they are called. Notice that the sh parameter is turned on because the actual printed banner is being generated on the fly by the filter.

```
#!/bin/sh
# Filename /usr/local/libexec/psbanner
# parameter spacing comes from if= filter call template of:
# if -c -w -l -i -n login -h host
# parsing trickiness is to allow for the presence or absence of -c
# sleep is in there for ickiness of some PostScript printers for dummy
do
      case "$1" in
      -n)   alogname="$2" ;;
      -h)   ahostname="$2" ;;
      esac
      shift
done
/usr/local/libexec/make-ps-header $alogname $ahostname "PostScript" |
\ lpr -P lpnobanner
sleep 10
cat && exit 0
```

Here is the `make-ps-header` listing.

```sh
#!/bin/sh
# Filename /usr/local/libexec/make-ps-header
#
# These are PostScript units (72 to the inch). Modify for A4 or
# whatever size paper you are using:
#
page_width=612
page_height=792
border=72
#
# Save these, mostly for readability in PostScript, below.
#
user=$1
host=$2
job=$3
date=`date`
#
# Send the PostScript code to stdout.
#
exec cat <<EOF
%!PS
%

% Make sure we do not interfere with user's job that will follow.
%


%
% Make a thick, unpleasant border around the edge of the paper.
%
$border $border moveto
$page_width $border 2 mul sub 0 rlineto
0 $page_height $border 2 mul sub rlineto
currentscreen 3 -1 roll pop 100 3 1 roll setscreen
$border 2 mul $page_width sub 0 rlineto closepath
0.8 setgray 10 setlinewidth stroke 0 setgray
%
% Display user's login name, nice and large and prominent.
%
/Helvetica-Bold findfont 64 scalefont setfont
$page_width ($user) stringwidth pop sub 2 div $page_height 200 sub
moveto
($user) show

%
% Now show the boring particulars.
%
/Helvetica findfont 14 scalefont setfont
/y 200 def
[ (Job:) (Host:) (Date:) ] {
    200 y moveto show /y y 18 sub def
} forall
```

```
/Helvetica-Bold findfont 14 scalefont setfont
/y 200 def
[ ($job) ($host) ($date) ] {
    270 y moveto show /y y 18 sub def
} forall

%
% That is it.
%
showpage
```

Here is the /etc/printcap file.

```
#
lp|local line printer, PostScript, banner:\
     :lp=/dev/lpt0:sd=/var/spool/output/lpd:lf=/var/log/lpd-errs:
     :if=/usr/local/libexec/psbanner:sh:mx#0:
lpnobanner|local line printer, PostScript, no banner:\
     :lp=/dev/lpt0:sd=/var/spool/output/lpd-noban:\
     :lf=/var/log/lpd-errs:sh:mx#0:
#
```

# PRINTER ACCOUNTING

The FreeBSD print spooler can manage accounting statistics for printer usage. The spooler counts each page printed and generates totals for each user. In this manner departments or individuals can be charged money for their use of the printer.

In the academic world, such as student computer labs, accounting is very political. Many schemes have been developed to attempt to gather statistics to charge people (generally students) for printing. Administrators in this environment who deal with printers can have almost as many accounting problems as printer problems. In the corporate environment, on the other hand, accounting is not as important. I strongly recommend against any corporation attempting to implement printer accounting on shared printers for a number of reasons.

**1.** The entire UNIX accounting system is based on ASCII printouts. It is easy to count the number of ASCII pages, form feeds, or text lines in a print job. In corporations, however, PostScript and HPPCL are generally the order of the day. It is almost impossible to figure out by examining the datastream how many pages it will occupy, and even if this could be done accurately, it wastes significant computational resources.

**2.** Banner pages aren't included in UNIX printer accounting counts. Therefore, someone submitting 20 two-page jobs uses much more paper than does someone submitting one 40-page job, yet both are charged the same amount.

> **NOTE** It is possible to get some PostScript printers to count pages, but doing so requires a bidirectional connection to the printer and additional programming on the UNIX system. This task is beyond the scope of this book.

**3.** The username of the submitter can be easily forged if the job is remotely submitted over the network from a client (practically all jobs in a Windows client printing environment are remotely submitted). Although some LPR clients can be set to authenticate, and the `rs` capability can be set to enforce authentication, not all can, especially Windows LPR clients.

**4.** It is more difficult for a submitter to hide the IP number or machine name of the remote client, but in a Windows environment there is no guarantee that someone was sitting at a particular desktop machine when the job was submitted.

**5.** A business generates no revenue by monitoring printer usage. In the academic community, however, when a student lab charges for printouts, the lab is actually extracting money from an entity (the student) that is separate from the lab. Within a corporation, the concept of department A getting revenue from user B is pointless and doesn't generate a net gain for the corporation as a whole.

For my printer administration, I have found that I can save more money on printing costs by purchasing supplies wisely than by attempting to discourage printing through "chargebacks." What is the sense of being miserly with printing while spending double on toner cartridges because no one is willing to comparison-shop, or signing a "lease" agreement that isn't beneficial for the printer? When you get down to it, corporate users don't care much for print-sharing anyway, and they generally agree to it only because the administrator can buy a far bigger, faster, and fancier printer than they can requisition.

**6.** Worse yet, if usage on a shared printer is charged, it encourages employees to look for other places to print. Inevitably, people buy cheap inkjet printers for their own use, and the business ends up spending more on paper and supplies for many poor-quality small printers than it would for a few decent big ones. Moreover, the inferior output of these printers makes the organization as a whole look bad.

**7.** The corporate spirit should be one of teamwork, not bickering. The surest way to kill a network in a corporation is to set up a situation that puts the administrator into the policeman position or pits one department against another.

The only justification I've ever seen for running accounting on corporate printers is using the accounting system to automate reminders to the administrator to replace paper or toner. Aside from this use, a corporation that implements accounting as a way of encouraging employees not to *waste* paper ends up defeating the purpose of turning on accounting.

## MICROSOFT NETWORKING CLIENT PRINTING WITH SAMBA

Although LPR is a time-tested and truly cross-platform printing solution, sites with a majority of Windows clients running Microsoft Networking have an alternate printing mechanism—Samba. Samba can provide print services to clients running SMB-compatible network clients. With a running Samba installation, the administrator may *share out* printers as well as filesystem directories from the FreeBSD system (Figure 8.6).

Printers accessed with Samba must be defined in both the `/etc/printcap` file and the `/usr/local/etc/smb.conf file`. If the individual printers are defined in the `smb.conf` file with the `printer driver=` statement set to the exact model name of the printer, the "Auto printer driver install" feature of Windows NT and Win95/98 is activated. This automatically loads the correct printer driver if the user clicks on the print queue in Network Neighborhood under Win95 or NT 4.0. The restriction, of course, is that the printer model must be in the Windows client driver database.

The `smb.conf` file also defines the `print` command used to pass jobs to the UNIX print spool. It is a good idea to redefine this via the `print` command option to `lpr -s -P %p %s; rm %s`. This turns on soft linking, so that large print jobs don't get truncated.

In operation, the SMB-networking client builds the print job on itself and then transfers the entire job over the network to the Samba server. On the

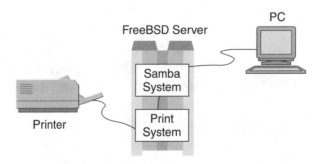

**Figure 8.6**  Samba printing

server, Samba has its own temporary print spool directory to which the job is copied. Once the job has been completely received, it is then passed to the UNIX print spooler.

## Client Access Issues

Because a Windows client formats print jobs before sending them to the server, the administrator may want to hide some of the specialty print queues on the server. For example, the queue that converts LF to CRLF for UNIX text printouts would probably not be shared out. To make such queues invisible, the `browseable=no` option can be turned on in the `smb.conf` file. Also, the `load printers` option must be set to no to allow individual printer definitions.

> **NOTE** In general, the only print queues that should be visible through Samba are the "raw" print queues that are set up by the administrator to allow incoming preformatted print jobs.

Windows clients that print to Samba print queues on the UNIX system can view and cancel print jobs in the print queue. They cannot pause them, however, which is a difference between Novell and Windows NT Server print queues. They also cannot prioritize print jobs from the print queue window, although the administrator can reprioritize print jobs that are in the queue from a command shell on the FreeBSD server.

## Printer Entries in Configuration Files

Following are listings of sample `/etc/printcap` and `smb.conf` files used on the system to provide print services. An explanation of the interaction of these files follows.

**Listing 8.1** `/etc/printcap`

```
#
#
# The printer in lpt0 is a PostScript printer. The nec-crlf entry
# is for testing the printer when it is switched into HP LaserJet III
# mode.
#
```

```
lp|local line printer:\
    :lp=/dev/lpt0:sd=/var/spool/output/lpd:\
    :lf=/var/log/lpd-errs:sh:mx#0:
#
nec-crlf|NEC Silentwriter 95 in ASCII mode with UNIX text filter:\
    :lp=/dev/lpt0:sd=/usr/lpdspool/nec-crlf:\
    :lf=/var/log/lpd-errs:sh:mx#0:\
    :if=/usr/local/libexec/crlfilter:tr=\f:
#
nec-raw|NEC Silentwriter 95 used for PostScript passthrough printing:\
    :lp=/dev/lpt0:sd=/usr/lpdspool/nec-raw:\
    :lf=/var/log/lpd-errs:sh:mx#0:
#
nec-ps-banner|NEC Silentwriter 95 with Postscript banner page created:\
    :lp=/dev/lpt0:sd=/usr/lpdspool/nec-ps-banner:\
    :lf=/var/log/lpd-errs:sh:mx#0:if=/usr/local/libexec/psbanner:
#
#
```

**Listing 8.2**   /usr/local/etc/smb.conf

```
[global]
comment = FreeBSD - Samba %v
log file = /var/log/samba.log
dont descend = /dev,/proc,/root,/stand
print command = lpr -s -P %p %s; rm %s
interfaces = 10.0.0.1 (the system IP number goes here)

printing = bsd
map archive = no
status = yes
public = yes
read only = no
preserve case = yes
strip dot = yes
security = share
guest ok = no
password level = 1
dead time = 15
domain master = yes
workgroup = WORKGROUP

[homes]
browseable = no
comment = User Home Directory
create mode = 0775
public = no

[printers]
path = /var/spool
comment = Printers
create mode = 0700
```

```
browseable = no
read only = yes
public = no

[lp]
printable = yes
browseable = no

[nec-raw]
comment = Main Postscript printer driver for Windows clients
printer driver = NEC SilentWriter 95
printable = yes
browseable = yes

[wwwroot]
path = /usr/local/www
read only = no
create mode = 0775
comment = Internal Web Server
```

### *Browsing Output*

Following is the output of a `net view` command executed at a DOS prompt under Windows 95.

```
Shared resources at \\SERVER

Sharename   Type    Comment
--------------------------------------------------------
nec-crlf    Print   NEC Silentwriter 95 in ASCII mode
nec-raw     Print   Main PostScript printer driver
tedm        Disk    User Home Directory
wwwroot     Disk    Internal Web Server
The command was completed successfully.
```

In the `/etc/printcap` file four print queues are defined, all tied to the printer plugged in to the parallel port on the FreeBSD server. The first is `lp`, the generic local line printer. Since this print queue generally has a filter placed on it to format jobs from the UNIX print queue properly, it should not be visible on the SMB network (i.e., visible in Network Neighborhood). The second queue, `nec-crlf`, has a filter that converts UNIX text to text that prints without stairstepping, so it also should be hidden from the SMB network. The third, `nec-raw`, should be visible on the network because this is the spool that the Windows clients use. The last queue, `nec-ps-banner`, is another specialty queue for UNIX local printing and thus should not be visible.

When the `smb.conf` file is parsed, the default entry `[printers]` is first read and used as a set of defaults for printers that are going to be shared out. Next, the `/etc/printcap` file is read to get a list of all printers on the server.

Last, each printer is checked for a service name in the smb.conf file that contains settings to override the set of defaults.

In the listing of what resources are visible on the network, both nec-crlf and nec-raw print queues are visible, and lp and nec-ps-banner are not. lp is not visible because there is a specific entry, [lp], in the smb.conf file that blocks it. nec-ps-banner doesn't have such an entry, but because the print queue name is not a legal length for an SMB name, it isn't shared out either.

The nec-crlf printer is visible so as to illustrate another point—comments. If a print queue has no entry in the smb.conf file and is built by scanning the /etc/printcap file and using the [printers] defaults, the comment is taken from the /etc/printcap file next to the queue definition name. Otherwise, if an entry is made for the printer in the smb.conf file, the comment is taken from the entry in smb.conf.

## PRINTING BETWEEN NT SERVER OR NETWARE AND FREEBSD

Up to this point in the chapter, our main concern has been FreeBSD and Windows NT printing interoperability with NT as a print client passing jobs to the FreeBSD system. What happens if the situation is reversed and the FreeBSD system is itself a printing client of another LPD server? This situation can arise in a mixed UNIX/NetWare or UNIX/NT environment. The administrator may elect to forego the use of Samba, and use an NT server to provide print services. Alternatively, the administrator may have existing DOS Novell IPX clients that they don't want to change, printing to an existing IPX Novell NetWare server. Many of the earlier hardware printservers, such as the Intel NetPort 1 and 2, were IPX only. A site with a large number of these hardware servers may wish to move the clients to TCP/IP but leave the existing IPX-based printing network intact.

With NetWare, it is possible to load an LPD NetWare loadable module (NLM) on the NetWare server that takes incoming LPR print jobs and prints them on IPX print queues. Later versions of NetWare may include this NLM, but it was an extra-cost add-on with NetWare 3.X.

With Windows NT Server, loading the TCP/IP LPR printing support also loads the LPD printserver on NT. By using LPR client programs on UNIX, it is possible to submit, view status, and remove jobs remotely from an NT server that has LPR installed as a port for its printers.

Following is a sample /etc/printcap file entry that defines a print queue named tank on the FreeBSD system pointed to an NT LPD server queue named sherman on an NT server named big.army.mil in the DNS. This uses the `rm` printcap capability. Unlike the earlier examples, the output print jobs are sent out not by the PC parallel port but over the network to the NT server.

```
#
tank|sample remote printer:\
        :rm=big.army.mil:rp=sherman:sd=/var/spool/output/lphost:\
        :lf=/var/log/lpd-errs:
#
```

> **NOTE** When using an NT server as an LPD server, it may be necessary to make the NT registry changes mentioned under Windows NT Registry Changes, earlier in the chapter.

## PRINTING FROM UNIX

Two commands used at the FreeBSD command prompt are intended as general-purpose print commands: `lp` and `lpr`.

### Lp

The `lp` command is simply a front-end command that calls the `lpr` command with appropriate options. Its main use is to allow the running of precompiled binary programs and scripts that assume that the `lp` command is the *official* printing command.

### Lpr

The `lpr` command is the main command used to print files from the command prompts under the FreeBSD operating system. It is frequently spawned off as a child program or used in pipes. For example, when the Netscape Web browser's Print button is clicked, Netscape may create the PostScript output, but the output goes through the `lpr` command.

The `lpr` command, like many UNIX command-line printing programs, assumes that the default print queue name is `lp`. When the FreeBSD machine is set up, the administrator usually sets the `lp` queue to print through a filter that allows raw UNIX text sent to it to print properly. For example, if an HP LaserJet printer that doesn't have PostScript is connected to the server, the `lp` queue specifies in the `/etc/printcap` file the CRLF filter listed earlier. On the other hand, if an Apple Laserwriter that doesn't support ASCII is connected to the server, the `a2ps` filter would be specified in the `/etc/printcap` for the `lp` queue.

When printing raw text files, usually the -p option is specified to lpr. When printing preformatted files, such as PostScript files, the -P option is used, which selects whatever queue is used to handle these job types.

## MANAGING THE UNIX PRINT QUEUE

Once the print jobs coming in from clients are received on the FreeBSD system and placed in the print spool, they are metered out at a slower rate to the various printers. If traffic activity is light and few print jobs get sent through, the administrator can probably ignore the print queue as long as it continues to work. However, a busy network printer running at an optimal rate of speed usually has a backlog of unprinted jobs in the queue waiting for print time. To keep all users happy and to provide for the occasional rush print job, the UNIX LPD/LPR printing system has several administration commands, which are described here.

### Viewing the Queue

On busy printers, and to troubleshoot stopped printers, users sometimes need to view the print jobs in the queue. Administrators also must view the queue to see what jobs may need to be expedited. This can be done from the workstation that remotely submitted the job if the LPR client has the ability to do it. The Windows 3.1 LPR client discussed earlier has this capability. Unfortunately, many LPR clients don't, which means that the administrator must Telnet into the UNIX machine that the print queues are on and view them there.

The UNIX shell command used to view the queue is the lpq command. It is frequently run as lpq -a, which shows jobs in all queues. The following is a sample output of the command.

```
# lpq -a
nec-raw:
Rank   Owner   Job   Files                          Total Size
1st    tedm    19    C:/WLPRSPL/SPOOL/~LP00018.TMP  105221 bytes
2nd    tedm    20    C:/WLPRSPL/SPOOL/~LP00019.TMP  13488 bytes
3rd    root    3     hosts                          1220 bytes
4th    tedm    1     Printer Test Page              765 bytes
5th    tedm    2     Microsoft Word - CHAPTE10.DOC  15411 bytes
#
```

The first two jobs and the last two jobs came from remote clients; the third came from the command prompt.

## Removing Print Jobs

Deleting unwanted print jobs that haven't yet printed from the queue can be done by the remote workstations that submitted the job if their LPR implementations have the necessary commands. The Windows 3.1 LPR client I detailed earlier has this capability. Many LPR clients don't, however, which means that the administrator must Telnet into the UNIX machine that the print queues are on and delete the jobs there.

The administrator can delete any print jobs from any queues by running the `lprm` command followed by the specified print queue and the job number. Below is a sample output of the command.

```
# lprm -P nec-raw 19
dfA019tedmitte dequeued
cfA019dostest dequeued
# lprm -P nec-raw 3
dfA003toybox.placo.com dequeued
cfA003toybox.placo.com dequeued
#
```

The `lprm` command is also used under UNIX to delete remote print jobs.

## Advanced Management

The administrator logged into the FreeBSD system as the root user can also perform several other operations that ordinary users cannot. These include turning the queues on and off and moving print jobs within the print queues. The command used to do this is the `lpc` command.

`lpc` has two modes of operation. In the first mode, the command is run by itself, which puts the administrator into an `lpc` prompt. Some general help is available for the commands, such as the following sample output.

```
# lpc
lpc> help
Commands may be abbreviated. Commands are

abort enable disable help restart status topq ?
clean exit down quit start stop up
lpc> help disable
disable    turn a spooling queue off
lpc> help status
status     show status of daemon and queue
lpc> exit
#
```

In the second mode of operation, the `lpc` command is just run by itself, followed
by the command and the print queue name. Following is a sample output.

```
# lpc disable lp
lp:
        queuing disabled
#
```

Under FreeBSD, there is no command that specifically allows the administrator to move jobs from one queue to another. This can be done, however, by
changing into the raw queue directory and then rerunning the `lpr` command.
Following is a sample run showing three print jobs moved from a dysfunctional
queue to a good one.

```
# lpq -a
lp:
Warning: lp is down: printing disabled
printing disabled
Rank   Owner    Job   Files                  Total Size
1st    root     51    hosts                  1220 bytes
2nd    root     52    services               60767 bytes
3rd    root     53    printcap               2383 bytes

# cd /var/spool/output/lpd
# ls
.seq                    cfA053toybox.placo.com  dfA053toybox.placo.com
cfA051toybox.placo.com  dfA051toybox.placo.com  lock
cfA052toybox.placo.com  dfA052toybox.placo.com  status

# lpr -P nec-raw dfA051toybox.placo.com
# lpr -P nec-raw dfA052toybox.placo.com
# lpr -P nec-raw dfA053toybox.placo.com

# lprm -P lp -

# lpq -a
nec-raw:
Warning: nec-raw is down: printing disabled
Warning: no daemon present
Rank   Owner    Job    Files                  Total Size
1st    root     5      dfA051toybox.placo.com  1220 bytes
2nd    root     6      dfA052toybox.placo.com  60767 bytes
3rd    root     7      dfA053toybox.placo.com  2383 bytes

#
```

**NOTE** Moving jobs from queue to queue is feasible only when all printers
are similar, as when all printers support PostScript.

### Remote Management

Just as the root user can manipulate remotely submitted jobs in the print queue, print jobs can be remotely managed by regular users with the LPR clients that created them. Unfortunately, some LPR clients, such as Win95, don't have enough programming to be able to do this. Others, like the Win31 client, can manipulate the print jobs remotely.

FreeBSD offers some level of protection against inadvertent deletion of print jobs from remote hosts by restricting manipulation of a job to the same host that originated it. Even if the owner of the job matches a local user account on the server, for an ordinary user to delete remotely submitted print jobs, the request still must come from the remote host.

## ADVANCED PRINTING TOPICS

The FreeBSD UNIX LPR/LPD printing system is very flexible and, with the addition of filters, can be adapted to very unusual printing environments. To enhance this flexibility several useful printing utilities are supplied on the FreeBSD CD-ROM, which the administrator might wish to install.

### Ghostscript

The `Ghostscript` program, invoked as `/usr/local/bin/gs`, is one of the most useful printing utilities that have been developed for the free software community. `Ghostscript` reads incoming PostScript data (or Adobe PDF files), interprets it, and outputs it as a raster image. This can be displayed on screen, for example, with the `GhostView` program under the X Window System, or printed on most graphics printers, such as Epson dot-matrix, HP DeskJet, or HP LaserJet. In effect, it is a way of adding PostScript printing capability to a printer that doesn't have PostScript firmware code. `Ghostscript` has been ported to numerous operating systems, including Windows.

The `Ghostscript` home page is located at http://www.cs.wisc.edu/~ghost/ and contains the most current version of the program. A prebuilt FreeBSD binary of `Ghostscript` is located in the Packages section of the FreeBSD CD-ROM. This can be installed on the FreeBSD system by selecting the package from the prepackaged software list that is accessed through the `/stand/sysinstall` installation program. Many packaged programs on the CD depend on `Ghostscript`, and so it may already be installed.

Installation of the packaged version of `Ghostscript` is recommended in the FreeBSD Ports Section because it has been tested with the other packages that require it. The package creates a directory containing some documentation files in /usr/local/share/ghostscript/X.XX/doc. Unfortunately, because of the packaging process on the FreeBSD CD-ROM not all the useful installation files are copied into this location. So, if the package is version 5.03 (for example), the administrator will also want to get the file ftp://ftp.cs.wisc.edu/ghost/aladdin/gs503/ghostscript-5.03.tar.gz, and unzip and untar it into a temporary directory.

Extracting the archive file creates a directory structure under the gs5.03 subdirectory. To install Ghostscript in the /etc/printcap file, read the gs5.03/devs.mak file to determine which printer driver definition works with your printer, and then use the instructions in Exhibit 8.5.

**Exhibit 8.5 Installing** Ghostscript **in the** /etc/printcap **file**

1. Change to the root user with su.
2. In the gs5.03 directory, copy the lprsetup.sh, unix-lpr.txt, and unix-lpr.sh files to /usr/local/share/ghostscript/5.03.
3. Change to the /usr/local/share/ghostscript/5.03 directory. Edit lprsetup.sh with a text editor such as vi.
4. Modify the DEVICES= entries to list your selected printer driver definitions per the instructions in unix-lpr.txt.
5. Modify the PRINTERDEV= to /dev/lpt0, the GSDIR= to /usr/local/share/ghostscript, and the SPOOLDIR= to /var/spool/output. Save the file.
6. Edit the unix-lpr.sh file and change the PSFILTERPATH= to /usr/local/share/ghostscript.
7. If the printer that you defined in the lprsetup.sh file is a monochrome printer, remove the "-dBitsPerPixel=${bpp}" and "$colorspec" entries on the gs invocation line and save the file. Otherwise, if it is a color definition, leave them in. For example, the following line is for a monochrome LaserJet.
   ") | gs -q -dNOPAUSE -sDEVICE=${device} \"
   Don't remove anything else. Exit the editor, and save the unix-lpr.sh file.
8. Copy the unix-lpr.sh file to the parent directory, /usr/local/share/ghostscript, and set the execute bit on it.
9. Set the execute bit on lprsetup.sh with chmod and run the file by typing ./lprsetup.sh.
10. Follow the instructions for creating the Spool directories. If you will be using accounting and a separate log file, run the touch command to create the empty files per directions in script output.
11. The sample /etc/printcap is located in the current directory; the filename is printcap.insert. Use this as a template to modify the /etc/printcap file. A sample /etc/printcap file for a LaserJet 3 follows:

```
#
#
ljet3.raw|Raw output device ljet3 for Ghostscript:\
      :rm=big.army.mil:rp=sherman:sd=/var/spool/output/ljet3/raw:\
      :mx#0:sf:sh:rs:
#
ljet3|Ghostscript device ljet3 (output to ljet3.raw):\
      :lp=/dev/null:sd=/var/spool/output/ljet3:\
      :lf=/var/log/lpd-errs:mx#0:sf:sh:rs:\
      :if=/usr/local/share/ghostscript/filt/indirect/ljet3/gsif:\
      :af=/var/spool/output/ljet3/acct:
#
#
```

## A2ps Filter

Another handy utility is the a2ps, short for ASCII-to-PostScript. This program takes an incoming ASCII datastream and converts it to PostScript. It can also print multiple pages on a single sheet of paper by shrinking them down. It is a useful tool for a printer that cannot interpret ASCII, such as a PostScript-only printer.

a2ps is not installed in the FreeBSD system by default; it is located in the ports section /usr/ports/print/a2ps43. A prepackaged binary can be installed with /stand/sysinstall, but I have had problems with that port. It is best to install it by running make in the a2ps43 Ports directory, as follows.

```
/etc/printcap
#
lp|local line printer with output dumped through a2ps for raw
        listings:\
    :lp=/dev/lpt0:sd=/var/spool/output/lpd:lf=/var/log/lpd-
        errs:sh:mx#0:\
    :if=/usr/local/libexec/ascii2postscript:
#

/usr/local/libexec/ascii2postscript
#!/bin/sh
#
# Simple filter that converts ASCII to PostScript for basic stuff like
# directory listings.
#
/usr/local/bin/a2ps && exit 0
exit 2
```

Read the system manual page for a2ps to see the options available with this program, and remember to set the filter script ascii2postscript all-executable.

## Miscellaneous

The large number of other printing utilities cannot be covered here. Some add features such as automatic job type sensing; others handle bidirectional communication between the server and the printer. There are also a few other experimental LPR printing replacement systems. Commands such as `Ghostscript` and `a2ps` can also be used in pipes that create pretty output on an ordinary impact printer.

One last hint: The system manual pages can be printed with the `-t` option, which turns their ordinary ASCII output to beautifully formatted PostScript. Try the `man -t man` command, and send the output through `Ghostscript` or a PostScript printer for easier-to-read manual pages.

# Chapter 9

# Electronic Mail

Building a complete e-mail server on FreeBSD is probably the most advanced and professionally satisfying task you can perform. It can also become the most complex operation you do on FreeBSD because e-mail tends to be as complicated as the organization's network. The e-mail server is also usually the single most important information systems server in the network. FreeBSD makes an excellent platform for this task and has mature and reliable tools available for the job.

Running Microsoft's Internet Mail program on FreeBSD brings the following advantages to the organization.

- The Internet Mail protocol—Simple Mail Transport Protocol (SMTP)— is already the de facto standard for exchanging messages between companies. Since an organization is generally required to make the time and monetary investment to field SMTP, why make the same investment to support an additional, proprietary mail system, such as Microsoft Exchange, internally? It's better and easier to make the internal and external systems the same.
- Lower-cost training—the organizational e-mail system uses the same e-mail clients that employees use at home with their personal ISPs.
- With a well-designed mail client, the user is not aware of any delays in mail transmission from the mail program to the mailserver. Thus, the mailserver can be located geographically distant from the user or connected via a slow or intermittent link, such as a remote asynchronous or ISDN dialup.
- Internet e-mail is a store-and-forward operation. If it uses dial-on-demand SMTP ETRN or UNIX-to-UNIX-Copy Program (UUCP), the organization

is not required to have a permanent connection to the Internet to exchange
e-mail.

- Since such a system uses TCP/IP, it can use the public Internet as a transport between offices of a spread-out company without bothering with an
  expensive virtual private network (VPN) or another tunneling solution.
  For example, many remote sales representatives who work out of their
  homes use Internet mail over an ISP as their exclusive e-mail connection
  with their employers.

- Internet Mail allows the number of users who use a mailserver to be enor-
  mously increased because clients connect to the mailserver only when
  there is mail to be sent or when polling for incoming mail, not all the
  time. A single FreeBSD server with proper configuration can support up
  to 65,000 users without significant modifications to the mail system.

- The mailserver's resources are used only to manipulate and transfer mail.
  They are not wasted on NFS mounts, SMB shares, or client record locking or other connections.

- Since users do not need shell accounts on the mailserver, its security is
  vastly improved.

Because e-mail is a complex subject, this chapter is one of the most complicated and advanced chapters in the book. It is not necessary to implement every
item listed in this chapter to have a running mailserver. The systems and features
listed here are a fairly complete inventory of features found on larger corporate
mailservers; smaller organizations may find it easy to do without many of them.

## FUNDAMENTALS OF MICROSOFT INTERNET MAIL

*Internet Mail* is a mail system, not a product. Microsoft implements Internet
Mail inside of Exchange Server, along with other mail systems. Internet Mail
protocols are built around several basic concepts, chief among them being simplicity. Next in importance is the proper division of labor: the mail system processing is done both at the server and in the client, which makes it a true
client-server mail system.

### Simple Transport

Internet Mail messages are passed between servers, mail clients, and mail programs using the basic protocol of SMTP. One protocol is used between server
and server, between client and server, and between remote and local clients.
Clients do not require a filesharing connection to the server. Clients also are not

required to authenticate between themselves or the server to send mail via SMTP, nor are servers required to authenticate between each other. When an SMTP-enabled program wants to send a mail message, it attempts to contact the destination host or a mailserver, which relays the message to the destination host. After connection, it opens a channel and—with minimal handshaking—transmits the message. All handshaking and message transmission takes place in ASCII; in fact, an administrator can connect to a mailserver's SMTP port via Telnet and simulate a mail client, which greatly simplifies debugging. Under FreeBSD, a user can see this exchange by running /usr/bin/Mail with the -v option.

The strength in simplicity is that little can go wrong. An SMTP message transfer session requires just three things: the sender's address, the recipient's address, and the message itself. Everything else (e.g., date, type of mailer) is dictated by standards but is not actually required by the software for it to operate.

Contrast this with the proprietary Exchange Connector protocol used by Microsoft Exchange Server and its mail clients. This protocol, based on NT NetBIOS, cannot work through a Network Address Translator (NAT), and requires NT domain authentication. Setting up remote TCP/IP clients to use Exchange Connector over a dialup link is extremely complicated, requiring a WINS server and often a VPN.

Perhaps the biggest downside to SMTP—and a constant point of contention—is that it may be too open. The historical implementation of SMTP, particularly Sendmail, has been permissive, with no authentication. Only recently have methods been added to deny incoming e-mail from unverified IP numbers, and it wasn't until Sendmail version 8.9 that blind relaying was disabled by default. Even worse is that every SMTP implementation written since Sendmail has followed this lead. To this day, SMTP commercial mailserver programs are in use (i.e., Microsoft Exchange Server 5.0) that have *no way* of locking down blind relaying without a *forklift upgrade* (i.e., purchasing a brand new, expensive replacement). As a result it is child's play to forge e-mail messages, which is a serious problem on the Internet because forging is the principal means of hiding e-mail spammers' identities.

## Return Receipts

Internet Mail assumes that if it successfully contacts the destination mailserver, transmits the message, and successfully closes the TCP connection, the mail message has been received. However, just because the destination *machine* received the mail message, there is no guarantee that the destination *user* received the message. Thus, there is a quality of unreliability to the transmission of an Internet Mail message.

Some proprietary mail systems implement a function known as Return Receipt Requested (RRQ). With these systems, a sender can mark the message RRQ and when the recipient opens the message, a response is transmitted back to the sender. This attempts to add a reliability component.

Although RRQ may seem to be a useful feature, I have found that it suffers from a human engineering problem. Simply put, in my experience as a network administrator, most RRQ messages sent to a recipient contain information that the recipient doesn't want to hear; the sender turns on RRQ because messages are being ignored by the recipient. The sender forwards the receipts to supervisors and managers along with a complaint that they are being ignored. Eventually, recipients learn to delete unread messages that have the RRQ symbol. When the sender eventually complains, the recipient claims he or she never got the message and blames it on the e-mail system and mail administrator, thereby creating a three-ring circus that burns up a huge chunk of the mail administrator's time. Even if this doesn't happen, at best an RRQ on a message carries the implication that the sender doesn't trust the recipient, which is hardly a helpful idea to communicate.

Besides the social flaws, RRQ has many technical ones. Originally, Sendmail tried to support RRQ functionality with the user-added header `Return-Receipt-To:`. A number of problems developed with this header. First, the receiving Sendmail issued the receipt, and not all SMTP Internet Mail installations supported it. Next, with automated listservers, if a user posts a message to a list with this header set, an avalanche of returns can flood the listserver system. It is also insecure because a spammer can use it to find out hidden addresses on mailing lists.

When Sendmail 8.7 was released, support for this header was dropped. Instead, a new kind of RRQ functionality was added called Delivery Status Notification (DSN). DSN is part of the Extended SMTP (ESMTP). To get an RRQ message with ESMTP, during the SMTP handshake, this addition is made: `RCPT TO: <mailaddress@example.org> NOTIFY=SUCCESS`. The additional keywords `FAILURE` or `DELAY` are allowed instead of the keyword `SUCCESS`. Despite the DSN additions, it is still the responsibility of the recipient's mailserver to issue the return receipt on successful delivery.

Return receipts can also create a tremendous problem for users who post to mailing lists or other mass-distribution aliases. A user could send an RRQ message to an `ALL_USERS` alias for a company of 500 users and receive 500 replies in return, thus snowing the mailbox. For this reason, a mechanism is provided to shut off RRQ under Sendmail 8.8 and later by using the `*.mc` directive `define('confPRIVACY_FLAGS', 'authwarnings, noreceipts')`.

mc directives are covered later in this chapter (see Exhibit 9.1). Users should understand that RRQs don't have much meaning in electronic mail. E-mail lacks the fundamental guarantee of message reception; unlike certified mail delivered by the post office, there is no human involved to testify that the recipient did indeed get the message. Users should not substitute e-mail for communication that should be carried out on the phone or face to face.

## Split Processing

Internet Mail is client-server software, in that mail processing and handling are done both at the mailserver and at the user's mail client. In Internet Mail terminology, the server part is referred to as the Mail Transfer Agent (MTA), the user part is referred to as the Mail User Agent (MUA), and the part that delivers mail from the MTA to the user's mailbox is the Mail Delivery Agent (MDA). Additionally, many mailservers have a daemon that is used to transfer the contents of the user's mailbox to a remote client via POP3 or IMAP (Figure 9.1).

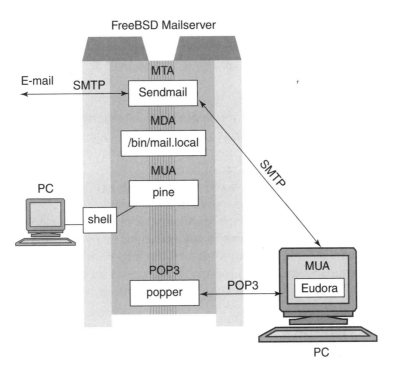

**Figure 9.1** Internet Mail processing under FreeBSD is done at both the mailserver and the mail client.

### Mail User Agent

The MUA is the software program in the mail system that is responsible for the following.

- Setting up a user-friendly editor or other means of typing in the mail message.
- Properly formatting the mail message and adding its header.
- Any spell-checking, message footer addition, or other message preprocessing.
- Managing the user's address book or providing access to a systemwide address book.
- Transmitting the message to the MTA.
- Receiving, sorting, and displaying received mail messages for the user. Some UNIX client-based MUAs (e.g., Pine) copy the messages to user mail directories. PC POP3-based mail clients copy the message via Post Office Protocol (POP) 3 to the user's PC and then delete it from the server. In general PC IMAP-based clients don't copy the message to the user's PC but leave the message on the server and manipulate it there.

### Mail Transfer Agent

The MTA is the software program in the mail system responsible for the following.

- Looking up the destination mailserver and determining a route to it.
- Additional processing of the mail message, such as rewriting headers.
- Temporarily storing the message if the destination mailserver is unable to accept it at the time of transmission.
- Returning the message marked undeliverable if there is an error in the address or the user is no longer in the system.
- Making the network connection to the destination mailserver.
- Reformatting the message in any particular manner if it has to be transmitted via a non-Internet Mail network transport, such as UUCP.
- Filtering incoming mail messages that are undesirable, such as unsolicited commercial e-mail, also known as junk mail or spam.

## ASCII and Eight-Bit Character Sets

Because SMTP originated on a scientific computer network in the United States it used the language of computer science, English. As a result, SMTP implementations were originally in seven-bit ASCII. This caused problems when Internet Mail spread to the rest of the world because some alphabets, particularly Asian languages that use symbols, are not completely representable in ASCII. Kanji, for example, uses double-byte characters that require almost the entire 256-digit byte space.

As a result there are two ways that foreign languages are represented in Internet Mail. The first is to encode foreign languages in MIME messages. The second is to use ASCII and the higher-numbered bytes above the ASCII range. Neither method makes messages representable in many U.S. ASCII mail clients.

More important, the ASCII limitation affects e-mail addresses. Because the part of the e-mail address to the right of the @ symbol is the destination machine hostname, this part of the address is restricted to ASCII characters. The username should also be restricted to ASCII because some mailers cannot digest non-ASCII usernames. Also, some ASCII symbols (e.g., the underscore "_") are prohibited in hostnames, so it is prudent to avoid them in usernames.

Unless and until a significant percentage of the Internet's MTAs (e.g., Sendmail) are changed, it is strongly recommended that foreign, and even internal, e-mail addresses (both username and hostname) conform to the U.S. ASCII standard. The safest course is to restrict usernames to eight characters, from letters A through Z, with as few alternative characters as possible (e.g., the period and hyphen are OK, but characters such as umlauts aren't). Restrict hostnames to a maximum of 256 characters, containing only periods for domain separators, hyphens (underscores are illegal hostname characters), the letters A through Z, and numbers. Both hostnames and usernames should be considered case insensitive because to most e-mail systems e-mail addresses such as "FreD" and "fred" are identical. Keep the special characters in the body of the e-mail message.

It is important to understand that this is not "United States bigotry." When SMTP was developed, the line had to be drawn somewhere, and at that time computer systems based on foreign languages were rare to nonexistent. Besides, most foreign languages also use the Roman alphabet.

## Case Sensitivity

Arguments often surface over the area of case sensitivity in e-mail addresses. Allowing case sensitivity in the username greatly increases the number of potential usernames and can provide a slippery solution to the problem of users who both want the same username (e.g., in a case-sensitive system Mark and mark would be different accounts). Since UNIX itself is case sensitive in filenames, it is easy to be confused about what is case-sensitive and what is not.

Under strict interpretation, RFC1035 dictates the following for the hostname part (i.e., the part to the right of the @ symbol) of the e-mail address.

*Character Case*
For all parts of the DNS that are part of the official protocol, all comparisons between character strings (e.g., labels, domain names, etc.) are done in a case-insensitive manner. At present, this rule is in force throughout the domain system without exception. (from RFC1035, p. 9)

In other words, the hostname or domain name part of the e-mail address is *case insensitive*.

Less clear is the status of the username. Under UNIX, it is quite possible to have case-sensitive usernames. In other words, the username `Tedm` is distinct from `tedm`.

Under Sendmail, by *default*, usernames are *case insensitive*. This means that if two users, `Tedm` and `tedm`, are added to the server, the destination of e-mail to `Tedm@XXXX` is undefined. The same is true of mail to `tedm@XXXX`.

A flag can be set in the Sendmail configuration file to make usernames case sensitive. Since this flag is not set by default, it is probably safe to assume that the vast majority of recipients' mailservers on the Internet do *not* have this flag set and thus treat usernames as case insensitive.

Common sense would dictate that a deviation from how most systems handle Internet e-mail would be asking for trouble. Certainly, there are a great number of mail gateways and other oddball mail systems on the Internet that are unable to distinguish between case-sensitive e-mail addresses. This is likely to be tremendously confusing for most users. In addition, several of the popular listservers are unable to distinguish between case-sensitive usernames. For these reasons it is a very poor decision to make usernames case sensitive.

As a point of style, the convention is to print *all* characters in the e-mail address in *lowercase*. The absence of capitalization immediately distinguishes the e-mail address as an electronic label identifier.

## Mail Address Usernames

In a typical mailserver installation the administrator sets the username in the e-mail address to be the same as that used to log in to the mailserver. For example, `Sam Smith` might have a login name of `sams`, and so his e-mail address would be `sams@whateverdomainname`. In larger organizations this practice can lead to some duplication. For example, username `Scott Williams` and `Scott Wallace` might end up with the duplicate username `scottw`.

A variety of schemes have been proposed in an attempt to guarantee uniqueness of usernames. Some organizations concatenate a number to the name, but who wants to be known as `scott465`? Others use the last name, but this doesn't prevent duplicates either because in a large organization a duplicate might be created by `Sara Smith` and `Sam Smith`. This method also makes it difficult to guess the e-mail address, which is the point of a username like `sams` in the first place.

Some organizations use a scheme with the entire full name, such as `Sara.Smith@example.org`. This scheme requires either a separate alias entry for every user or the addition of the Lightweight Directory Access Protocol (LDAP), NIS, or other mechanism to automate the mapping, which increases administration overhead and complexity. It also doesn't prevent duplication because many large companies have people with the same first and last names.

No less than Eric Allman, the author of Sendmail, advocates that people be allowed to choose their own usernames. This is the approach used by most major commercial ISPs. However, it makes it difficult to guess the e-mail address, and many people still try to use the first name and last initial and thus the administrator ends up with the same problem.

My own approach and recommendation is to use first name and last initial. The probability of duplication is far less than you might think, and no scheme is completely free of duplication anyway. The point of the username assignment should be to make it easy for the user, not the administrator. If a duplicate arises, add an additional last name initial, (e.g., `scottwi` and `scottwa`). These are fairly easy for other users to guess, and most people can remember that the "first" Scott might be using `scottw` and the "newer" Scott would use `scottwa`. If a full duplicate arises, use a nickname. Even if you do set up a situation where the two Scotts get each other's mail on occasion, it's a small price to pay for making things easier for everyone else on the mailserver. In any case, most users have personal address books that list the full name of the person. Other benefits to this approach are that users feel that their names do count for something among the impersonal business machines and that troubleshooting is eased for the administrator.

Regardless of the username scheme selected, because people's real names contain spaces and are much longer than the eight-character (15 characters in current FreeBSD versions) login name limit, a table of names cross-referencing identifiers is created. This is sometimes loosely referred to as a directory and can be present as a personal directory file or accessible from the mailserver via a directory access protocol.

## Attachments

Because of the ASCII limitation, when people began to send binary attachment files through e-mail they had to encode them. Two binary-to-ASCII encoding schemes are used to do this, Uuencode and MIME. Uuencode was the first scheme, but it was never completely standardized, and some older mail gateways use an incompatible variation of it. Uuencode is the standard encoding scheme used in products such as Microsoft Mail SMTP gateway and Lotus cc:Mail SMTP gateway. It is also used for Usenet news and in other applications unrelated to mail.

MIME is the newer method, and it has been standardized in RFC1341. It was first popularized in the Eudora mail client, and today all major e-mail clients support MIME transmission. With both encoding schemes, binary attachments are converted to ASCII representations and e-mailed as a regular message. This conversion increases the size of the e-mail message, for example, a 5MB binary attachment file may produce 7MB e-mail messages. This is an important consideration if the mailserver is set to limit messages by size.

MIME encoding also supports the concept of *multiparts*, which is useful if the attachment file is very large and must traverse a relay or mail transport that trims large messages. For example, many Bitnet relays would chop a message larger than 64K. Some modern mail clients, such as Microsoft Outlook, provide for specifying a default message split size in a MIME encoding. The only problem is that the recipient MUA must be able to put the message parts back together, and many cannot do this. In general, unless there is a known size restriction in the mailserver, the multiparts feature should be turned off in any mail client.

## Mail Directories under FreeBSD

Under FreeBSD, there are several directories related to the mail system.

- `/var/mail` Unread user e-mail. Mail that has been read usually is moved to mail directories under the user home directories or transferred to other systems via POP mail.
- `/var/spool/mqueue` Spooled e-mail, or mail that hasn't been transmitted to other systems. It may also be received mail that hasn't been copied to the user e-mail directory yet.
- `/etc` or `/etc/mail` The location of the system mail alias file.
- `/etc/mail` The location of various filters and things related to Sendmail.
- `/usr/local/majordomo` The Majordomo listserver files usually go here.

> **NOTE**   In default FreeBSD installations, /var is usually set to be a sepa-
> rate partition of 50MB or so. On corporate mailservers supporting many
> users, this space is inadequate because corporate users often share large
> documents with each other via e-mail. FreeBSD systems set up as mail-
> servers should set up /var to be much larger. One rule of thumb is for POP
> servers to set it to 10MB per user that the server is expected to support, for
> up to 100 users. From 100 to 400 users, set it to 5MB per user; from 400
> to 1,000 users, set it to 4MB per user and start monitoring the size of user
> mailboxes. For example, a 350-user mailserver should allocate 1.7GB to
> /var. For IMAP-based clients, this figure should be much, much higher.

Although SMTP doesn't require a file-based connection to the mailserver,
some early diskless/NFS UNIX client workstation schemes used the concept of
a *shared mail directory*. Occasionally there are references to this idea in some
of the mail literature. The basic scheme is pretty simple: export the user mail
directory /var/mail via NFS from the mailserver, have UNIX client workstations mount the exported directory in place of their own user mail directories,
and allow users to run their mail programs on the remote UNIX clients to
access the central mailserver shared directory over the network. This scheme
really works only via NFS from commercial UNIX systems that support full
NFS file locking, which is a requirement for remote mounting of the user mail
directory. I have seen only one PC-client mail program, LAmail, supplied with
the OS/2 TCP/IP add-on for early OS/2 versions, that supports this from a non-
UNIX OS.

## INTERNET MAIL PROTOCOLS

The basic concepts of Internet Mail are implemented on the standardized protocols described in this section.

### SMTP

SMTP is documented in the standards documents RFC821 and RFC1123,
which cover addressing and the SMTP handshake protocol.

### POP3

Post Office Protocol 3 is documented in RFC1081 and RFC1082. This simple
protocol allows remote clients to authenticate themselves to the mailserver in

order to access specific user mailboxes to obtain received e-mail and delete it from the server. POP3 clients all *transmit* e-mail via SMTP and *receive* e-mail via POP3. Most POP3 clients transmit passwords in plain text; they do not wire-encrypt passwords. The lack of wire encryption may be an issue in campus networks that permit shell accounts and these accounts use the same username or password as the mail system. (Here is another reason that strong-security networks should use switching network hubs, which usually defeat packet sniffers.) If this is a problem for a user, the administrator can set up `ssh` and allow the user to Telnet into the mailserver and run Pine or Elm. Alternatively, the user can poll the mailserver frequently for e-mail and have no shell access allowed, or the administrator may disable POP3 and use a secured POP such as APOP or IMAP. The mail clients must, of course, support it.

POP3 was developed when PCs and Macintosh computers began to be used on networks. Previous to this time, the usual procedure was for UNIX client workstations to remain continuously powered up on the network, running a Sendmail process that listened for any incoming e-mail. UNIX systems had to have a static IP number assignment and be named in the DNS. By contrast, PCs and Macs that were placed on TCP/IP networks were usually turned off at day's end and were usually assigned dynamic IP numbers (e.g., with DHCP), which complicated their listing in the DNS. Thus, it was impossible to use SMTP to transmit mail to PC and Mac clients because if the mailserver attempted to transmit the mail and the client system wasn't powered up, the mailserver would bounce the message. As a result, POP3 was devised, which allowed the mail to stay on the mailserver until the client could retrieve it.

## IMAP

Internet Message Access Protocol (IMAP) version 2 is documented in RFC1176; version 4 is documented in RFC1731 and RFC1733; and version 4 revision 1 is documented in RFC2060. Many extensions were added since then that are documented in various RFCs. Unlike SMTP or POP3, IMAP is a kind of "kitchen sink" of mail client protocols that is anything but simple. IMAP's main strength is that it addresses the deficiencies of POP3, allowing users to access a single mailbox from many different clients and to store e-mail on the server. Because of its increased complexity, however, IMAP installations can have greater administrative overhead.

Because IMAP supports a far richer set of command syntax than POP3 it presents a higher workload to the server. It does allows Kerberos wire encryption of the password, which may be useful on some insecure networks. The main thrust seems to be to get the server to do as much work on behalf of clients as possible. Its drawbacks are that it may be more difficult to troubleshoot and that the storage of e-mail messages on the server can rapidly consume all available space if users often mail each other large attachment files. From a user's point of view, one big advantage of IMAP is the ability to access one's e-mail from multiple machines and see a consistent view.

## IMAP versus POP3

The question of whether to use IMAP4 or POP3 has been and still is hotly debated. Each approach arises from a different philosophy. POP3 is simple, has low server overhead requirements, and has few commands; its main thrust is to get e-mail off the server as soon as possible. Sorting, redirecting, forwarding, addressing, and so on are all left as the mail client's responsibility. POP3 is ideally suited to large mailservers, where it is important to keep the server from being bogged down by client activity.

In my opinion, commercial corporate networks gain a tremendous *technical* advantage by forcing users to download e-mail to their local workstations using POP3. In all commercial e-mail servers I have administered that allow mail storage on the fileserver, the mailserver consumes all free space on the hard drives at approximately 6-month intervals. The administrator then wastes time chasing down the bad citizen users and getting them to delete their junk or must set arbitrary limits to mailbox size. The main cause of this problem is users' propensity to e-mail each other giant presentation, graphic, and other document files. It happened as much five years ago under proprietary mail systems (e.g., cc:Mail and Microsoft Mail) as under open Internet mail systems today. It is an axiom that users rarely delete old e-mail unless they are forced to do so; therefore, making them store e-mail locally instead of on the server means that if they don't delete old mail, they fill their own drives instead of affecting mail delivery for others.

From a political or business standpoint, however, there are many reasons that a commercial organization may want to keep user mail on the server with IMAP. Ease of support is one: some rather backward mail clients cannot handle multiple POP3 accounts (think of subordinates needing access to their bosses' e-mail during vacations), and in a large organization with users regularly destroying their desktop hard drives, keeping at least some of the data out of harm's way is a good thing.

Another issue is that with POP3, users must understand that backup and permanent archival of their e-mail messages doesn't happen on the mailserver. Instead, users must make provisions for this, and if they can't, then there is little point in running POP3. It is important to be familiar with where the client e-mail program stores its mail on the local hard drive. For example, Microsoft Outlook running on NT uses the user profile directories, so if the user's profile gets trashed, all the stored e-mail is lost.

The biggest drawback to POP3 for corporate organizations, however, is the organizations' failure to control e-mail. Within the last few years lawyers have discovered a boundless font of trouble in stored e-mail messages. Probably the most visible example of this occurred during the Microsoft antitrust trial. Microsoft had to provide mountains of stored e-mail messages during the trial discovery phase. The government's lawyers then had a rich database of stored e-mail to comb through looking for damaging items, which they eventually found. (This is not to say that Microsoft used POP3, it merely illustrates the potential damage from storing sensitive e-mail.) In a POP3 system, since the e-mail is stored on client systems, it's very difficult for the administrator to enforce a mandatory deletion time limit. In an IMAP system, since mail is not stored on user workstations, it is simple to enforce a mandatory storage limit of 90 days or so.

## MIME

Multipurpose Internet Mail Extension (MIME) is documented in RFC2045. MIME is the recommended standard for encoding binary data in seven-bit ASCII, as well as being a standard for a number of other things. Whereas MIME defines a bunch of file types, in general with e-mail work, all encoding is encoded binary.

## Uuencode

Uuencode, Uudecode, and their variants are programs released with the original UNIX distributions and widely copied. Versions are available for all operating systems, including DOS. Well-designed modern e-mail clients should never *send* messages in Uuencode—they should use MIME. However, they should be able to *receive* and decode Uuencoded messages.

## UUCP

UNIX-to-UNIX-Copy-Program, which was first documented in AT&T's original SVR3 UNIX distribution, is a non-TCP/IP transport used for long-haul mail, news, and file transfer. There are many different variants of UUCP today, and some are not interoperable. The original and most common UUCP protocol was the "g" protocol. Telebit made modems for a while that would *spoof* UUCP-g connections for increased throughput (assuming Telebit modems were on each end of the connection). The Taylor UUCP supplied with FreeBSD implements all major known UUCP protocol variants, and uses an alternative—the "i" protocol—which is much faster than "g." UUCP mail transfer is documented in RFC976 and is still used as a long-haul intermittent e-mail protocol today. It has largely been replaced by SMTP ETRN for local intermittent mail connections, such as dialup ISDN. UUCP is used for intermittent unattended dialup connections, whereas SMTP is used for continuous unattended TCP/IP connections.

## LDAP

Lightweight Directory Access Protocol, documented in RFC1777, is used to implement a centralized e-mail address directory. LDAP is a relative newcomer on the scene, and only recently have e-mail clients implemented support for it. Currently, Eudora (http://www.eudora.com), Mulberry (http://www.cyrusoft.com), Netscape Mail, and Microsoft Outlook e-mail clients support LDAP.

LDAP servers can be set up in a global listing of LDAP servers or as private standalone servers for their organizations. They can also replicate between each other. Many educational institutions run publicly listed and accessible LDAP servers. (At this time there is no single, recognized, central LDAP e-mail directory on the Internet itself and there is unlikely to ever be one.)

If a commercial organization runs a public LDAP server, it must take care to permit the public to make only specific full-name queries against the database. Allowing wildcard or partial name queries can let a spammer romp through the entire corporate database and collect large numbers of e-mail addresses. This is sad, but until spamming is made illegal, an organization should never publish internal e-mail addresses of its employees on publicly available electronic media. Electronically accessible e-mail addresses should always be aliased in the system so that the mail administrator can set up tight antispamming filters on them, and users can set up rulesets on their mail clients to sort incoming public e-mail automatically.

Although LDAP is handy on a corporate network, it is possible to use personal address books instead of LDAP. The key to solving this problem is understanding that for the vast majority of mail users, they use just a few dozen addresses repeatedly.

## Ph

Ph is a directory lookup protocol that Qualcomm used for its Eudora client e-mail program. It was developed at the University of Illinois at Urbana–

Champaign's Central Computing Service Organization. Although it hasn't really caught on, a Ph-to-LDAP converter can be used with an LDAP database if desired.

## Whois

Whois is a UNIX command that determines who owns a particular domain name. It can also be used to look up the e-mail address of the technical contact of the domain. Whois is used primarily in troubleshooting.

## Finger

Finger is a program that is used to determine the e-mail address for a user. The `finger` program can take the full name or part of a name and return all user accounts that list this name or part of name. The user running Finger can then choose the user account he or she wants to mail to and construct the e-mail address by adding the host part with an @ symbol.

Unlike LDAP, it is not possible to send `finger` a global search and obtain a list of every username e-mail address on the server, so it is much safer to run a Finger server on a publicly accessible mailserver. It is, of course, still possible for a spammer to send a list of common names to the Finger server and get exact e-mail addresses, but because this is a painstaking operation, a spammer is unlikely to waste time on it—not to mention that it could trigger an alert to an administrator.

Major mail clients, such as Eudora, support `finger`, and Windows has a standalone `finger` client program that can be run on Windows systems to supplement POP3 clients that don't support `finger`.

## PoPassd

PopPassword (PoPassd) is a short protocol that allows remote users to change their passwords on the mailserver. It has two parts: a daemon program that runs on the mailserver and a client program that runs on the remote POP3 client. Eudora implements the client program, as does a standalone Windows program at http://www.tip.net.au/~mphillip/. The daemon program is located in the FreeBSD Ports directories. This protocol is not standardized in an RFC, but the source code for the daemon is publicly available and can be easily implemented. Like POP3, passwords are sent in cleartext.

## COMMON INTERNET MAIL ADMINISTRATIVE TASKS

In a standard Internet Mail organizational setup there are a number of administration procedures that the postmaster must perform. Some of these daily chores follow.

1. Add and delete accounts to and from the mailserver by using either the `vipw` program, the `adduser` program, or an administrative interface such as `webmin`. For nonshell POP3 accounts, the shell must be set to `/sbin/nologin`.
2. Add and delete groups to the alias file and maintain lists of usernames in group aliases. This is done by editing `/etc/aliases` with a text editor and running the `newaliases` program.
3. Monitor the status of mail items in the mail spool. FreeBSD produces nightly reports on the mail server status that are mailed to the administrator.
4. For remote users, delete e-mail messages that are too large for them to download. Typically, this is done by editing their `/var/mail` user mail file and truncating the offending message, which corrupts the attachment file and, if not done right, the entire mailbox.
5. Repair invalid headers of e-mail messages that may affect POP3 clients. For example, a mail message with a `<>` in the `From:` line causes the original Microsoft Win95 Exchange POP3 client to abort download. To remedy this, the administrator can edit the `/var/mail` user mail file with a text editor and fix the header.
6. Tracing the source of offending spam mail by reviewing the mailserver log `/var/log/maillog` or looking at the headers of the offending message. This assumes that the user retains the real header, which seldom happens.
7. At the sender's request, deleting mail messages in the system that were sent in error. This is done by editing the `/var/mail` user mail file of the recipient and removing the message before the recipient downloads it. The same warnings in item 4 apply here. The recipient should probably be locked out of the system while this is going on, and the server administrator should verify the authenticity of the requester.
8. Helping users to archive mail messages or transfer their saved e-mail to new systems or to backup.
9. Installing and upgrading user mail client programs.

Whenever the administrator is directly editing a user mail file in `/var/mail`, the mailbox should be backed up. It is also safest to work on a copy of the mailbox, and when the box is repaired `tail` both the copy and the actual box to make sure no new mail has arrived while the box was being edited. Then immediately copy the repaired box over the user's existing box.

# WINDOWS INTERNET MAIL CLIENT INSTALLATION

The last few years have seen a burst of freely available e-mail clients for Windows that are capable of handling Internet Mail. Commercial and shareware clients have also appeared, but their growth has been somewhat discouraged by the quantity and quality of the free offerings. In this section I cover Microsoft, Netscape, and Eudora clients.

Before installing any of the e-mail clients described in the next section, the administrator should test POP3 and SMTP connectivity to the mailserver. This is easily done with the Telnet program on the workstation on which the mail client is to be installed. Start by Telnetting into the SMTP port on the mailserver and then into the POP3 port, using its fully qualified DNS name. If a login banner is presented on both ports, the mailserver is ready to serve client computers with mail user programs installed on them.

## Microsoft Internet Mail Clients

### The 16-Bit Client
Microsoft has two free offerings for 16-bit Internet Mail clients. These run on WfW 3.11 with MS TCP/IP, Win31 with the free Novell 16-bit Winsock stack covered in Chapter 8, or Win31 with Microsoft TCP/IP dialup adapter. The first free client is the independent Internet Mail and News program released with Microsoft Internet Explorer Web browser version 3.0. It is a basic, stripped-down, 16-bit POP3 mail program. The second is the Outlook Express for Win31 client that is the successor to the Internet Mail and News program. It is the most desirable 16-bit Win31 Microsoft client to use for Internet Mail.

There is also a client in the integrated e-mail support in the Microsoft Web browser itself.

### The 32-Bit Client
Compared to 16-bit clients, 32-bit clients have a much better selection of free and commercial Microsoft clients for Internet Mail. A list of them follows in order of their general release date.

**Microsoft Exchange**   The Microsoft Exchange client included in the shrink-wrapped copy of Win95. This client originally had no support for Internet Mail, but soon after the release of Win95, Microsoft released the Internet Mail connector in the Win95 service patches library, which added POP3/SMTP support.

**Windows Messaging**   Microsoft renamed the Microsoft Exchange client to the Windows Messaging client version 4, and released it as a general upgrade for Win95. This client, along with the Internet Mail Connector, was present in the so-called OSR-2 release of Win95, replacing the original Microsoft Exchange client. Both the original Exchange client and its Windows Messaging client contained some bad bugs and should be avoided in production environments.

**Office 97 Windows Messaging**   The Windows Messaging plus Internet Mail Connector client reached its zenith in version 5, which was released as part of Microsoft Office 97. On normal installation of Office 97, if Windows Messaging version 4 was present and configured on the Win95 desktop, *and* if "Additional support for Windows Messaging clients" was selected in the Outlook 97 submenu, this client would be installed.

Of the three major versions of Windows Messaging, version 5 is the most desirable because it automatically wraps lines at 79 characters, terminating them with a hard return. The previous versions of messaging clients would not do this, which was a major bug and source of complaints.

The Windows Messaging version 5 client and the full-blown Outlook 97 program (also released with Office 97) are the same program. The difference is that depending on which icon is run, either version 5 messaging or the Outlook interface is presented to the user.

All Windows Messaging and Outlook 97 clients store all mail and folders in a single `*.pst` file, and store all addresses in a `*.pab` file. Outlook 97 allows both its Contacts folder and the `*.pab` file to be user selected as separate and independent address books. It also has an import procedure that allows data to be copied from the `*.pab` file to the Contacts folder, which makes it easy for the administrator to distribute an organizational master address book if either the Messaging version 5 or Outlook 97 clients are used.

**Outlook 98**   Microsoft released an update to Outlook 97 named Outlook 98, which was a free program to all for several months. It remains a free update but only to Office 97 users. Outlook 98 does not include the Windows Messaging version 5 client, and it changes the mail storage file format. It was introduced with a security hole, which was later corrected with a patch from Microsoft. It does not install support for dual address books, but it does support them if installed over Outlook 97. The original free version of Outlook 98 would install on any 32-bit Windows client, including NT. The update available from the

Web site tests for the presence of Office 97. Presumably, the CD version of Outlook 98 does not test for Office 97.

Outlook 98 does introduce a very useful capability: it allows the user to import address book updates selectively, rejecting any duplicates. The updates must be in comma-delimited format to allow the duplicate rejection to operate. This allows an administrator running a network of all Outlook 98 clients to distribute address book updates via e-mail and have users import them directly into their contacts databases without creating inadvertent duplicates. Outlook 98 also allows MIME type specification to be selected by the user (i.e., it can be set to U.S. ASCII). Outlook 97 defaulted to ISO-8859, which can disrupt how some mail clients display received messages.

> **NOTE**   It must be understood that Microsoft seems to be deliberately pushing users into using Outlook as their mail client, as a replacement for Schedule Plus and for prior e-mail clients. It is doing this because the Exchange Server that Microsoft sells contains shared scheduling hooks into the Outlook client, and Microsoft is hoping to sell Exchange Servers into organizations that use Outlook. Also, the original Schedule Plus allowed shared network scheduling without an Exchange Server or a Microsoft Mail server being present on the network. The new Outlook client does not allow shared network scheduling merely with a single shared schedule file. It either requires an Exchange Server or at the very least an older Workgroup-style original Microsoft Mail post office mapped to the drive letter M:. If Microsoft can replace Schedule Plus shared scheduling, it helps them sell Exchange Servers into an organization.

**Outlook Express**   In tandem with the introduction of the commercial version of Outlook, Microsoft released the free Outlook Express as part of the Internet Explorer version 4 browser. Outlook Express is certainly much better than Internet Mail and News, but compared to the commercial versions of Outlook, the free Outlook Express is a pale imitation. It also uses a radically different mechanism for storing e-mail and address books, thereby making it complicated to move users rapidly from one system to another, as is often done by support desks in a corporate setting.

Outlook Express is the default e-mail client included with Win98. It also supports LDAP for centralized directory lookups. Although Outlook Express is better than nothing, a commercial organization that deploys Windows desktops and Microsoft Office would be well advised to use the full-blown Outlook 98 client instead of the Outlook Express client.

**Outlook 2000**   With the release of Office 2000, Microsoft also released Outlook 2000, which is basically the same thing as Outlook 98.

## Microsoft Internet Mail Gotchas

Because of the complexity of the Microsoft Internet Mail clients and their interaction with the Microsoft browsers and Office 97, it is easy for the administrator to make errors in option selections during installation that in effect destroy the client Windows machine's original settings. Some of this may have been done deliberately by Microsoft in an attempt to manipulate organizations into a situation where they are forced to purchase an expensive Exchange Server. Others are probably design flaws and overlooks created because of unfamiliarity with SMTP mail in 1995 and 1996. Here are the *gotchas* that the administrator should be aware of when dealing with the Microsoft Mail client software (i.e., once you start using it, you can't go back).

- The original Exchange and Windows Messaging clients supplied in Windows 95 and 95b/c do not wrap outgoing mail messages with hard carriage returns. This is contrary to most default Internet e-mail transmission, and so it makes the message unreadable to many other e-mail clients, such as Netscape. Some clients, such as Eudora, wrap the received message automatically. Avoid the original Microsoft clients in a heterogeneous environment if possible.

- The original Exchange and Windows Messaging clients are unable to download e-mail messages that have the unusual construct `<>` in their `From:` headers. This bug also prevents downloading additional messages from the user account. If someone using this client complains of being unable to retrieve e-mail, check for this condition in the current e-mail message on the server.

- The original clients, through Outlook 97 and Outlook 98 in "Workgroup mode," do not have a progress bar that shows the status of messages during downloading. If the user is dialed in to the mailserver via modem and the client attempts to download a mail message with an attached file larger than 1MB, the client appears to have frozen. In extreme cases, the end user reboots, which breaks the connection and causes the POP3 server to requeue the message. When the client next logs in, the server freezes and the entire process repeats itself. Outlook 98 in "Internet Mail Only" mode *does* have a progress bar.

- Do not install Office 97 unless it is at least the SR-1 version. Many bugs in the original Office 97 version are corrected in SR-1, some of which affect Outlook. If you have a non-SR-1 version of Office installed, immediately install the SR-1 patch from Microsoft, followed by the rest of the Office 97 patches.

■ Installation of Office 97 with Outlook 97 default settings on a clean Win95 system doesn't install support for `*.pab` files, thus rendering dual-address book support nonfunctional. (Exchange Server has a mechanism for a centralized address book.) In this case, `*.pab` support can be added back in with a patch from the Microsoft Web site.

■ Installation of Office 97 with Outlook 97 default settings on a Win95 system with Windows Messaging installed deletes access to the Windows Messaging interface, unless the additional forms support is checked in the `Office97/Outlook97` subinstallation folder. This forces the user to use Outlook 97 as the primary mail interface instead of the Windows Messaging interface.

■ If Schedule Plus is installed on the user's machine, default installation of Office 97 overwrites the Schedule Plus program and subsumes its schedule file into Outlook. Unlike the Schedule Plus program, Outlook cannot access a schedule file shared over the network from another user.

Originally, Schedule Plus schedules were intended to be shared via a Microsoft Mail post office through a MAPI interface. However, with the release of Office 95 and Win95 a loophole was created: the Windows Messaging client implements a MAPI interface under Win95 rather than on a post office, and Schedule Plus runs in network-enabled mode. If the schedule file is then placed on a network server and a workstation is designated as the owner of the schedule file, other workstations can use Schedule Plus to access the network schedule file in shared mode, for group scheduling. Outlook removes this support, forcing group scheduling to take place through an Exchange Server or an older workgroup-style shared MS Mail post office.

The fix on a clean system is to install Outlook 97/Office 97, followed by Schedule Plus.

■ The Outlook Express installation automatically imports all contacts and e-mail from an original Windows Messaging installation. However, this is one-way only: if the user doesn't like Outlook Express, it is not possible to go back to the original client. If the organization uses Microsoft Office, avoid Outlook Express if possible in favor of Outlook 97, 98, or 2000.

■ Outlook 98 imports mail and addresses from all previous versions of the Microsoft mail clients, including Outlook Express. However, do not install Outlook 98 without installing the security patch released by Microsoft for Outlook 98.

■ Some Microsoft clients are known to produce e-mail messages with identical message IDs. This is a gross violation of the RFC mail standards, and it wreaks havoc with mailing listservers. Non-SR-1 Outlook 97 and some earlier Exchange Servers reportedly have this bug.

■ Some Microsoft clients, such as Outlook 97, produce e-mail messages that use the mail account name to produce a section of the message ID. This allows crackers to gain access to the user account name, which may be a security hole if the organization is trying to hide them through an alias file (i.e., using e-mail addresses such as `john.smith@xxx.com` instead of `jsmith@xxx.com`).

- Some Microsoft e-mail products, such as Exchange Server 5, in certain circumstances can produce an illegal `RCPT TO <'user@domain'>` instead of the correct `RCPT TO <user@domain>` in the SMTP handshake. This can be filtered with the following Sendmail ruleset.

```
O OperatorChars=.:%@!^/[]+'
S3
R<'$+@$+'> <$1@$2>
```

- Most Microsoft Internet Mail clients use ISO 8859-1 as the default character set for text characters in MIME-encoded e-mail messages. Default should be set to U.S. ASCII (i.e., plain text) for maximum compatibility with all e-mail clients. MIME encoding should always be enabled by default. In Outlook 97, if this setting is available it is located under Tools, Options, Internet E-mail, Character Set. Unfortunately, depending on the DLL versions used to transport Internet Mail, this setting may not appear in both Outlook 97 and Outlook 98. If Outlook is running in this mode, all that shows up if MIME encoding is selected is ISO 8859-1. The only other option is to select Uuencode. Of course, if the user is not mailing to U.S. UNIX users, ISO 8859-1 must be used to handle the extended text characters used in languages other than English.

- The newer Microsoft mail clients "HTMLize" outgoing e-mail messages by default. Using HTML coding is a nonstandard Internet Mail extension that Netscape introduced, and it can wreak havoc on HTML-cognizant e-mail clients and annoy users of text-only mail clients. This extension should always be turned off by default by the administrator on installation of the mail client. The user should enable it only for specific clients.

- Microsoft clients all make the POP3 e-mail polling interval changeable by the user. The administrator should be aware that some users go so far as to set this to poll for one-minute intervals! If even just a few users change this interval to a minute, it can cause a great deal of harm when a large number of clients in the organization access the server.

- If Outlook 98 is installed on a clean system, during installation it asks what mode of installation to use. The mode can be Internet only, workgroup and Internet, or workgroup only. If the Internet-only mode is installed, support for LDAP is integrated and the progress bar is automatically installed. IMAP support is also installed. If Workgroup-only mode is selected, the LDAP support is *not* installed and must be separately installed from an options directory on the Outlook CD, from the `O98ldap.exe` file. IMAP support is also not installed, and no Microsoft add-in file exists to install it. Workgroup-only mode also changes the properties of the Outlook client to be much like Outlook 97 and the earlier Windows Messaging. One disadvantage of the Internet-only mode is that it effectively requires users to save their passwords in the mail client, which is insecure.

An IMAP-to-MAPI provider called IMAPSP can be used to implement IMAP for workgroup mode. The main use for the Workgroup mode of installation is to access Microsoft Exchange Servers or Microsoft Mail servers.

Outlook does not ask what type of installation to use if the Windows Messaging client was previously installed on the system; it simply installs in Workgroup mode.

## Eudora

Eudora was one of the first free e-mail clients. It originated on the Macintosh as a university project and later was made commercial by the software company Qualcomm. Eudora is available in both a commercial and a free version for Mac and Windows platforms. The older Lite (free) version is located at `ftp://ftp.qualcomm.com/eudora/eudoralight/windows/english/306/eul306.exe`.

Eudora is available in both a 16-bit version and a 32-bit version. The commercial version supports all the usual Internet Mail client features, including spelling, MIME, and Uuencoding, as well as the ability to present an MAPI interface to the client, as the Windows mail client can do. The commercial version also has Pretty Good Privacy (PGP) hooks to allow sending and receiving of PGP-encrypted messages. The free version does *not* support Uuencode or Uudecode.

Eudora version 4.3 replaces the separate commercial and Lite versions. It installs in *sponsored* mode, with flashing advertisements. The advertisements can be turned off after installation by switching on the Lite (free) mode or by purchasing the full product.

## Netscape Messenger

The Netscape Messenger mail client is a basic Internet Mail client that is released with the suite of Netscape programs in Netscape Communicator. This suite includes the browser, calendar (which requires a calendar server for shared calendaring), Net Meeting, and some other programs.

Netscape has an advantage over other programs in that it supports more operating system platforms, including the X Window System under FreeBSD. Organizations may want to deploy Netscape in order to standardize across platforms. The Netscape Mail client imports all common mail file formats, which makes it easy to install over other Internet Mail client programs.

Netscape's Internet Mail client has several settings that should be changed after installation. The biggest problem is that by default, the mail client uses HTML coding for outbound e-mail; this setting should be switched off. The Netscape Mail client is even worse than the Microsoft Internet Mail clients in this regard. Although Microsoft clients send a copy of both the normal and the HTML version of the mail message (by default), the Netscape mail client *only* sends the HTML version. A switch sets it to send both HTML and normal, the same way that Microsoft does, for a little better compatibility, but it's best to turn off this feature entirely.

The other problem with the Netscape client is that by default, it doesn't line-wrap received e-mail. This makes it difficult to receive e-mail from some other Internet e-mail clients that don't properly wrap outbound mail messages. All other Internet e-mail clients in use today line-wrap received mail by default. In the most current version of Netscape, a checkbox can be set to enable wrapping of incoming mail messages to window width, but older versions do not have this setting. This should be turned on.

In my experience, the Netscape Messenger client also has a higher incidence of developing corrupted e-mail storage folders and inboxes than do other clients. (Some of this can be alleviated by using IMAP instead of POP3, and it may be corrected in newer versions.) Netscape provides a utility to correct this problem.

Current versions of Messenger also appear to permit support for only one POP3 mailserver, although they permit multiple IMAP servers.

## Other Mail Client Programs

There are numerous other e-mail client programs on the Internet. For example, the University of Washington puts out one named PC-Pine, at `http://www.washington.edu/pine/pc-pine/`. PC-Pine is an IMAP client. The University of Washington also sponsors development on one of the more popular IMAP servers for UNIX. FreeBSD has this IMAP server in the Ports directories.

## Hard and Soft Returns

Hard and soft returns are also likely to affect the interaction of Windows Internet Mail clients with the rest of the world. Under the original Internet Mail formatting standards, a sent e-mail message was composed of lines of text, each line of which was no longer than 80 columns and ended with a newline character. Under UNIX, newline is an ASCII linefeed, but under DOS and DOS-based systems such as Windows, newline is an ASCII linefeed followed by an ASCII carriage return character.

When the MIME standard for mail was proposed, proportional fonts had already begun to be used under X Window on UNIX. The designers of MIME realized that the old standard of 80 columns (which originated from ASCII terminal days) would become a problem with proportional fonts and borrowed an idea from word processing—a *soft* end-of-line character. This is codified in RFC2045 and RFC1521, as follows.

> If longer lines (more than 76 characters) are to be encoded with Quoted-Printable encoding, "soft" line breaks must be used. An equal sign as the last character on an encoded line indicates such a non-significant ("soft") line break in the encoded text. (RFC2045, pp. 20–21)

The purpose of this encoding protocol is to allow the preservation of the sender's original line breaks in cases where the Quoted-Printable encoding has bloated the line length beyond the maximum. Because MIME is such a superior attachment encoding protocol, practically all Windows Internet Mail clients today by default produce messages that are MIME encapsulated. This includes the text part of the message. Some older e-mail clients cannot deal with soft returns and display text where each line terminates in an =20 sequence (i.e., encoded space).

In general, it is prudent whenever possible to transmit messages with each line wrapped at 68 characters with a hard return. Some clients, such as Outlook 97 and 98 in Workgroup mode, continue to use soft returns even when *specifically configured not to*. Novell GroupWise clients also have this problem, but Novell has released a patch in its service pack to correct it. Most major listservers cannot digest soft returns properly and may garble such messages. One quick hack for noncompliant Microsoft mail clients is to train the users to press the Enter key at the end of each line of text, which inserts a hard return.

## BASIC SENDMAIL INSTALLATION ON FREEBSD

Installation and configuration of Sendmail on the FreeBSD server is only part of what must be done to set up the server as a main mailserver. Configuring a FreeBSD server connected to the Internet to process e-mail has four major parts.

- Properly configuring Sendmail
- Setting up user accounts on the server
- Properly configuring the POP3 server program
- Registering the mailserver in the DNS

Some organizations may want to undertake the further step of setting up an LDAP server to handle e-mail addresses, which is discussed later in this chapter. Like most UNIX systems, FreeBSD comes with Sendmail installed in the OS and a generic Sendmail configuration file. This configuration file is optimized to use the FreeBSD UNIX system as a workstation client system. FreeBSD does not come with a POP3 server installed by default.

Before beginning Sendmail configuration the administrator should have a client workstation set up with an Internet Mail client to use for testing and a user account on the FreeBSD system to use as the mailserver. The FreeBSD system should also have access to a nameserver, which can either be running on the mailserver system or on another system reachable over the network from the mailserver. This nameserver should be able to resolve names fully and should not be an *internal fake root* nameserver *unless* the mailserver is on an internal network with no connection to the Internet, such as a UUCP-connected mailserver configuration. Often, organizations run a secondary nameserver on the primary mailserver. If access to a nameserver is not possible, even a fake root one, hosts files on the clients and mailserver can be used. This is not recommended due to the large amount of administrative work it requires.

The instructions shown in Exhibit 9.1 for Sendmail configuration assume a FreeBSD server directly connected to the Internet that has been set up roughly according to the instructions in Chapter 5. The intent is to configure Sendmail to allow for incoming and outgoing e-mail traffic for a typical main mail hub.

**Exhibit 9.1  Sendmail configuration instructions**

1. Start by logging into the server as the root user and running /stand/sysinstall.

2. Select Do Post-Install configuration of FreeBSD.

3. If needed, select View/Set various installation options.

4. If needed, select Change the Installation Media Type.

5. Select Install Additional Distribution Sets.

6. Select Sources for Everything but DES.

7. If on FreeBSD 2.2.8 or below, select only the smailcf (Sendmail configuration macros) and press Enter. If on FreeBSD 3.X, select /usr/src/contrib.

8. Press Enter, and the Sendmail configuration macros are installed for the version of Sendmail that ships with the FreeBSD used on the server. For example, Sendmail version 8.8.8 ships with FreeBSD 2.2.7, and version 8.9.3 ships with FreeBSD 3.4. Note that a production mailserver exposed to the Internet should be running FreeBSD 4.X or later.*

9. Exit /stand/sysinstall.

10. If a newer version of Sendmail is used, go to the /usr/src/usr.sbin directory and place the new Sendmail distribution file here. This should be unzipped and untarred with the command cat sendmail.8.9.3.tar.gz | gunzip | tar xf -. This creates the subdirectory /usr/src/usr.sbin/sendmail-8.9.3 with the extracted Sendmail version in it.

11. Compile this version by changing into sendmail-8.9.3/src directory and running the command sh Build. This creates the executable Sendmail file in an obj directory under the src directory.

**Exhibit 9.1**  *(continued)*

12. Change directory to this object directory and run the command `make install`. This copies the new version of sendmail to `/usr/sbin` as well as the new manual pages.

13. In a new Sendmail installation, change to the `mail.local` directory (`/usr/src/usr.sbin/sendmail-8.9.3/mail.local`) and run the `sh Build` command. This creates a new `obj` directory and makes a new version of the `/usr/libexec/mail.local` program, which is only compatible with BSD UNIX systems, such as FreeBSD. Install this program by changing into the `obj` directory and running `make force-install`.

14. If the mailserver is to run UUCP, the administrator may want to install a new `rmail` program. To do this, change to the `rmail` directory (`/usr/src/usr.sbin/sendmail-8.9.3/rmail`) and run the `sh Build` command. This creates a new `obj` directory and makes a new version of the `/bin/rmail` program. Install this program by changing into the `obj` directory and running `make force-install`.

15. Next, change to the `cf/cf` directory (`/usr/src/usr.sbin/sendmail-8.9.3/cf/cf`) or (`/usr/src/usr.sbin/sendmail/cf/cf`) and create a new `sendmail.mc` file. A sample `sendmail.mc` file follows.
```
VERSIONID('@(#)tcpproto.mc      8.10 (Berkeley) 5/19/98')
OSTYPE(bsd4.4)dnl
FEATURE(nouucp)dnl
MAILER(local)dnl
MAILER(smtp)dnl
FEATURE(always_add_domain)dnl
FEATURE(local_lmtp)
define('confME_TOO','True')dnl
define('confMAX_MESSAGE_SIZE','7000000')dnl
define('confMCI_CACHE_SIZE','6')dnl
Cw mail.example.org
Cw example.org
```
A description of the lines in this `mc` file is located in the `cf/README` file.[†]

16. Build a `sendmail.cf` file with the command `make sendmail.cf`.

17. To complete the installation, copy the `sendmail.cf` file to `/etc`, and kill and restart Sendmail.

---

*If the version of Sendmail used on the FreeBSD system isn't the most current, the administrator should obtain the most current version and use this instead of using the Sendmail configuration macros, so steps 2 through 9 may be of dubious value. As of this writing the most current version of Sendmail is version 8.9.3, available via anonymous FTP from ftp://ftp.sendmail.org/pub/sendmail/sendmail.8.9.3.tar.gz.

[†]If the mailserver must be configured to accept fully qualified domain names in the e-mail addresses (i.e., username@example.org), it must list both the mailserver hostname and the mailserver domain name in the `Cw` directives in the `*.mc` file, as the sample file in step 15 does.

It is also possible to use a form to generate a `sendmail.cf` file instead of the `*.mc` method. A Web site at http://www.harker.com/ has such a generator. FreeBSD ships with a standard `*.mc` file that is used to create its `sendmail.cf`, and for most mailservers running current FreeBSD versions, it should be sufficient. To build it, change directory to `/usr/src/etc/sendmail` and run `make SENDMAIL_CF=myhostname.cf`.

One can generate the `sendmail.cf` directly by hand, without using the `*.mc` file, by simply modifying the existing `sendmail.cf` file (Costales & Allman, 1997).[1]

## The Difference between From, From:, and Reply-To:

The administrator on an operating mailserver may need to troubleshoot e-mail messages that users receive, which requires access to the *message header*. The header is normally stripped from messages by e-mail clients when these messages are displayed to the user. Some clients allow the user to view the header. For example, Eudora has a button labeled *Blah Blah Blah* that displays the header when clicked. Microsoft clients often display the header by viewing the Properties of the message.

One of the first things the administrator may notice is that most messages have two lines labeled `From` and some messages may have an additional line labeled `Reply-To`. Correct addressing must appear in these lines for the user's mail client Forward and Reply buttons to work. This is as important for inbound e-mail as it is for outbound e-mail. An explanation of these lines and how they are generated follows.

### From

The *From* line is the first line listed when a message header is displayed. Note that no colon follows the word. This *envelope address* is passed to the mailserver during the initial SMTP handshaking negotiation, but it is not part of the actual header in the message. The address in this line can be forged, but additional explanations usually follow, such as the statement that the forged address doesn't match the IP number it originated from. Forging is commonly done by spammers to hide their true identity and the origin of the message.

The envelope address is generated when the transmitting mailserver takes the user account name that sent out the mail and tacks it onto the hostname that the mailserver thinks it has. If the message originates from a POP client, the transmitting mailserver by definition is the actual client system that the user composed and sent the message from. Some Windows POP3 mail clients take the user account name and attach it to the hostname entered in the TCP/IP properties to generate the envelope address; others use a user-set "from" name. The way a mail client generates the envelope address is not standardized and thus undefined. Ideally, the envelope address should be set to the user's official name and the official hostname of the originating machine.

---

[1]Bryan Costales and Eric Allman, *Sendmail, Second Edition*. O'Reilly & Associates, 1997.

### From:

The *From:* line, like the non-colon From, contains the real e-mail address of the sender. This line is generated by the direct control of the user, who must set it with a mail client setting. It is part of the mail data section and is not determined by the SMTP handshake protocol.

On incoming messages, the `From:` line is used by most mail clients to generate a proper reply address. If the user wants to reply directly to the person the mail originated from, the client generally uses this line as the e-mail address. Ideally, the `From:` line should be the user's official e-mail address. If the user's official e-mail address contains only a username and domain name, the `From:` line should be set to it. If the user's official e-mail address is aliased to an account name, the `From:` line should contain the aliased name, not the account name.

### Reply-To:

The *Reply-To:* line was added because some people get stuck behind broken mailservers or mailservers that are configured in such a way that they wreck the correct `From:` addresses. If the user has no control over an incorrect `From:` e-mail address being applied to outgoing e-mail, he or she can override this with a `Reply-To:` line.

The `Reply-To:` line can also make replies go to a different account. For example, a user might send personal e-mail from a work mail system and want the response to go to the home e-mail address. A corporate user might send a message to `ALL_USERS` with `Reply-To:` set to a general corporate mailbox.

When the Reply button is clicked, a well-written Internet e-mail client ignores the `From:` address if there is a `Reply-To:` entry in the header, but many mail clients are not well written. Also, few Windows POP3 mail clients allow resetting of `Reply-To:` on the fly when the message is being composed, although they may have a static configuration that can be modified.

## Masquerading

*Masquerading* is a configuration setting that the administrator can apply to the mailserver (Figure 9.2). What it does is simple: all mail passing through the server that originates with specific criteria has the From header rewritten to a different e-mail address. Careful use of the masquerading function can prevent mistakes in the From address in outgoing e-mail, help to switch to a new domain name rapidly, and help to route responses to a specific mailserver.

For example, consider how mail routing might be affected in the following scenario. Suppose an administrator is in charge of a large corporate network with many different e-mail clients. The administrator sets up a master

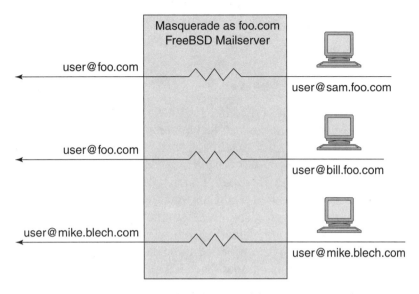

**Figure 9.2** Masquerading only affects mail from systems in the masqueraded domain.

mailserver, sets up POP3 accounts on it for all users in the organization, and then changes the corporate DNS so that the master mailserver is the highest-priority MTA for inbound e-mail to the domain. Many people in the organization have UNIX systems using stock mailer configurations. Some of those systems may create a mail message with the line `user@machine.example.org`. Other systems are Windows POP clients, which send e-mail with the address of `user@example.org`. To make all mail match `xxx@example.org`, the administrator might define the following `*.mc` file directives:

```
MASQUERADE_AS(example.org)
MASQUERADE_DOMAIN(example.org)
FEATURE(masquerade_entire_domain)
```

Now, all mail from `anyusername@anyhost.example.org` is shortened to `anyuser@example.org`.

Masquerading can also help if a domain name is changed. A masquerade directive can be added that replaces the old domain name on all outgoing e-mail messages with the new one. Masquerading is applied only to mail that has a From address within the domain to be masqueraded—it is not applied to every single piece of mail passing through the server. Individuals can also choose to direct outbound e-mail to other hosts than the mailserver and thus avoid having their outbound mail masqueraded. Masquerading should really be used only as a temporary measure; the user's mail client should properly generate a correct From address.

## The Qualcomm POP3 Server

The POP3 standard (detailed in RFC1081 and RFC1082) originated in 1988. It was the result of work done at the University of California, Berkeley, based on earlier work done at other universities and research laboratories. One of the first servers to implement POP3 was the popper server, written for BSD UNIX. Of course, a server by itself wouldn't have been any good, and so a corresponding e-mail client based on a HyperCard stack was created for the Macintosh. This client program later grew into the Eudora e-mail program.

Eudora and the POP3 mail system grew popular enough that UC Berkeley decided to turn over further maintenance of Eudora to a private company, Qualcomm. Since this company needed a server for the Eudora clients to use, they also took over maintenance of the BSD `popper` code. Because all the server code originated under the BSD license with freely available source code, Qualcomm wisely decided to follow a *razor-blade* approach to marketing Eudora: it would continue to publish the full `popper` server source code, including all enhancements Qualcomm had added; give away the server code for free; and charge for the clients. This strategy has helped to make the POP3 standard the de facto client-server Internet Mail standard. Qualcomm has continued to maintain the code, performing numerous bug and security fixes, and to serve as a clearinghouse for contributed patches, enhancements, and fixes to the code.

The `popper` server of today, Qualcomm's version 3.1 for UNIX, is heavily debugged, extremely stable, rather simple, and takes little server resource to operate. It is ideally suited for heavily used mailservers. In addition, the POP3 paradigm gives users little incentive to store e-mail on the mailserver, thus most users collecting POP3 mail immediately delete it from the server after download. This saves space on the hard drive, which is very important on a heavily used mailserver. Since the POP3 server is not tremendously complex, it is easy to port to other UNIX operating systems, which is an important reason for its popularity.

## Status Line

To support the POP3 standard fully, when an account mailbox is first opened in the `/var/mail` directory, the Qualcomm POP3 server adds a *status* line to the message header. This line is removed from the message when it is transferred to the POP3 client program. It is present if the system administrator uses an editor to look at the raw mail file in /var/mail for the specified user. Normally, the status line is added if the mailbox is opened but the e-mail in it is not downloaded to the POP3 client.

The status line is useful for troubleshooting at times. A feature of many POP3 clients is the ability to prevent a large message (typically, one with a large attachment) from being downloaded to the POP3 client. If a user receives such a message and doesn't download it, the message sits in the mailbox until the user connects to the server and the client issues a Delete command. If the user never adjusts the client to delete large messages and never downloads them, after a number of them are received, the /var/mail directory may become very full. Eventually the popper server runs slower and slower when transferring that user's e-mail.

Periodically, as part of good housekeeping, the system administrator should go through the /var/mail directory and look for unusually large mailbox files. Checking the status lines of the messages in these mailboxes reveals whether the message has ever been read. Unread messages have a status line of Status: U.

## CHANGING USER PASSWORDS

On any larger mailserver with many users, an administrator gets occasional requests from users to change the passwords on their mail accounts. Users may suspect that someone is stealing their e-mail, or these users may be more security conscious than most.

Since the POP3 server uses the FreeBSD /etc/passwd file, if the password is lost because the user forgot it, there is no way to *decrypt* the password and get it back: UNIX encryption is one-way only. To change a lost password, the root user must log in and run passwd username to replace the existing password with a new one. If the user remembers the old password, it's a waste of the administrator's time to change the password when it is easy to set up a system to allow the user to change it. The popassd password-changing server is a de facto standard from Qualcomm. The source of the server is ftp://ftp.eudora.com/eudora/servers/unix/password, but use this site for reference only—on FreeBSD this server should be installed from /usr/ports/mail/poppassd Ports directory.

Once the server is installed, it sets up a server run from inetd on TCP port 106. Users who want to change a password can access this server a number of ways. The first and most obvious is to use the password-changing function within the Eudora mail program. If the user is running Windows and doesn't have Eudora loaded, the Windows password-changing program at http://www.tip.net.au/~mphillip/ can be used.

However, it may be inconvenient for users to run either of these programs. It is possible to set up a simple Web page that runs a CGI script allowing the user to change his or her password. The CGI program calls the `poppassd` program directly (see <u>http://www.freebsd-corp-net-guide.com</u>). This script and Web page is also available from <u>ftp://ftp.atlantic.net/pub/src/mp/wwwpass2.tar.gz</u>.

It's also possible to insert a JavaScript into the password-changing Web page that generates a random password the user can select or override. Here is a JavaScript function that creates passwords of half letters and half numbers, leaving out the lowercase L (to prevent confusion between number 1 and lowercase L).

```
function randpswd()
{
        var randpswdstring = '';
        var charlist =
            'a1b2c3d4e5f6g7h8i9j1k2m3n4o5p6q7r8s9t1u2v3w4x5y6z7';
        var multiplier = charlist.length - 1;

        for (var i=0; i < 8; i++)
        {
                randpswdstring +=
                   charlist.charAt(Math.round((Math.random() *
                   multiplier)));
        }
        return randpswdstring;
}
```

Both `popassd` and the Web interface transmit passwords in cleartext. It may be safer to block off `popassd` access and run the Web interface under an SSL server.

## DIRECTORY SERVICE USAGE

E-mail for a large organization can be difficult to manage if users lack a listing of e-mail addresses or names of people in the organization. An employee in a large company with several thousand employees cannot remember the proper spelling of every other employee's name, let alone their e-mail addresses. A searchable table—or directory—of full names and their corresponding e-mail addresses must be created. Organizations that use a full-name convention for usernames, such as `firstname.lastname@organizational.example.org`, are not excused from the need to maintain a central directory. The directory must exist even though the mapping between full name and e-mail address may be closer and more obvious.

Proprietary e-mail systems, such as Microsoft and Lotus cc:Mail, have a central file that clients open with a filesharing lock. Remote clients receive copies of this directory on installation and thereafter receive directory updates. The clients then add or delete directory entries in their local directories based on information in these update messages.

Internet Mail protocols contain a directory access protocol known as LDAP. LDAP replaces the central shared directory file used by proprietary systems and is used for Internet Mail clients that are permanently connected to a LAN. Remote Internet Mail clients, in contrast, may contain LDAP support, but they must depend on a remote address book to store e-mail addresses. Thus, there are two major directory mechanisms under Internet Mail: a local directory and LDAP.

## The Local Directory Mechanism

Remote Internet Mail clients must use a personal address book, known as a local directory, to store e-mail names and addresses. A remote Internet Mail client is a POP3-based e-mail client run on a computer, such as a laptop used for traveling, that is not connected to a network every time the user composes e-mail.

For example, a salesman may run Microsoft Outlook on a laptop while traveling on a plane. During his trip he responds to a number of e-mail messages and clicks the Send button. Outlook knows that it is not connected to a mailserver, so it places the e-mail message in an outbox. Once the salesman arrives at a hotel, he uses remote networking to establish a connection to the Internet or to his organizational network. He clicks the Send and Receive button on Outlook, and the Outlook client sends the messages pending in the outbox, downloading any new messages via POP3.

Because the salesman is replying and composing messages while on the plane, he cannot use LDAP to obtain e-mail addresses from the central directory. Thus he relies on the copy of the directory stored in his local Outlook client, in this case, in the Contacts folder. The same mechanism is used with Eudora, Netscape Mail, or any other POP3 mail client.

## The LDAP Directory Mechanism

Local Internet Mail clients can use LDAP to obtain e-mail addresses. They may also use a directory access protocol, such as Finger or Ph, to get the same information. These clients run on a system, such as a desktop computer, that is continuously connected to the network. For example, an inside saleswoman may run Microsoft Outlook on her desktop computer. When she composes an e-mail message to someone in the organization, she looks in the central address book on the server via LDAP.

The desktop user may still require functionality for a local address. The inside saleswoman may e-mail a contact at another company, who is not listed in the organization's LDAP server. Therefore, the inside saleswoman must retain an address entry for the recipient in her own Contacts folder.

## Address Book Replication

One of the few advantages of proprietary e-mail systems is that they handle directory updating for remote clients automatically. For example, when an address is deleted from the central directory under cc:Mail, a special directory update message is automatically created and propagated to remote clients. (A directory update server must be purchased and running continuously on a separate PC.)

Organizations contemplating a switch to Internet Mail protocols can do something similar, but it requires some discipline on the part of the administrator. In general, here is how address books are replicated on Internet Mail.

1. A standalone workstation is created and specially designated as an address book system. A copy of every e-mail client program supported by the organization (e.g., Outlook, Netscape Mail, and Eudora) is loaded on the workstation.
2. To add a user to the system, the administrator goes to this workstation and performs the following procedure for each client.
   a. Enters the new user into the client's address book.
   b. Exports the client's address book to a comma-delimited file.
   c. Opens the comma-delimited file with a text editor and deletes all entries except for the new ones.
   d. E-mails the delimited file to the All Remote Users alias.
3. When clients receive the address book, they import it into their own local address books, where the new entry is added to existing entries.
4. To send out deletions, the administrator e-mails All Remote Users with the deletion entry, and the users open their local directories and delete the entry.
5. To set up new users, the administrator makes a copy of the address book for the preferred client from the address book system and uses this for the initial address book for the new client.

I recommend the comma-delimited format for Outlook because the Outlook client allows the user to specify duplicate rejection if the imported contact file is comma delimited. Also, comma-delimited files can be added manually by any user not running a standardized mail client version. Sites that don't use Outlook may prefer exporting in the LDAP Directory Interchange Format (LDIF), which is used by Netscape, or the HTML format, which is used by Eudora. Exporting in LDIF may also be useful for administrators who are populating an LDAP server (see Populating the Database in the LDAP Server section, later in this chapter). With a little effort, an administrator could also use a text editor and a template file directly at a Telnet command prompt on the mailserver to generate the export file.

Certain programs and scripts are available on the Internet to convert between address book formats. One such is located at `http://www.interguru. com/mailconv.htm`. This shareware site accepts uploads of address books, which it converts and sends back. The Perl5 code that the conversion engine is built on is also available for any organization that wants to use it as a base for customized automatic directory update message generation. The nightly scripts that run under FreeBSD track password file changes, and it should be fairly easy to use these as input to a Perl script that creates automatic update messages.

## Finger

Long before LDAP was developed, the Finger protocol was created to serve as a central directory access mechanism. Eudora, for example, still supports Finger natively in its program, and Chapter 2 of this book lists a location for a standalone Windows Finger client.

Unfortunately, the output of a Finger is not explicitly defined as it is in LDAP. As a result, it is much harder to use Finger natively in a mail client as an e-mail address lookup tool. For example, under Outlook 98, if a user enters a name in the Send To box, the client can be set to query a LDAP server and automatically fill in the e-mail addressing information. With Finger, the user reads the full output of a `finger` command and selects the e-mail address from it—a somewhat clunkier operation.

Another problem with `finger` is that if a user has shell access to the mailserver, he or she can put a `.plan` file in the home directory that can cause trouble. The `.plan` file is supposed to be used as a short informational message, but a malicious user can place a pipe or a very large file in the `.plan` file in an effort to prevent people from fingering him or her. When setting up users, an administrator may want to put a read-only `.plan` file into their home directories, owned by root, containing `email: user@emailaddress`. This may help novice users to know what the correct e-mail address is, as well as preventing user mischief.

## Installing the Reference LDAP Directory Server

Installing the LDAP server on FreeBSD can be a bit tricky. The instructions shown in Exhibit 9.2 make use of the existing port, with a few modifications. This port is for the *original reference implementation* of LDAP and is old code; a newer server is the Open LDAP server. One problem with the reference LDAP server is that some of its configuration is hard-coded into the source and should be modified before compiling and using it on a production system. It also has several bugs and some assumptions that hinder portability; however, unlike Open LDAP, it is *not* under the GNU software license.

### Exhibit 9.2  Reference LDAP Directory server installation instructions

1. Make sure the Ports collection is installed on the FreeBSD server; if not, use `/stand/sysinstall` to install it.

2. Change to `/usr/ports/net/ldap` and run the command `make`. This downloads the current version of the LDAP server, extracts it, and compiles it. Do *not* run `make install` at this time.

3. Change to the `/usr/ports/net/ldap/work/ldap3.3/include` directory. Edit the `ldapconfig.h.edit` file, and add your organizational name, as in the following example for Cool Dudes Inc. in the United States.
   ```
   #define DEFAULT_BASE    "o=Cool Dudes Inc, c=US"
   ```

4. Change back up one directory level to `/usr/ports/net/ldap/work/ldap-3.3` and run `make` again.

5. Run the `make test` command, which builds the test suite and tests all components. Unfortunately, as of this writing the `slurpd` directory replicator does not run properly (see Open LDAP for a fixed version), although it does build. This is not normally an issue with a single master mailserver with an LDAP server running on it. It matters only if a network of LDAP servers was set up using the replication daemon in the LDAP distribution.

6. Change back to the `/usr/ports/net/ldap` directory and run `make install`. This installs all binaries into `/usr/local/bin` and configuration files into `/usr/local/etc/ldap`.

7. Change to `/usr/local/etc/ldap`, edit `slapd.conf`, and make the following changes.
   a. Change the suffix entry to the organizational name and country used in the `ldapconfig.h.edit` file modified in step 3.
   b. Change the directory entry to the future location of the database files.
   c. Change the referral line to the hostname of the mailserver on which the LDAP database will run.
   d. For testing purposes, comment out the `rootdn` and `rootpw` entries.

8. Create the directory listed in the `slapd.conf` file.

9. Change to `/usr/local/etc/rc.d`, create the file `slapd.sh`, and set it executable. It should contain the following lines.

```
#!/bin/sh
echo -n ' Slapd'
/usr/local/etc/ldap/slapd
```

10. Change back to `/usr/local/etc/ldap` and create a test database named `test.ldif`. For the organization Cool Dudes Inc., the test database would look like this.

```
dn: o=Cool Dudes Inc., c=US
o: Cool Dudes Inc.
objectclass: organization

dn: cn=Ted Mittelstaedt, o=Cool Dudes Inc., c=US
cn: Ted Mittelstaedt
sn: Mittelstaedt
givenname: Ted
objectclass: top
objectclass: person
mail: tedm@agora.rdrop.com
o: Cool Dudes Inc.
```

11. Create the binary database files with the `./ldif2ldbm -i test.ldif` command.

12. Start up the server with the `/usr/local/etc/rc.d/slapd.sh` command.

13. Run the `/usr/local/bin/ldapsearch -h 127.0.0.1 'objectclass=*'` command, which should dump the contents of the database that you just built.

## Installing the Open LDAP Directory Server

Open LDAP has fewer installation problems than the reference LDAP server. The instructions shown in Exhibit 9.3 detail this port installation under FreeBSD 4.0 with the Open LDAP 1.2.9 version.

### Exhibit 9.3  Open LDAP Directory server installation instructions

1. Make sure the Ports collection is installed on the FreeBSD server; if not, use `/stand/sysinstall` to install it.

2. Run the command `make`. This downloads the current version of the LDAP server, extracts it, and compiles it.

3. To verify server operation, run `cd /usr/ports/net/openldap/work/openldap-1.2.9/tests`. Run `make`, and all tests should complete successfully.

4. To install the server, run `make install`. The server should be installed in `/usr/local/bin` and its configuration files in `/usr/local/etc`.

**Exhibit 9.3** (*continued*)

5. Change to `/usr/local/etc/openldap`, edit `slapd.conf`, and make the following changes.

   a. Change the `suffix` entry to the organization's domain name. For example, for the domain `booboo.com` the line would read

```
suffix "dc=booboo, dc=com"
```

   b. Change the `rootdn` line to have the same dc's as the suffix line, as in this example.

```
rootdn "cn=Manager, dc=booboo, dc=com"
```

   c. Change the `rootpw` line to a password other than "secret."

   d. Change the directory entry to the future location of the database files (e.g., `/var/openldap`).

6. Create the directory listed in the `slapd.conf` file.

7. Change to `/usr/local/etc/rc.d`, create the `slapd.sh` file, and set it executable. It should contain the following lines.

```
#!/bin/sh
echo -n ' Slapd'
/usr/local/libexec/slapd
```

8. Move to the location specified in the `slapd.conf` file, and create a test database named `test.ldif`. For the organization Cool Dudes Inc. and domain `booboo.com`, the database looks like this.

```
dn: dc=booboo, dc=com
dc: booboo
o: Cool Dudes Inc.
objectclass: organization
objectclass: dcObject

dn: cn=Ted Mittelstaedt, dc=booboo, dc=com
cn: Ted Mittelstaedt
sn: Mittelstaedt
givenname: Ted
objectclass: top
objectclass: person
mail: tedm@agora.rdrop.com
o: Cool Dudes Inc.
```

The dn line's dc must match that used in the `slapd.conf` file *exactly*.

9. Create the binary database files with the `/usr/local/sbin/ldif2ldbm -i test.ldif` command.

10. Start up the server with the `/usr/local/etc/rc.d/slapd.sh` command.

11. Run the `/usr/local/bin/ldapsearch -h 127.0.0.1 -b "dc=booboo, dc=com" "(objectclass=*)"` command. This should dump the contents of the database that you just built.

> **NOTE**   When testing the LDAP server lookup with programs such as MS
> Outlook and Netscape, the configuration on these mail clients *must* have
> the Search Base set to the *same* line as that specified in the `suffix` line of
> the `slapd.conf` file (e.g., dc=booboo, dc=net).
>
> The Web interface to the LDAP server can be found at http://www.tu-
> chemnitz.de/~fri/web500gw/.

## Populating the Database in the LDAP Server

When entering data into the LDAP server built using one of the previous examples, the administrator has a number of options.

- Use a client X.500 directory user agent that runs under Windows, such as
  waX.500 (available from http://www.umich.edu/~dirsvcs/ldap/
  wax500/), to create entries and upload them to the LDAP server. Authentication must be set up on the server and the client. One way of doing this
  is a Kerberos authentication package available for use with this program
  and Windows clients. Authentication is discussed in the administrator's
  guide located at http://www.umich.edu/~dirsvcs/ldap/doc/guides/.
- Telnet into the mailserver and use the command-line `ldapadd`,
  `ldapdelete`, and `ldapmodify` programs to manipulate the database.
- Maintain the data in an arbitrary format and run it through the `ldif` program
  to convert into LDIF, and then use the `ldif2ldbm` to build the database.
- Maintain the database in LDIF directly, and use `ldif2ldbm` to build the
  database.

LDIF is not difficult to deal with, and it is convenient to be able to Telnet
into the mailserver and do a quick edit on an ASCII database file. An administrator may want to populate the database with an LDIF file if an address book
exists because the Netscape mail client, Netscape Messenger, can save its
address book directly in LDIF. Some conversion programs convert from many
of the popular address book formats, such as Microsoft's `*.PAB` file and
Eudora's HTML format, into the Netscape format. In addition, the current version of Netscape Messenger can import and read a wide variety of competing
address book format files. Another advantage of directly editing a master LDIF
file and regenerating the LDAP database from it is that if the LDAP database is
ever corrupted, it is easy to recover.

Assume that the administrator allows users to modify the LDAP database
file remotely using a directory tool and wants to maintain the database using
LDIF as a master file. Before editing the LDIF file, the administrator must run
the `ldbmcat` program to propagate changes made in the LDAP database back
into the LDIF master ASCII file.

If Netscape Messenger's address book is used to generate the LDIF file initially, several changes must be made. Unfortunately, the address book does not
save in a true LDIF file format (despite what it says in the documentation), so
the administrator must massage the file before actually using it as a source for
generating the LDAP database file.

Here is a sample raw Netscape Messenger `*.ldif` file.

```
-------------BEGIN FILE-------------
dn: cn=Ted Mittelstaedt,mail=tedm@cooldudesinc.com
cn: Ted Mittelstaedt
sn: Mittelstaedt
givenname: Ted
objectclass: top
objectclass: person
mail: tedm@cooldudesinc.com
o: Cool Dudes Inc.
xmozillanickname: tedm
xmozillausehtmlmail: FALSE
xmozillauseconferenceserver: 0
dn: cn=Sam Smith,mail=sam@cooldudesinc.com
cn: Sam Smith
sn: Smith
givenname: Sam
objectclass: top
objectclass: person
mail: sam@cooldudesinc.com
o: Cool Dudes Inc.
xmozillanickname: sam
xmozillausehtmlmail: FALSE
xmozillauseconferenceserver: 0
-------------END FILE-------------
```

There are several problems with this file.

- The file is missing an entry for the organization itself.
- Each directory entry is missing the organization and country on the `dn:`
  line.
- The mail entry should not be on the `dn:` line.

Here is the same file after modification for use in populating an LDAP database.

```
------------BEGIN FILE------------
dn: o=Cool Dudes Inc., c=US
o: Cool Dudes Inc.
objectclass: organization

dn: cn=Ted Mittelstaedt,o=Cool Dudes Inc., c=US
cn: Ted Mittelstaedt
sn: Mittelstaedt
givenname: Ted
objectclass: top
objectclass: person
mail: tedm@cooldudesinc.com
o: Cool Dudes Inc.
xmozillanickname: tedm
xmozillausehtmlmail: FALSE
xmozillauseconferenceserver: 0

dn: cn=Sam Smith,o=Cool Dudes Inc., c=US
cn: Sam Smith
sn: Smith
givenname: Sam
objectclass: top
objectclass: person
mail: sam@cooldudesinc.com
o: Cool Dudes Inc.
xmozillanickname: sam
xmozillausehtmlmail: FALSE
xmozillauseconferenceserver: 0
------------END FILE------------
```

## Setting Up Outlook 98 to Use LDAP

If a central master LDAP directory server and database are created using exactly the template used in the Installing the Open LDAP server section, it is possible to activate an automatic directory lookup feature in Outlook 98 that is extremely valuable for a large organization. What this feature does is simple: when a user composes an e-mail to other organization members, he or she types in the first name, or part of the first name, in the `To:` line of the Outlook message composing window. As soon as the user clicks on the body of the composing window to write the message, Outlook queries the LDAP server for the correct name and e-mail address of the user. Usernames can be separated by commas, and Outlook queries the LDAP server for each username. Conflicts or misspellings are easy to resolve: the Outlook client underlines the name and, when the user right-clicks on the name, a list of possible usernames to choose from appears.

The following instructions for Internet-installed Outlook activate the automatic directory lookup feature.

1. Run the full Outlook 98 client.
2. Select Tools-Accounts and click the Directory Service tab.
3. Click Add->Directory Service and type in the LDAP server name (the mailserver, usually).
4. Click the Yes button when asked if you want to check addresses using this directory service, and then click Next.
5. Choose a name, such as Organizational LDAP server, and click Next, and then Finish.
6. In the listing of Directory Services, highlight the one that was just created. Click Properties and then push the Advanced tab.
7. Enter the name of the organization and the country into the Search Base window (e.g., `o=Cool Dudes Inc., c=US`).
8. Click OK and then Close.

If Outlook was installed in Workgroup mode, LDAP support must be installed with a separate patch file from Microsoft; this was mentioned in the Microsoft Internet Mail Gotcha's section earlier.

## Setting Up Netscape Messenger to Use LDAP

Netscape's mail client through version 4.06 does not have an autocompletion addressing window—or at least not that I was able to activate. What it does have is an address book that can be set to query the LDAP database specified if the Find button in the address book is used. The address can then be selected to use in the To: line.

Like the Outlook client, the LDAP server and the search base must be specified in the Netscape settings. Failure to specify the search base on the client properly results in failure to look up names. Be sure to use the same organization and country used in the Search Base window.

## Setting Up Eudora with Ph to Use LDAP

Eudora is a popular mail program that exists in two versions: Eudora Pro and Eudora Lite. The Lite version is a free program, but it does not (as of this writing) support LDAP lookups. Eudora Pro version 3.XX and earlier also does not support LDAP. Eudora Pro version 4.X does support LDAP, but sites may need to support the Lite clients as well as the earlier Pro clients.

Fortunately, Qualcomm's FTP site has a Ph-to-LDAP server program that can be installed under FreeBSD and used with the LDAP database created in the installation example for Open LDAP cited earlier. The older Pro and the Lite versions of Eudora support Ph and can work with this program to use an

LDAP database. The current version of the Ph-to-LDAP program is located at ftp://ftp.qualcomm.com/eudora/servers/unix/ph2ldap/ph2ldap-1.0b3.tar. Use the instructions in Exhibit 9.4 to set up this program on a FreeBSD server that has the LDAP distribution installed.

### Exhibit 9.4 Ph-to-LDAP setup instructions

1. Make sure LDAP is installed and running.

2. Obtain the ph2ldap-1.0b3.tar file and place it in /usr/ports/distfiles.

3. Untar the file with the tar xf ph2ldap-1.0b3.tar command, which creates the /usr/ports/distfiles/ph2ldap-1.0B3 directory.

4. Modify the following in the Makefile.
   ```
   LDAPDIR = /usr/ports/net/ldap/work/ldap-3.3
   LEX = flex
   LEXLIB = lfl
   ```

5. Move to the Include subdirectory in the Distribution directory and locate the qiapi.h file.

6. Delete line 200 in this file, which contains the directive extern char *sys_errlist[];.

7. Go back to the Distribution directory and modify the conf.c file. Change the MAILDOMAIN and ADMIN lines per the README and INSTALL file instructions.

8. Run the make command and build the ph2ldap program.

9. Create the directory /usr/local/ph2ldap, and copy both the ph2ldap executable and ph2ldap.cfg configuration file into it.

10. Change the ownership and group on ph2ldap and ph2ldap.cfg to bin, group bin.

11. Modify the /etc/services file and change line 205 from
    ```
    csnet-ns    105/tcp to ns    105/tcp.
    ```

12. Modify /etc/inetd.conf and add the following line.
    ```
    ns stream tcp nowait bin /usr/local/ph2ldap/ph2ldap ph2ldap -d
    ```

13. Send a hangup (HUP) signal to inetd with the kill command to make it reread its configuration file.

14. In the /usr/local/ph2ldap directory, modify ph2ldap.cfg using the following example as a guide.
    ```
    BASE_DN o=Cool Dudes Inc., c=US
    QUERY_FIELDS sn,mail
    ```
    The BASE_DN must *exactly* match that compiled into the LDAP server mentioned in the Installing the Open LDAP section.

15. Test the server with a Eudora client by selecting "Tools-Directory Services" and doing a Ph lookup on an entry. Eudora allows the user to click the To: button and automatically selects the e-mail address from the results of a Ph lookup, unlike the results of a Finger lookup done with Eudora.

# CONNECTING THE MAILSERVER TO THE INTERNET

Now you know how to set up the mailserver software on the FreeBSD system designated as the organization's mailserver and how to set up a POP3 mail client. This section presents the steps needed to get the mailserver to process incoming mail. Assume that the mailserver is on a dedicated connection to the Internet that is continuously operable.

## Circuit and Routing Issues

For a mailserver to receive e-mail from other mailservers on the Internet, it must be reachable. In other words, a system must be able to send traffic to port 25 of the IP number that is listed for the mailserver from any point on the Internet.

An organization that uses "legal" routable IP numbers on its internal network and that connects to the Internet typically uses an access list in its router as a firewall. If this is done, a hole must be opened for the internal mailserver. For example, the following statement in a Cisco router applied to the input side of the interface connected to the Internet would allow incoming e-mail to a mailserver located at IP number 192.168.5.2.

```
access-list 101 permit tcp any host 192.168.5.2 eq smtp
```

If the organization is using FreeBSD with a modem on a PPP connection to the ISP and is using `ipfw` to provide packet filtering, a similar statement must be added to the `ipfw` configuration file.

## NAT Considerations

ISPs usually assign a small range of IP numbers rather than a subnet large enough to cover the entire organization to an organization that directly connects. It is then expected to implement NAT or a proxy in conjunction with RFC1918 numbers on the internal network to establish connectivity for its inside hosts. NAT implementation on FreeBSD is covered in Chapter 5. NAT can also be implemented right on the router the organization uses to connect, for example, Cisco routers have supported NAT since IOS version 11.2.

If the organization uses a proxy server to handle its circuit connection, such as SOCKS5 running on FreeBSD, the mailserver must be located either right on the proxy server itself or on the *outside* network between the proxy and the router to the Internet.

If the organization uses NAT, which is more popular, several approaches can be taken.

- Locate the mailserver on the outside network (i.e., the network between the NAT and the router to the Internet). This assumes that NAT is performed on a router, firewall, or PC that is connected to a network, which is connected to a router that the organization uses to connect to the Internet (i.e., a DMZ network).
- Run NAT right on the mailserver. This also requires a DMZ network; the mailserver does double duty as the NAT device.
- Locate the mailserver on the inside network behind the NAT device and create a static IP translation map entry for it in the router. The router (e.g., Cisco) can be the NAT device here.
- Locate the mailserver on the inside network behind the NAT device and create a static PORT translation entry for port 25 on the router. The router is the NAT device here. Unfortunately, early Cisco IOSs don't permit port-to-IP number map entries in the NAT code; IOS version 12.0 must be used.
- Run a relay mailserver on the NAT—not Cisco—and relay incoming mail to the real mailserver on the inside network.

## Cisco NAT Configuration

Because Cisco routers are ubiquitous and are preferred by ISPs and customers connecting to ISPs, running NAT on a Cisco is probably the most popular option for organizational connections on leased-line circuits of speeds 128K and above. Cisco NAT code can be used with static IP-to-IP number maps to support incoming SMTP and Web server access.

The following sample Cisco configuration shows how an organization can program its router to perform NAT and place both a Web server and a mailserver on its internal network. With this configuration, the ISP has assigned a *classless* subnet to the organization consisting of six legal TCP/IP numbers. These numbers are as follows.

| | |
|---|---|
| 209.193.241.40 | Network number |
| 209.193.241.41 through 209.193.241.46 | Legal IP numbers |
| 209.193.241.47 | Broadcast address for this subnet |
| 255.255.255.248 | Subnet mask |

The organization has decided to use the number range of 192.168.1.0, subnet mask 255.255.255.0, from RFC1918 to make all assignments for internal devices. This is a *classful* address assignment.

The mailserver on the inside is assigned 192.168.1.2, and the Web server is assigned 192.168.1.3. They are assigned external legal IP numbers from the

ISP's assigned range that map to these internal IP numbers. The DNS entry for the mailserver assigns the name `mail.foo.com` to the external IP number and `postoffice.foo.com` to the inside IP number. Desktop clients on the network use the name `postoffice.foo.com` as their POP3 and SMTP server to ensure that client mail traffic doesn't unnecessarily pass through the router. Mail originating on the Internet is directed to mail.foo.com, so that the reachable external IP number for the mailserver is used.

The ISP can elect to assign a small subnet to the serial link between itself and the organization, and many do. Generally, these are class C addresses that are broken up with a subnet of 255.255.255.252. Some ISPs don't want to waste subnet numbers on serial links. In that case, the subinterfaces of the serial link have the statement `ip unnumbered Ethernet0` in place of a statement assigning the serial link network IP number to the interface. In the example code (see next page), the ISP has split up the Class C network 199.2.3.0 specifically for serial links.

If the ISP is running "IP unnumbered" on the serial link and if the router must be reachable from the outside (e.g., for Telnet access for programming), the Ethernet interface of the router at the organization also must be assigned a legal number from the subnet. Even if the router doesn't need to be reachable, diagnostic tools and Internet Control Message Protocol (ICMP) traffic, such as MTU Path Discovery, can be disrupted if no legal IP number is mapped to the Ethernet interface of the router. In this example, the serial interface of the router has a legal IP number and the Ethernet interface is assigned 192.168.1.1, which is an illegal number from the RFC1918 range used on the internal net. This makes it reachable from the inside, which is required for a gateway, but it is also mapped to a legal number. The translation map in Table 9.1 is thus created on the router at the organization's site.

This map can create problems with DNS because, depending on what network a client is on, a DNS lookup will return a different IP number for the same

**Table 9.1**  Router Translation Map

| Outside Numbers | Inside Numbers |
| --- | --- |
| 209.193.241.41 | IP numbers 192.168.1.4 through 192.168.1.254 |
| 209.193.241.42 | 192.168.1.1 (router) |
| 209.193.241.43 | 192.168.1.2 (mailserver) |
| 209.193.241.44 | 192.168.1.3 (Web server) |
| 209.193.241.45 | Unassigned |
| 209.193.241.46 | Unassigned |

name. If the organization does not run a DNS server, the DNS server managed by the ISP lists the legal, external IP numbers and the DNS translation in the router (part of the NAT translation) handles everything fine. However, if the organization does run an internal DNS server and inside hosts are pointed to the internal DNS server, they get the external rather than internal numbers when doing a lookup, thus causing needless traffic through the router. In this instance, the organization may need to run duplicate DNS servers: one for the outside, listing the legal outside numbers, and one for the inside, listing the illegal inside numbers. That way there is no replication from the inside illegal server and the outside legal server and lookups do not become inconsistent.

A fraction of the ISP's router configuration is shown here.

```
!
interface Serial2/0.4 point-to-point
  description    To foo.com
  bandwidth    384
  ip address 199.2.3.1  255.255.255.252
  frame-relay   interface-dlci    666
!
ip route 209.193.241.40  255.255.255.248  Serial2/0.4
!
```

The configuration used on the organization's router follows.

```
!
version 11.2
no service password-encryption
no service udp-small-servers
no service tcp-small-servers
!
hostname org-int-rtr
!
enable password foo
!
ip subnet-zero
no ip source-route
ip nat pool net-208 209.193.241.41 209.193.241.41 netmask
255.255.255.248
ip nat inside source static 192.168.1.1  209.193.241.42
ip nat inside source static 192.168.1.2  209.193.241.43
ip nat inside source static 192.168.1.3  209.193.241.44
ip nat inside source list 1 pool net-208 overload
ip domain-name foo.com
ip name-server 200.0.0.1
!
interface Ethernet0
  ip address 192.168.1.1 255.255.255.0
  ip nat inside
  no ip route-cache
  no ip mroute-cache
```

```
 !
 interface Serial0
  description Circuit ID 12345678PNB
  no ip address
  no ip directed-broadcast
  encapsulation frame-relay IETF
  no ip route-cache
  no ip mroute-cache
  bandwidth 56
  no fair-queue
  frame-relay lmi-type ansi
 !
 interface Serial0.1 point-to-point
  description to Internet Service Provider
  ip address 199.2.3.2   255.255.255.252
  ip nat outside
  no ip route-cache
  bandwidth 56
  frame-relay interface-dlci 16 IETF
 !
 interface Serial1
  no ip address
  no ip route-cache
  no ip mroute-cache
  shutdown
 !
 router rip
   redistribute static
   passive-interface Serial0
   passive-interface Serial0.1
   network 209.193.241.40
 !
 ip classless
 ip route 0.0.0.0 0.0.0.0 Serial0.1
 no logging console
 access-list 1 permit 192.168.1.0 0.0.0.255
 !
 line con 0
 line aux 0
  transport input all
 line vty 0 4
  password eatme
  login
 !
 end
```

> **NOTE**   SMTP e-mail is supposed to be delivered according to the MX record, not the A (address) record. However, this is not 100 percent guaranteed: *many* broken mailserver software programs operate on the Internet.

## Listing the Mailserver in the DNS

Once circuit path connectivity to port 25 has been verified, the only remaining task is to list the mailserver in the organization's DNS record. A fragment of a DNS zone file for the domain `foo.com` is shown here.

```
        IN NS ns.foo.com
        IN NS ns.isp.net

mail    IN A  209.193.241.43
        IN MX 10 mail.foo.com.
        IN MX 100 backupmail.isp.net
```

Note that the MX records for `mail.foo.com` list a backup mailserver to be used if the link to `mail.foo.com` happens to go down. A backup mailserver is a good idea. The ISP must make an entry in its *allowed relays* file for the backup to work, so you must coordinate efforts with the ISP.

If `foo.com` wishes to receive e-mail addressed to a domain (`user@foo.com`), an additional MX record must be added.

```
        IN NS ns.foo.com
        IN NS ns.isp.net

        IN MX 10  mail.foo.com.

mail    IN A  209.193.241.43
        IN MX 10 mail.foo.com.
        IN MX 100 backupmail.isp.net
```

Note that this is an *MX* record for the *domain—not* an address record.

Unfortunately, many ISPs use an address record in the DNS when setting up domains, as in the following.

```
        IN NS ns.foo.com
        IN NS ns.isp.net

        IN A  209.193.241.43

mail    IN A  209.193.241.43
        IN MX 10 mail.foo.com.
        IN MX 100 backupmail.isp.net
```

Because a standard MX record is missing, mailers typically make a last-ditch attempt to look up an address record for mail routing. Since an address record does exist, it appears that everything works, but it can create problems, as shown in Exhibit 9.5.

**Exhibit 9.5  A typical DNS problem**

Organization `foo.com` wishes to set up a Web server for its Web site with a URL of
`http://www.foo.com`. This server uses IP number `209.193.241.44`. Thus, the address
record is added to the domain as follows.

```
       IN NS ns.foo.com
       IN NS ns.isp.net

       IN MX 10  mail.foo.com.
 mail  IN A  209.193.241.43
       IN MX 10 mail.foo.com.
       IN MX 100 backupmail.isp.net
 www   IN A  209.193.241.44
```

Everything works as expected until a user on the Internet mistakenly enters the URL
`http://foo.com`. Because the DNS is improperly set up, the browser issues an address
lookup for `foo.com`. Since an address record for `foo.com` doesn't exist, many browsers
silently insert a "www" into the URL (if `www.foo.com` was selected previously) and do a
second DNS lookup. This is a feature or misfeature that some current browsers support, and
it is widely misunderstood.

Suppose, however, that the ISP has mistakenly used an address record for `foo.com`, as
follows.

```
       IN NS ns.foo.com
       IN NS ns.isp.net

       IN A  209.193.241.43
 mail  IN A  209.193.241.43
       IN MX 10 mail.foo.com.
       IN MX 100 backupmail.isp.net
 www   IN A  209.193.241.44
```

The browser makes its query on `foo.com` and comes back with an address. So, the user is
actually redirected to the mailserver when seeking the Web page.

The ISP gets a complaint about this and decides to "fix" it by doing the following.

```
       IN NS ns.foo.com
       IN NS ns.isp.net

       IN A  209.193.241.44
 mail  IN A  209.193.241.43
       IN MX 10 mail.foo.com.
       IN MX 100 backupmail.isp.net
 www   IN A  209.193.241.44
```

Now the browser gets the right IP number, but what about mail? Since no `MX` record
appears for the domain, e-mail for `user@foo.com` is suddenly redirected to the Web site
rather than going to the mailserver. The ISP decides to be clever and makes the following
change.

```
       IN NS ns.foo.com
       IN NS ns.isp.net

       IN A  209.193.241.44
       IN MX 10 mail.foo.com.
```

```
mail   IN A  209.193.241.43
       IN MX 10 mail.foo.com.
       IN MX 100 backupmail.isp.net
www    IN A  209.193.241.44
```

The problem appears to be fixed for a few weeks. Inevitably, though, the postmaster receives intermittent complaints that e-mail to `user@foo.com` is not going through.

---

The cause of the type of problem shown in this exhibit is that some e-mail software is *not* compliant; that is, it does address lookups instead of MX lookups. As a result, some mailers attempt to send mail to the Web server. The moral of this tale is simple: *never use address records for domains!*

Constructs such as `http://foo.com` are confusing to users in any case, leading users to develop the mistaken impression that `http://foo.com` and `http://www.foo.com` are the same thing. It is also very easy to have one TCP/IP address for `http://foo.com` and a completely *different* TCP/IP address for `http://www.foo.com`.

## InterNIC Registration

The last thing to do to turn on incoming e-mail to the mailserver is to be sure that the organization's domain is listed in the root nameservers. This is done by the nameserver administrator for the domain. If the ISP is the nameserver administrator, it handles this task. If the organization is the nameserver, a registration form must be sent to `hostmaster@internic.net` or to the registry that the organization uses (see Chapter 2).

One of the most important issues with DNS registration is that the contacts listed on the domain be reachable. Hundreds of thousands of domains are registered in which the e-mail addresses listed as the domain contacts are invalid and the telephone numbers listed for the administrative and technical contacts are disconnected. Companies that have had domains for years have usually undergone internal reorganizations, changing phone numbers and the like, and not updated the domain records.

When the payment for the domain registration runs out, the Registry issues a bill to the billing contact listed in the domain record. If this bounces or is not received, the Registry generally does not attempt to contact the domain holder and the domain is eventually turned off.

## Troubleshooting

The following are some common problems with bringing up mail services that the administrator may encounter.

- Mail to the domain bounces with the error message "Cannot talk to myself" or similar message. This is very common and is caused by listing a mailserver as the highest-priority mailserver for the domain in the DNS files but failing to list that domain in the `sendmail.cf` file. For domains receiving mail to `user@example.org`, the shortened "`example.org`" *must* be listed in the `sendmail.cf`, or the `sendmail.cw` file if that is being used, as well as the hostname of the mailserver. This is also true for all *vanity* domains that the organization registers.

- Occasional bounces from the secondary mailserver. Most mailservers on the Internet used to *blind relay* mail with no problem. It was very common for administrators to list the ISP's mailserver as the backup relay, and mail to the domain would spool on the backup if the primary mailserver was down. Today, the postmaster should *never* list an arbitrary mailserver as the backup mailserver for a domain without contacting the administrator of that mailserver. Most mailservers have antispamming, antirelaying filters and do not relay mail arbitrarily.

- Laptop "road warriors" who use personal ISP accounts cannot transmit mail when on the road. To remedy this problem, a small organization, which does not field its own modem bank and has employees that travel with laptops, can set up access to a national ISP, such as AT&T Worldnet, on the laptops. These ISPs have 800 numbers to dial in to for access. When the laptop is docked at the company net, it uses the network to send mail to the mailserver, and when on the road, it relays mail through the national ISP's mailserver.

## MAILING LISTS

A mailing list is a general term for an e-mail address that expands to a list of user mail addresses. There are two general types of mailing lists: alias lists and listservers. *Alias lists* are usually manually created by the administrator and are defined in the file `/etc/aliases`, which must be rebuilt with the `newaliases` program whenever the file is modified. *Listserving* is the process by which a group of e-mail users are subscribed or unsubscribed to a mailing list, under the user's control. Alias lists are simple; listservers are more complicated. E-mail messages, called posts, mailed to either kind of list are forwarded to all users on the list.

Listserver software can also provide gateway services, such as a mail-to-fax gateway or a mail-to-Usenet news gateway. For example, listservers can receive Usenet news postings and transmit them via an e-mail mailing list or forward mail messages to Usenet for posting as news articles. The listserver can also run additional processes, such as *digesting*, whereby the day's postings to the mailing list are formatted into a single e-mail message. This message goes to the subscriber that requests the e-mail in digest form rather than as individual postings.

Listservers can be modified to include special commands, such as redirection of mail. For example, a user going on vacation may want all mail forwarded to a subordinate to handle. The administrator sets up a listserver with a redirector command so that the user sends a mail message to the redirector, which automatically forwards the mail. A second command turns off the redirection on the user's return. Several safeguards are needed to prevent forged mail.

Two major UNIX listserver packages are available. The oldest is ListProc, which is written in the C language. In 1993, the ListProc code rights were purchased by CREN and taken into the commercial realm (see `http://www.cren.net`). Versions of ListProc up to and including 6.0c fall under the original publicly available copyright and are free to use. A mailing list provides a support forum for the original version of ListProc at `unix-listproc@boldfish.com`. The code itself is located at `ftp://cs-ftp.bu.edu/pub/listserv/`. The licensing agreement in ListProc version 6.0 prevents modified code from being distributed except from the author of ListProc, thus, the free version of ListProc is strictly a do-it-yourself installation.

The second major free listserver package is Majordomo. Majordomo is written in Perl, a scripting language, and is becoming more popular. Majordomo's main advantage is that it can be easily modified and extended, assuming the user knows Perl. There is a Web front-end for it in the `webmin` software package. Its drawback is that it is not well suited to large lists and can create a security hole if configured wrong, but it is the most popular listserver.

Other mailing list packages, such as mailman, are available as well.

## Alias Mailing

The simplest mailing list is an *alias* list entry. The `/etc/alias` file normally contains a list of all system aliases, such as an alias for the postmaster pointing to the regular e-mail account of the system administrator. This file can also contain a list of e-mail addresses separated by commas, such as

```
All-Users: fred,sam,jill,bob,sammy@davis.com,freddy@kruegar.com.
```

Such a list does not have automatic addition and deletion of addresses but must be maintained manually by the system administrator.

The alias list must be rebuilt whenever it is edited. This is done by running the `newaliases` command right after the alias file is edited. Unless `newaliases` is run, any changes to the alias file will not take effect in the mail system.

Since it can become awkward to continue to add names to the line, separated by commas, it's possible to rewrite the alias list as a single entry pointing to a list of names in a separate file. For example, the previous list could be written as

```
All-Users: :include:/etc/mail/allusers-list
```

The file `/etc/allusers-list` would then contain

```
fred
sam
jill
bob
sammy@davis.com
freddy@kruegar.com
```

A simple alias list can be posted to by any users, whether they are listed in the list file or not. Thus, such a mailing list is unsuitable for large numbers of users because it can attract spammers.

## Installing the Majordomo Listserver

For a large list with automatic subscription and unsubscription, the Majordomo listserver is more practical. Majordomo is a set of Perl scripts wrapped around a compiled C program that handles the remailing. In effect, it manipulates a list referenced in the alias file. It handles housekeeping tasks, such as inspecting incoming mail to make sure that only subscribed or other authorized users may post to the list. It also allows list members to add or remove themselves from the list.

To install Majordomo, change into the `/usr/ports/mail/majordomo` directory and run `make`, followed by `make install`. Under FreeBSD version 3.4, Majordomo 1.94.4 is retrieved and installed. Majordomo's Web site is located at `http://www.greatcircle.com/majordomo/`, along with list configuration instructions and documentation.

Under FreeBSD 3.4 running Sendmail 8.9, it is also necessary to remove the group-write bit on the lists directory and any list files. Be sure that any parent directories do not have the *group* or *other* write bits set. If Majordomo is working correctly, group write permission is not necessary and could cause Sendmail to issue errors such as "Cannot open `/path/name`: Group writable directory" or "Aliasing/forwarding loop broken."

With Majordomo it is especially important to define all the lists in `/etc/aliases`. If lists are defined in a separate alias file, Sendmail does not rebuild the `aliases` file when `newaliases` is run unless this separate alias file is also defined in the `sendmail.cf` file. Unless there are hundreds of mailing lists on a server, it is best to leave the lists in the mail alias file.

Mhonarc is an e-mail-to-Web converter that is used in conjunction with a list manager, such as Majordomo, to create HTML mail archives that are indexed and have mail thread linking. Its home page is located at `http://www.mhonarc.org/`. Obviously, the mailserver running the list manager must have a Web server installed and operating on it to use it. Mhonarc is currently the most popular of the Web-to-mailing list archive interfaces. An add-in named Wilma uses Mhonarc to allow users to browse the traditional list archives produced by Majordomo (see the Web site). Mhonarc is available in the FreeBSD Ports directories under FreeBSD 4.X at `/usr/ports/www/mhonarc`.

## WEB MAIL INTERFACE

It is becoming more and more common for ISPs and others operating mailservers to install a Web interface on the server. This allows mailserver users to access their e-mail from remote locations where they do not have any network access other than Web browsing access, such as the floor of a trade show or the offices of another company. The user goes to a special Web site and logs in, reading, deleting, and composing messages in the mailbox from the Web browser. The messages are retained on the mail server until the user returns to the network, where they can be downloaded normally via POP3 to an Internet Mail client program.

Usually, the Web mail interfaces are implemented as a CGI program that uses IMAP to access the user's mailbox, assuming the mailserver supports IMAP. There are a few, however, that require only POP3.

On any IMAP mailserver the administrator must periodically check the mail directories and e-mail users who have exceeded a reasonable size limit for mail. IMAP allows users to store mail on the mailserver, and stored e-mail can be a time bomb for an ISP or an organization because it is frequently subpoenaed in court cases. The administrator is well advised to require deletion of any mail messages older than 60 days.

A variety of Web mail interfaces are available. Pointers to many interesting ones are at `http://www.cru.fr/http-mail/`. Because most interfaces depend on IMAP, it must be installed as well. FreeBSD has an IMAP server in its Ports directories, located at `/usr/ports/mail/imap-uw`.

Following are summaries of some Web interfaces listed on the overview Web page that are applicable to FreeBSD.

- Acmemail at `http://www.astray.com/acmemail/`   Requires Perl, a POP3 or IMAP server, and a Web server running on the mailserver. Written entirely in Perl, it can send and receive e-mail.
- AtDot Webmail at `http://www.atdot.org/`   Requires Perl, a POP3 server, and any Web server, which does not need to be on the mailserver. Written entirely in Perl, it can send and receive e-mail and uses DBM calls.
- FocalMail at `http://www.focalmail.com/home/`   Requires Apache, PHP3, Mysql IMAP, and a number of other things. FocalMail is very full featured and can have an address book and user-customizable settings.
- IMP at `http://web.horde.org/imp/`   Requires a Web server and IMAP, which does not have to be running on the same Web server. It makes use of most of the IMAP features and yet does not go too far into offloading many user-specific things onto the server.
- IMHO Webmail at `http://www.lysator.liu.se/~stewa/IMHO/` Requires a special Web server, the Roxen server (freely available), as well as IMAP. Very full-featured, with support for user personal information.
- MUMail at `http://user.cs.tu-berlin.de/~marktop/MUMail/`   A Java applet that requires the Web server to be on the mailserver for normal usage. It completely offloads processing onto the client Web browser and can access the mailserver via POP3. MUMail is very simple to install.
- TWIG at `http://twig.screwdriver.net/about.php3`   TWIG is an entire groupware messaging interface, a kind of stripped-down Lotus Notes. It requires IMAP, mySQL, PHP, and a Web server on the mailserver, and it supports personal user settings.
- WebMail at `http://jwebmail.sourceforge.net/`   Implemented as a server-side Java application, it requires IMAP on the mailserver. WebMail supports user-customizable settings and the usual features supported by other WebMail interfaces.

## VACATION AUTORESPONDER

The `vacation` program, located in `/usr/bin/vacation`, is a useful UNIX utility for people who are going to be off the system for a while. It replies to the senders of incoming mail messages with a message about the user's absence. `Vacation` is designed to issue a single reply to prevent mail loops. It stores a list of all senders who have been informed in a small file kept in the user's home directory.

To use `vacation`, the user logs in to a shell prompt on the FreeBSD system and initializes the `vacation` program with the `vacation -i` command.

The user creates a file in the home directory named `.forward` that contains
`\username, "|/usr/bin/vacation -a username"`. Next, the user creates
a `.vacation.msg` file that contains a mail message such as this.

```
From: username@mailaddress.com
Subject: Out Of Office
Precedence: bulk
X-Mailer: The vacation program


I'm out of the office until May 31.
```

There must be at least *one* blank line between the `X-Mailer` and the first
line of the message. When incoming mail is delivered to the mailbox, the
`vacation` program autoresponds with this message. It continues until the user
deletes the `.forward` file from the home directory.

## HYLAFAX

E-mail-to-fax services are a valuable addition to any mailserver. This is yet
another area where a FreeBSD mailserver is in advance of Microsoft Exchange
server running on NT—Exchange Server has no faxing capability. (The
Microsoft SBS server does have it, but it's limited to 50 users.) To add faxing to a FreeBSD mailserver, use the `HylaFAX` program at http://www.
hylafax.org.

`HylaFAX` enables the imaging, transmission, and reception of faxes through
a fax or modem. It uses the PostScript interpreter, `Ghostscript`, as the imaging engine. `HylaFAX` can receive incoming faxes and image them into TIFF
files. These files are then mailed to a designated person, who forwards them to
the appropriate recipients or prints them out. The TIFF graphic image format
can be viewed with the Windows Imaging program included on Windows 95,
98, and NT installation CDs.

HylaFAX also images ASCII e-mail messages from users and transmits
them as faxes. Documents that contain graphics can be converted to PostScript
by selecting Print to File on a PostScript driver on a Windows machine or by
creating PostScript files on UNIX, OS/2, or Mac clients. These are e-mailed to
HylaFAX to be imaged and faxed.

HylaFAX can also be set up as a fax server. It can receive fax jobs over the
network that originate from a Print-to-Fax printer driver installed on Windows
clients using the WHFC software located at http://www.transcom.de/
whfc/.

Source code and documentation is available from the HylaFAX home page at http://www.hylafax.org, but it is simplest to install it from the FreeBSD Ports directory /usr/ports/comms/hylafax.

HylaFAX depends on three utilities: bash, Ghostscript, and the Adobe Font Metrics. The bash utility is a Bourne shell lookalike that supports job control, such as C shell, as well as the ability to use the arrow keys to repeat any command, DOSKEY style.

Although the port builds both bash and Adobe Font Metrics, it does not install Ghostscript because there are a number of different versions. The administrator must install Ghostscript before building the port, thus it is best to install HylaFAX as one of the last utility programs on the server. Make sure that all other utilities you want to put on the server that may require Ghostscript are installed, such as apsfilter, latex2html, and graphics utilities.

HylaFAX requires a fax modem, preferably a Class-2 modem, to be installed on the mailserver (see UUCP, earlier in this chapter).

Instructions to set up HylaFAX as a fax gateway are available on the HylaFAX Web site at http://www.hylafax.org/faxgateway.html; these use Sendmail. A contributed script at ftp://ftp.sgi.com/sgi/fax/contrib/dirks-faxmailer/ extracts a MIME attachment file from an e-mail message and faxes it. This script can fax out only attachments that are in the FIG file format. This script can, however, be used as the basis for creating a script that sends out PostScript, LaTeX, or HTML attachment files, using the html2ps or LaTeX converters to convert the attachments into PostScript files and pass them to HylaFAX.

Once HylaFAX is installed, it can be integrated into the mail system in one of two ways.

- The administrator can create individual alias entries for every fax recipient. In this scenario, the user e-mails the fax recipient and the recipient's phone number to the administrator, who enters a line in the alias file for the recipient. The only advantage to this is that the sendmail.cf file doesn't need modification. For example, to enter an alias for a recipient named Sam located at fax number 5551212, you would edit the /etc/alias file and insert

```
"sam: "|/usr/local/bin/faxmail | /usr/local/bin/sendfax -d
sam@5551212 -"
```

If the alias file is located on the machine named mail1.mail.com, any mail addressed to sam@mail1.mail.com is sent out via fax.

- The administrator can make a modification in sendmail.cf that results in the creation of the pseudo-domain .FAX on the mailserver. Mail to this fictitious domain would be passed to the fax subsystem.

In Eudora, for example, the user's To line might read `To: "Joe Shmoe"` `<joe@1234567.FAX>` or `joe@1234567.FAX`. If automatic cover-sheet generation was enabled, either `Joe Shmoe` or `joe` would go on the cover sheet. In this case Sendmail disassembles the address and sends it to the fax subsystem. To set up the pseudo-domain `.FAX`, do the following.

1. Change directory to `/usr/local/lib/fax` and create a file called `mailfax` containing the following lines.
   ```
   #! /bin/sh
   /usr/local/bin/faxmail | /usr/local/bin/sendfax -d "$1@$2" -f "$3" -n
   ```
2. Change the attributes of this file to world-executable with the `chmod a+x mailfax` command.
3. Add the following to your `sendmail.mc` file immediately under the `MAILER(uucp)dnl` line: `MAILER(fax)dnl`.
4. Remake and install `sendmail.cf` and kill and restart the Sendmail daemon.
5. Send a test fax by logging into the mailserver as an ordinary user and typing `mail mytest@8675309.FAX`. A test fax is sent to the person named `mytest` at the fax machine numbered `8675309`.

These instructions disable automatic cover sheet generation with the `-n` option. To enable it, remove the option from either the mailfax script, or the `/etc/aliases` file.

## POPPER BULLETIN BOARDS

If the organization is running QPopper as the POP3 server on the FreeBSD mailserver, a useful feature called Bulletins can be turned on. What this does is during the POP3 session that follows authentication by the user, the server copies bulletins placed in a special Bulletin directory (e.g., `/var/spool/bulls`) to the user's message spool. In effect, it's a big alias list with an entry for *all* users and every user on the server is in the list.

Normally, the QPopper server figures out the last bulletin read by placing a `.popbull` file under the user's home directory that contains the last bulletin number read. Any bulletin in the special Bulletin directory with a number greater than the one in the `.popbull` file is copied to the user's message spool. With a large ISP, users may not have home directories on the server, so the compile option BULLDB can be set to use a central database located in the Bulletin directory instead of a user's home directory. BULLDBDIR can be defined in the `makefile` if an alternate location for the bulletin database is desired. When new users are added to the mailserver, on the first invocation of the POP server they are sent all old bulletins.

# FreeBSD Advocacy

Some readers may wonder what a chapter as political as this one is doing in a technical manual, but what I discuss here is central to the FreeBSD Project and why FreeBSD exists. The information covers the history of FreeBSD and how it relates to other operating systems (OSs), as well as the state of the OS software market today, and how that market affects FreeBSD. In this chapter, I list all the arguments I'm aware of for using FreeBSD instead of any other OS. If you're a system administrator who is attempting to convince upper management in your organization to look at FreeBSD, you should be able to find something you can use here. My list is not exhaustive, however, and I would greatly appreciate hearing any additional arguments that readers develop for using FreeBSD.

## HISTORY OF FREEBSD

In addition to PC hardware's role in the story of FreeBSD, the history of the OS—in short, the history of Berkeley Software Distribution's UNIX itself—has helped put FreeBSD where it is today. FreeBSD is the child of many BSD UNIX operating systems—far older than any other PC OS available today, except for commercial UNIX PC operating systems, such as Solaris and SCO, which are built on AT&T System V UNIX.

BSD UNIX has had many thousands of human-years of testing and refining, more than younger systems, such as Windows, which goes back only a little more than a decade. FreeBSD's story begins with a version of UNIX known as the

Berkeley Software Distribution (BSD), which originated with the Computing Science Research Group (CSRG) at the University of California, Berkeley (UCB). Versions of FreeBSD from 1.0 to 1.1.5.1 were built on the BSD 4.4 (also referred to as Net/2) release; versions from 2.0 onward were built on the BSD 4.4 Lite release. Many commercial versions of UNIX, such as Sun's SunOS, were built on BSD versions 4.3 and earlier. Today, except for BSDi, the commercial UNIX market has mainly turned to the SYSV release of UNIX. How this came about, and how UCB/CSRG came into the UNIX market, is a difficult story to piece together.

The history of UNIX itself begins with the C programming language, which was based on earlier programming languages. One of the earliest of these related to C was ALGOL 60 (1960), followed by Cambridge's CPL (1963), Martin Richard's BCPL (1967), and Ken Thompson's B language (1970) at Bell Labs. In 1972, Dennis Ritchie wrote the first C compiler, which was intended for use with an OS he was writing for a DEC PDP-7. That operating system, written in 100 percent assembler language, was the first UNIX kernel. Later, Ritchie and colleagues were able to obtain a DEC PDP-11, with a whopping total of 24KB (this is kilobytes, *not* megabytes) of RAM, and began writing parts of their operating system in B, and then later on in C. The OS kernel (essentially all UNIX applications programs), as well as the C compiler itself, were written in C. The severely limited RAM in the original PDP resulted in a system with a small, tight kernel, and all utilities were implemented as separate, standalone programs. The original kernel was only 11KB, and even today a typical FreeBSD kernel with only the required drivers loaded consumes less than 2MB of RAM. This version ultimately evolved into Version 6 UNIX.

The UNIX operating system design philosophy stands in sharp contrast to many commercial OSs, such as WinNT. NT itself was based on both OS/2 LanServer and ideas from the older DEC VAX VMS operating system.[1] The VAX system took many ideas from the ancient Multiplexed Information and Computing Service (MULTICS) operating system. The name UNIX is not, in fact, an acronym for anything. The original name was UNICS, for Uniplexed Information and Computing Service, and it got changed in the telling to UNIX. The AT&T lawyers were convinced that UNIX was an acronym and the engineers never bothered to correct them. So, AT&T went ahead and actually registered UNIX as a trademark written with all capital letters.

UNIX was actually a pun on the name MULTICS.[2] MULTICS was a multiuser OS, and the first version of UNIX was single-user. A MULTICS Web site

---

[1] NT through version 4 even ran command-line OS/2 programs, and NT3.5 also had as an alternative the OS/2 HPFS filesystem driver.

[2] In some ways, the UNIX versus NT rivalry existed long before NT was designed, and can also be viewed as a fundamental difference of opinion among computer scientists on how best to design an OS.

is at `http://www.multicians.org/`. MULTICS and similar derivatives put huge numbers of system functions into their kernels (witness the extensive graphics system in modern Windows NT). UNIX separates many of these functions into system *libraries*, located in the `/usr/lib` directory, and many system utilities are separate programs. Each system utility is designed to accept input from standard input, known as *stdin*, and send output to standard output, known as *stdout*. This scheme is known as *piping*, and is so important that it has been copied by many other operating systems, such as MS-DOS.

When UNIX was first being developed, some people at Bell Labs had contacts in the university system, and word of the V4 and later V6 UNIX OS began to spread, along with copies of the source code. Chief among the schools that began using it was UCB. UC Berkeley's first copy, V4, booted up in early 1974; V6 followed in May 1975. The UCB computer science students liked UNIX so much that they began heavily modifying it. A tight-knit community developed with ideas crossing between the UCB version and the Bell Labs version. From 1976 to 1977, UNIX was ported to the Interdata 7/32 computer at the University of Wollongong in Australia—this port was referred to as 32V. Around 1977, the UCB modifications were christened Berkeley Software Distribution, and 1BSD for the DEC PDP-11 was born. In January 1979, version 7 was released; universities were charged $100 for the source code, and everyone else was charged $21,000. At this time distribution was done mainly on nine-track tape cartridges, so the cost to universities pretty much covered distribution. In late 1979, Bill Joy released 3BSD for the VAX 11/780.

In 1979, Bell Labs created its UNIX Support Group (USG), which later spun off as UNIX System Laboratories (USL). USL began supplying source code to a number of UNIX vendors, such as Sun, Digital Equipment, and others. Eventually, this source code evolved into the System III UNIX kernel in 1982. All this was copyright AT&T, including the name UNIX; as a result, the Berkeley BSD code began to diverge from the commercial AT&T code. After this, in 1983–1984, AT&T/Bell Labs went through *the* Breakup. System III was later followed by System V, then System V, Version 2—which was released in 1984. Several revisions of USL followed, notably Revision 3.2 The most current revision is System V, Release 4, often shortened to SVR4. Today, all major UNIX vendors use SVR4 with the exception of HP/UX, which has a distant BSD base.

System V has been licensed by many commercial UNIX companies for use on their own proprietary hardware. Some of these are Sun, with the Solaris Sparc version, IBM with System/370 and AIX on RS/6000, and DEC (now Compaq) with OSF on its Alpha line. There have also been many commercial ports to the Intel architectured systems, but until the 80386 processor was released, none of these had any serious commercial advantage. This is because of the fact that earlier Intel chips did not implement memory protection in hardware, thus application programs could overwrite memory used by the kernel and crash the computer. Some of the vendors who implemented early Intel UNIXs were Interactive Systems Corporation's PC/IX and Microsoft Corporation's XENIX. (Yes, believe it or not, Microsoft actually did produce a version of UNIX at one time that was spun off later as SCO.) There were even a few notable early commercial PC clones of SYSV, such as Mark William Co.'s Coherent and Prentice-Hall's Minix system.

At Berkeley in 1980, BSD passed under the control of the Computing Science Research Group, which applied the Berkeley copyright to all the kernel source and many of its utilities, such as Sendmail. In late 1980, they released 4BSD. In 1981, the next release was named 4.1BSD. From 1982 to 1984, UCB made many changes to the Berkeley Software Distribution software—BSD 4.2 was released in 1983, BSD 4.3 was released in 1986. By 1989, UCB released Net/1, which consisted mostly of the networking code written at UCB. This code became the basis of a number of commercial versions as well, such as SunOS and HP/UX.

During this time, AT&T/USL also took a number of improvements that were made in the BSD source and folded them back into the SYSV source. Chief among these was the TCP/IP networking code (Net/1), which was developed on BSD. Other improvements were Sendmail, a number of UUCP variants, utilities like the `vi` editor, and numerous other utilities and kernel modifications.

By 1990, seeing the handwriting on the wall, some in the CSRG decided to release a version of BSD with all USL code removed. Keith Bostic was instrumental in this, collecting volunteers to rewrite the myriad of utility programs—such as `cat`, `ls`, `more`—that actually make UNIX UNIX. At the 1990 UK UNIX users group conference, Chris Torek (one of the BSD fathers) referred to this project as "detoxification." Others in CSRG decided to begin work on forming a new corporation separate from UCB, which eventually became BSDi.

After the BSD 4.3 kernel release, problems began to develop between the BSD and SYSV groups. AT&T had decided that it wanted to get out of the UNIX market and started looking for a buyer for USL.

The rise of multiprocessor UNIX servers had caused Symmetric Multiprocessing (SMP) support to be added to SYSV, and UNIX vendors were starting to turn away from the BSD source because, at that time, it didn't have SMP. UCB became uncomfortable with the idea of carrying on the responsibility for maintaining control over what had turned into a commercial source for code. The UNIX market was also doing some serious soul-searching at the time. People could see that Intel-based PCs were rapidly becoming powerful enough to displace workstations, and the UNIX market recognized a threat to their proprietary workstation hardware from PC servers. Santa Cruz Operation, Inc. (SCO) had announced a version of UNIX that would run on an Intel 80386, and this had some UNIX vendors, like Sun, concerned. The UNIX community was also concerned about the overall image that the two major variants of UNIX were presenting to commercial customers, and a number of misguided UNIX pundits had embarked on a campaign to attempt to standardize on SVR4, for no other reason than that AT&T seemed *bigger*.

One of the more damaging things to happen to the commercial UNIX community was when AT&T finally sold USL to Novell in 1992. (It wasn't that it was damaging to sell it, what was damaging was who bought it.) This was the beginning of the end for USL; ultimately Novell as a corporation couldn't make the transition into the UNIX realm and it sold its UNIXware to SCO a number of years later. USL ended up in pieces spread around between various other major UNIX vendors, including Sun.

In May of 1991, a number of Berkeley CSRG's key people left to found BSDi, with the purpose of selling a 80386 port of BSD UNIX. A month later, UCB/CSRG released Net/2, which was the result of the detoxification project begun the previous year. Net/2 (BSD 4.4) wasn't a complete, working BSD UNIX operating system; at the time, UCB was merely interested in getting out a newer version of BSD that did not contain any proprietary USL code. In fact, the only program in the distribution that contained any USL-copyrighted code was cpio (CoPyInput2Output), which AT&T had earlier asked to have included in the distribution.

Because UCB seemed to be less and less interested in maintaining the BSD sources as time passed, a number of people communicating via the Internet began to discuss the possibility of an open port of the BSD 4.4 source to the Intel 80386. They knew that, if the effort was made, the source would become so important to the hobbyist community that it wouldn't disintegrate. Also, it would provide a cheap supply of UNIX workstations to computer science students who were searching for UNIX systems that they could learn on. By December 1991, there was a crude alpha-quality port of BSD to the 80386 that filled in the missing USL code—created by William Jolitz—and a beta version became available in early 1992.

The 386BSD project cumulated with the Herculean efforts of William and Lynne Jolitz, who wrote a series of now-famous articles for *Dr. Dobbs Journal* detailing the creation of 386BSD version 0.0—released in March 1992. This was followed later by version 0.1. This source was the first that could actually be used to boot up a 386 into BSD UNIX. Bill Jolitz, in particular, made many mentions in the 386BSD source about how it wasn't intended as production source and that the goal was to produce a version of UNIX that could be used in computer science classes and by researchers. (Some of the older device drivers, such as the LPT driver in FreeBSD 2.2.8, still carry Bill's ranting against commercial use of the code in their headers.)

The publishing of 386BSD touched off a powder keg of excitement and interest. Bill's stated goals—386BSD being a research operating system only—were soon trampled by numerous developers who began to rapidly churn out patches and new utilities. At that time, the first serious split occurred in the BSD community when the NetBSD group separated from the 386BSD project. NetBSD wished to decouple BSD from the Intel 80386.

After the first release of 386BSD, Bill Jolitz trademarked the 386BSD name to block BSDi from appropriating the name. Then, in 1992, he was occupied for a number of months handling family affairs, and decided to withdraw from the BSD project "public life" to work on 386BSD 0.2. However, by then, the BSD community was moving so fast that the *patchkit* for 386BSD grew so much that it became unmanageable. Many community members tried working with Bill to get the 0.2 release accelerated, but no release was forthcoming. Eventually, they gave up waiting for him and went forward with the next 386BSD release. At that time, Bill agreed to allow the 386BSD trademark to be used; however, before the release was finalized, Lynne Jolitz created a firestorm on Usenet with her infamous quote: "One-third of the patches in the patchkit are good, one-third are benign and do nothing, and one-third are harmful." In the aftermath of the bad feelings this generated, Bill withdrew permission for use of the 386BSD name and, since the 386BSD name was trademarked, the others had to find a different name. Thus, the FreeBSD name was coined and FreeBSD 1.0 was released in late 1993. Bill then dropped out of the BSD picture to concentrate his energy on creating a company named Telemuse.

As they contemplated the horrifying thought that the commercial UNIX vendors planned to keep the Intel hardware out of the UNIX workstation market, all the excitement rang alarm bells in USL as well. At that time all major UNIX vendors, with the exception of SCO, sold proprietary workstation hardware. In 1992 the BSDi group, which had left CSRG, released its version of a patched Net/2 tape as BSDi and began to advertise it extensively as a commercial System V alternative.

The excitement of the BSD community was dealt a last thrash of the commercial UNIX vendor's stranglehold on UNIX when, in April 1992, AT&T announced it was filing a lawsuit over the UNIX kernel source against BSDi[3]

---

[3]BSDi's phone number then was 1-800-ITS-UNIX, and many jokes were made that ITS should also have filed suit against BSDi. The court later did enjoin BSDi's use of the UNIX trademark in its phone number.

alleging copyright violations, unfair competition, trademark infringement, and false advertising. AT&T wanted to "pretty" up USL for its buyer, Novell, which was very concerned about the disgusted reaction of its customerbase to Net-Ware version 4. Novell envisioned SVR4 becoming the basis for a "super NOS" New NetWare OS. AT&T told anyone who would listen that they were only suing to be able to serve up an unencumbered USL to Novell, but there was much more at stake here. AT&T wanted the BSD kernel source gutted so that it would take a long time for anyone else to get a running kernel out of BSD and UNIX development would be controlled by USL through SVR4.

In July 1992, AT&T/USL dragged the Regents of the University of California (UCB) into the suit, adding breach of contract and misappropriation of trade secrets to the complaints. This was because BSDi argued that UCB made the source code available with AT&T's approval. In October 1992, UCB attempted to make a behind-the-scenes deal with AT&T/USL—in effect to "sell out" and agree with AT&T—in order to extricate itself from the lawsuit. This plan failed when Rick Adams of Uunet blew the whistle via e-mail. A gigantic firestorm of complaints to the university forced it to abandon the attempt.

The lawsuit dragged on, and in January 1993, the judge ruled against AT&T/USL on all but two claims, which were to be resolved in court, and refused their demand for a preliminary injunction. His ruling stated two main points: (1) AT&T/USL failed to demonstrate that a successful likelihood existed that they could defend their copyright in 32V, and (2) they had failed to demonstrate they could succeed with their claim of misappropriation of trade secrets. Following this, UCB refiled the lawsuit against USL in the state court system. This meant the dispute was now to be resolved in California, which greatly benefited UCB.

This initial ruling and the refiling threw AT&T/USL's lawyers into a panic. If they continued to proceed with the case, they would most likely fail, and then the entire AT&T/USL source to Revision 3.2 could be exposed. Worse, shortly after the new filing, Novell completed the purchase of USL and started pressuring the USL lawyers for immediate resolution. As a result, USL decided it would be in its best interest to settle the suit out of court to prevent a ruling that could be used later as legal precedent. So, they began meaningful negotiations with BSDi and UCB, which ended in February 1994 when all parties agreed to a settlement.

The settlement between Novell/USL and UCB meant that UCB would modify the BSD 4.4 sources by removing certain kernel files (mainly dealing with the scheduler and virtual memory). This new distribution was to be labeled BSD 4.4-Lite. In addition, USL was prohibited from suing anyone using BSD 4.4-Lite as a basis for a commercial OS. BSDi's agreement with USL was confidential, although, as in cases of this type, it very probably required them to license modifications they had made back to USL. BSDi also did announce that it would shift to BSD-Lite. In addition, USL, as part of the settlement, agreed that it would affix the UCB copyright notice to certain files distributed with future releases of the System V UNIX OS.

BSD-Lite did not contain enough of a kernel to boot it out of the box, but it was blessed by the lawyers as "unencumbered of USL" source code. By July 1994, FreeBSD had reached version 1.1.5.1 with the now-encumbered Net/2-BSD4.4 code and was widely regarded as stable enough for production use. Because of the lawsuit, the FreeBSD Project elected to avoid the legal morass of distributing it on CD, and to uncouple FreeBSD from the encumbered Net/2 code—the 1.X release tree was at an end. The FreeBSD group began work on FreeBSD 2.0 then. Released in January of 1995, based on the unencumbered BSD-Lite release that came out in 1994, 2.0 was much more unstable than 1.1.5.1 and not as suitable for production use. This release was later followed by 2.0.5, which soon began to be used as the production replacement for 1.1.5.1.

In 1995, 4.4 BSD-Lite version 2 was released by CSRG, which subsequently disbanded—this action was not without controversy. Many people felt that BSD would be harmed by the lack of a central authority overseeing code changes. But the root of the issue was that most active BSD development had left UCB and was now being done within the NetBSD, FreeBSD, BSDi, and later OpenBSD groups. The only group that appears to be doing any active BSD work at Berkeley now is CSUA, which runs a number of FreeBSD systems for the general undergraduate community.

**NOTE**    Since the breakup of USL, there is no single central authority for System V UNIX either; in addition, the incredible power of the modern desktop computer has made UNIX OS research into a pursuit that can comfortably be done at home.

In August of 1996, FreeBSD version 2.1.5, which contained many departures from 2.0.5, was released. The 2.X series finally reached the stability of the 1.1.5.1 release with 2.1.6, which was released in January 1997. The 2.1.X series ended with version 2.1.7.1.

The FreeBSD Project had hoped that the 2.1 series would be the end, and the next series would be 3.X, but the addition of Symmetric Multiprocessing and a later rework of the SCSI subsystem proved too much to manage this quickly. So the next release was the 2.2X series. It started with FreeBSD 2.2.1 in April of 1997 and ended with FreeBSD 2.2.8 in December of 1998. One notable addition to 2.2X was Divert Sockets, which permitted NATs and fire-walls to be built using FreeBSD. By November 1998, FreeBSD 3.0 was released.

The production kernel 4.0 was shipped in March 2000. Major improvements over 2.2.X are the addition of SMP, better PPP dialup connectivity allowing IP dial-on-demand, and significant changes to the Adaptec 2940/3940 PCI SCSI card drivers—very popular for Usenet news servers. FreeBSD remains a rock-solid BSD UNIX operating system.

Since first running in 1977 on the PDP-11, BSD UNIX has come a long way. When BSD was born the few personal computers that existed were mere toys, and serious computing was done on terminals that were hardwired into mainframes such as the PDP series. At that time there was no Internet, and long-distance connectivity consisted of 110- and 300-baud acoustically coupled modems, as well as mailing nine-track tapes between sites. Today, serious computing is done on desktop computers, mainframes have turned into "server farms," and the Internet makes file transfers in seconds.

The future of FreeBSD is exciting. The 3.X series of kernels broke the old BSD bugaboo of no multiprocessor support with SMP support built in. A port now exists to the DEC/Compaq Alpha chip. Even better, the UNIX community has finally begun to realize that it has more to fear from Windows NT and has begun to stop infighting. In addition, the tremendous growth of Linux has taken the commercial UNIX market by total surprise, and begun to provide validity to the concept of a commercial organization using a free OS. Another exciting development is the merger of Walnut Creek CD-ROM and BSDi, which was announced in March 2000.

## FREEBSD'S RELATIONSHIP TO LINUX

Like it or not, Linux and FreeBSD are intertwined. Linux has successfully captured the market as the most widely used Open Source UNIX-like OS, and the attention it has generated has helped increase interest and use of all Open Source operating systems. From a commercial and marketing viewpoint, Linux is a rocketing success. From a technological perspective, however, FreeBSD is far more successful than Linux, which does not have the history and pedigree of FreeBSD. Most of the utilities and programs in the various Linux distributions originated from the earlier BSD distributions. Many of the more advanced Linux technological development ideas are borrowed from earlier work in the BSDs. Last, although there is a good argument that BSD and FreeBSD are the *real* UNIX, separated from System V merely by a legal copyright definition, Linux can never hold this distinction. The Linux kernel was developed independently from the AT&T/USL/BSD kernels, and it is an emulation. This was done to avoid copyright infringement, but it crippled early versions of Linux with unstable, buggy, and weak kernels.

Today, there is a good deal of crossover between the Linux and FreeBSD projects. The biggest issue, of course, is that both OSs are utterly dependent on GCC, the GNU C compiler. At one time BSD did have its own C compiler, but both BSD and Linux use GCC now. Another dependency is XFree86, and both systems use XFree86 for their X Window System implementations. There is also a lot of sharing of device drivers, and FreeBSD contains a Linux emulator, sometimes called the *Linuxulator*, which allows Linux binaries to execute on FreeBSD.

Beyond the crossover between OSs, there is a tremendous idealistic difference between the BSD and Linux Open Source camps regarding licensing. Virtually all of Linux is licensed under the GNU license, whereas most of FreeBSD is under the BSD license. FreeBSD is a better choice for commercial products based on an Open Source OS because GNU requires redistribution to modifications of GNU software, but BSD does not. A commercial entity can take the FreeBSD source, modify it, and then redistribute binaries of its results for a fee. GNU software, on the other hand, requires that source modifications be made available along with the binaries.

GNU's main goal is to continue to improve GNU software by folding all good ideas back into the distribution. BSD's main goal is to have BSD software used as widely as possible, both in commercial products and in Open Source products. In this it's been very successful because practically all commercial OSs, from Windows to Apple, contain Berkeley code in them and display Berkeley copyrights. The idea is that wide utilization forces a de facto standard in areas that are too controversial for a recognized standard to gain acceptance. Although BSD never successfully applied this idea to the overall BSD operating system software to force BSD to be a de facto UNIX implementation, its validity has been upheld by many other commercial and Open Source software projects, as well as subsystems within BSD, such as Sendmail and TCP/IP.

## WHY USE FREEBSD?

The question of why to use any free OS rather than a Microsoft or Novell software product really combines two questions. Why use UNIX instead of NT or NetWare? And, why use a free OS, such as FreeBSD, instead of a commercial UNIX? The implication is that it's abnormal to use a free operating system and that a commercial OS is better no matter how *better* is defined. The argument usually boils down to whether or not the profit motive of a commercial entity is enough to ensure that it supports its customers. In this regard, it's useful to recall the thousands of recent corporate mergers in which the acquiring company jettisons the acquired product line, thereby making product support unavailable.

Many administrators are concerned about using UNIX as a PC server OS because NT Server and NetWare are much more popular. There are a variety of reasons for this popularity besides the obvious one of more advertising money being spent to push these server OSs. The simple desire to do what everyone else does is often behind this line of reasoning. To argue against this attitude, in this section I compare an out-of-the-box NT server to an out-of-the-box UNIX system.

It is only recently that PCs have become powerful enough to consider using UNIX running on a PC as a server OS. NetWare began its life on the 80286 CPU, which does not allow for memory protection, so to run UNIX on this architecture required severe compromises. Processor speeds were very slow compared to higher-end workstation hardware, and the ISA bus is a bottleneck compared to workstation hardware.

During the early PC-server years, the most popular NOS was Novell NetWare, because its DOS client was fast, trouble free, and didn't occupy large amounts of RAM and because the server itself made the most of the limited hardware resources by concentrating almost exclusively on filesharing. (Thus, to this day the design of NetWare concentrates almost all the computer's resources on fileserving.) When the 80386 was released, Microsoft began work on NT Server, but it wasn't until the rise of the Internet protocols that NetWare was seriously challenged. Today, for many enterprise NetWare sites, even if the entire company agreed to switch away from NetWare tomorrow it would take years before the NetWare network could be taken apart. Experience with many large, entrenched NetWare sites shows that when their administrators ask why they should be forced to switch away from NetWare (to Windows, usually), they are really trying to figure out how to avoid doing so because of the effort involved.

For sites that are honestly willing to consider using a different NOS, there are many benefits to using UNIX. Unlike NetWare and Windows, UNIX allows for real process and job control. Processes can be started, suspended, and terminated under UNIX without affecting the OS kernel. Although processes can be stopped and started under Windows, they can crash the server or have other undesirable side effects. Because fileserving and printserving, as well as Web, FTP, shell, and so on, are not part of the kernel, the administrator can often change services on a running server without taking it down. NetWare does allow for processes to be started and stopped by loading and unloading NLMs; however, experienced NetWare administrators generally do not willingly unload NLMs from a running NetWare server. They have learned that doing this can sometimes terminate the server with an abnormal ending (abend) error. Windows is even worse in this respect: many Windows services, such as file-serving, cannot be started or stopped without damage, or even modified without rebooting the server.

UNIX also allows processes to be prioritized, unlike the cooperative nature of Novell and Windows 3.1 multitasking. The `nice` command can be used to place a fine granularity of control over how much CPU time a program is allotted. Both Windows and NetWare have no equivalent to this command.

UNIX provides superior diagnostic tools compared to Windows or Net-Ware. Programs like `ps` and `top` can be used to examine how much memory a process is using, whether it is swapped out or not, and what parent and children processes exist. Rogue processes can be killed by the administrator without rebooting the system. The network can be sniffed by a bpf client. Processes have ownership and can be subjected to fine limits and controls.

While add-in programs for NT exist that can remedy some of these deficiencies, they are not written by the manufacturer of Windows NT and thus do not have the same level of integration and safety. Many are also quite expensive.

UNIX is much easier to manage remotely than NetWare or Windows. An administrator can sit at home during off hours and manipulate every aspect of the server exactly as if he or she was sitting at the console. This is done by using a PC with a modem to either dial into a shell prompt on the UNIX system or to dial into a PPP line and then use a Telnet program to access the server. Windows does have a remote administration module, but it only allows addition and removal of users and servers from the NT domain and some hard drive administration. Windows Net Meeting does allow some other remote management, but it is not possible to add and delete hardware interfaces, change IP numbers and network settings, or perform other lower-level administrative tasks without sitting at the Windows console (otherwise, Net Meeting can disconnect). UNIX servers can be patched and application programs can be added remotely without rebooting. This has particular importance if the organization has many servers spread out over a large geographical distance. The network administrator does not need to be physically at the server to manage it.

UNIX scripting is also superior to other PC NOSs. Perl, one of the most flexible and popular scripting languages, was developed under UNIX and is now so important that ports have been done to NetWare and Windows (although the ports lack many Perl features due to OS peculiarities). The other shells, such as tcsh, bash, and sh, and the many utilities—for example, awk and sed—allow powerful scripts as well. In fact, for many years the most popular news server software on the Internet, C-News, had most of its functions implemented in scripts. For administrators who manage a large number of repetitive tasks, scripting is a necessity.

Administrators sometimes are concerned about using UNIX because there is a perception that UNIX is more difficult to understand and learn. This perception is untrue, and it arises because the UNIX OS is made up of the kernel and many hundreds of utility programs. A UNIX user or administrator will never use 90 percent of these utility programs; they are there for historical reasons or because someone at one time thought they might be a good idea. Also, there is a disturbing tendency for commercial UNIX systems to not install the online manual pages in the default installation selection. So, many running UNIX systems don't have online documentation, which can be intimidating to new UNIX users.

Another issue that is sometimes raised is that UNIX doesn't have a graphical interface. This is because unlike Windows, the graphics driver in a UNIX system is not built into the kernel. The perception is that without a graphical interface the server is somehow harder to use. In fact, Microsoft has taken considerable heat for allowing things such as the video subsystem into the kernel because of its destabilizing effect on Windows Server. This seems to be an example of making the graphics subsystem the most important single piece of the server.

It is possible to set up a UNIX system so that the user sees a graphical login screen, followed by a graphical desktop, by using the X Window System. The big issue here, though, is what exactly is this server really supposed to be doing? A corporate server concentrates the company's most valuable assets in one location. Ideally, it should sit isolated in the server room, not out on the floor where anything could happen to it. Since a good server is never going to be touched except through the network, why must it have a graphical interface? Novell NetWare doesn't have a graphical interface. Graphics require a lot of CPU power to run, and with a server the CPU should concentrate on file and network serving rather than drawing cool-looking screensaver displays. In fact, *Network Computing* magazine recently discussed a problem where a company was prepared to spend $12,000 on a more powerful Windows Server because the administrator hadn't realized that Windows basically grinds to a halt when running open-GL screensavers. (Microsoft later documented this in Knowledge Base, article Q121282.) Even FreeBSD has this problem with some of its graphical screensavers.

Another area of concern is the shortage of administrators who know UNIX. There is also a shortage of *good* Windows server administrators, so what's the difference? My experience as an IT director has been that about only one out of ten system administrator candidates who claim Windows experience are actually technically competent. By contrast, about one out of two candidates claiming UNIX experience are technically competent. Generally five times the number of candidates claim to know Windows alone, compared to those who know only UNIX, so the actual number of technically competent UNIX administrator candidates turns out to be the same as the number of technically competent NT candidates.

In addition, virtually all UNIX administrators know quite a bit about Windows, whereas the vast majority of Windows administrators know nothing about UNIX. The reason is probably intellectual laziness: people starting out in the administration business who know Windows can usually find enough work in Windows-only networks so that once they learn how it works, they don't want to learn anything else. By contrast, most UNIX administrators also deal with a mix of Windows clients on their networks, so the UNIX administrator community contains a much higher percentage of people who want to know how all tools work in order to use the best ones for the job.

Imagine a woodworker who used only one tool, a chisel, and one material, wood. A chisel can be used to cut boards in half, but a board cut with a chisel would be a mess. A cabinet put together using such pieces without hinges, screws, or glue would fall apart. Similarly, an administrator who knows how to use only Windows or NetWare and is unwilling to learn UNIX tends to see all problems as solvable by Windows or NetWare. If the NOS is unable to solve the problem, they are helpless or, worse, they label the problem as insoluble. These administrators are the equivalent of the woodworker who can only use a chisel. Most companies would be wise to avoid using such people to run their corporate networks rather than seek them out.

Most UNIX administrators are just as interested in Windows as they are in UNIX. For proof, look no further than the pages of *SunExpert*, one of the bastion publications of the UNIX community. This magazine, a major proponent of Sun's Solaris UNIX, has a large NT section every month. No recognized PC magazine that sings the Windows mantra the way that *SunExpert* sings the Sun mantra has anything to say about UNIX.

Support is almost always raised as an objection to moving to UNIX. It is true that commercial UNIX vendors often do not give support unless the company purchases a service contract that's over and above the cost of the UNIX OS. However, Novell is the same way, as is Microsoft. Unlike most UNIX vendors, both of these companies use barely trained support technicians as their *weed-out* front-line support. It is very common to call either of these companies about an issue and spend a week tossing the problem back and forth before getting referred to an experienced support staff member. The reason for this practice is that most calls they receive are RTM (Read-the-Manual) questions, which can waste the time of an experienced technician. Even when an experienced technician admits that the problem is due to a bug, repairing it can take months, if it can be done at all without requiring a version upgrade.

With corporate server software support, it usually boils down to "do it yourself or do without," whether the server software is commercial or free. Fixing problems is, after all, what a network administrator is paid to do. If the administrator simply doesn't know enough to support whatever server software is in use, and is unwilling to learn, the company would be better served using a commercial computer consulting company. Many professional FreeBSD consultants are available and are listed on the FreeBSD Web site (`www.freebsd.org`). FreeBSD phone support lines for commercial users are also available from BSDi.

UNIX is often considered more expensive than NT Server or NetWare. This is because, for many years, PCs were weak compared to UNIX workstations. The majority of UNIX vendors, such as Sun, HP, and DEC, made lots of money selling proprietary workstation and server hardware to run their UNIX OSs. In some ways, these companies merely looked at the UNIX operating system as a necessity for selling hardware. Needless to say, these vendors had little interest in doing good ports to Intel. Even when they did do these ports, such as Solaris x86, Sun never applied the same pressure to UNIX ISVs to do ports of its software to the x86 version as it did for the Sparc version.

The rise of the Intel Pentium and later chips has solved the expense issue. Commercial UNIX systems like Solaris x86 and SCO UNIX are now challenging the older UNIX workstation model, which puts Sun in a very interesting position.

If the UNIX-versus-NT/NetWare question is answered, the next question is this: Why use FreeBSD instead of a commercial UNIX or even its biggest free OS competitor, Linux?[4] Opinions vary, but the following are the reasons that are important to me.

- One great thing about a free OS is that it only costs a bit of time to evaluate. If a commercial UNIX purchase is contemplated, try out a free UNIX first. If it works out, you will save the purchase price. Even if you do end up buying a commercial OS, experience gained on the free OS isn't wasted. You have nothing to lose.
- FreeBSD does useful work with lower-end hardware. It is quite possible to serve light-duty tasks, such as mail, for dozens of people from a 386 with 8MB of RAM. (Remember the 11KB UNIX kernel.) FreeBSD has faithfully incorporated the original goals of the UNIX designers.

---

[4]Linux and FreeBSD do not really compete in the true sense of the word. The usual answer to the question of which is better is to try out both and see for yourself.

- Source code is very expensive for a commercial UNIX. If the plans include modification of the OS, a considerable amount of money can be saved by use of FreeBSD.
- Many people feel that FreeBSD is far and away the most stable of the free UNIX-like OSs.
- FreeBSD and Linux borrow a lot of each other's driver code. Interesting hardware drivers often migrate between systems.
- Technical support for FreeBSD is free and simple; just read the source code. An active user base on Usenet and on the mailing lists can help out those who cannot figure out what the C code is doing. Commercial FreeBSD consultants are also available at http://www.freebsd.org, and BSDi now offers phone support for FreeBSD.
- FreeBSD is a low-cost way to learn what other solutions are out there. For example, many administrators were unable to field Internet Web servers until Microsoft released the built-in Web server for NT. While UNIX-enabled organizations got a competitive head start of more than a year on the Internet, organizations managed by NT-only administrators fell behind. This isn't a fluke; almost any new server system was first implemented on UNIX.
- Scalability. Simply put, FreeBSD can scale to virtually any size. For example, Yahoo!, the largest search engine on the Internet, runs entirely on FreeBSD.

Expense is a whole category by itself. When the number of users to support becomes very large, the licensing costs of commercial server NOSs can become astronomical—by far the single biggest expense of the server. FreeBSD has been proved to support many thousands of simultaneous user connections on appropriate hardware. Even making an allowance for the additional cost of training, such as reading this book, a large NetWare or NT Server network is going to cost much more than FreeBSD. Table 10.1 shows the going costs of NetWare and NT as listed in the June 1998 *MicroWarehouse* catalog) and Windows 2000. As you can see, the costs haven't gone down over the last two years, they have increased.

By contrast, the Walnut Creek FTP server (ftp://ftp.cdrom.com) can support a total of 5,000 simultaneous users. It runs on a Micron NetFRAME 9201 Xeon 500Mhz with 4GB of main memory and 500GB of RAID-5 hard drive space. This server runs FreeBSD UNIX. The Free Software FTP server at ftp://ftp.freesoftware.com is also a Xeon 550Mhz with a 5,000-simultaneous user limit and 400GB of RAID-5. Novell NetWare doesn't even produce a server license that goes that high, it would have to be built by adding twelve 250-user licenses to the base 250-user server; therefore, the total cost of

**Table 10.1** Comparison of Server Costs

|  | Windows NT Advanced Server (full package) | Novell IntranetWare (NetWare 4.11) (full package) |
|---|---|---|
| 5 users | $ 700 | $ 730 |
| 25 users | $1,300 | $2,400 |
| 100 users | $3,550 | $4,700 |
| 250 users* | $8,050 | $8,400 |

| | |
|---|---|
| *Windows 2000 Cost* (from the current *MicroWarehouse*) | |
| Windows 2000 Server with 5 client licenses | $ 800 |
| Windows 2000 Advanced Server with 25 client licenses | $3,300 |
| *NetWare Cost* (from the current Novell site) | |
| NetWare 5.1 Server plus 5 connections | $1,000 |
| NetWare 5.1 Server with 5-connection additive license | $1,000 |

*A 250-user license for either operating system is at least double the cost of the hardware needed to support that many users.

the server software alone would exceed $100,000. Windows NT would have a similar cost after adding in the required Client Access licenses.

The cost of FreeBSD software for this large a server is zero. For the $100,000 cost of software for a commercial server, an organization could afford to hire someone for a year to work solely on the FreeBSD server. When the site decides to add multiple servers, the cost savings become even greater.

## Deciding to Use FreeBSD in Production

Running an Open Source operating system, such as FreeBSD, in a production environment for the first time can be very scary to many administrators, even if they are convinced of the technical merits of the system. For a FreeBSD novice, the biggest fear is this: What if it goes down and I can't fix it immediately? This is a legitimate fear when dozens to hundreds of fellow employees at an organization will be using the system for mission-critical applications such as e-mail.

A true FreeBSD novice should probably refrain from running FreeBSD in a production environment until he or she has had some time to "play" and learn the software at home, or at work. However, for an administrator who has had time to do this and yet still hesitates, there are three major reasons for these feelings of apprehension in my experience.

**1.** The administrator is in an environment that provides no support from upper management for trying anything new. This situation can be real or imagined. It is sad that there are working administrators who feel this way. There is a tremendous demand for and shortage of qualified administrators, and no one working as an administrator should tolerate this atmosphere. A competent administrator can walk out the door and within a week be working elsewhere, often for more money.

Although it's one thing for a larger organization to have a defined set of policies for introducing anything new into the network, it's quite another for a large organization to shut the door on innovation. If this is the case where you work, there's really only one answer: quit and go elsewhere. By staying, you are merely enabling the status quo. Plenty of other companies are nowhere near as restrictive and want and deserve open-minded administrators. Others might tell you to sit down with your boss and discuss it, but I feel that's a waste of time. From a human standpoint, an experienced technician can determine in the first half hour of work if the IT department is innovative. Most novices can figure it out in a week, and most users can figure it out in a month.

I've worked in IT and as an IT manager for several large and small organizations. I know that the only reason a large IT organization isn't innovative is because the IT director doesn't want it to be innovative. The responsibility for encouraging innovation in the staff and selling it to upper management rests on the IT director's shoulders. You're wasting your breath attempting to convince an IT director who wants to hold on to the status quo to change; both of you will be much better off if you find another organization. There are plenty of innovative IT directors who are firing lazy technicians in frustration. You owe it to yourself and to those IT directors to make yourself available to them.

**2.** The administrator feels that he or she doesn't understand FreeBSD well enough to troubleshoot it if a problem develops and wants the extra security of being able to pick up the phone and call a technical support person. No problem! BSDi offers FreeBSD support contracts, as well as per-incident support.

In any case, if the administrator knows nothing at all about the OS, it is generally not possible to just pick up the phone and get an answer with a commercial operating system either—*when it is being used as a server*. Many intricate interactions take place in the server's own hardware, and with other devices on the network. It is simply not possible for a remote technical support person to have a strong grasp of how an organization's network and servers are set up. If a technical support call cannot be answered in the first 15 minutes on a server problem, in most cases it cannot be answered by a technical support technician without hours, or perhaps days of testing and troubleshooting, and in some cases not even then. It is no different from calling a FreeBSD consultant or asking a question on the FreeBSD Usenet news groups or mailing lists.

There is only one significant difference between the person receiving the technical support call and the person making the call. The technical support engineer is confident that he or she can solve the problem, and the end user isn't. There is no reason that administrators cannot do their own troubleshooting as long as they have a good solid education in the PC field. If they don't, they had better learn if they want to stay in the field. Successful troubleshooting relies on three things: persistence, education, and common sense. It's not rocket science; anyone can learn to do it.

**3.** The administrator is suspicious that the FreeBSD system can actually perform as advertised. This is certainly a healthy and good attitude. It is also valuable to apply this attitude to commercial OSs. No commercial server OS sold today contains a warranty that the software can work as advertised, or even that it can work at all. All software disks come with a big disclaimer, written all over the package, stating that the manufacturer is not responsible for problems caused by the software. This does *not* mean that the manufacturer is only excused from liability if someone installs it wrong or misapplies the software; it means that the manufacturer is *also* excused from liability if the software is full of bugs or doesn't work at all.

There is no guarantee that FreeBSD will work. However, this does not mean that there *is* a guarantee that a commercial software package will work. In reality, there is also no guarantee that a commercial software package will work—it's printed right on the box! In this respect, FreeBSD is no different from a commercial piece of software.

Even if you do have a written guarantee for some piece of software (e.g., you get a special letter from the vendor), it will be limited to getting your money back if it doesn't work. Getting that money is a different thing altogether: It will undoubtedly involve a court case if the cost of the software is more than a few thousand dollars—to define "doesn't work." Walnut Creek offers the same guarantee: If you want your $40 back, return the FreeBSD CD-ROM—no questions asked.

## Freeness

Yes, the FreeBSD OS is free, but building any kind of serious server involves many costs other than the OS. There is the cost of hardware, the cost of rent on the room in which to run the server, and the cost of ongoing maintenance.

Other costs include the cost of backup tape media, off-site storage, and spare parts on the shelf, but the biggest single cost is that of the person sitting in the chair managing the server.

Microsoft and Novell both make the argument that their NOSs are easy to understand and use and thus easy for practically anyone to manage. To prove how simple their products are to use, both companies have done demonstrations in which someone who has never seen a server installs it. The unspoken idea here (directed at the IS vice president, usually) is that the products are so simple to use that you don't have to pay someone a lot of money to manage them—just use any temporary employee who can turn on a computer.

In truth, it is almost impossible to build a solid and stable server of any complexity with no training, no matter how simple the server NOS appears. If the office has ten users or less, someone can throw together a Novell NetWare 3.X server with no prior training and learn along the way. To build anything large, however, the administrator must be prepared to make a serious commitment to learning the system in depth, no matter how simple it appears to be on the surface. Managers who embrace the *zero administration initiative* are best cured by the experience of going out and attempting to do it.

Novell NetWare and Windows are *not* simple to install and configure for networks with multiple servers. There are user account replication issues, network issues, and many other factors to understand. To run a large network well, a number of experienced administrators must be at the helm. UNIX, whether it is a commercial UNIX, such as Sun's, or a free UNIX, such as FreeBSD, is no more complex than these NOSs in this environment. However, it is precisely these environments where the cost differential between a free operating system, and a commercial NOS becomes so great. Since the administrators are going to be just as expensive no matter what NOS is used and are going to spend just as much time in the care and feeding of the servers on the network, doesn't it pay to at least give the free OS a shot? The true administrative costs are the same, so why not save on licensing fees?

## Supportability and Liability of Open Source Packages

When Open Source software is used, no one—including its author—owes anyone anything. There isn't even the implication that it will work at all. Although commercial software also has no guarantees that it will work, because of truth-in-advertising laws, there is always an alternative through the court system. The various Y2K lawsuits demonstrate this: the courts are saying that if the software vendor sells software and collects money for it, there is an implicit promise that the software will work. If it doesn't work due to glitches, the vendor must take it back and refund the purchase price, even if that price includes many hundreds of thousands of dollars' worth of labor to install.

Although this idea of workability hasn't yet spread from the Y2K case law to general software case law, it is quite possible that lawsuits will ultimately result in a definition that will, in essence, completely invalidate and outlaw *shrink-wrap* licenses on commercial software. It will probably take another decade for this to happen, but commercial software vendors may someday be held to the same standards of workability as food product manufacturers. It may become a violation of fair trade practices to sell buggy and defective commercial software. In a way then, the commercial software user does have one advantage over a FreeBSD user: an organization is somehow liable for making it run, and that organization could be forced to make the product work with an expensive lawsuit.

With Open Source software, no organization is responsible for making it work. Ultimately, there is only the administrator. So, it is a mistake to think of actually getting something completely free. In actuality, the organization *is* paying for a piece of Open Source software when it uses the software. The difference is that with commercial software, money is the cost; with Open Source, the currency is the time needed to install it, learn how to use it, and support it. The Open Source user *is* the technical support department. Deciding if it would be worth the time to support an Open Source software item running under FreeBSD requires a good sense of the administrator's skill level, persistence, and the host of other factors that go into good troubleshooting.

Other than the *cost = time* factor, Open Source software right now is no different than commercial software. There are pieces of Open Source code that simply aren't worth the time to learn how to use, just as there are pieces of commercial software out there that aren't worth the price. Some Open Source software is extremely buggy; ditto for commercial software.

Even if commercial software is used, the technical support department for that software package expects the organization to do *some* of the troubleshooting (i.e., take some responsibility for getting the software to work). The only way that an administrator can get totally off the support and troubleshooting hook is to pay someone else to do *everything* associated with the network. Most organizations can't afford this.

Nobody knows whether they have made a good investment in a piece of software until they try it out. There are commercial packages that some people think are fantastic and there are Open Source packages that some people feel are fantastic. Plenty of people think that these same packages are worthless.

I have discovered that when talking to people who ask why they should use a particular piece of Open Source software in a production environment when it is not supported, the real issue usually has nothing whatsoever to do with support. Usually, the problem is one of the following.

- Someone with an agenda is looking for a reason to kill the project. We have all heard about the manager who insists on using MS products for everything just because he or she thinks that nobody has gotten fired for using Microsoft. In reality, incompetent system administrators get fired every day, whether they have used Microsoft products or not.
- There is a lack of faith that the software works at all. This is an emotional reaction since, plainly, there are people using the software, thus the software obviously does work, at least to some extent.
- Some lack self-confidence. This is usually tied up with a fear of the unknown. My answer to that is simple—if you work in high-tech at all, you had better learn to be a little nervy now. No other industry has more new things happening faster. If you are an administrator, doesn't that at least prove that you are more trainable than the average user? Why are you afraid that you might not be able to handle something complicated? Weren't you afraid, at least a little bit, the first time you ran `format C:` on a disk?

To sum up, the only proper answer to the question of why to use a particular piece of Open Source software in a production environment when it is not supported goes like this:

> "I am not concerned with the supportability of this product because I have confidence in myself. I can support it—given that full source code comes with the package—and I *am* confident that the package works. If you don't feel that you can trust me to make this determination, we have some other issues in the employee-employer relationship that we need to discuss. Otherwise, let me have the freedom to implement it, quit worrying about everything that is supposed to go wrong, and start looking forward to everything that is going to go right."

## WHAT IS FREEBSD ADVOCACY?

Advocacy is a negative word to many people in the high-tech industry, conjuring up images of system administrators so far off the deep end that they refuse to consider any other solution than their own. Most people in the industry have encountered "Microsoft bigots," or Macintosh or NetWare bigots, who are so dedicated to "their" OS that they use it as a solution for every problem. I have had people tell me with a straight face, completely believing what they say, that

Windows NT is perfectly capable of handling 100,000 fileserving connections in a large corporation. This of course is impossible because the network infrastructure needed to support that many simultaneous users on a single server at Ethernet speeds would be economically unfeasible. I have also heard similarly wild claims for OS/2, NetWare, Appleshare, and UNIX from people who typically have little administrative experience. A common source of such bias is the neophyte systems administrator with two or three successful WinNT installations under his belt. His comfort level with NT starts rising, and from that point on the administrator is completely unwilling to look at any other solution to a problem.

A FreeBSD advocate is not someone who believes that if every computer used FreeBSD the world would be a better place. Even technically inferior computer OSs, such as Win95/98, have their place in the industry. What I mean when speaking about a FreeBSD advocate is someone who feels that, for most important network serving, UNIX is simply the best choice and FreeBSD is the best UNIX; this person attempts to use FreeBSD whenever possible. This preference does not preclude the use of WinNT or Win2K when called for: after all, NT is a pretty basic OS, and people who know UNIX thoroughly could probably install Windows NT in their sleep. The same is true of NetWare, OS/2, and the rest of the non-UNIX network OSs. None of these other systems stacks up against FreeBSD, in my opinion (see Why Use FreeBSD? earlier in this chapter).

The high-tech industry continues to expand and change rapidly. As long as the current pace continues, there will be far more inexperienced, unskilled system administrators than knowledgeable and experienced ones. The companies that write operating systems for money know this. If they write an OS that is flexible and can be used to solve many problems, it will be complex. If they write an OS that is rigid and limited in its problem-solving ability, they can make it simple—thus, they can sell more copies. Inexperienced administrators want simple answers despite the fact that, historically, *complex problems do not have simple solutions.*

Inexperience and limited skills by themselves are no crime—many system administrators are pressed into the role because nobody else is available—but closing one's eyes to the rest of the industry is inexcusable. There are valuable lessons and techniques to be learned from *all* computer OSs, *even old ones.* Despite the fact that Win31 is obsolete, it did some things that the later Windows OSs abandoned because they weren't applicable to 90 percent of users. If you're in the 10 percent that those things were applicable to, however, you can benefit from learning how they worked and may want to carry them forward to a current system.

So, FreeBSD advocates have their eyes wide open to the industry; are familiar with all OSs, including FreeBSD; and can see the flaws. I am confident that anyone who weighs all of these factors will reach the same logical conclusion as I have—FreeBSD is the best computer and network OS.

## The Role of Hobby Users in Software Development

The story of FreeBSD has many threads, one of the most important being the PC market itself. This market wouldn't exist today in its current form if not for volunteer (hobby) efforts. I do not mean to say that businesses have had no place: certainly they have funded the industry. Most early PC customers, however, were *hobby* users, not businesses. Commercial desktop computing got its seed money from the pockets of hobby users, not from other businesses. It wasn't until much later, when IBM got involved, that businesses started looking seriously at desktop computing. Here are some reasons hobby users played such an important role in the PC market.

Most serious computer users know how the PC came to be—the creation and sale of the personal computer to the hobbyist user sparked the industry into flame. Steve Jobs, Bill Gates, and the other "captains" of the PC industry might be credited with building the industry out of their garages, from thin air. The truth is, however, that these people didn't create the industry—they happened to be in the right place at the right time and made good decisions for a few years. In actuality, the army of programmers and hardware engineers working under them created the industry. Those who created the Macintosh and Windows OSs two decades ago came straight out of the hobbyist ranks of a decade earlier.

To understand the position of Open Source software today, it is critically important to understand this group. Not many of them had earned B.S.s in computer science. For the most part, they were people who had been marginalized by society, dismissed as dreamers—people who might have been more interested in destroying the system, not helping to build it. Most of the "old boys" network of that day dismissed them—only a few in the corporate world realized what was going on and took advantage of it. Yet it was the hobbyist group—not the people running corporations—who might be said to have created the software industry out of thin air. In fact, if IBM, which dismissed PC software, had not had some insightful managers to work on creating the PC, the hobbyists might have created the PC *hardware* industry as well! The hobbyist users were well on their way to doing it when IBM got involved. In some ways, the current proliferation of computer clone builders can be seen as a part of this industry, reverting to the way it was originally.

What happened then made history. When the UNIX operating system was first written and cast into the technical community, the hobbyist group came out of the woodwork and began using it and adding to it. This effort wasn't limited to UNIX alone—a few years later the same group began contributing to early DOS development. If the hobbyist users and academic system administrators hadn't begun using UNIX, it might have remained a laboratory curiosity. Today, 20 years later, the PC industry is completely different. Microsoft has unseated IBM and placed itself on the same throne, in the process becoming larger than its predecessor. In doing so, Microsoft has put itself out of reach of most of the hobbyist group.

Nonetheless, a hobbyist group of dedicated dreamers remains active. These people are no longer wiring computers, such as the Altair, because computer hardware has gotten so ridiculously inexpensive and its complexity has outgrown a basement workbench. Instead, hobbyists are pursuing the only avenue still open to them in the industry—software. There are now two arms of software development: the commercial for-profit arm and the hobby not-for-profit arm. The "products" of the hobby arm show up as shareware, and some of it has made a lot of money for its developers, despite the ease of copying. However, just like the original army of hobbyists in the 1970s, there is a core group of idealists who still want to shake up the establishment and unseat its ruler—Microsoft. They are helping drive the success of the free OSs, such as FreeBSD. FreeBSD has been in use since 1993 and required some four or five years of polishing before it was ready for commercial use. But, there is simply no way that this work could have occurred if idealism wasn't driving it.

In my experience, many of the software developers and others working to create and enhance the FreeBSD and Linux OSs have a common goal. In Tolkien's *Lord of the Rings*, the characters want to destroy the Dark Lord and leave no one to replace him. Similarly, the core group of the FreeBSD and Linux supporters want to render Microsoft or its successor incapable of dictating policy in the software industry, leaving no single organization or individual with the ability to rule it. Regardless of whether you agree with this philosophy or not, being able to use software other than Microsoft's is one of the motivational forces behind FreeBSD. This seems to be even more true of the Linux supporters, whose rhetoric is far more anti-Microsoft than that of the BSD group. Twenty years ago it was the dedication of people like them that built the desktop PC industry. Today, these dedicated people are building the Open Source software industry.

## The Engine That Drives Development

There is no question that the large number of hobby users writing software and using FreeBSD supplies the raw talent for the effort, but hobbyist use can take a project the size of FreeBSD only so far. One of the big problems with depending on their efforts is that most hobby users pursue hobbies precisely because they want an alternative to work and drudgery, but a project with the magnitude of FreeBSD necessarily involves some drudgery. It may be fun to write a cool new program for FreeBSD, but someone must test it to shake out all the bugs and security holes. Here is where one's hobby turns professional, and a lot of hobbyist users won't cross that line.

With a commercial OS effort, the problem is easily solved by paying people. Pay enough and you attract people who will do it well, which is exactly how Microsoft has been so successful in grabbing market share from Novell. MS recognized early on how to win the war against Novell: just pay a tremendous amount of money for the best people you can find. The company that pays the most in developers' salaries can purchase the best commercial software development talent. Do it long enough and eventually you probably will beat out everyone else who is trying to do the same thing. Novell's key problem was that upper management could never let go of control, so the company was never permitted to grow to the size it needed to be to pay the highest price for talent.

With an Open Source effort, however, no one's paying for software talent. Most of the time nobody gets paid anything for creating the stuff; if they are paid, it's for applying the software to solve problems. This is alien to most commercial organizations: "Nobody makes money by selling it," they think, "so this Open Source stuff must be amateurish junk." The solution to this problem is to meld advocacy and hobbyist efforts. This melding is being made possible by one of the greatest data networks ever built—the Internet. Using the Internet, effective communication and sharing of code between *all* participants in the FreeBSD Project is possible. Hobbyist users work on improving FreeBSD because they like it, and they share their efforts with hapless advocates like me; those who are motivated to bring down whoever is the Dark Lord of the day are willing to put in the drudgery needed to turn FreeBSD into a professional, polished product.

## THE MICROSOFT ANTITRUST TRIAL

### Failure of Microsoft to Partner in the Industry

In many ways the antitrust trial was the turning point in the history of Microsoft as a force in the computer market. Before the trial, the company was seen as invincible. If Bill Gates, or any major Microsoft company officer, said anything computer-related, it was seen in the industry as the Way, the Truth, and the Light. This power sparked the term *FUD*, meaning fear, uncertainty, and doubt. Basically, FUD is successful rumor-mongering by a company to affect a market, particularly when the company spreading the rumors has no real tangible alternative to effect change. For example, making an announcement of an imminent product release is FUD, especially when the announced product did not actually exist, even as a prototype. In addition to FUD, the term *Wintel* was coined by Microsoft as a result of the company's tremendously close relationship with Intel.

Since the trial, the world has changed—at least, the world from the computer industry's point of view has changed. As soon as the finding-of-fact—that Microsoft is a monopoly—existed, all of the pressure on OEM computer hardware manufacturers to deliver only Windows on their machines vanished. As soon as the verdict—Microsoft had committed a crime—came down, in a split second they lost their close relationship with Intel.[5] As soon as the break-up remedy judgment was announced, practically all power to issue FUD was removed from MS's marketing department. Instead of being able to issue FUD, the company was now a victim of it. And, as a final straw, the company's stock valuation went down by billions of dollars, reducing the personal fortunes of company principals immensely (and souring most investors on Microsoft stock).

What is even more fascinating is that all this damage occurred even before the case has really been settled, because everyone knows that all parties are going to insist on dragging an appeal to the U.S. Supreme Court. However, the computer industry moves fast, incredibly so. Historically, there are very, very few computer software companies that have been able to reverse a downward spiral. The Microsoft antitrust trial is the equivalent of a 200-ton locomotive smashing into an immovable wall at 200 miles per hour. The company has stopped, and begun to back up a bit. If the principals don't handle this carefully, that backing up is going to get faster and faster until they will be heading lickety-split down the road to unprofitability and eventual corporate death. It was not too long ago that IBM was in the same position as Microsoft, and even though they are now profitable, IBM has little influence in the computer market today. A few mistakes now, such as failing to gain market share for the Win2K product, could do the same to Microsoft.

In addition to all the visible damage that has been done to Microsoft, the trial has been extremely effective at highlighting some other more subtle flaws of the entire software industry. Although these flaws are visible in all commercial software, they are magnified in Microsoft due to its large size in comparison to other software companies. These flaws don't exist in noncommercial, Open Source software projects like FreeBSD, and thus the MS antitrust trial provides a perfect example for comparison and contrast of FreeBSD and Windows. These flaws are described in the following sections.

---

[5]It was the Intel vice-president's testimony against Microsoft that helped lead to the court's ruling early in 2000.

### Flaw #1: The Myth That Centralized Control Is Best

There is absolutely no question that Microsoft is managed by a single individual at the top of the company, the CEO Bill Gates. This model is very common in small businesses but is generally outgrown as the company gets larger. Microsoft has never outgrown this management style. This model has one obvious benefit—it provides a consistency and seamlessness to the product line that is impossible to duplicate under any other model. In a divisional, or subsidiary company, model, different parts of the company are free to design products that don't interoperate with each other (but sometimes do), as long as they gain more market share by competing with each other than by working with each other. Microsoft has never done this; all of their products are interrelated.

The Achilles heel of this model is that if one division makes a mistake, it could pull the entire company down with it. The antitrust trial's roots began with earlier litigation between the U.S. Department of Justice and Microsoft that concerned distribution and trade agreements. At the time, monopolization of the Internet by MS's Web browser product wasn't even an issue. Once it became one, the trial enveloped the rest of the company.

FreeBSD, by contrast, has a very loose central control. The FreeBSD core group has responsibility for coordinating only the results of others' efforts, not planning and directing them. A single individual dying in a car crash won't bring the effort to a screeching halt.

### Flaw #2: You Can Fence Yourself In, But You Cannot Fence Out the World

One of the older business philosophies is to find a niche in a market, be the best in that niche and push out all competitors, and then raise the prices because everyone has to buy from you. This is where the incentive to build monopolies comes from, and this is why laws have to exist to make them illegal.

In the past, Microsoft's business philosophy has been to build a system close to the accepted standard, then modify it just enough to be slightly incompatible. This forces competitors to retool their products, which makes them lose ground. Microsoft then considers their modifications proprietary, and either requires licensing fees or withholds information, forcing a competitor to reengineer using *clean room* to emulate the Microsoft interface. For example, Microsoft delayed release of the modified Win2K Kerberos implementation. This modification broke UNIX-to-Win2K Kerberos interoperation. No wonder there was so much support in the industry for a trial.

Since the trial, the company has been bending over backward to make new products as compatible as possible—they must have seen the damage that forcing proprietary standards can do. Although customers may not care, it alienates the rest of the industry and could force all competitors to bond together to oppose Microsoft. Together, the companies may be strong enough to retaliate and pull Microsoft down. Microsoft's refusal to accept governmental regulation just gives ammunition to its detractors because every other major company of its size works with regulators.

In contrast, FreeBSD is written to open standards, not modified versions.

### *Flaw #3: Software Doesn't Wear Out*

Unlike a car or mechanical device, software doesn't wear out. The business model of continuing to sell copies of software year after year only works if people can be convinced to upgrade. If their computer and software are running fine, then why buy a new copy?

The trial introduced FUD that makes system administrators delay purchase of new Microsoft OSs. Since Windows 2000 came out during the trial, the FUD generated by the trial contributed significantly to an industrywide delay in adopting Win2K. It is ironic that the same weapon used by Microsoft in the past to destroy competitors is now being used to harm it.

The Win2K adoption delay has had a number of significant effects. For starters, it is far more likely that companies will continue to maintain an existing Microsoft network on older WinNT Servers in conjunction with newer Windows 2000 Servers. As a result, the newer server will operate in backward compatibility to the older NT servers. Thus, UNIX programs, such as Samba, that could have been rendered unusable, are generally not affected in significant ways.

The adoption delay also makes it more attractive to start looking for other alternatives to a sole-source network operating system like FreeBSD. This is an obvious, easily understandable argument—why tie your infrastructure to a company that's going to be split up?

### *Flaw #4: Everybody Sees the Emperor*

In the story of *The Emperor's New Clothes*, the Emperor convinced himself, but not everyone in the crowd. Similar to this, Microsoft has managed to convince itself that most of the computer industry loves it and its products. What it failed to consider was that rather than everyone in the industry thinking it was the greatest thing since sliced bread, it may have been that everyone else in the industry simply may not have seen any other alternative.

I think that the speed with which people came out of the woodwork to testify against Microsoft in the antitrust trial really indicates something fundamental. Nobody likes being pushed into using a product they don't like, or feel is inferior. The support forums are filled with complaints about Microsoft; in fact, Microsoft was the first major software manufacturer to institute technical support for a fee. If the products were better, the company would not have had so many calls for support so that MS needed to charge money just to reduce the calls to a manageable number or to view them as a significant source of revenue.

Increasingly, the FreeBSD and Linux efforts, and their feedback into the commercial UNIX operating systems, is showing the industry that Microsoft's closed OS business plan has a fatal flaw. To put it simply, there's not enough money in the world to hire enough software developers needed to put the same number of eyes on the Windows code as those currently looking at Open Source code. As the Windows code bloats larger and larger, in an effort to support more and more "stuff," defects and bugs multiply a hundredfold. As the FreeBSD code bloats larger and larger, it does more things that draw more and more people into it. These people read the code, fix problems, and make contributions that advance the project further and further, attracting more and more contributions. In a way, it's a gigantic pyramid scheme.

The problem is most obvious during the FreeBSD beta cycles. With commercial software, such as Novell and Windows, none of the beta users can see a scrap of the code. So, if a beta tester has a problem, Microsoft must reproduce the problem and generate a fix for it. As a result, bugs are prioritized, and thousands of reported bugs designated as minor are never investigated or repaired before release, and sometimes not even during the lifetime of the software product.

With FreeBSD and other Open Source software, a beta tester who sees a problem often sends in the code fix along with the problem report! With commercial software, the larger the beta, the more problems that are discovered, which delays the release and thus represents a liability for a commercial software house. With FreeBSD, the larger the beta, the more code fixes that are contributed.

## Backlash against MS Windows

One more side effect of the antitrust trial worth mentioning is Microsoft's behavior during the trial. In the United States, regulation of larger companies is quite common. Every large company must clear merger deals with the Department of Justice before making them final, and large companies often agree to divest parts of themselves to permit a deal to go through. Generally, these issues are dealt with directly between Justice and the companies involved; rarely are they dragged into a court system.

Microsoft forced this trial into the courts. This move damaged its credibility and made it look like it wanted to operate differently than every other company of its size. As the trial progressed, this initial image strengthened.

Once the trial concluded, Microsoft insisted on appealing, without even making a good faith effort to work with the prosecution, thereby damaging its credibility even more. As a result of these actions, many people are now convinced that MS's aim was deliberate monopolization of the software industry.

It is hard to underestimate the destructiveness of this perception. Prior to the trial and the evidence released during it, Microsoft could have effectively argued that its software monopolization was not the result of deliberate planning, but an involuntary effect of its superior product. After many of the destructive internal Microsoft communications were made public during the trail, the credibility of this argument has been destroyed. Once destroyed, another thought starts nagging—that in fact, it could be argued that Microsoft has not had superior product offerings as its primary goal. If MS's goal was to build a monopoly at all costs, it follows that the products were designed from the get-go to lock the purchaser into that monopoly, with quality taking a back-seat.

There is no question that this perception in the software industry has begun to create a backlash against Microsoft Windows. Linux use is growing at an incredible rate—and as a desktop OS, no less. It seems that Microsoft's flagship product—the desktop computer OS—is being displaced.

## SOME FINAL WORDS ABOUT OPEN SOURCE SOFTWARE

At the dawn of the computer age, computers were huge, expensive things that were programmed directly in machine language. Programming them was a difficult, tedious task requiring tremendous skills. It was perfectly understandable to pay programmers huge sums of money to do it, and because there was little use for the computer, other than perhaps calculating weapon payloads for the military, the narrow market meant that the cost of buying software was very high.

It wasn't long before economists took note of this and began to work out how it would fit into classic economic theory. It was obvious that the computer would someday take the same path of all other technical advances. The hardware would get cheaper and faster, the devices would be used more and more, and more effort would be required to program it. This and other technical advances led to the Information Age, as well as to the idea that the next generation of products of a dominant economy would be those of the mind, not of the hands.

The idea of software as a product and a commodity item came out of this philosophy and is almost universally accepted today. This is why so many people have difficulty understanding Open Source—the very idea of it on the surface seems to be completely counter to the idea of information as a commodity item. "Since no one gets paid for writing it," people surmise, "either the people writing it are incapable of producing code anyone would want to buy, or they are doing a haphazard, shoddy job."

The Free Software Foundation, author of the GNU license, has further muddied the waters on this issue. GNU operates under the assumption that although the base software may be free, modifications to it must be purchased. In a perfect GNU world, most programmers would make their daily bread by modifying and customizing GNU software for their clients. GNU applies the classic economic approach to software and comes up with writing custom modifications to the software as the commodity item. However, this is still classic Information Age philosophy.

The problem with all these approaches is that they rest on the assumption that people are basically lazy, that work is a thing that people don't normally want to do, and that the only way to get them to work is to pay them. Producing or modifying software is seen as work that people won't do unless paid for it. This is classic Puritan thinking—the concept of work in complete opposition to the idea of play. The drudgery of writing software is the penance that the software developer (sinner) must pay for redemption.

It is possible, however, to enjoy work on more than just a superficial level, and to find that work and play can be indistinguishable from each other. This idea can work hand in hand with the increased communications infrastructure that allows people with similar hobbies to find each other and to create a new market for each other's services. In addition, many labor-saving machines have been invented that eliminate true drudgery.

Software development is benefiting from these ideas and advances: many programmers have fun doing what they do, and to them, writing code is an artistic expression that they love. When these people go home, they don't want to stop having fun, so they continue to write code. Huge amounts of this code show up in the shareware market, a lot of it in GNU. The most altruistic of these programmers put their code into the BSD license, and it shows up in FreeBSD.

Commercial software vendors don't quite know what to make of this. These companies operate on classic economic theory, and it is quite beyond their comprehension that some programmers write code that is in direct competition with them and then give it away. For years most commercial vendors completely ignored it. Today, most of them are grudgingly acknowledging its existence. Some of them, like Netscape, even support it with their products.

Without a doubt, though, virtually all commercial software vendors make the same mistake with free software—they completely underestimate the future threat that free software poses to their markets. Unlike commercial software, Open Source software never goes away. A commercial vendor, such as Microsoft, can make a current software package obsolete with the stroke of a pen: they just stop selling the current version and start selling the next version. Open Source software, on the other hand, cannot be withdrawn from the market. Once it's out there, it never goes away.

Suppose that 20 years from now, someone wants to run Word 6.0 on a contemporary OS: it would not run, so this wouldn't be an option. If, however, MS Word was Open Source software, a recompile would bring the program forward in time by 20 years. When a programmer contributes code to an Open Source project, such as FreeBSD, that code becomes a permanent part of history; it cannot be thrown away like a commercial binary-only version of software can. In a way, it's a chance for immortality.

The fundamental drive to make a difference, to change the way the computer industry operates, does not fit the neat economic mold of the Information Age, where all software packages are commodity products of companies competing against each other. Assumptions based on classic economics—Open Source is inferior because it's free—simply do not apply. Instead, Open Source software packages are almost religious in nature; they represent humanity's efforts to achieve perfection in software. This is really why FreeBSD is an Open Source software package—people are proud when they create a thing of beauty, and it's the most human of desires to want to show it to the world.

# Index

D
daily logs, 138
dashes, 222
database manager, 9
databases, 9
data encryption, 78–79, 127–128
data fields, 186
daylight savings time, 83, 159–160
DC3/DC1, 125–126
dd, 133
DEC (Digital Equipment
       Corporation), 359
defect remapping, 70–71
delete key, 17
Delivery Status Notification (DSN),
       298
deltree, 133
Department of Justice, 384–386
dependencies, 86
DES cryptographic software, 78–79
DES encryption, 127–128
Deskpro, 20–21
device drivers, 216
device files, 216–218
DHCP, 3–4, 31–34, 37
DHCP Server Failover, 33
diagnostics, 368
diagnostics partition, 73–74, 76
dialup, 4–5, 99–100, 140
dialup PPP, Microsoft, 57
dialup PPP-only Winsock, 56
digesting, 349
digital subscriber lines (DSL), 4–5,
       193
dir, 133
directory services, 49, 328–339
directory standard (X.500), 49
discovering the network, 160
Diskcopy, 133
Diskfix, 71
DISK Geometry:, 75
diskless boot, 102
DiskManager, 66
divert sockets, 65, 365
dmesg printout, 90, 155
DMZ (demilitarized zone)
       networks, 149–153
DNS (Domain Naming System),
       3–4
    compared with WINS, 41–45
    debugger, 85

and DHCP, 37
on DMZ networks, 152–153
dynamic, 4
hierarchical structure, 42
and ISPs, 35–36
listing, Internet Mail, 345–347
maintaining control of, 147–148
numbering, 79–80
servers, 35–47
-WINS interoperation, 42–43, ch
       7
*DNS & BIND*, 36*n*.3, 43
domain name, 45–47
domain, NetBIOS, 222
domain (term)
    as used by Microsoft, 42
Doom (game), 85
DOS, 223–226
    and character case sensitivity,
       132
    command files, 268–269
    commands, 132–134
    and FTP software, 53
    loading MS Networking client,
       223–226
    and TCP/IP, 52–54
DOS-only workstations, 52–54
DP1, 274
*Dr. Dobbs Journal*, 361
drive letters, 216
drive partitions, 75–78, 216
drive-testing utilities, 70–72
DSL (digital subscriber lines), 4–5,
       193
DSN (Delivery Status Notification),
       298
dual-booting, 23, 65–66, 75–76
dumb signaling cable, 103
dumb terminals, 27
dump, 136
dump/restore, 135
Dunlap, Kevin, 36
duplicate IP numbers, 31
dust, 72
dynamic DNS, 4
Dynamic Host Configuration
       Protocol. *See* DHCP

E
ECC memory, 72
ed editor, 208

edit, 133
editors, 207–209
ee, 133
ee editor, 208
80386 processor, 359–362
EISA, 73
Elm mail program, 87
Emacs editor, 85, 208–209
Emacs/WE, 207
e-mail
    archiving, 307–308
    forging, 297
    HTML-coded, 317
    Mail Exchanger queries, 40
    polling, 317
    server programs, 8
    storage and archiving, 307–308
    TCP/IP services, 49
    -to-fax, 353–355
    usernames, 302–303
    *See also* Internet Mail
encryption, password, 327–328
end-node hardware routing,
       193–196
envelope address, 323–324
environment setup, 118–122
environment variables, 120–121
Erase, 133
error messages
    "cannot find system", 82
    compilation, 90
    Too many open files, 45
escape codes, 17
escape key, 17
ESDI drives, 70
established (keyword), 164
Ethernet, 4–5
Ethernet interface, 342
Ethernet interface names, 155
Eudora, 8, 309, 318, 326, 338–339
Exchange Connector protocol, 297
Explorer, 206
external internet Web server, 205
externally accessible Web servers,
       199
EZ-Disk, 66

F
fake root nameserver, 41
fax services, 353–355
fax software, 85

# We're Everywhere!

800-580-BSDi (2734)
daemon@bsd.com
www.bsd.com/daemon

# CD-ROM WARRANTY

*Miscellaneous Hardware Support:* Standard IDE and SCSI disk, tape and CD-ROM peripherals, ESDI disk, floppy drives, ATAPI/IDE CD burner and tape drive support, multisession CDR support, Sony CDU 31/33 CD-ROM, Mitsumi FX001 or FX003D, Matsushita CD on "Soundblaster" interface card, IDE CD-ROM, 2/4/8/16 port serial cards from BOCA, Cyclades and Digiboard, Wangtec/Archive QIC drives on QIC-02 or QIC-36 controller, Creative Labs Video Spigot, Matrox Meteor, Bt848 cards, Connectix Quick-CAM, Sound Blaster 16/SB PRO/AWE32, ProAudioSpectrum, Gravis Ultrasound/MAX, MS Sound Source, Sound Blaster PCI 128, Ensoniq AudioPCI, Neomagic sound controllers.

*Hard Disk Controllers:* AdvanSys SCSI controllers, QLogic SCSI controller, any ESDI WD 1007 compatible, Adaptec 152x/151x/ AIC-6360, 154x ISA, 174x/274x/284x EISA, 294x/39xx PCI, 789x on board, DPT III and IV series SCSI RAID, BusLogic 742/545x ISA, 445x VLB, 747x EISA, 946x/956x PCI, NCR 53C810/825/875 PCI, Tekram DC390 and DC390T (and other AMD 53c974 based boards).

*Networking:* ATM networking support (HARP), SMC Elite 16/Ultra, SMC9432TX and most WD80x3 clones, ISOLAN AT 4140-0, Isolink 4110, Novell NE1000/2000/2100, 3Com 3C501/3/7/9, 3C579, 3C590/3C905, DEC DC 21040/21041/21140 PCI, DEFPA, DEFEA, Fujitsu MB86960A/MB86965A, Intel Etherexpress Pro/100 and Pro/10, Znyx ZX34 series PCI, Texas Instruments TNET 100, IBM Etherjet, SDL RISCom N2pci sync serial card. SMC EZ Card 10/100 PCI 1211-TX and other RealTek 8129/8139 and Accton MPX 5030/5038 based cards. Adaptec Duralink cards, AIC-6950, LinkSys LNE100TX, NetGear FA310TX Rev. D1, Matrox FastNIC 10/100 and other PNIC based cards. ASIX Electronics AX88140A based cards, Macronix 98713, 98713A, 98715, 98715A, and 98725 based cards, SiS 900 and 7016 based cards, SK-984x, ST-201, Winbond W89C840F, VIA Technologies VT3043 "Rhine I," VT86C100A "Rhine II." Tigon 1 and 2 based gigabit Ethernet cards.